A HISTORY OF THE
RUTGERS UNIVERSITY GLEE CLUB

A HISTORY OF
THE RUTGERS UNIVERSITY

GLEE CLUB

David F. Chapman

Rutgers University Press
New Brunswick, Camden, and Newark, New Jersey, and London

Library of Congress Cataloging-in-Publication Data

Names: Chapman, David F. (David Francis), 1954– author.
Title: A history of the Rutgers University Glee Club / David F. Chapman.
Description: New Brunswick : Rutgers University Press, 2022. | Includes bibliographical references and index.
Identifiers: LCCN 2022007511 | ISBN 9781978832237 (hardback) | ISBN 9781978832244 (epub) | ISBN 9781978832268 (pdf)
Subjects: LCSH: Rutgers University. Glee Club—History. | Glee Clubs—New Jersey—New Brunswick—History.
Classification: LCC ML28.N29 G544 2022 | DDC 782.80609749/42—dcundefined
LC record available at https://lccn.loc.gov/2022007511

A British Cataloging-in-Publication record for this book is available from the British Library.

References to internet websites (URLs) were accurate at the time of writing. Neither the author nor Rutgers University Press is responsible for URLs that may have expired or changed since the manuscript was prepared.

♾ The paper used in this publication meets the requirements of the American National Standard for Information Sciences—Permanence of Paper for Printed Library Materials, ANSI Z39.48-1992.

www.rutgersuniversitypress.org

Manufactured in the United States of America

The publisher wishes to thank

ROBERT E. MORTENSEN

Rutgers University Class of 1963 and
Glee Club member 1959–62,
whose support of this book
made its publication possible.

For my wife,

SEIRAN

whose love and support greatly facilitated
the writing of this book.

CONTENTS

PREFACE

Presenting the history of an organization such as the Rutgers University Glee Club can serve a variety of intersecting purposes. An endeavor of this kind can function as a practical narrative, chronicling the exploits of the group and its important actors. Such an account can provide the background information necessary for the continuation of a long-standing tradition so that the customs and practices of the past can underlay the more modern versions of glee club culture in a meaningful way. To this end, the narrative must contain a balanced and authoritative assortment of facts blended with pertinent reminiscences that, when taken as a whole, supply the necessary historical context for present-day interested parties. It is the purpose of this book to provide just such a presentation to the reader.

In so doing, the chronicle that follows highlights the continuity of purpose and sense of dedication to oft-stated goals that have served as guideposts for the Club's activities from its inception. Therefore, in conjunction with the historical narration, a focus on the group's most important artifacts—that is, the musical works and the circumstances of performance under which those works arose and are offered—in the narrative that follows illuminates this devotion to purpose and persistence of tradition in relation to the prevailing historical conditions. It is in this light that the fruits of these performance traditions and artistic achievements—indeed, the essential rationale for the Club's existence—can perhaps be seen most clearly, particularly concerning the very tangible and productive results that the Club has consistently achieved on behalf of its alma mater over the past century and a half.

From the time of its humble beginnings as a student-run organization in 1872, the Rutgers Glee Club has considered its association with the college/university to be its most elemental and therefore indispensable affiliation. One of its earliest functions was to provide the college songs necessary to the proper presentation of that new and vital collegiate institution, the game of football. In later years, however, as the Glee Club matured into a musical entity that was renowned for its accomplishments throughout the nation, the role of the group as an ambassador for Rutgers and all that the college/university could offer to prospective attendees was a most crucial one. This was a responsibility that all directors, officers, and members of the group shouldered with pride.

Anniversaries are excellent occasions for reflection on the traditional features of such a well-established symbol. Thus the 150th-anniversary year of the Glee Club, which will be celebrated during the 2021–22 season, has served as the impetus for the composition of this volume. This detailed history is the brainchild of current Glee Club director Patrick Gardner, whose dedication to the traditions of the Rutgers University Glee Club is outlined in the narrative that follows. Gardner secured funding for this book from his close friend and Glee Club alumnus Robert Mortensen, '63, and then brought the project to the Rutgers University Press for publication. As a colleague of Gardner's in the Rutgers University Music Department of the Mason Gross School of the Arts, I was asked to do the research and present my findings in this format.

As I became more engaged with the project over the past months, I was struck by the enormous popular acclaim afforded to the Glee Club almost from the beginning of the Club's existence, both locally and, later, nationally and internationally. Indeed, the willingness of the group's leaders and members to adapt to advancing social and artistic styles and tastes over its long history in service of maintaining and, to be sure, expanding its popularity is one of the hallmarks of this organization. Throughout the various changes to its size, composition, and musical repertory that have taken place over the last 150 years, however, the group's dedication to its core mission—that of advancing the argument for the exceptional nature of the institution that it so proudly represents—has remained intact.

It is my hope that the narrative that follows not only embraces the historical facts of the group's development and maturation but also captures some of the sense of pride and purpose at the core of this organization that so clearly emerges in the various press accounts and oral histories that I have consulted in preparing this volume. In reading what follows, I ask that you look beyond the details of repertory and performance venues to observe the long arc of the group's development, to see how the Rutgers Glee Club is truly "ever-changing, yet eternally the same" with regard to its core mission and principles.

David F. Chapman
New Brunswick, New Jersey
May 24, 2021

A HISTORY OF THE
RUTGERS UNIVERSITY GLEE CLUB

INTRODUCTION

The institution that is today known as Rutgers, The State University of New Jersey was founded in 1766 as Queen's College, so named after Queen Charlotte of Mecklenburg-Strelitz, queen consort of the British king George III. Financed by the Dutch Reformed Church in the Netherlands, the mission of this enterprise, as stated by its most ardent advocate, Dutch American Dutch Reformed minister Theodorus Jacobus Frelinghuysen (1691–1747), was to establish "a university or seminary for young men destined for study in the learned languages and liberal arts, and who are to be instructed in the philosophical sciences."[1]

As such, Queen's College joined the ranks of Harvard (1636), William and Mary (1693), Yale (1701), and their later analogue institutions—such as the College of Philadelphia (1740, later the University of Pennsylvania), the College of New Jersey (1746, later Princeton), King's College (1754, later Columbia), and the College of Rhode Island (1764, later Brown)—as one of the nine institutions, including Dartmouth (1769), now known as the colonial colleges. Established prior to the onset of the Revolutionary War, these academies—unlike the European universities on which they purported to model themselves and despite the religious principles on which they were founded—were required to cater to the sort of theological heterogeneity that the American colonies, by their very nature, manifested.[2]

Beset by the problems of the Revolutionary War and subsequently by various fiscal crises of the early nineteenth century, Queen's College suffered two extended periods of closure before reopening permanently in 1825. At that time, members of the General Synod—a general assembly of the Dutch Reformed Church in America that was all but independent of the Classis of Amsterdam—and the board of trustees, the governing bodies of the college, felt that it would be appropriate to institute a change of name, recognizing the new circumstances in which the college resided as a fully American entity. Thus Queen's College passed into dim memory and Rutgers College emerged. The new designation was in honor of Colonel Henry Rutgers (1745–1830), at that time perhaps the most prominent layman in the American Dutch Reformed Church and a distinguished elder in a New York parish of that denomination—a man, by all accounts, of impeccable Christian qualities. Colonel Rutgers was also a wealthy landowner in New York, and the board may well have had some idea of financial support when bestowing this honor upon the venerable Rutgers; this expectation was realized, if somewhat modestly.[3]

Following the American Civil War, Rutgers College was a distinctly different institution than its earlier nineteenth-century incarnation. Ties with the Dutch Church had been all but severed, and a new spirit of academic inquiry was evident. Rutgers was designated as the land-grant college of New Jersey in 1864 and, as a direct result, established the Rutgers Scientific School, which featured departments of agriculture, engineering, and chemistry. This new curriculum brought with it an infusion of dynamic new professors keen on promoting their specific disciplines. After the reception of generous endowments from many quarters, new buildings were appearing with some regularity on campus. As former Rutgers president and renowned historian Richard P. McCormick says of this period, "The foundations were laid for a new Rutgers."[4]

By the 1870s, a new crop of students had made their way to the Rutgers campus. These young men came to avail themselves of the training in the new disciplines that were now being offered, and they assimilated quickly and completely into the old college ranks. Labeled "the Scientifs" by their fellow classmates in the well-established Classical Department, these new arrivals provided fresh blood for the many literary societies and fraternities that had arisen over the last several decades on campus.[5] In 1872, out of this spirit of academic and social renaissance, the Rutgers College Glee Club was formed.

Student organizations of all stripes emerged and perished from year to year during this period. In 1872, *The Scarlet Letter*—the student-initiated yearbook for the college that had begun publication only the previous year—listed such social groups as the Skating Club of '75, the Chess Club, and the Ancient Order of Eaters. There was also a Bible society and a boat club.[6] Indeed, the college boasted its own campus newspaper, the *Targum*, at this point a monthly publication. Founded in 1869, though a slightly earlier date has been posited in some versions of its history, the *Targum* is often described as the oldest continuously active student organization at Rutgers.[7] It is true that the *Targum* has been managed since its inception by a student-run editorial board; that fact seems clear in all versions of its history. However, during World War II, there was a gap of nineteen months during which the *Targum* was shut down due to wartime exigencies (from February

1944 to October 1945).[8] This, then, makes the Rutgers University Glee Club—which suffered some setbacks during World War II but remained in operation, albeit on a greatly reduced scale—the rightful claimant to the title of the oldest continuously active student-run organization at the institution.

The Rutgers College Glee Club was a manifestation of the very popular *Männerchor* tradition that had arrived in early nineteenth-century America via the large influx of German immigrants during this period. Also very influential in the development of this type of musical organization was the tradition of the British catch and glee clubs of the late-eighteenth century that, like the German practice, made its way to American shores. The narrative that follows outlines these influences and their effect on singing organizations in this country, particularly regarding collegiate groups. The Rutgers College Glee Club was a very early entrant in the ranks of such institutional organizations.

The Rutgers College Glee Club is often identified as being the eleventh oldest collegiate glee club in the United States. Its antecedents with similar all-male configurations at their inceptions include the clubs at Harvard (1858), the University of Michigan (1859), Yale (1861), Wesleyan (1862), the University of Pennsylvania (1862), Amherst (1865), Cornell (1868), Union College (1869), Lehigh (1869), and the University of Virginia (1871). However, some researchers have pointed to glee clubs at other such institutions whose dates of initiation intersect the above-cited list. Among these are male singing clubs at Kenyon College in 1866 and Williams College, Boston College, and Dartmouth, all in 1868.[9] How long and in what form any of these clubs may have survived throughout the years is clearly a mixed bag; some, like the Yale Glee Club, exist today as mixed-voice ensembles, while some of the organizations listed have become dormant. With regard to the historical placement of the Rutgers College Glee Club, it suffices to say that it is, indeed, one of the oldest such institutions in the United States.

The narrative that unfolds in the following chapters begins with some brief comments on the customs and practices that fed into the development of the collegiate glee club model of the nineteenth century. The *Männerchor* and catch club traditions are highlighted as forerunners of this style, with an emphasis on their impact on collegiate organizations such as the Rutgers College Glee Club. The balance of the extended narrative consists of a chronological account of the various iterations of the Rutgers Glee Club throughout its 150-year existence. From its inception in 1872 as a student organization begotten by the sophomores of the class of 1874 through its various configurations and focuses, the history of the Club is given in as much detail as is practicable. This includes a thorough examination of

3

the conditions of the group's genesis and the immediate aftermath of its organization.

The examination of the Glee Club's history explores the work of the various leaders /directors of the Club and their relationships to the group; the college/university; the community of New Brunswick, New Jersey, which contained the original college and now plays host to much of the expanded university; and the greater universe of choral music, particularly TTBB (tenor/tenor/bass/bass) organizations, throughout the United States and the world. This material includes details on the lives and careers of these directors: the flamboyant and occasionally erratic minstrel performer and composer Loren Bragdon (1856–1914), the group's first professional leader; his eventual replacement, the staid and circumspect church musician and renowned music educator George Wilmot (1858–1933); the founder of the Rutgers College Music Department and the man who oversaw the expansion of the Club into new avenues of repertory and performance practice, Howard Decker McKinney (1889–1980); McKinney's protégé and eventual replacement, Francis Austin "Soup" Walter (1910–2000), who facilitated Glee Club participation in performances, on the Rutgers campus and elsewhere, with world-class symphony orchestras and conductors and instituted a regimen of international travel for the Club; and Patrick Gardner (b. 1953), the Glee

Club's current director, who has taken the multifaceted tradition that these colorful and capable directors fashioned over the years and turned the Rutgers University Glee Club into a preeminent TTBB ensemble recognized the world over as a premiere professional-caliber organization.

When details of the exploits of these colorful leaders become too far-reaching, the narrative is supplemented with sidebars. These excursions from the basic chronology allow the reader to engage with greater details concerning the life and work of the various individuals and how they exerted an impact on the Glee Club. Naturally, in addition to the personalities of the leaders, there are a variety of customs and traditions that also require extended explication outside of the chronology. Issues such as the genesis and development of the signature Rutgers anthem "On the Banks of the Old Raritan" and the yearly extended-rehearsal excursions in the mid-twentieth century to the resort area of Lake Minnewaska, New York, receive detailed accounts. The long-standing tradition of the Christmas in Carol and Song concerts at Kirkpatrick Chapel on the Old Queens campus is more intimately examined in this fashion as well. There is also a discography of the recordings that the Club has participated in over the course of its existence, from its initial venture along these lines in 1943 to the present day.

Throughout the narrative and, indeed, within the more comprehensive and detailed sidebars as well, however, there is an overarching theme: the existence of the Rutgers University Glee Club as an extension of the institution that it represents. The available historical record makes it clear that the main mission of the organization, from its inception as a modest and somewhat slapdash student group in 1872 to its current poised and polished iteration, has always been to represent Rutgers as an exceptional entity, an entity with which association is a thing to be coveted and admired. The Glee Club has and always will represent the finest example of what it means to attend Rutgers. For the men who participated in its performance tradition, the memories of some of the events and performances recounted here will last a lifetime. And for all Rutgers-affiliated nonparticipants who basked—as students, alumni, or faculty—in the finished product of the group's diligent preparations, the Glee Club stands as a cherished link to their alma mater and the treasured memories of their associations therewith.

To avoid terminological and chronological confusion when reading the narrative that follows, two editorial points should be mentioned at the outset. The first concerns references in the general narrative and sidebars to the annual student yearbook of Rutgers College/University, *The Scarlet Letter*. First appearing in 1871, this yearbook was subsequently published every year—with the exception, due to wartime constraints, of the years 1944, 1945, and 1946—until 2005. *The Scarlet Letter* is an excellent resource for engaging with the traditions and customs of the various organizations that played such an important role in the life of Rutgers College/University from any given period. The narrative that follows makes ample use of this resource.

However, when considering references made to material taken from this source, please keep in mind the following circumstance. Between the years 1886 and 1931, *The Scarlet Letter* was published by the junior class. Thus the edition with the senior class of one year would have a publication date of the year following; for example, the senior class of 1888 would be represented by an edition of *The Scarlet Letter* dated 1889. This being the case, a reference in the following narrative to the list of officers for the Glee Club in the graduation-class year of 1895 might have a noted citation from *The Scarlet Letter* from 1896. This becomes even more convoluted when this procedure was abandoned in 1932; there are actually two 1932 editions of *The Scarlet Letter*, one published by the junior class and featuring the senior class of 1931 (published in 1932) and one published by and featuring the senior class of 1932.[10] Therefore, when the

5

narrative cites material from an edition of *The Scarlet Letter* published between 1886 and 1931, the accompanying note will refer to the year of publication, not the graduating class. All possible efforts are made in the narrative to identify the material according to the appropriate class year, so, in some cases, the cited yearbook date may seem incongruous. The reader should guard against faulty conclusions based on these inconsistencies.

One other editorial matter deserves brief mention. This introduction begins with a discussion of the establishment in 1766 of Queen's College, the precursor institution of Rutgers College/University.

All historical references to this as the original name of Rutgers College (Queen's College) appear with an apostrophe. However, throughout the narrative, there are also several references to Queens Campus or Old Queens Campus. These terms refer to the collection of buildings and the grounds on which they stand that constituted Rutgers College by the end of the nineteenth century. These structures include Winants Hall, Kirkpatrick Chapel, and the Old Queens Building—the oldest extant structure on today's Rutgers campus—among others. When referring to the Old Queens Building or to the campus itself (Queens Campus), no apostrophe is used.[11]

1 EARLY HISTORY

There is not any Musicke of Instruments whatsoever, comparable to that which is made of the voyces of Men, wher the voyces are good, & the same wel sorted and ordered.

—*William Byrd*, Psalmes, Sonets, and Songs
of Sadnes and Pietie, made into
Musicke of Five Parts

Choral singing with male voices is a tradition that can be traced back to the art forms of antiquity. Such configurations played a particularly strong role in the dramas that defined the arts in Periclean Greece. By 600 BCE, these stylized choruses had reached the level of true art music.[1] The dithyramb, a predramatic choreographed chorus that depicted the adventures of the fertility goddess Dionysus, is known to have been customarily composed of about fifty members, all men and boys.[2] The choirs organized by the Levites for temple services, as described in the Old Testament (First and Second Chronicles), were traditionally made up of adult males, though Levite boys were often allowed to participate, to "add the sweetness of their voices to the singing," and women were almost certainly included in choral singing in some capacity.[3] With the advent of Christianity, church leaders encouraged the incorporation of the Hebrew choral tradition into their services. However, St. Paul's admonition concerning the participation of women in church services laid the foundation for hundreds of years of their exclusion from sacred choirs.[4] From the papacy of Gregory I (590–604) through the Renaissance, the Roman Catholic Church, the main patron of choral music during this period, maintained this exclusion of women; during the lifetime of the Italian composer Giovanni Pierluigi da Palestrina (1525–94), the papal choir at St. Peter's Basilica in Rome employed only male singers, with boys taking on the soprano and alto parts.[5] While the quote above from William Byrd, Palestrina's contemporary, may not specifically use the term *men* to mean "male," there clearly would have been ample precedent for the performance of the works from his collection, *Psalmes,*

Sonets, and Songs of Sadnes and Pietie (1588), in an all-male format.[6]

The *Männerchor* Tradition and the English Catch Clubs

By the eighteenth century, the use of male voices to cover all registers in choral art music for church establishments was ubiquitous. That this tradition remained in force can be seen in the works of Johann Sebastian Bach, *Kantor* of the *Thomasschule* in Leipzig from 1727 to his death in 1750, who routinely used boys from the school establishment in his concerted choral works.[7] And in England, the tradition extended to performances of Handel's oratorios; his standard arrangement was to utilize boys as sopranos and men for the alto roles.[8]

The pervasiveness of this all-male musical texture in sacred vocal music during the eighteenth century had an influence on less exalted artistic expressions as well. In Germany and Austria, male choruses flourished. Scholars point to the German *Meistergesang* tradition as having had an impact on the development of the late-eighteenth- and nineteenth-century male chorus associations.[9] From the fourteenth to seventeenth centuries, German citizens banded together in guilds for the purpose of the composition and performance

of *Meisterlieder*. These *Meistersänger* were generally from the middle and lower classes, though participation by the professional classes (teachers, lawyers, the clergy, etc.) was also common.[10] The popularity of fraternal organizations, particularly the Freemasons, further fueled the composition of works for male groups. W. A. Mozart was an enthusiastic member of the order[11] and contributed to this repertory.[12] The result of these activities can be seen in the many male chorus organizations that flourished in Germany during the nineteenth century, including groups that were related to the German *Männerchor* tradition, such as the *Liedertafel* and *Liederkranz* societies.[13]

In eighteenth-century England, the male chorus found a home in clubs that were dedicated to the genres of the catch, the canon, and the glee. A catch could most simply be described as a humorous round for male voices, usually in three or four parts. The earliest catches appeared in the late sixteenth and early seventeenth centuries.[14] In the mid-eighteenth century, the interest in these popular and lively part-singing vehicles led to the development of a variety of gentlemen's clubs dedicated to their propagation. One of the first significant organizations of this type was the Noblemen's and Gentlemen's Catch Club, which was established in London in 1761. What differentiated the Catch Club (as it came to be called) from its contemporaneous counterparts, among which were the Madrigal Society (founded in 1741) and the Anacreontic Society (founded in 1766), was the institution in 1763 of annual prizes, one each in the classifications of catch, canon, and glee.[15] The response to this offer of remuneration was overwhelming, resulting in the production of works in these categories by the thousands during the course of the nineteenth century.[16]

An inherent problem existed, however, within the genre itself and therefore in the constitution of a club dedicated to it; the subject matter of the catch was not appropriate to all situations. Musicologist David Johnson states the matter thus: "The essential characteristic of the genre is its humour: catches were a celebration of irresponsible male leisure time, spent out of reach of the demands of women and children. Their words are usually on such subjects as drink, tobacco, music, different trades and their shortcomings, poor service in taverns, and especially, sex in its most ridiculous and least mentionable forms, the bodily functions of women being described with schoolboyish gusto. Occasionally the mixed blessings of fatherhood are also discussed."[17]

Notwithstanding the bawdy nature of much of the material, evidence indicates that members of the Noblemen's and Gentlemen's Catch Club, who were often of the noble classes, expected and, indeed, were provided with performances of these works that were of the highest quality. Much effort went into securing highly esteemed professional singers, often through the expedient of providing these professionals with honorary memberships.[18] The roster of the Catch Club boasted composers of considerable talents as well. In the early years of the Club's existence, many of the prizes for composition mentioned earlier were awarded to Samuel Webbe (1740–1816), a professional composer, organist, and accomplished bass singer, who served as the secretary of the Club from 1784 to 1812. Webbe produced hundreds of catches, canons, and glees for the Club during his years of involvement.[19]

The Glee Club of London (1787)

As mentioned previously, so keen was the vogue for such organizations in London during this period that independent clubs catering to similar pursuits also flourished. Such was the case with the Glee Club of London, which began offering memberships in 1787, making it one of the last major clubs to be established in that city in the eighteenth century.[20] There were, of course, connections to the earlier clubs, particularly to the Catch Club; Webbe, for example, was a founding member of the Glee Club and served as its initial librarian.[21] Beginning in 1790, every session of the Glee Club would be opened with the singing of Webbe's *Glorious Apollo*, a work that would become synonymous with the glee tradition.[22]

But the Glee Club also boasted strong connections to the Academy of Ancient Music, a London organization founded in 1726 and dedicated to the revival of sixteenth- and seventeenth-century sacred music and madrigals.[23] Though details of the repertory of the Glee Club are scarce, indications are that the interests of this new society lay more toward older and less controversial literature than did the Catch Club.[24] However, the core repertory still consisted of the genres of the catch, canon, and glee.

While a catch is a relatively straightforward form, often utilizing somewhat inappropriate texts, a glee frequently employs more sophisticated compositional methods and more elegant and idyllic (English-language) texts. The term *glee* is taken from the Anglo-Saxon words *glíw* or *gléo*, meaning "entertainment" or "merriment."[25] Originating in seventeenth-century England, a glee is a secular vocal composition for three or more voices. At its inception, the genre connoted participation by male voices only; upper parts were performed by male altos in three-voice configurations, and in later periods, boys were utilized for soprano parts, though female participation was occasionally seen.[26] In contrast to the catch and the canon, the texture of a glee was primarily homophonic, with relatively simple harmonizations.

That the glee tradition should migrate to the newly established American republic comes as no surprise. Despite the political tensions of the times, cultural ties between Britain and America remained strong. Glee clubs in Philadelphia, Boston, New York, and elsewhere in the former British colonies were founded roughly contemporaneously with (or slightly later than) their English counterparts.[27] Boston was particularly active in the realm of glee clubs, boasting the Junior Glee Club, the Boston Senior Glee Club, and later the Handel and Haydn Society, established in 1815 as one of these choral societies and still in existence today as a premiere historically informed performance ensemble.[28] It is therefore not surprising that when Harvard instituted the first collegiate glee club in the United States in 1858, it relied heavily on the tradition of the English Glee for its base repertory.[29] Indeed, Webbe's *Glorious Apollo*—a work that falls into the "harmonized song" category of glees as described above—was immediately embraced by the group and has been a standard of the Harvard Glee Club to the present day.[30]

But there was another strong influence in North America on the development of the glee club during the nineteenth century—that of the German *Männerchor* tradition. A large influx of German nationals following the Napoleonic Wars brought with them vestiges of the cultural artifacts of that community. The German singing societies are, indeed, thought by some scholars to be not only an extension of the

Meistergesang heritage but also a direct offshoot of the English catch and glee vogue of the eighteenth century.[31] Thus the confluence of styles, particularly in populous urban areas of the early nineteenth century, would seem to be a natural occurrence. This synergetic merging of traditions would, indeed, lead to changes in the concept of the glee genre. Questions of performing forces, repertory, proper venues, and so on, would all evolve in the midst of the cultural pluralism that was prevalent in early nineteenth-century America, particularly in the Northeast and Midwest regions, where the influences of the above-mentioned traditions were strongest.[32]

Collegiate Glee Clubs in America

One of the most important and enduring adaptations of these cultural artifacts can be found in the mid-nineteenth century establishment of collegiate glees clubs. During this period, college men—and the vast majority of contemporary American college students were men[33]—embraced both elite and popular song styles, reflecting the general tastes of society at large.[34] This can be seen in the numerous publications containing collections of college songs for all occasions; Yale College, for example, produced the first volume dedicated to the songs involved in the lives of students (*Songs of Yale*) in 1853.[35] This volume was marketed to the general public as well as to students; the editors suggest in the preface that the presentation of material was "thus affording amusement to outsiders who may be curious in such matters."[36] Further, technological improvements in the printing process at this time greatly enhanced the opportunities to produce such material efficiently and inexpensively.[37] With access to printed collections to enhance the male chorus traditions that were, by this time, firmly in place in American society, mid-nineteenth century college students had many options available to them. It is not surprising that many were drawn to the fraternal and convivial nature of both the glee and the *Männerchor* traditions. Thus the glee club was well positioned to become an enduring part of American collegiate life.

The first collegiate glee club in America was founded at Harvard College in 1858. Following rapidly in Harvard's footsteps, glee clubs appeared at the University of Michigan in 1859 and at Yale College in 1861.[38] Wesleyan College and the University of Pennsylvania both initiated glee clubs in 1862.[39]

The American Civil War (1861–65) did much to popularize the type of singing embraced by these groups; singing was a most favored activity among the various military regiments.[40] The conclusion of the Civil War saw the emergence of several new entrants into the realm of collegiate glee clubs: Amherst College (1865); Kenyon College (1866); Hampton Institute (1868); Cornell University (1868); Williams College (1869); Boston College (1869); Dartmouth College (1869); Union College (1869); and Wooster College (1870).[41]

Birth of the Rutgers College Glee Club

Rutgers College joined the ranks of collegiate glee clubs in 1872. While it led a somewhat tenuous existence in its early stages, contemporary accounts attest to the enthusiasm that this group engendered, not only from Rutgers students and faculty, but among the general public as well. Some of the highlights of the Rutgers University Glee Club are presented below for your consideration.

The Rutgers College Glee Club is first listed as an official student organization in the college yearbook, *The Scarlet Letter*, in 1872. It is therein identified as being incorporated under the auspices of the class of 1874—that is, the sophomore class. The vocal contingent of the group at this initial stage consisted of eleven members; the arrangement of voices was four sopranos, two altos, one first tenor, one second tenor, one baritone, one first bass, and one second bass. All members of the group were Rutgers College students, some of whom served as officers of the Club and also doubled as instrumental accompanists.[42] The list of Club officers indicates that Amos Van Etten served as the Glee Club's first leader, with George W. Van Horne serving as the group's inaugural president. As a sophomore, Leader Van Etten was active in several student organizations. He was a member of the Delta Kappa Epsilon fraternity,[43] a pitcher for the sophomore contingent of the Rutgers College (RC) Base Ball Club (Classical Section),[44] and was a member of Ye Jolly Boys' Cassino Club, where he is listed under the nickname "Bub."[45] As a senior, Van Etten was awarded the Bradley Prize for Mathematics from Rutgers College.[46]

The date of inception for the Glee Club can be corroborated from statements found in the 1874 issue of *The Scarlet Letter*. In that volume, the graduating class lays claim to the founding of the group in their opening "History of '74" section. They recount that during their freshman year, "a calithump in honor of the return of a respected Professor"[47] gave rise to the eventual formation the following year of the Glee Club.[48] This witty account contains partially obscured, yet easily decipherable, references to both President Van Horne and Leader "Bub" Van Etten and states unequivocally that the Glee Club was founded *non sibi, sed omnibus* (not for ourselves, but for all).[49]

GLEE CLUB OF '74.

OFFICERS.

GEO. W. VAN HORNE, *President.*
WM. STODDARD, *Vice-President.*
G. D. W. LYDECKER, *Secretary.*
JOHN OPPIE, *Treasurer.*
AMOS VAN ETTEN, *Leader.*

CHOIR.

JAS. PARKER, 1st Tenor.   H. N. FULLER, Soprano.
G. D.W. LYDECKER, 2d Tenor.   G. S. JONES, Alto.
P. J. FULLER, Soprano.   WM. STODDARD, Alto.
W. F. GASTON, Soprano.   A. VAN ETTEN, 1st Bass.
J. R. DURYEE, Soprano.   G. W. VAN HORNE, 2d Bass.
S. B. VREELAND, Baritone.

INSTRUMENTALISTS.

JOHN OPPIE,   } Organists.
G. W. VAN HORNE, }

H. N. FULLER, } Flutists.
P. J. FULLER, }

A. VAN ETTEN, Pianist.
JAS. PARKER, Cornet.

Leadership of the Glee Club appears to have been quite fluid in the group's nascent years. The 1874 edition of *The Scarlet Letter* lists William Hubert Osbourne as leader, with Edwin E. Colburn serving as president. Both officers played active roles in the ten-member ensemble. Osbourne sang second tenor while Colburn is designated as a first bass; Colburn is also named as a pianist for the group. The organization is listed in the 1874 edition as a sophomore group ('76 Glee Club), as it was in the inaugural 1872 yearbook.[50]

The following year yielded further changes. The group is listed in the 1875 issue of *The Scarlet Letter* as simply the "Rutgers College Glee Club." While still comprised mainly of members from the class of 1876, other classes are also represented. Now listed as president of the organization is Isaac D. Vanderpoel; the position of leader is filled by William R. Taylor. The roster indicates that Colburn now serves on a three-member executive committee, while still assigned a part in the ensemble (now second bass).[51]

With the graduation of the founding '76 members, the listing in the 1877 yearbook also indicates significant changes. Again open to all classes, the group now boasts sixteen singers. The posts of leader and president are no longer active; Henry Veghte is designated as the director of the ensemble, with E. Carman

The Scarlet Letter (1872), 46. Roster of the original Rutgers College Glee Club. Special Collections, Rutgers University Libraries.

Scudder serving as pianist and John Vanderpoel as organist (Vanderpoel is also listed among the singers).

Some of the above information is contradictory to the standard version of the genesis of the Rutgers College Glee Club, a version that seems to be inextricably bound to the legend of the composition of the most identifiable of all Rutgers songs, "On the Banks of the Old Raritan." The song's composer, Howard Newton Fuller, '74, was an important figure in more than one pivotal moment in the history of Rutgers College (see chap. 1 sidebar, "Howard Newton Fuller [1854–1931]"). And he was an active member of the original '74 Glee Club.[52] The main elements of this generally accepted account appear, among other places, in a 1947 article by Rutgers staff librarian Oliver Kip Westling.[53] The specifics of this tale are as follows.

The *Carmina Collegensia*, a compendium of contemporary American college songs proclaimed by its editor, Henry Randall Waite, to be definitively "complete," first appeared in 1868.[54] Waite declared in his preface to the volume that "every college in the United States has been solicited to contribute its songs, and two years have been occupied in making the collection. Nearly, perhaps all, of the colleges having songs are represented on the following pages."[55] Rutgers College, however, was not represented in this publication.

The Scarlet Letter (1874), 60. Glee Club roster for the 1873–74 academic year. Special Collections, Rutgers University Libraries.

'76 Glee Club.

Officers.

E. E. COLBURN,	PRESIDENT.
C. C. VAN DEUSEN,	VICE-PRESIDENT.
I. D. VANDERPOEL,	SECRETARY.
J. D. PRINCE, JR.,	TREASURER.
W. H. OSBORNE,	LEADER.

LE ROY BRUMAGHIM,	1st Tenor.	E. E. COLBURN,	1st Bass.
J. E. LYALL,	1st Tenor.	W. R. TAYLOR,	1st Bass.
I. D. VANDERPOEL,	1st Tenor.	H. C. KELLEY,	2nd Bass.
W. H. OSBORNE,	2nd Tenor.	JOHN LEFFERTS, JR.,	2nd Bass.
C. C. VAN DEUSEN,	2nd Tenor.	J. D. PRINCE, JR.,	2nd Bass.

Quartette.

C. C. VAN DEUSEN.	W. R. TAYLOR.
W. H. OSBORNE.	JOHN LEFFERTS, JR.

Pianists.

E. E. COLBURN.

W. R. TAYLOR.

Whether Rutgers was solicited by Waite to submit songs to the edition and simply did not respond or was not, in fact, approached to contribute is unclear. Nonetheless, it is evident from contemporary accounts that Rutgers by this time did, indeed, have a substantial body of school songs that would have warranted inclusion in such a collection.[56]

Distressed by this situation, a committee to develop a songbook for Rutgers was appointed in 1873. The hope was that such a collection of Rutgers songs would be wholeheartedly supported by the general college community. Further, the committee solicited submissions of songs from students, graduates, faculty, and trustees and encouraged all to participate in the compilation and eventual distribution of the finished product.[57]

The committee that was formed included the following members: Alexander Johnston, '70; John Oppie, '74; Howard N. Fuller, '74; Edwin E. Colburn, '76; John Lefferts, '76; and John W. Searing, '74.[58]

In the standard telling of the story, the group that is identified as the Glee Club of '76 was formed as a result of the songbook effort; Colburn and Lefferts are identified as being included in this ten-member ensemble.[59] Howard N. Fuller, composer of the text for "On the Banks of the Old Raritan," is not listed as a member of the '76 Glee Club, though Westling does note that he participated in the '74 Glee Club. It is further documented by Westling that the Glee Club of '76 performed in various locations under that name.[60] This much would seem to comport with the information from the yearbooks cited previously. However, several subsequent sources have stated that this group formed the initial iteration of the Rutgers College Glee Club and have cited Colburn as the founder of the group.[61]

Considering the information provided, it would seem that the sophomores of the 1872 yearbook can justifiably lay claim to being the original Rutgers College Glee Club, with "Bub" Van Etten and George V. Van Horne recognized as the founding leader and president, respectively. Colburn, as a member of the class of '76, was not yet a student at the college. Nor do any of the '74 Glee Club members appear to have participated in the '76 Glee Club. The impact of the Colburn and Lefferts group is, of course, undeniable; their efforts to organize and popularize the group, through the Rutgers songbook as well as public performances, are extremely important to the legitimization of the Glee Club in the eyes of the college and the larger collegiate universe. Indeed, the 1876 edition of the *Carmina Collegensia* includes several Rutgers songs, for which members of this group can claim direct credit.[62] And Fuller's contribution is equally important. But the role of founders should be rightly attributed to the members of the '74 Glee Club.

Composition of "On the Banks of the Old Raritan" (1873)

The most emblematic and most easily recognized song in the Rutgers Glee Club repertory is without a doubt "On the Banks of the Old Raritan." As stated in the narrative above, the appearance of this song in 1873 came at an important moment for the group, which was still in its infancy. It was immediately incorporated into Glee Club programs and has remained there throughout the many changes that have occurred around it, eventually becoming the college/university's alma mater (see chap. 1 sidebar, "Alma Mater").

The man responsible for the creation of the song was Howard Newton Fuller of New Baltimore, New York. Fuller held several distinctions as a Rutgers College student. He was an avid participant in the areas of class governance, the arts, and other activities throughout his time at Rutgers. Additionally, his contributions to the field of intercollegiate sports are well documented (see chap. 1 sidebar, "Howard Newton Fuller [1854–1931]"). But perhaps his most lasting contribution was the composition of the lyrics for the iconic "On the Banks of the Old Raritan." As with some of the details concerning the genesis of the Glee Club, Fuller's account of the circumstances surrounding the composition of the song and the obtainable facts do not always correspond. In 1906, Fuller

presented in writing his version of the events leading up to the writing of "On the Banks" to William Clinton Armstrong, editor of the volume *Patriotic Poems of New Jersey*; Armstrong included Fuller's lyrics in his publication. The essence of this story, as related by Fuller and appearing in that volume, is as follows:

At approximately 3:00 p.m. on a winter afternoon in 1873, Edwin E. Colburn, president of the '76 Glee Club, visited Fuller in his room at 41 Schureman Street in New Brunswick. Apparently, the Glee Club had scheduled an engagement for that evening in the town of Metuchen, New Jersey; in this account, this is the Glee Club's first performance. Colburn was eager to have ready a song that ably represented the college for this important event. Further, Colburn indicated that the song must be produced by no later than 5:00 p.m. so that the Glee Club would have the necessary time to prepare it for performance. Fuller then composed his lyrics and set them to the contemporary popular tune of "On the Banks of the Old Dundee." The result was an immediate success, drawing an extremely favorable reaction from that evening's audience. The song was subsequently scored for publication by John Oppie, '74, who had served on the songbook committee.[63]

Other sources, however, offer facts that would seem to contradict elements of this narrative. It can be verified that the '76 Glee Club gave a performance on

December 11, 1873, in Flatbush, Long Island. According-ing to a report in the *Kings County Rural Gazette*, eight of the ten members of the Glee Club participated in this performance, which occurred at the private residence on Fenimore Street of Mr. John Lefferts, father of a prominent member of the Glee Club. Among other selections, "On the Banks of the Old Raritan" was featured in this performance.[64] Westling suggests that in offering his account years later, Fuller conflated the Flatbush performance, possibly the first public appearance of the Glee Club, with the performance that took place on March 17, 1874, in Metuchen, possibly the first performance of the entire ten-member ensemble.[65]

However, it should also be noted that there are indications that performances prior to December 11, 1873, may have occurred. An article in the *Targum* of April 1873 states the following: "Never has any class in Rutgers kept a Glee Club alive, and in such a flourishing condition, as long as the Freshman. Some of the best singers in College are '76 men. As soon as the weather becomes sufficiently agreeable, and plenty of new and comparatively unheard of songs have been practised, they intend to sing in the principal towns in the State, and whatever compensation may be received it shall be devoted to the advancement of the Club. They have our best wishes, and with the talent they possess, shall they not be glorified?"[66]

Though no records of concerts between April and December of 1873 have been found, it would seem that, at the least, the intention of the Glee Club to perform existed prior to the December 1873 concert. Therefore, an 1873 Metuchen performance cannot be ruled out. Still, the performance at Metuchen on March 17, 1874, is described in such detail in the *Targum* as to suggest that this is the concert to which Fuller may have been referring in his narrative some years later. Again, Westling's theory of a conflation of stories seems to account for all these facts. But given the inconsistencies that are present, it is not unreasonable to assume that other aspects of the story of the genesis of "On the Banks" may also be apocryphal.

HOWARD NEWTON FULLER

(1854–1931)

Howard Newton Fuller was, by any standard, an important figure in the history of Rutgers College. Born in New Baltimore, New York, in 1854, he began his studies at Rutgers in the fall of 1870. He and his brother, Perry James Fuller—who, like Howard, was a prominent member of the class of '74—shared rooms together at 41 Schureman Street in New Brunswick for most of their college days.[67]

The Fuller brothers asserted a strong presence in their class from the very beginning. In their freshman year (1870–71), Perry served as class president while Howard filled the post of class historian; Howard would continue in this post through his senior year.[68] In his sophomore year (1871–72), Howard became a member of the fraternity Zeta Psi and served as one of four directors of the Rutgers College Targum Association, the student newspaper that then published monthly.[69] He was also associated with the Rutgers Chess Club[70] and, of course, was a member of the inaugural iteration of the Glee Club, singing soprano.[71]

In 1873, Howard Fuller would participate in two pivotal moments in Rutgers history. It was in that year that he and fellow Rutgers College Glee Club member John W. Searing served as representatives at a conference in New York City. Initiated by Yale College, the purpose of the conference was "to organize the first intercollegiate football association and define a uniform game."[72] Fuller's credentials for this assignment were excellent; he was an outstanding student athlete and served as president of the Rutgers College Foot Ball Association in his senior year (1873–74);[73] he also played center field for the Rutgers College Base Ball Association.[74] And in 1873, so the story goes, Howard Fuller composed the lyrics for "On the Banks of the Old Raritan" in a matter of hours (see chap. 1, "Composition of 'On the Banks of the Old Raritan' [1873]").

In addition to these accomplishments, in his senior year, Fuller served as an editor of the class yearbook, *The Scarlet Letter*.[75] Along with Perry, he was a member of the Rutgers Philoclean Literary Society;[76] Howard was also elected to the post of president of the Rutgers College Temperance Society.[77] His breadth of interests and wealth of skills truly distinguished Howard Fuller from many of his less-accomplished classmates.

Upon leaving Rutgers, Fuller attended medical school for two years. Unfortunately, it became necessary for him to abandon his career in medicine and assist his father in his flour and feed business. He eventually pursued a career in banking, becoming the director of the Home Savings Bank in Albany in 1902 and vice president of the bank in 1910. Fuller attained the position of president of the bank in 1923. He died on February 28, 1931, survived by his brother, Perry, and several nieces and nephews.[78]

1872–79: Fits and Starts

It seems that once established, the Glee Club of Rutgers College had great difficulty achieving any sort of continuous existence. Contemporary records are replete with references to attempts at forming an ensemble that failed to take hold as well as to a general lack of organization and even apathy when it came to presenting the Rutgers College Glee Club as an organization worthy of representing the college.

As discussed previously, the very popular and widely praised '76 Glee Club had an impactful reign. This apparently began in their freshman year, as the *Targum* noted that the Glee Club was hopeful of presenting performances in the spring and fall semesters of 1873.[79] These are admirable sentiments and very much in keeping with what we have previously heard concerning the Glee Club of '76. Further, the fall semester of 1873 led to the formation of the committee to compile the *Rutgers Songbook* and the putative inaugural performance of the Glee Club in Flatbush. Making good on the promise to explore as many performance venues as possible, the '76 Glee Club planned to make its first appearance in the city of Newark "shortly after the Sophomore Exposition" of 1874,[80] scheduled for February 23 of that year.[81] The much-discussed concert at Metuchen of March 17, 1874, caused considerable excitement in the college community; that month's edition of the *Targum* delayed publication until details of that concert could be printed.[82] This very successful venture was followed up by an equally well-received event at Somerville, New Jersey, the following June.[83] Thus the anticipated success of the Glee Club seemed by the end of the 1874 academic year to have been at least partially realized.

The year 1875, however, does not appear to have lived up to this promise. A brief statement in the January 1875 edition of the *Targum* expresses hopes for a forthcoming concert, the proceeds of which are designated to be dedicated to the Rutgers College Boating Association.[84] Notwithstanding, there is no further mention of this concert (or any other) in subsequent issues of the student newspaper that year. Nor does it appear that 1876 fared any better for the Glee Club. Though still a viable entity with nine singers and Edward Colburn as a member of that year's executive committee, public performances were lacking.[85] Despite the publication of a new edition of the *Carmina Collegensia* in January of that year containing Rutgers school songs, there appears to have been little interest, within the college walls or outside of them, in the Club.[86] An article in the *Targum* bemoaning the general apathy of the student body toward their collegiate organizations specifically mentions the Glee Club: "Once there was a glee club. Only once. They sang! They sing no more."[87] By May of 1876, the hopes for a viable iteration of the Glee Club had been transferred to the freshman class ('79); a *Targum* article from that date states that

> the idea of a Glee Club is [not] anything particularly original or remarkable in itself, but it is very appropriate at the present time, because no such organization now exists in our College. The '76 Glee Club has long been a thing of the past, and neither the Sophomores nor Juniors have vim enough to get their singers together and practice. The consequence is, the singing of College songs by us is almost a lost art. . . .
>
> It seems too bad to have the old practice die out. . . . The organization of a Glee-Club by the Freshmen is one step toward the desired end. We hope it will not be the last.[88]

The following academic year (1876–77) began with renewed hopes of a viable Glee Club being established.[89] The role of leader (or now director) of this newly constituted ensemble went to Henry Veghte, '77. Veghte was, like so many prominent Glee Club members, an active and influential student at the college. In his sophomore year, he was selected to be class treasurer[90] and won the Rutgers College prize for grammar.[91] He served as class president in his senior year[92] and acted as an editor of that year's edition of *The Scarlet Letter*.[93]

It is indicated that Veghte was a capable director for the ensemble and that he had the confidence of the group and the college community overall, at least in the early part of his tenure. Further, he seems to have aimed high with his musical aspirations for the group. A brief mention in the *Targum* attests to these sentiments: "The Glee Club are very ambitious. They are now murdering parts of Mozart's first Mass. Well, we think Veghte will get them through alright."[94] And yet it would seem that inactivity still ruled the day for the Glee Club. In February of 1877, the *Targum* was moved to comment thus: "The Glee Club still howleth. The general inquiry is 'When will be the first Concert?'"[95] And by June, the *Targum* put the following question to the student body: "The Williams College Glee Club has made a successful tour of several large cities. Why can't we have such a Glee Club[?]"[96] So it would seem that the promising start to Henry Veghte's Glee Club did not live up to college expectations.

Following the graduation of Veghte in June of 1877, the academic year 1877–78 gave rise to evermore impassioned pleas for a viable Glee Club, encouraging participation from the current class of freshmen.[97] This appeal would seem to have been heeded; the March 1878 issue of the *Targum* announced the formation of a Glee Club by the first-year students.[98] But to judge by a rather lengthy article in the *Targum* from the following academic year (December 1878), the Glee Club purportedly organized by the freshmen in the spring of 1878 failed to take root.[99]

The academic year 1879–80 seems to have begun with an established Glee Club in place. It would also seem that the ideal of travel, which was an aspiration for the group that had been previously expressed in print, was now being addressed by this new iteration of the Club. The November 1879 edition of the *Targum* contains the following announcement: "The Glee Club will give a concert in Norwich, Ct., during Thanksgiving recess, instead of at Poughkeepsie, as first proposed. The Club has tendered its services for the Hospital benefit concert, to be given soon."[100] The Glee Club also had a performance in New York scheduled for January of 1880.[101] In May, an announcement was made in the *Targum* to the effect that a new Glee Club had been formed "under the leadership of J. Andrus Cowles" and that it was "the intention of this club in due time to give concerts."[102] It was also noted in the *Targum* at this time that other collegiate glee clubs, particularly that of Amherst College, were in the habit of traveling to diverse locales to offer performances. The author of the article offers these facts "for the encouragement of our own Glee Club, which has recently been revived."[103]

Thus by the summer of 1880, this nascent Club was far from a settled entity. However, circumstances that would arise during the following academic year would place the Rutgers College Glee Club on a new and much more structurally sound footing.

1880–95: Stable Leadership

As we have seen, the early groups that were formed at Rutgers College to explore the glee club tradition sought the laudable goal of enhancing the college's reputation and standing throughout the collegiate universe. These groups were, at least at the time of their formation, well received, often highly regarded, and to some extent, well supported by the Rutgers College community. However, it would also appear that the various early incarnations of the Glee Club were all too often lacking in focus and clarity of purpose. The songbook that was proposed in 1873 was by 1880 still forthcoming. The presentation of public concerts by the Glee Club between 1874 and 1880 would seem to have been sporadic at best. Further, the nature of the group as an entirely student-oriented ensemble—with officers and a leader all recruited from the student ranks—made certain that some organizational and structural problems would be transferred from iteration to iteration as graduation took its toll. The situation, as perceived some forty years after the 1880–81 season, was described as follows: "For many years previous there had been class [Glee] clubs, organized by those musically inclined, and devoted entirely to their own interests, but these had no official sanction."[104]

These circumstances came to an end, however, in the academic year 1880–81. It was at this time that Loren Bragdon took the reins of the Glee Club as its leader;[105] he would continue in this position for the next fourteen years. During this period, Bragdon's musical expertise and organizational skills would propel the Rutgers College Glee Club to a prominent position in the burgeoning world of collegiate singing societies. Placing an emphasis on public concerts and travel to as many locations as practicable given the nature of the group, Bragdon raised the profile of the Glee Club to the world at large while solidifying its position as a cherished institution within the college.

Early in the academic year of 1880–81, lack of support from the college community was still apparently holding back any efforts to offer a stable and productive Glee Club:

> A few of our enterprising men, upon close consideration last Spring, thought it would be possible to organise and establish a College Glee Club. The project was set on foot, and all was done that good leadership and the few that cooperated in the matter could do. But there was a lack of sympathy and support by many of the good singers in College, which was very

discouraging, and which hindered it from thriving as it should. We heartily endorse the effort made and believe that it will be a great addition to the College. It is a thing greatly needed, and of which we have been in want for a long time. It should have the support of all the College; of those who have good voices, by their becoming members of it, and of others by their support financially. We are glad to say that it is still intended to push forward the project. Let us have a rousing Glee Club, and there is no doubt but that happy results will follow.[106]

It would seem that a visit to the Rutgers campus by the Princeton Glee Club during the fall semester of 1880 served as a catalyst for the efforts to invigorate the group that the above quote encourages. In an effort to improve the organizational structure of the group, a new business manager for the Club, George B. Fielder, '81 (apparently the first man to officially hold this position), was elected.[107] Further, the outside interest stimulated by this visit from the Princeton club led to the formation of a committee to reconstitute the entire organization under new operational procedures. The students who made up this committee were J. Russell Verbrycke, '81; Alfred F. Skinner, '83; and J. Waterbury Scudder, '83.[108] Thus launched in December of 1880, the familiar sense of optimism toward this latest incarnation is again prevalent in the college colloquies:

> There really seems to be an air of earnestness about the latest glee club. We give it, as we have always given its predecessors, our best blessing, and hope that in our next number we shall not have to write its obituary. Let the good of the club be preferred to all personal considerations, and one of the rocks on which former clubs have split will have been removed. If it be necessary to remove a member, do not be too tender hearted to do it. As soon as the students see that it will be an honor to sing in the club they will be ready and anxious to fill vacancies. Perhaps the best thing for the club would be for the managers of some charity to again invite the glee club from some other college to sing in our city.[109]

There were, however, reports of "early trouble" within this group.[110] A retrospective analysis of these difficulties, in which a lack of strong leadership is identified as the culprit, is presented by the Glee Club in the 1884–85 edition of *The Scarlet Letter*.[111] This was solved, according to the account in that yearbook, "by securing the services of Mr. Loren Bragdon, '76, as leader; and from this time the prospects of the club

began to brighten."[112] By January of 1881, a new governing structure for the group had been announced. The elected officers were first listed as follows: Cornelius I. Haring, '81, president; Alfred F. Skinner, '83, secretary; William C. Miller, '83, treasurer; and George B. Fielder, '81, was retained as the group's business manager. Named to a three-man board of directors are Fielder, J. Russell Verbrycke, '81, and Loren F. Bragdon.[113] This list is emended in an account in the *Targum* several weeks later to indicate that Mr. Bragdon had been elected musical director in January and, in accepting the office, had resigned his position on the original board of directors. He was replaced on the board by Howard M. Lansing, '82, who also served as the assistant business manager for the group.[114] It is this latter configuration, and particularly the appearance of Loren Bragdon as the newly installed musical director (or leader), that would at last provide the structure and cohesion necessary to form a permanent Glee Club of which the entire college could be proud.

Success was immediate. A concert on January 19, 1881, was presented in Bound Brook to a "numerous and enthusiastic audience." And plans for another concert at the Pitman M. E. Church in New Brunswick on February 2, 1881, were announced amid calls for "every one of the 145 students of the College [to] be in attendance and make the thing live."[115] At this latter event, "the audience was surprised to find so much musical ability and cultivation displayed."[116] According to a contemporary account of this concert, the Club consisted of sixteen members at this point, with Professor Bragdon—as he is identified in the 1885 Glee Club essay—as leader and Cyrus C. Smith, '83, serving as pianist for the group.[117] Evidence of Bragdon's influence on the repertory of the Club can be seen even at this early juncture. While most of the selections on the program were college airs, two of Bragdon's compositions, "Golden Wedding" and "Annie of Lindenthal," were featured and very well received. The latter was a musical setting by Bragdon to words by Rutgers College student James MacMullen, '83. All of this served to impress and please Dr. William Henry Campbell, president of Rutgers College, who was in attendance; it was reported that he seemed "much gratified" by the effort put forth by "his boys."[118]

A performance at the Jersey City Tabernacle on February 28, 1881, for the benefit of the First Union Sunday School produced similar praise. An account in the *Jersey City Evening Journal* from March 1 states that "the programme rendered was a fine one, embracing college songs, glees, and chants that are world wide." Again Bragdon's talents are spotlighted; he sang "Annie of Lindenthal" for this performance also, and his "remarkable vocal abilities" were the subject of comment in the *Evening Journal* article.[119] Bragdon, identified in this article as musical director of the

group, also performed two piano duets with accompanist Smith, which were described as "superbly executed." It is notable that the evening concluded with a rendition of "On the Banks of the Old Raritan" (identified in the account as "On the Banks of the Raritan").[120]

At this time, plans for a grand concert at the Opera House in New Brunswick were announced. A large advertisement was placed in the March 11, 1881, *Targum* edition, stating that on Monday, March 28, the Glee Club would perform "a new programme . . . comprising selections from the most popular authors, and never before rendered by any college glee club." The Glee Club would be assisted in this performance by the well-known New York soprano Miss Nettie Balmor.[121] The concert received a glowing review in the April 15 edition of the *Targum*, in which it was noted that "an audience of nearly 500 persons greeted the appearance of the Club, and showed by its applause its appreciation of the efforts made for its entertainment."[122] In addition to the generally favorable remarks about the ensemble, the great skill and musicality of accompanist Cyrus Smith were again noted, as were the efforts of Bragdon, "to whose efficient leadership the Club so largely owes its success."[123]

This article also mentions the tour that was undertaken by the Glee Club during the spring recess of 1881, which took the form of a series of concerts at

GRAND CONCERT

·¡· BY THE ·¡·

Rutgers College Glee Club,

(Assisted by Miss Nettie Balmor, of New York,)

At the Opera House, New Brunswick, N. J.,

ON MONDAY EVENING, MARCH 28th, 1881.

ADMISSION,   -   -   FIFTY CENTS.

Tickets are exchangeable for Reserved Seats without extra charge, at Kilmer's Drug Store, on and after March 23d.

Opera House concert, March 28, 1881, ticket. Rutgers University Glee Club Archives.

different locations along the Hudson River. Towns in which the Club performed included Yonkers, Fishkill (Matteawan), Poughkeepsie, Hudson, and Kingston. An extended account of this tour can be found in the May 6, 1881, edition of the *Targum*, which takes pains to note that, though arduous, the singers maintained a level of excellence in performance that was a tribute not only to their dedication to the tour and the Club in general but also to their affinity for their leader, Loren Bragdon. The article concludes with an evaluation of these conditions and a look ahead:

In the Concerts given by the Glee Club up to this time we have had every reason to feel flattered by the receptions we have received at the hands of those living in the places visited. Everywhere the Glee Club has compelled the respect of others, both on account of gentlemanly behavior and on account of our good entertainments. That we have been able to give the latter is owing to the time and labor spent by our leader, Mr. Bragdon, '76, in training the voices up to their present state of culture and in the

25

sixteen concerts that have already been given, nothing but praises have been heard both for the able way in which he has led the Glee Club and for his own effective singing in rendering "Gone Forever," "The Italian Opera," and his imitation of the cornet. Mr. Bragdon's three original pieces, "Bow-wow-wow," "Rhyme of the Revellers," and the "Vocal Waltz," have always met with the highest appreciation, especially the latter, which has been pronounced by connoisseurs as one of the finest productions of this kind in music. The Glee Club, as is stated in another column of this issue, is to give several concerts before June. Mr. Bragdon also hopes to train several new voices, both to sing in our final Concert in the Opera House at Commencement, and to fit them for a position on the Glee Club next year.[124]

A complete list of the concerts given by the newly established Rutgers College Glee Club under the direction of Loren Bragdon during its initial semester in the spring of 1881 can be found in the 1882 edition of *The Scarlet Letter*.[125] This list includes twenty-two performances, including those from the Hudson River tour. In addition to those mentioned above, this schedule included excursions to Mount Holly, New Jersey (Concert Hall, April 23), Brooklyn, New York (Music Hall, April 28), Philadelphia, Pennsylvania (Association Hall, May 13), and Trenton, New Jersey (Taylor Opera House, May 30). The academic year 1880–81 concluded with the performance at the Opera House in New Brunswick on June 20 mentioned in the prior quotation from the *Targum*, at which the Glee Club was assisted by the well-known contralto Mrs. Belle Cole of New York,[126] an artist with whom the Club would have occasion to work in future performances.[127]

In the midst of the great success of the 1881 season, the Glee Club took the opportunity to further solidify its organizational structure. An election of officers was held in early May, resulting in the retention of all officers from the January election save for the position of business manager, which was now filled by Abram B. Havens, '83. The position of secretary was added, filled by Myron T. Scudder, '82.[128] It was also at this time that the group undertook to adopt a constitution and to make provisions "for the permanent welfare of the Club."[129]

It seems that a further step toward professionalization of the club was taken at this time, perhaps as one of the aforementioned provisions. The final concert of the season on June 20 was to have been given as part of the commencement week ceremonies for the college. However, according to at least one account, this concert had another purpose as well. The *Targum* ran the following item in its May 6, 1881, issue: "Concerts of the Glee Club: In Philadelphia, on May 13th, and probably in Burlington, N. J., on May 12th. Arrangements are being completed by the Business Manager for concerts at New York, Plainfield, Rahway, Jersey City, Morristown, Orange, Newark, and New Brunswick again during Commencement week. The proceeds of the latter concert are to go for the purpose of repaying in part the inestimable services rendered the College by Mr. Bragdon, '76, in training the Glee Club as ably as he has done." Thus the position of leader was now placed on a paying basis; Mr. Bragdon, the only nonstudent involved in the venture, became the person on whom the responsibility for the tutelage and presentation of the Club had fallen, and for these duties, the Club had decided that he should be compensated. The custom of bestowing the proceeds from the annual commencement concert on the Club leader would endure for many years.[130] This is a stark departure from the student-centered organizational strategy of the previous incarnations of the Rutgers College Glee Club, one that would have far-reaching implications for the continued existence of the organization.

While tremendous progress had been made during the spring semester of 1881, there were apparently still some rough edges to be planed in terms of the presentation of the Glee Club. Appraisals of the concert that was given at the Opera House in New Brunswick on December 19, 1881, draw attention to some of these defects. In a *Targum* article describing this performance, the sparse audience is commented on and compared unfavorably to the turnout at a Glee Club event at Association Hall in Philadelphia on December 15, which drew an estimated crowd of 1,800.[131] It was clear from the *Targum* account that an effort was made to present a program that was "new and entertaining."[132] Indeed, the featured soloist was Miss Anna Teresa Berger (1853–1925), a well-known cornet soloist who traveled extensively in the United States and abroad.[133] But there were quibbles concerning some aspects of the evening's proceedings. It was commented that, though the program was presented, for the most part, "under Mr. Bragdon's able leadership . . . with such skill and good taste as to be beyond criticism," there was "some dreadful screeching . . . amongst the first Tenors." Bragdon himself is criticized for his participation in a duet, during which he "sang so loud as to entirely drown out Mr. Smith's fine tenor." Exception was taken to some of the musical selections as well; the piece "Come Along, Sinner" was described as "little less than disgusting, and . . . wholly beneath the dignity of College students."[134]

A communication to the *Targum* editor, published in the "Campus Echoes" section of the student journal, also points to some general failings in Mr. Bragdon's leadership of the Club:

> Mr. Editor,
>
> There is nothing to criticise in the appearance of our Glee Club on the stage—they are orderly yet not too stiff, and seem perfectly at home. The leader, however, and we do not say it in a grumbling spirit of fault-finding, succeeds in making himself a little too conspicuous by his continuous rambling in and out and about the stage. An audience will appreciate his merits all the more if he can manage to restrain himself and act with some propriety.
>
> B. Y.

Despite these minor issues, the reputation of the Glee Club as a worthy institution continued to grow. A concert at the New Brunswick Opera House featuring the Hungarian violin virtuoso Eduard (Ede) Reményi (1828–98) in January of 1882 included the Glee Club,[135] apparently by special invitation from the artist himself.[136] And other concerts from the spring semester of that year met with high praise and favorable reviews. The *Targum* states that by June of 1882, "the Glee Club, under efficient management, is flourishing and highly complimented on their concerts."[137]

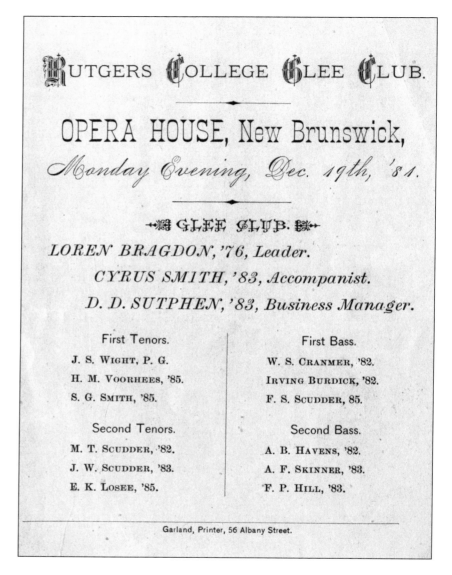

The 1881–82 Glee Club was a twelve-member ensemble, with all singers filling posts as officers. Though primarily made up of currently enrolled students, two members of the Club are listed as postgraduates, though their names do not appear on the roster

PROGRAM.

PART I.

Piano Duett,—"Rutgers Glee Club Galop."	Bragdon.
Messrs. SMITH & BRAGDON.	
March,	Becker.
Rutgers Co-education Song,	———
Solo by Mr. SKINNER, '83.	
Menu,	Karl Merz.
Duet,—"Fisherman,"	Gabussi.
Messrs. SMITH, '85 and BRAGDON.	
Medley,	Carmina.
Cornet Solo,— "Young America Polka,"	Levy.
ANNA TERESA BERGER.	
O Summer Night,	Donizetti.
Fra Diavolo,	Carmina.
Solo by Mr. Scudder, '82.	

PROGRAM.

PART II.

My Bonnie,	Carmina.
Solo by Mr. SMITH, '85.	
Quartette. { a. Sweet and Low,	Barnby.
{ b. The Little German Band,	Anon.
Messrs. WIGHT, BRAGDON, SCUDDER, '82, SKINNER.	
Come along, Sinner,	———
Solo by Mr. WIGHT.	
Solo—"Yeoman's wedding song."	Poniatowski.
Mr. BRAGDON.	
Cornet Solo—"Russian Fantasie."	Levy.
ANNA TERESA BERGER.	
Fatinitza,	Von Suppe.
Messrs. BRAGDON, WIGHT, SCUDDER, '82.	
"Bolumkus,"	Anon.
Conducted by Mr. SCUDDER, '82.	
Good bye, Mavourneen,	Allendorf.
Solo by Mr. Bragdon.	

Program, New Brunswick Opera House, December 19, 1881. Rutgers University Archives.

of postgraduate students for this academic year.[138] This twelve-member format seems to have been adhered to in subsequent years as well, with occasional deviations, and the addition of graduate students and postgraduate members becomes less frequent as the years progress.

By the late 1880s, the Glee Club held a secure and stable position as one of the premiere organizations of the college. This reputation was also known to the public at large through the successful tours and other excursions to venues outside of the Club's local environs. Travel was still an integral part of the Club's charter in the academic year 1887–88; before the Christmas holiday of 1887, performances were given in Brooklyn, New York (November 18); Gravesend, New York (November 30); Bloomfield, New Jersey (December 2); Newark, New Jersey (December 5); Jersey City, New Jersey (December 6); and Philadelphia, Pennsylvania (December 10).[139] A Rutgers College commencement concert featuring the Glee Club was rapidly becoming a tradition; they appeared at the Opera House in New Brunswick on June 18, 1888, as the finale to the commencement exercises. The following account of the concert speaks to the Club's continued popularity and also to the expanded scope of their travels during this period:

Program, Taylor Opera House, November 21, 1881.
Rutgers University Glee Club Archives.

+GRAND CONCERT+
—BY—
Rutgers College Glee Club
AT TAYLOR OPERA HOUSE,
Monday Evening, Nov. 21st, '81.
———
PROGRAMME.--PART I.

PIANO DUET, · · · · · · ·
 MESSRS. SMITH AND BRAGDON.
LAURIGEE HORATIUS, · · · · Carm. Coll.
BOW, WOW, WOW. · · · Loren Bragdon
 SOLO BY MR. BRAGDON.
SPEED AWAY, · · · · · Woodbury
 MESSRS. WIGHT, BRAGDON, SCUDDER, SKINNER.
MEET ME BY MOONLIGHT ALONE, · Carm. Rutgersensia
OH, NO, SIR, NO, · · · · Carm. Rut.
 SOLO BY MR. SCUDDER.
FATINITZA, · · · · · Von Suppe
 MESSRS. WIGHT, BRAGDON, SCUDDER.
NOAH HE DID BUILD AN ARK, · · Carm. Rut.
OH, SUMMER NIGHT, · · · · Donizetti

PART II.

PIANO DUET, · · · · · ·
 MESSRS. SMITH AND BRAGDON.
MARCH, · · · · · · Becker
ANGELS, MEET ME AT THE CROSS ROADS, · ·
 SOLO BY MR. WIGHT.
YEOMAN'S WEDDING SONG, · · ·
 MR. BRAGDON.
MEDLEY, · · · · · · Carm. Rut.
QUARTET, { a—Sweet and Low, · · Barnby
         { b—Three Chafers, · · Truhn
 MESSRS. WIGHT, BRAGDON, SCUDDER, SKINNER.
BOHUNKUS, · · · · · ·
 CONDUCTED BY MR. SCUDDER.
DUET, · · · The Fisherman, · · Gabussi
 MESSRS. SMITH AND BRAGDON.
ON THE BANKS OF THE OLD RARITAN, · Carm. Rut.

LEADER—LOREN BRAGDON, '76.   ACCOMPANIST—CYRUS SMITH, '83.
D. D. SUTPHEN, BUSINESS MANAGER.

1ST TENORS.	2D TENORS.	1ST BASS.	2D BASS.
J. S. WIGHT, P. G.,	M. T. SCUDDER, '82.	W. S. CRANMER, '82,	A. B. HAVENS, '82,
H. M. VOORHEES, '85,	N. D. W. PUMYEA, '82.	IRVING BURDICK, '82,	A. F. SKINNER, '83,
S. G. SMITH, '85.	E. H. LOSEE, '85.	F. S. SCUDDER, '85.	F. P. HILL, '83.

MacCrellish & Quigley, Printers.

More popular still [than the Class Day exercises] was the glee club concert tonight [June 18]. The glee club has won fame and fortune. The men spend their Summers singing at Summer resorts from Mt. Desert [Maine] to Old Point Comfort [Virginia] or St. Augustine [Florida], and their Winters are given to the city audiences. The rest of the year is spent in study. Tonight, their annual concert was given under the leadership of Prof. Loren Bragdon, and the whole town was there. The programme was a very pretty one, the most striking thing being the neat localizations of the famous songs of [the comic opera] "Erminie," the parodies being by Howard MacSherry. A college "Erminie" proved most amusing.[140]

The spring semester of 1889 featured another extended tour to the upstate New York region. Beginning on April 2, 1889, the group traveled to Walden, New Paltz, Nyack, Tarrytown, Altamont, Amsterdam, and finally Albany, wrapping up what was described as an enjoyable and successful excursion.[141]

Novelty songs, parodies, and humorous pieces were very much staples of the repertory of the Rutgers College Glee Club during this period. And many of the programs featured guest soloists and the works of Mr. Bragdon, who was himself also a featured performer. The following program from the commencement concert of June 16, 1890, illustrates these programming features:

PART I.

1. Chorus, "Kerry Dance,"   Wiske
2. Solo, "Nobody Knows," (Local Topical Song).
   [Music from "Oolah." Words by Howard
      MacSherry.]
   Mr. Bragdon.
3. Whistling Obligato, "Evening Song,"   David
   Mr. Sherwood.
4. Chorus, "Wild Man of Borneo,"   Driskel
5. Solo, "Sognai," (Reverie)   Shira
   Miss Mary J. Dunn.
6. Chorus "Chestnuts," (Fresh)   Songs of Rutgers
7. Selection, "L'Ingenue,"
   Stevens Institute Banjo Club.
8. Chorus, "Skippers of St. Ives,"   Roecke

PART II.

1. Chorus, "Simple Simon,"   Macy
2. Solo   Selected
   Mr. Smock.
3. Selection, "The Darkies Patrol,"
                       Stevens Institute Banjo Club
4a. "Good Morning,"   Greig
   b. "The Ferry to Shadowtown,"   De Roven
   Miss Mary J. Dunn.

5. Chorus, "Medley." (New)   Bragdon
6. Whistling Solo, "Kiss Waltz,"   L. Arditta
    Mr. Sherwood.
7. Selection, "Nadjy Waltz,"
              Stevens Institute Banjo Club.
8. Chorus, "Good Night, My Love!"   Loud[142]

Loren Bragdon's Leadership in the 1890s

Along the lines of the retrospective analysis found in the 1885 edition of *The Scarlet Letter* (see note 111 in this chapter), the 1891 edition of the yearbook called attention to the achievements of the Rutgers College Glee Club by providing a synopsis of its accomplishments over the past several years. Titled "Ten Years of the Glee Club. 1881–1891," this five-page essay outlines many of the facts concerning the early history of the group but posits, as the title suggests, that the Rutgers College Glee Club has its origins in the 1880–81 academic year.[143] Though, as we have demonstrated, the Glee Club had a considerable, if fitful, history before this date, any references to earlier manifestations of the Glee Club are not included in this narrative. Many of the key figures in the group's history are mentioned by name, but none of the pioneers of the Club from before 1880 are included in this retrospective piece.[144] Nevertheless, the article is

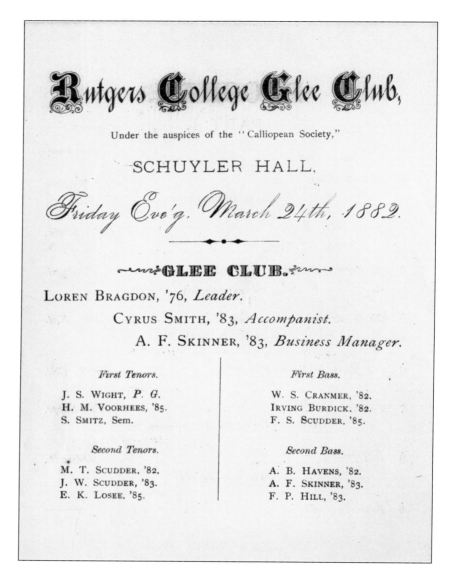

justified in calling attention to the achievements of the Club under the leadership of Loren Bragdon that began in that 1880–81 academic season.

This account also attests to the ever-expanding scope of the concert excursions by the group. It offers

PROGRAM.

PART I.

1 *Chant,* . . . . . *Anon.*

2 *Bow-wow-wow,* . . . *Loren Bragaon*
Solo by MR. BRAGDON.

3 *Jingle Bells,* . . . *Carmina Rutgersensia.*

4 *Co-educational Song,* . . . *Gabussi.*
MR. SKINNER, '83.

5 *Oh, no, sir—no!* . . . *Carm. Rut.*
Solo by MR. SCUDDER, '82.

6 *Old Noah, he did build an ark,* . . *Carm. Coll.*

7 *Fatinitza,* . . . . *Von Suppe.*
MESSRS. BRAGDON, WIGHT, SCUDDER, '82.

8 *Fra Diavolo,* . . . *Donizetti.*
MR. SCUDDER, '82.

9 *Four Jolly Smiths,* . . . ———

PROGRAM.

PART II.

1 *March,* . . . . . *Becker.*

2 *Golden Wedding,* . . . . *Bland.*
Solo by MR. WIGHT.

3 *Menu,* . . . . *Carl Merz.*

4 *Solo—"Yeoman's wedding song."* . *Poniwoski.*
MR. BRAGDON.

5 *Peter Grey,* . . . *Carm. Coll.*
Solo by MR. HAVENS.

6 *Quartette—a. "Speed Away,"* . . *Woodbury.*
MESSRS. WIGHT, BRAGDON, SCUDDER, '82, SKINNER.

7 *Bolumkus,* . . . . . ———
Conducted by MR. SCUDDER, '82.

8 *Medley,* . . . . *Carm. Rutgersensia.*

9 *Banks of the Old Raritan,* . *Carm. Rutgersensia.*

Program, Schuyler Hall, March 24, 1882. Rutgers University
Glee Club Archives.

Rutgers College Glee Club, 1888–89 season as depicted in *The Scarlet Letter*. Director Loren Bragdon is seen in the center of the middle row. To his left at the end of that row is future director and current first tenor George Wilmot. Special Collections, Rutgers University Libraries.

the following statement: "Before we close we feel compelled to speak of the enjoyable trip taken last summer to the blue grass region of Kentucky; all united in declaring it the most delightful experience of their lives. The trip by steamer from New York to Newport News, Va., thence over the picturesque Chesapeake and Ohio to Lexington was only surpassed by the return journey, when their hearts were filled with gratitude toward their hospitable Kentucky hosts."[145]

This quote from the *Scarlet Letter* essay was not the only way in which the tenth anniversary of the Glee Club—that is, the Bragdon Glee Club—was marked during the academic year 1890–91. On January 20, 1891, Leader Bragdon held a banquet at his home for the Club. These informal gatherings had apparently become a yearly event by this time; however, this year's event was of a much more elaborate nature than the standard *fête* for the students. The guest list for this celebratory occasion was comprised of several prominent members of the faculty, including Dr. T. Stanford Doolittle, professor of rhetoric, logic, and mental philosophy; Dr. Jacob Cooper, professor of Greek language and literature; and the newly elected Rutgers College president, Dr. Austin Scott (1848–1922), who had been a Rutgers College faculty member since 1883.[146] According to a contemporary account of this affair, no expense was spared in assembling the elements of the banquet; the

decorations were quite opulent, and "the affair had been made more pleasant by the employment of an orchestra."[147] Dr. Scott was honored as the dedicatee of Mr. Bragdon's latest composition, "Regina: A Mazurka Caprice," and was presented with an ornate copy of the work "bound . . . at one end with scarlet ribbon, and at the other by the Fraternity colors of its intended possessor."[148]

Following a dinner period characterized by the "wit and humor" of the conversation, the Club provided a bit of entertainment, offering performances of "Suwanee River," "Over the Beautiful Sea," and "My Old Kentucky Home," the last with whistling accompaniment. The evening was capped by a series of toasts. Perhaps the most impressive of these was that by Dr. Scott, who "characterized the Glee Club as the '[a]rch which bridged the chasm which existed between the Students and the Faculty.'" Dr. Scott expressed his wish that, during his upcoming tenure as president, such lines of communication could continue to improve. He concluded his remarks by paying tribute to Mr. Bragdon's work with the Club, stating that "[Bragdon] had done more for the College than he was aware of, and the whole College should be proud to show a high appreciation of Mr. Bragdon's work."[149]

As might be expected, the Glee Club was quite naturally enlisted as an element of Dr. Scott's official inauguration, which was marked by an elaborate ceremony at the New Brunswick Opera House on February 4, 1891. The Glee Club's role in these proceedings was significant. Following a welcoming address presented on behalf of the faculty by Dr. T. Stanford Doolittle, the Glee Club was called upon to deliver a rendition of "On the Banks of the Old Raritan," setting the proper tone for the welcoming speech on behalf of the students, presented by Mr. John H. Raven, '91. Immediately preceding the concluding doxology and benediction, the Glee Club was once again employed, this time presenting an "inaugural song, composed for the occasion by William Armitage Beardslee, '88 . . . [set to] the music by Loren Bragdon."[150]

While cementing its role as an indispensable element of life at Rutgers College, the Glee Club was still expanding its reach outside of the college's halls. Indeed, the schedule for the Club's travels during the academic year 1891–92 can only be described as extensive; no less than forty-two concerts were given during this period, some of which included audience members of the highest stature. *The Scarlet Letter* of 1892 puts the matter thus: "We have given more concerts this year than ever before. Twelve of these were during the ever-memorable Southern trip, during the Christmas holidays, when we gave a private concert before President Harrison, in the White House, ate our Christmas dinner in Cincinnati and spent [the] New Year in West Virginia."[151]

Academic year 1892–93 saw yet another increase in the number of concerts given, fifty-three in all, with yet another southern trip undertaken during the Christmas holidays. However, the year 1893 was a difficult one for the country and the world outside of Rutgers. The Panic of 1893 sent shock waves across the globe. The most extensive depression the United States had yet faced, it would produce profound economic disturbances, including an unemployment rate of over 10 percent for nearly five years. The political and social responses to this calamity, including violent strikes and the rise of the populist movement, set the stage for far-reaching political and intellectual developments of the twentieth century.[152]

The Glee Club of Rutgers College was, of course, not immune to these circumstances. Academic year 1893–94 saw a substantial reduction in the number of performances undertaken. The performances listed in that year's *Scarlet Letter* number only twenty, two of which were given with reduced forces ("Double Quartette").[153] The "Glee Club History" accompanying this list in the yearbook puts the matter thus: "The hard times have affected us considerably, yet the club has never been on a firmer financial footing than it is at present. The concerts have not been as numerous thus far as in some preceding years, but we rely on our worth and popularity for a very successful season."[154]

It is a valiant sentiment to put forth at this time; indeed, in the face of such political and economic upheaval, the default position is often to try to stay the course and preserve that which is clearly worth preserving. Much of the two-page "History" in the '95 *Scarlet Letter* emphasizes such continuity. "Lorie is still with us," the reader is informed, "to which may be attributed much of our success." And to be sure, the Rutgers Glee Club still claims Loren Bragdon as their musical director in that year's *Scarlet Letter*.[155] Thus the twelve-member ensemble had attained remarkable consistency and stability for a period of fourteen years (1880–81 through 1894) and achieved a level of notoriety and overall success that the '72 Club would have envied (and no doubt did). But change comes to all things, and the Rutgers Glee Club is no exception.

To all appearances, the academic year 1894–95 began for the Rutgers Glee Club much as it had over the past fourteen seasons. Three new singers were added to the ensemble to cover losses of personnel due to graduation and resignations. The outlook was optimistic for another fine year: "The Club, despite the fact that Case and Johnston have resigned[,] is commencing well and looks forward to a successful season. Rutgers, though she sometimes fails in other departments, is always 'on top' as regards singing."[156]

Travel was still part of the Club's charter, but the need to bow to the new economic realities was becoming a fact of life for the group:

> The Glee Club gave a concert in Media, Pa. last Friday evening [November 9, 1894].
>
> The usual southern holiday trip of the club will be postponed until the spring vacation and will be substituted by a tour through New York.[157]

Despite these attempts to retain the integrity of the Club in the face of trying economic times, however, the following curt announcement appeared in the *Targum* on January 9, 1895: "Loren Bragdon has resigned the leadership of the Glee Club. Mr. Bragdon has held this position since the organization of the Club in 1881, and to his untiring efforts is undoubtably due a large share of the success which it has attained. Mr. Wilmot has been selected to succeed him and knowing his ability and reputation we may feel sure that the Club will be none the less popular in the future than in the past."[158] Thus the tenure of Loren Bragdon as leader/musical director of the Rutgers College Glee Club came to an end. This announcement indicates that Bragdon's term with the Club in this role extends only through the fall semester of 1894, not until 1896 as is often reported.[159]

LOREN BRAGDON

(1856–1914)

Loren Bragdon is without doubt one of the most influential personalities in the history of the Rutgers Glee Club. Taking over leadership of the still-nascent Club during the academic year 1880–81, he is generally credited with providing the stability and artistic guidance necessary for the group to attain a high level of performance as well as a distinctive presence in the world of collegiate glee clubs. By most accounts, he was extraordinarily successful in these efforts, expanding the scope of the group's performing opportunities exponentially during his fourteen-year tenure as musical director/leader. However, Bragdon appears also to have been somewhat of a flamboyant character; he was reported to have "delight[ed] audiences [in New Brunswick] by appearing in women's clothes at concerts and singing in a falsetto voice."[160] It should also be noted that on more than one occasion, he found himself in disagreeable circumstances. The events of his life, chronicled fairly extensively in periodicals both local and national, make for fascinating reading.

Bragdon appears to have been a native of New Brunswick, New Jersey. There is little, if any, information on him before his taking over the Rutgers College Glee Club in 1880–81. It is documented that he lived for many years

Loren Bragdon, circa the early 1880s. Special Collections, Rutgers University Libraries.

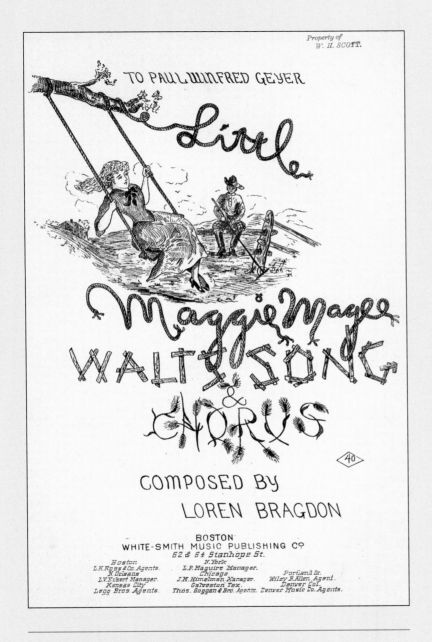

Sheet music for "Little Maggie Magee" by Loren Bragdon.
New York Public Library Archives.

in a house on George Street in New Brunswick, though when he may have first occupied this residence is not clear.[161] In the various listings of his activities during his tenure as Glee Club leader, he is often referred to as Professor Bragdon, '76. However, his name does not appear in any of the yearbooks for Rutgers College during the years in which he would have had to attend the school to obtain a baccalaureate. Further, Bragdon is not listed in the 1916 publication *Catalogue of the Officers and Alumni of Rutgers College*, which is considered the definitive source for such information.[162] It is therefore uncertain exactly what circumstances, if any, led to the granting of his degree.

Bragdon was very active outside of his responsibilities for the Rutgers Glee Club, which, during his time as musical director, were extensive. He was a composer of some note and contributed many works to the collection of songs in the repertory of the Rutgers College Glee Club. Many of his other works were published by the firm of White-Smith Publishing in Boston. He was for many years employed as a chorister at the First Reformed Church on Bayard Street in New Brunswick, a position that paid him a yearly salary of $50; he would eventually become the choir director at that institution.[163] He was active in the New York metropolitan area, making frequent concert appearances as a vocalist.[164] He also made appearances in New York and elsewhere in the very popular minstrel shows of this period; he appeared at Carnegie Hall on November 30, 1892, in a benefit performance of this type for the aid of the New York Athletic Club. The event was described in the *New York Times* as "strictly burnt cork throughout. Young gentlemen with blackened faces sang, danced, and cracked jokes, and as many people as could get into the hall cheered everything they did." Mr. Bragdon played the part of Mrs. Guyer in an adaptation of a play by the American dramatist Charles H. Hoyt, "amended to suit changed conditions, and entitled 'Coons' Trip to China-town.'"[165] Such entertainments were also presented in New Brunswick, some "under the . . . management of the Rutgers Glee Club."[166]

As noted in the general narrative, copious praise was bestowed by Rutgers students, faculty, senior administration, and the general public on Mr. Bragdon, or "Lorie," as he was often called. However, by the late 1880s, certain incidents began to cast a shadow on his career. In 1889, while conducting private dance classes for young men in New Brunswick, Mr. Bragdon informed one of the pupils that the young lady he had brought as a partner to class was not socially acceptable; the young woman is described in the account as "a young villager." The male dance pupil took exception, as did many of the young women of New Bruns-wick. This resulted in a general boycott by the female factory workers in the vicinity against the male members of Brag-don's dancing-school organization.[167]

More serious problems were yet to surface. It is unclear what specific circumstances led to these actions, but in the

The *New Brunswick Daily News Times*, March 6, 1894. Minstrel performance "under the . . . management of the Rutgers Glee Club."

latter part of 1894, Bragdon was forced to resign from his posts as choir director at the First Reformed Church and as leader of the Rutgers College Glee Club. Contemporary accounts state that he was asked to vacate these positions "on account of the public sentiment that was against him." So great was the animosity toward this once-popular figure in

New Brunswick social circles that, when he appeared, apparently uninvited, at a dance for the Alumni Association of the Sacred Heart School in New Brunswick, his presence was deemed objectionable. In fact, the musicians at the affair, led by violinist Fred Hart, left the hall in protest and refused to return until Bragdon had agreed to leave the premises.[168]

However, Bragdon seems to have emerged from beneath the shadow of this scandal to continue his career as a performer with a good deal of success. In the early 1900s, he set off on the road, appearing in a variety of American cities from coast to coast with an act that featured himself and three young brothers from the Carr family of New Brunswick. Calling the act "The Four Bragdons," the troupe presented "a ragtime operetta and a farce comedy entitled 'A Manager's Troubles in a Vaudeville Employment Agency.'"[169] Other variations of the ensemble act involved the boys playing cornet, violin, and clarinet while accompanied on the piano by Bragdon. The act often featured a duet with Bragdon and his "dog mascot, the latter howling in unison with the musical chords."[170]

This enterprise, however, was also wracked by controversy. In order to travel the country with the underage Carr brothers, Bragdon had apparently struck a deal with the boys' father, John Carr. In February of 1903, Carr hired an attorney to begin proceedings against Bragdon.[171] Carr stated that "he has a verbal contract with Mr. Bragdon whereby he is to receive compensation for the use of his sons." Failing to resolve the matter, Carr recalled his sons to New Brunswick. The two older sons, Wilbur and Harold, returned, but Bragdon and Clifford Carr, the youngest son, fled to California against the elder Carr's wishes. John Carr accused Bragdon of kidnapping Clifford and, after a two-month search, authorities traced the pair to Watsonville, California. It is unclear what subsequent actions were taken against Bragdon, if any.

Loren Bragdon died of pneumonia on March 12, 1914, at the age of fifty-eight in the Polyclinic Hospital in Chicago after a ten-day illness.[172] Despite his troubles and quirks of personality, he was still remembered fondly by the New Brunswick citizens who at one time held him in great esteem. "The last time he was in New Brunswick," his obituary states, "he went about with a pet dog and monkey. He was always eccentric in dress and habits, and had a warm heart and was generally liked."[173]

THE RUTGERS SONGBOOK
Songs of Rutgers

As stated in the accompanying narrative, the desire to implement a plan directed at the compilation and dissemination of a collegiate songbook along the lines of the 1868 *Carmina Collegensia* was cited as a major factor in the organization of the first Rutgers College Glee Club in 1872. However, the circumstances examined below give some insight into the reasons for the considerable gap in time between the formation of the committee dedicated to the production and dissemination of this songbook in 1873 and its eventual publication in 1885.

It may have been that the publication of a new edition of the *Carmina Collegensia* in 1876 alleviated some of the urgency for a purely Rutgers-centered publication.[174] This volume contained several Rutgers songs, including the original "Alma Mater" (words by W. R. Duryee, '56), the marching song "Bow-Wow-Wow" (composed by Loren Bragdon, '76), the "Rutgers Foot-Ball Song" (words by Alexander Johnston, '70), and of course, "On the Banks of the Old Raritan" (words by Howard Fuller, '74). However, contemporary accounts point to a certain lack of focus in the organizational structure of the early incarnations of the Glee Club, as well as a general apathy toward such projects by the Rutgers College student body during this period, as probable elements contributing to this delay. Whatever the motivations, or lack thereof, in the early years of the Glee Club's existence, the new sense of energy and purpose instigated by the formation of the Club under Loren Bragdon's leadership seemed to focus this effort to the point where pleas for the songbook became much more visceral.[175]

By the spring of 1882, it would seem that these imprecations had been heeded at last, and progress had been made. *The Scarlet Letter* of that year states the following:

Many times of late, has a notice appeared in the *Targum*, to the effect that "A Song Book" compiled for Rutgers College students, including many compositions both original and selected, would shortly be offered for sale. The non-appearance of this pet child of the Senior Class has given rise to the rumor that it is abandoned. The truth of the matter, however, is that the copy is all prepared; but like so many other things in this world, the one thing needful to its completion, namely *money*, is lacking. Philanthropical alumni and others are invited to contribute. One dollar will purchase one song book.[176]

Again, the publication of a related edition may have quelled the urgency to produce an all-Rutgers volume, for in January of 1882, *The American College Song Book*, also containing Rutgers songs, was released. Claiming to offer "a collection of College Songs more creditable to our [current]

College World than the somewhat limited and time-worn collections in existence" could, the publishers of *The American College Song Book* presented the latest college songs from fifty selected universities throughout the country. Each school was invited "to contribute four of her best songs, original as far as possible, for such purpose."[177] The chairman of the music committee in charge of submitting the songs for Rutgers was Myron T. Scudder, '82.[178] It is interesting to note that of the four songs submitted by Myron Scudder, three are credited to Loren Bragdon, including the rather lengthy (five pages) "Vocal Waltz."[179]

This is perhaps the place to say a word about the Scudder family and its associations with Rutgers College. Myron T. and Frank S. Scudder were brothers. They were both born in Palamanir, India, to Christian missionary parents.[180] Myron was the elder brother by three years, making it possible for them to attend Rutgers College simultaneously during the academic year 1881–82. During this period, they were both involved with the newly established Glee Club under Bragdon's leadership; senior Myron served as vice president and sang second tenor, while freshman Frank sang first bass.[181] Thus it is natural that the brothers should both be involved in the compilation and publication of what is often referred to in its early days before its eventual publication as the *Carmina Rutgersensia*.[182]

Once the decision had been taken to mount this project, Myron Scudder stood out as a logical choice to implement the details of the enterprise. His involvement with the Glee Club throughout his time at the college together with his role in the compilation of Rutgers songs for *The American College Song Book* project were both strong factors in his favor. And he served as an associate editor on the student newspaper, the *Targum*, at the time of the project's inception. The matter is stated thus in the *Targum*:

Messrs. [Myron T.] Scudder and [Will S.] Cranmer have entered upon the work of immortalizing their College, and perhaps themselves, by the publication of a little book of College songs. Carmina Rutgersensia, we believe, is the sonorous title. These will consist, principally, of Rutgers songs, both old and new, (since the book is intended to meet the wants of Rutgers men,) and also the choicest of other glees and choruses appropriate to college use, including of course Mr. Bragdon's popular songs and music. This task is no light one; but if successfully accomplished, all the more credit will be due to the gentlemen who have assumed it. Their well-known business ability and critical musical taste would lead us to expect the best possible College Song Book, both in point of compilation and general appearance. Let a thorough canvass of the College and the Alumni be made, in order to secure the issue of a large edition. Send in your subscriptions before commencement, and set the work a booming.[183]

Though the above announcement represents an auspicious start to the enterprise, it seems to have taken some time before any substantial progress was made. Perhaps the graduation of Myron Scudder in the spring of 1882 served as a stumbling block to such progress. This necessitated the transfer of the responsibility for the compilation and editing of the work to the Glee Club. A five-man committee drawn from the Club's ranks, including Frank S. Scudder, was assigned this task in 1882 and, according to a contemporary account, "the MSS. were then carefully revised and several attempts were made to publish the book, with no better success."[184]

Though the hope of publishing a songbook before the end of the 1883–84 academic year would not come to pass, 1884 did see the formation of another committee charged with "perfecting a plan for issuing the College Song Book at an early date."[185] This committee consisted of several members, all of whom, like the previous committee, had ties to musical organizations at Rutgers College; Frank S. Scudder was again a member.[186] The efforts of this committee proved successful; in April of 1885, the *Targum* announced the publication of this collection, now titled *Songs of Rutgers*. A brief article goes on to state that "the Editor, Mr. F. S. Scudder, '85, has spared neither pains nor expense in making this one of the very finest of College Song Books."[187] The following, more detailed, account, presented in the same issue of the *Targum* under the heading "Songs of Rutgers," provides insights into the volume's contents:

The "Songs of Rutgers" is published in the same style as "Yale Songs"—a book pronounced by Ditson & Co. to be "the finest bound collection of college songs yet published." Having been in the process of compilation for over four years, during which time seven members of the Glee Club have been engaged in the work, each song contained in the "Songs of Rutgers" has been submitted to severe criticism, and has been included only on the ground of true merit and popularity among alumni and undergraduates. A number of new Rutgers songs have been included and the Rutgers arrangements claim credit for their originality. The style of paper, type and binding is exceptionally good. On the face of the cover is an elaborate design of "Songs of Rutgers" stamped in gilt, and on the back is placed the college seal. With the taste which has been exercised in the selection of college songs, glees and serenades, the "Songs of Rutgers" can not but be appreciated, even outside the circle of our Alma Mater's friends.[188]

ALMA MATER

The term *alma mater* (Latin: "benign mother") is used by alumni to refer to their school or college. The term can also be used to describe a school hymn or anthem that is utilized in ceremonial, festive, sporting, or other school events that call for an evocation of devotion to or enthusiasm for the institution, a display of school spirit.[189] By the mid-nineteenth century, many American colleges had a variety of songs in general circulation that fit the basic criteria for use at just such occasions. College presidents, often eager to foster feelings of camaraderie among the students as well as fealty to the institution, actively encouraged the dissemination of these "presentation songs," as they have been described, through the various college songbooks that were launched during this period.[190] As a subset of this collection of songs, selections designated "alma mater" were frequently included. Often set to borrowed music, the original lyrics would customarily depict the idyllic nature of collegiate life and, for alumni, nostalgia for a return thereto.

Songs of Rutgers, first issued in 1885, includes presentation songs, among which is an excellent example of the type of alma mater described above. The tune is derived from a musical setting by the Irish composer Sir John Andrew Stevenson of a poem by the Irish writer and lyricist Thomas Moore, "Oft in the Stilly Night." Titled "Alma Mater," the lyrics are credited to W. R. Duryee, '56. Appearing on page 46 of *Songs of Rutgers*, the poem speaks of the delight that images of the college ignite in the souls of students and alumni alike:

> *Deep in our heart of hearts*
> *Enshrined in love unbroken*
> *Old Rutgers' name imparts*
> *A joy by lips unspoken*

However, as the years progressed and the Rutgers Glee Club rose to ever-greater prominence as the premiere student group representing the college, the song that was most closely associated with the group—"On the Banks of the Old Raritan," the song that had been especially prepared for the group in order that they might put their best foot forward in their nascent performances—overtook the quaint "Stilly Night" adaptation as the official alma mater of Rutgers College. Exactly how and when "On the Banks" was so adopted is somewhat unclear. *The Scarlet Letter* for the 1966 bicentennial year of Rutgers states that, following its composition in 1873, "the song became popular and was soon chosen as the University's Alma Mater."[191]

The original incarnation of the song by Howard N. Fuller, '74, consisted of six verses in all; it is this version that is included in the 1885 *Songs of Rutgers* publication. The lyrics are as follows:

My father sent me to old Rutgers
And resolved that I should be a man
And so I settled down
In that noisy college town
On the banks of the old Raritan
   Chorus

On the banks of the old Raritan, my boys
Where old Rutgers evermore shall stand
For has she not stood
Since the time of the flood
On the banks of the old Raritan

As Fresh, they used me rather roughly
But I the fearful gauntlet ran
And they shook me so about
That they turned me inside out
On the banks of the old Raritan
   Chorus

I passed through all these tortures nobly
And then, as Soph, my turn began
And I hazed the freshman so
That they longed for heaven, I know
On the banks of the old Raritan
   Chorus

And then I rested at my pleasure
And steered quite clear of Prex's ban
And the stars their good-bye kissing
Found me not from Euchre missing
On the banks of the old Raritan
   Chorus

And soon I made my social entrée
When I laid full many a wicked plan
And by my cunning art
Slew many a maiden's heart
On the banks of the old Raritan
   Chorus

Then sing aloud to Alma Mater
And keep the Scarlet in the Van
For with her motto high
Rutgers' name shall never die
On the banks of the old Raritan
   Chorus

These verses are replete with contemporary cultural references, both general and particular, to the college. The term *Prex* in verse 4, for example, was apparently the students' nickname for the president of the college, at that time William Henry Campbell (1808–90).[192] "Euchre" in the same verse was a popular trick-taking card game among the students during this period.[193] And of course, the overall theme of the lyrics, with references to hazing activities and the general rambunctiousness of young men, reflects the nature of Rutgers College as an all-male institution typical of its time.

Fuller had gone on to a successful career in banking following his college years. Despite his personal success, he maintained an active interest in the affairs of Rutgers College. He was appointed to the board of directors of the school in 1906, which solidified his relationship with the president of the college at that time, William Henry Demarest. The two men often corresponded by mail, and in a letter concerning an unrelated matter dated February 1, 1914, Fuller raised the matter of the lyrics to "On the Banks."[194] Apparently, the overall tone of the 1873 lyrics gave Fuller pause in later life. He had come to believe, he told Demarest in a subsequent letter, that the original words to the song had been written "in the prankish spirit of my college days," and that, in particular, the four internal verses did not express "the true sentiments of affection and veneration I have always felt, and which every loyal alumnus must feel, for the dear old college."[195]

In a return letter, Demarest agreed with Fuller's assessment but also asserted that the original lyrics should be preserved and used for internal College functions only. However, Demarest asked Fuller to prepare alternate lyrics for use at alumni affairs, public ceremonies, and so on.[196] Fuller complied, sending along a rough draft of the revised lyrics. Over a correspondence of fifteen letters, the two men sorted out details, paying close attention to matters of grammar, rhyme scheme, and overall appropriateness. Finally, the revised lyrics, shown below, were sent to Demarest in a letter dated April 4, 1914:

My father sent me to old Rutgers
And resolv'd that I should be a man
And so I settled down
In that noisy college town
On the banks of the old Raritan
   Chorus

On the banks of the old Raritan, my boys
Where old Rutgers evermore shall stand
For has she not stood
Since the time of the flood
On the banks of the old Raritan

Her ardent spirit stirred and cheered me
From the day my college years began
Gracious Alma Mater mine
Learning's fair and honored shrine
On the banks of the old Raritan
   Chorus

I love her flaming far-flung banner
I love her triumphs proud to scan
And I glory in the fame

That's immortalized her name
On the banks of the old Raritan
   Chorus

My heart clings closer than the ivy
As life runs out its fleeting span
To the stately ancient walls
Of her hallowed, classic halls
On the banks of the old Raritan
   Chorus

Then sing aloud to Alma Mater
And keep the Scarlet in the Van
For with her motto high
Rutgers' name shall never die
On the banks of the old Raritan
   Chorus

These lyrics were first presented at an alumni event in April 1914 and were apparently well received.[197] They would subsequently become standardized as the new version of "On the Banks" through the revised 1916 edition of *Songs of Rutgers*, compiled by Howard McKinney. The entire Fuller letter from April 4, 1914, with the new lyrics, is reproduced in that edition,[198] as are words of praise for this publication and its contents from President Demarest.[199]

However, though "On the Banks" has pride of place in this new edition, appearing as the first selection in the volume, it is followed immediately by two songs that are titled "Alma Mater." For the first of this pair, the words and music are ascribed to E. J. Meeker, '96. The opening verse and chorus are presented as follows:

In a quaint old Jersey town
That I long to call my own,
Stands a college that has long been known to fame
Where the hardy ivy clings
To the walls of ancient stone,
Ever changing yet eternally the same.
   Chorus

Alma Mater, Alma Mater
Plucky college by the gentle Raritan,
You're the apple of my eye
Brightest star in all the sky,
Rutgers college by the gentle Raritan.

The second is the "Alma Mater" from the original 1885 publication, based on "Oft in the Stilly Night." It would seem, therefore, that by 1916, "On the Banks" had yet to be firmly established as the official alma mater of Rutgers College, nor had any song that exclusive right at this time. Indeed, press accounts over the course of the early twentieth century present a divergent picture as to what specific song could rightly lay claim to the title of the Rutgers "Alma Mater."[200]

Thus the question of which song represented the true alma mater of Rutgers University remained an open one, at least through the decade of the 1960s. It seems reasonable to assume, considering the evidence presented, that Rutgers students, alumni, and faculty considered the selections that carried the designation "Alma Mater"—either explicitly or by custom or preference—to be in the category of "presentation songs." In that regard, they were functionally interchangeable; any of the songs cited above could, at any time, be used as the alma mater of the college/university and engender the necessary acceptance in that capacity among the intended audience.

Throughout the early twentieth century, however, during the period in which the revisions to *Songs of Rutgers* that have been outlined took place, significant social changes had developed, both within the college/university and outside of it. As detailed in the narrative, the New Jersey College for Women was established in 1918 as a coordinate women's college affiliated with Rutgers; such a relationship was common at the time, as with Harvard and Radcliffe or Columbia and Barnard. Though still somewhat removed from a true coeducational experience, such an affiliation presented opportunities for interaction between male and female students at the individual schools, such as the combined efforts of the Rutgers vocal groups under the umbrella

designation of the University Choir in the mid-twentieth century (see chap. 5, "The 1950s: The University Choir").

By the 1970s, though, the idea of separate institutions for male and female students was being viewed as a relic of bygone years. Rutgers officially became a coeducational institution in 1972, and quite properly, the young women newly initiated into the Rutgers University system advocated for changes to existing school organizations and traditions that had heretofore served an all-male constituency. One of the issues raised by these women was that of Fuller's lyrics for what was, by the mid-1980s, widely known and accepted as the Rutgers alma mater, "On the Banks."

The fact that Fuller's lyrics represented a vision of Rutgers that was no longer applicable on many counts and were therefore in need of change had strong support from many quarters in the school, including the president of the university at this time, Edward J. Bloustein. In 1989, at Bloustein's suggestion, a committee was formed for the purpose of rewriting the lyrics. This committee solicited contributions via the mechanism of a $500 prize for the best entry. Four prizes were awarded in all, representing the winning revisions of the lyrics for use by the Rutgers Camden, Newark, and New Brunswick campuses, as well as a prize for lyrics for the university as a whole.[201]

The committee made its selections in 1990, resulting in new lyrics for all campuses. The new first verse of the version for Rutgers, The State University of New Jersey (i.e., the version for the University as a whole) for use at public events was revised as follows:

From New Jersey's northern lakes and mountains,
To our southern pines and gleaming shore,
Learning's fair and hallowed place
Joins us, every creed and race,
And we praise the name of Rutgers evermore.

This new verse was to be followed by Fuller's chorus, with the sole revision in that section being the change of "my boys" to the more gender-neutral "my friends."

The New Brunswick-campus revision retained Fuller's first verse (beginning "My father . . .") but also amended the ensuing chorus by replacing "my boys" with "my friends." However, a new verse was added to this revision:

Let's toast to Rutgers ever stronger
Since the time when Old Queen's first began
Here's to glory days of old
And a future bright and bold,
On the banks of the old Raritan.

It would appear, though, that the revisions to the version for general university usage had only a brief vogue. When first released in 1990, performances of the alma mater at commencement exercises consisted of two verses: the new

general-usage verse ("From New Jersey's lakes . . .") functioning as the first verse and Fuller's original final verse ("Sing aloud . . .") as the second. While the Rutgers College commencement programs printed the original first and final verses, the university-wide commencement ceremonies printed the new first verse for the next decade and a half. As current Glee Club director Patrick Gardner notes,

The singing of the verse starting "from New Jersey's lakes . . ." was required at the event which marked the legal graduation of all members of the Rutgers University student body, even though the individual colleges continued to print the original words and asked the Glee Club to present that version. The only time the "new" version was sung was at the University-wide commencement ceremony. Indeed, I never met anyone outside of the Glee Club that knew those words and the Glee Club had to hold a special rehearsal each year to remind themselves of the words sung for this singular occasion.[202]

As the new millennium got underway, calls for further revisions began to gain momentum. These calls came not only from female university students, faculty, and staff but from numerous other members of the community. Gardner notes, "It was clear to many that the first phrase of the alma mater, written when Rutgers was a relatively small men's college, did not represent fifty percent of the modern student body. It also held no relevance for those who were raised by same-sex parents. And, of course, it didn't celebrate the significance of the work of thousands of mothers who worked to send their children to Rutgers."[203]

In 2010, members of the Douglass College Governing Council—Douglass College having evolved from the New Jersey College for Women in 1955 as the women's coordinate of Rutgers—submitted a letter to the editors of the *Targum*, asking, among other things, "why perform the university alma mater that does not represent women as students or as active parents while we pride ourselves on being one of the most diverse institutions of higher learning in the nation?"[204]

Changes such as those requested in the above letter to the *Targum* editors were often suggested by a variety of interested parties to Patrick Gardner, who had become director of the Glee Club in 1993. Gardner was aware of the dissatisfaction that the lyrics had engendered among a variety of university constituencies. He noted that one solution, a cheekily rendered "or a woman" added after "and resolved that I should be a man" did not seem to fit with the dignity sought by Howard Fuller in his 1914 letter to President Demarest. Gardner was also aware of the fact that Rutgers was not the only institution to have experienced expressions of disapproval concerning the lyrics to time-honored college songs. Dartmouth, Princeton, Penn State, and even West Point had long since adjusted the lyrics to their school songs to remove any indications of gender bias.[205]

For Gardner, an important aspect of this matter was preserving the tradition of "On the Banks" while refurbishing the lyrics to better reflect the standards and attitudes of contemporary society. Additionally, how could a glee club—which by this time was welcoming transgender students to the ranks of alumni and current members and providing a place to sing for all gifted tenors and basses—continue to sing such constrained lyrics? Unless the song could be adapted to meet current needs, Gardner feared that "On the Banks" could be relegated to the historical trash heap. There were increasing requests to simply leave the alma mater out of important academic and alumni ceremonies. But if the alma mater was not to be sung at these gatherings, the tradition of celebrating community through song would be completely lost. Most students at the university experience the alma mater primarily through its performance at convocations, commencements, and sporting events. With requests to remove the alma mater from such occasions as a possibility, the urgency for a solution was apparent.

By 2013, Gardner had come to the conclusion that the lyrics of "On the Banks" must be adjusted to offer a vision that was more reflective of the university's current student community. Indeed, in that year, 53 percent of the total student population of approximately 65,000 students were women.[206] "We've had 20 years of intense wave[s] of people upset with the old lyrics," Gardner was quoted as saying at that time. "My thoughts always were, 'Well, how can we get this changed?'"[207]

The answer, it appears, lay with Gardner. Rutgers University president Robert L. Barchi agreed that the Rutgers Glee Club had the right to alter the lyrics of "On the Banks." Thus it fell to Gardner, in consultation with the Glee Club executive committee as well as other current and former Glee Club members, to put forth a more socially acceptable version.[208] While struggling to find new words, Gardner first seriously floated the idea of altering the lyrics to the executive committee throughout the spring of 2010; regular discussions were then held throughout the 2011 school year. Different solutions were considered in those conferences and in the meetings of the Glee Club as a whole. Also considered was the idea of adopting an entirely new composition, as there would surely be alumni who might not accept a revision of a song dear to them. However, Gardner felt strongly that in an era when community singing was no longer a part of daily life, introducing a new song would simply result in no one bothering to learn it. In that scenario, people would surely drift back to the "old alma mater" with the questionable first phrase.

While numerous adaptations of the first phrase were considered and subjected to extensive deliberation, Gardner finally designed a lyric that would both fit the original rhyme scheme and resolve the problematic social issues presented in the original text. The resulting change to the opening verse of Fuller's lyrics reflects, in Gardner's estimation, the consensus that arose from these deliberations:

From far and near we came to Rutgers
And resolved to learn all that we can . . .

Gardner's intent—and the intent of all involved—was to make the new lyrics blend in with the rest of the original opening verse and, of course, to address the inherent gender bias of the original;[209] it certainly succeeds on both counts.

Gardner's new version had its debut in early September of 2013, when the Glee Club performed it at the university's welcoming event for incoming freshmen. However, this new configuration got its first large-scale exposure when it was sung at the football game between Rutgers and Arkansas at High Point Solutions Stadium on September 28, 2013. As Gardner put it at the time, "We're [the] leaders in song at the university, and it was time for us to lead this."[210]

The 2013 version is now performed as the Rutgers alma mater at all major university events, printed in the convocation and commencement programs as the official alma mater, and broadcast on stadium jumbotrons when the alma mater is sung at football games. As of the writing of this book, over 50,000 students have learned the current words of the alma mater at their first-year convocation ceremonies. The 2013 version serves as the official alma mater of Rutgers University and is noted as such on the Rutgers University website (https://www.rutgers.edu/about/traditional-songs).

2 NEW DIRECTIONS

George W. Wilmot (Musical Director/Leader, 1895–1906)

As previously indicated (see the quote attached to note 158 in chap. 1), George W. Wilmot of New Brunswick assumed the leadership role of the Glee Club, replacing Loren Bragdon. Like his predecessor, Wilmot was not a student; in fact, he was not even a Rutgers College alumnus. He had, however, been affiliated with the Glee Club prior to Bragdon's resignation; his name appears on the roster of singers as a first tenor beginning in 1885,[1] and the yearbook for the 1895 class lists him among the first tenors and as a "Soloist."[2]

Wilmot was, in fact, a prominent citizen of New Brunswick and had been for some time when his appointment as leader of the Club was announced. He was employed by Christ Church in New Brunswick in 1885 as a professional chorister and choirmaster, a post he would retain for the next forty-five years. He is generally credited with establishing the fundamental artistic and organizational principles on which the present-day music program at Christ Church is based.[3] A student of the British composer and conductor Sir Joseph Barnby (1838–96), Wilmot was a published composer with several works under copyright.[4] Wilmot was also a prominent educator; he served as the music supervisor of the New Brunswick public schools for twenty-eight years beginning in 1900[5] and was a sought-after lecturer on the subject of music education in the American public school system.[6] He was, therefore, eminently qualified to take over the position of musical director for Mr. Bragdon.

That there was turmoil in the transition period is evidenced by the fact that, though the Glee Club is referenced tangentially in the 1894–95 edition of *The Scarlet Letter*, there is no dedicated section listing the officers and members of the Club, as had been the case since 1872. That is not to say, however, that the group was dormant during the spring semester of 1895 nor during the ensuing 1895–96 academic year. A concert was given on February 7, 1895, at the YMCA in Philadelphia, blizzard conditions of the evening notwithstanding.[7] Several other concerts were given in the spring of 1895, including appearances in Bound Brook, Westfield,[8] and New York City.[9] Perhaps most significantly, the Club appeared on Washington's birthday, February 22, 1895, at the Academy of Music in Brooklyn with the Sousa Band, led by the legendary "March King," John Philip Sousa.[10] Sousa's group traveled extensively throughout the world between 1892 and 1931, often showcasing the finest local talent, as in this case.[11] A performance of this nature attests to the fact that Wilmot was keen to maintain a prominent profile for the group during his tenure as leader.

Indeed, the value of the Club to the college is emphasized in *The Scarlet Letter* for the following year (1895–96). The first page of that volume bears this inscription: "We, the editors of the Junior Class, dedicate this volume to our Glee Club, through whose efforts the name and reputation of Rutgers has been made more prominent than through any other organization."[12]

For the academic year 1895–96, Wilmot's Glee Club retained the basic structure instituted by Bragdon. The group consisted of twelve vocalists, three on a part (first and second tenors, first and second basses); Wilmot sang first tenor in addition to his role as leader/musical director. All officers were again drawn from the ranks of the singers, with the exception of George

Glee Club director George W. Wilmot in later years.
Rutgers University Glee Club Archives.

The Rutgers College Glee Club, 1895–96, George W. Wilmot, director. The members are pictured as follows:
Back row: Ryno, '98; Francisco, '99; W. V. B. Van Dyck, '96; Wyckoff, '96; Rosencrantz, '96; von Gehren, '99; Girtanner, '99.
Middle row: Inglis, '96; Vaules, '98; George Wilmot, director; J. B. Voorhees, '96; Riggs, '98.
Bottom row: Gregory, '96 (auditor); Pool, '96; Nuttman, '96 (accompanist and auditor). Special Collections and University Archives, Rutgers University Libraries.

Winfield Nuttman, '96, the accompanist for the group, who also served as one of two auditors.[13] This basic framework would remain in place throughout Wilmot's time as director, though the number of participants in the ensemble would increase as the years passed.

Still the premiere musical organization on campus, it is no surprise that the Club was chosen to perform for the Charter Day exercises on November 10, 1895, at which President Austin Scott presented a narrative of the college's founding in 1766.[14] It is also interesting to note that the Club participated in a combined concert with the Rutgers College Banjo, Mandolin, and Guitar Club at Evelyn College (the coordinate women's college for Princeton during this period) on

December 9, 1895.[15] This was the first year of the latter club's existence,[16] and the combined concert marked a precedent that would have profound implications for the future of both clubs.

The academic year concluded with the Glee Club playing its traditional spotlighted role in the commencement ceremonies. The program featured selections by the popular contralto Eva Hawkes. The Club presented several old favorites ("Bow-Wow-Wow," "Old Folks at Home") and offered a new medley arranged by Director Wilmot. And of course, the program concluded with "On the Banks of the Old Raritan." The Mandolin Club was also an integral part of the performance, with several selections by them on the program; they assisted the Glee Club in the finale. Of this concert, the *Targum* noted, "The concert given by the Rutgers College Glee Club on Friday evening, June 12, was one which was never excelled and rarely equalled [*sic*]. The appreciation of the audience was shown by the fact that almost every selection was encored once at least. The Mandolin Club fully did justice to itself, and with the special artists gave a most pleasant evening's entertainment."[17] Thus the 1895–96 version of the Rutgers Glee Club came to an impressive end, and the yearbook contains the group's sentiments concerning the nature of this success: "The program of the season has been pronounced by 'experts' as the finest ever put forth by the Club, and to Mr. Wilmot the whole credit of this is due."[18]

Academic year 1897–98 saw a significant increase in the number of performances given by the Club over the preceding few years. The southern trip was reinstated, with engagements at Richmond, Virginia; Winston, North Carolina; Columbia and Charleston, South Carolina; and a finale to the tour on New Year's Eve in Raleigh, North Carolina.[19] Concerts by the Club to New Jersey locales remained a prominent part of the group's profile as well: nineteen such performances were given. Occasional excursions to Manhattan and Philadelphia and one appearance at Newtown on Long Island brought the total number of performances for the year to thirty-one, much on par with the best seasons of the Bragdon ensemble.[20] A similar southern sojourn was undertaken in the following year, this time accompanied by the Mandolin Club.[21] Including these concerts, the group appeared twenty times during the academic year 1898–99.

Though the southern trip was discontinued after the 1898–99 season, the Club maintained an active schedule of events within the greater New Brunswick area, extending to Manhattan and Brooklyn. It was also at this time that the Club began to regularly present concerts given by a quartet (or occasionally a double quartet) of their best vocalists in lieu of the entire group; the quartet performances usually included Wilmot as first tenor.[22] During the 1899–1900 season, the Club gave twenty performances. Twelve of these featured the entire ensemble, and seven were presented with the quartet; a concert in High Bridge, New Jersey, on March 24, 1900, was given by the double quartet.[23] The 1900–1901 season offered thirteen concerts with the full ensemble and four with the quartet.[24] In 1901–2, there were twelve programs featuring the whole group, with again four appearances by the quartet.[25] And during the 1902–3 academic year, another variation was added to the schedule; nineteen concerts were given, four of which were combined efforts with the Mandolin Club. No quartet performances occurred during this season.[26]

In academic year 1903–4, the basic configuration of the Club began to change. For one thing, the alliance with the Mandolin Club seems to have abated, if not outright disappeared. More significantly, as stated previously, the usual complement of the ensemble was twelve singers, three on a part. Though this number fluctuated from time to time throughout the life of the group to this date,[27] the twelve-member format was the most common. During this year, the number grew to fourteen singers; the arrangement of voices was then four first tenors, four second tenors, three first basses, and three second basses, with Wilmot still serving as a first tenor. Eighteen concerts were presented by the group in this season, with four additional performances by the quartet.[28] In the year 1904–5, the Club began to officially maintain a coterie of four substitute singers, owing, no doubt, to conflicts among the regular members given the wide-ranging schedule of performances.[29] The singers listed on the Glee Club page of *The Scarlet Letter* for this year appeared in the following configuration: four first tenors (including Wilmot), five second tenors, four first basses, and four second basses.[30] This list includes the substitutes that were now considered part of the ensemble, bringing the total number of singers to seventeen.[31] Twenty-six performances were given by this group, with five additional concerts by the quartet. A Christmas-holiday excursion to upstate New York was undertaken as part of this schedule, with appearances at venues including Yonkers, Poughkeepsie, Liberty, Kingston, Catskill, and Hudson.[32]

The employment of substitutes became further integrated into the Club's practices in the following year. The arrangement of singers for the 1905–6 Club was now five first tenors (including Wilmot), four second tenors (with two more designated as substitutes), three first basses (with one designated substitute), and three second basses (with one designated substitute). This then brought the official number of singers in the ensemble to nineteen, though it is probable that full-ensemble performances employed the twelve-man contingent as a base model whenever possible.

A word about the terminology used to designate the vocal parts of the ensemble may be in order here. In the first Rutgers College Glee Club of 1872, the designations were soprano, alto, first tenor, second tenor, baritone, first bass, and second bass, conforming to the standard division of vocal parts.[33] This quickly gave way in 1874 to an arrangement of first and second tenors and first and second basses.[34] This would come to be the usual designation for the vocal parts, but with some variations over the years. The first basses were sometimes designated baritones; this was occasionally the case under Wilmot's direction.[35] Further, the terminology for the bass parts varied from year to year as well. The term was *basses* in 1872, *bassos* in 1882, *bass* in 1885, and by 1906, at the end of Wilmot's time as musical director, *bassos* seems to have won the day.[36]

The Club by this time had established an excellent reputation as a premiere ensemble, a reputation that had been in place for more than a few years, as we have seen in the previous discussion. Still, the desire to maintain a solid financial footing, so that the Club could continue the good work of serving as the ultimate representation of collegiate achievement, meant that all means of increasing revenue had to be considered. To that end, advertisements were placed in the *Targum* and elsewhere alerting individuals and institutions to the availability of the group for performances. These notices appeared periodically in the *Targum*, soliciting all interested parties to contact the business manager concerning estimated prices for individual events.[37]

The Glee Club had maintained a business manager since the beginning of the Bragdon group in 1880. It is

THE RUTGERS COLLEGE GLEE CLUB

is ready to maintain the high standard of excellence attained in previous years.
CATCHY COLLEGE GLEES.
POPULAR SONGS AND CHORUSES,
SOLOS AND QUARTETTES,
READINGS AND RECITATIONS.
For particulars as to dates, terms, &c., address
J. HARVEY MURPHY, Business Manager,
New Brunswick, N. J.

Glee Club advertisement, *Targum* (October 6, 1904).

obvious from the various newspaper accounts and histories recounted in *The Scarlet Letter* over the years that this was a vital position, especially as the need to travel became ever more imperative. In the Wilmot years, however, it became customary for the Club to employ auditors as well; two members of the group are usually assigned to the task during this period. However, there are years where no auditors are listed.[38] Also, the appointment of a reader, or elocutionist, was implemented in the years 1904–5 and 1905–6 under Wilmot's leadership. The reader would present the very popular recitations that were a vital part of many Club performances.[39] All of these adjustments to the basic format of the Club speak to the willingness that the group demonstrated to modernize and adapt in response to the tremendous interest that the organization had generated for itself, both within the college community and with the public at large.

Academic year 1905–6 saw a decrease in scheduled performances; there are only fifteen events scheduled for the full ensemble, with two additional quartet appearances. This may reflect the fact that, by the spring of 1906, a long-standing political struggle within the college community involving the leadership of Director Wilmot had come to a crisis, culminating in his resignation from these duties pursuant to a request from the entire Club membership. The circumstances are as follows.

Wilmot appears to have been in active control of the ensemble until at least May 8, 1906. The group, again in connection with the Mandolin Club, presented a concert at the Parish House of the Trinity Church in Elizabeth, New Jersey, on that date. Mr. Wilmot directed the Club and sang, both as a soloist and as a member of the quartet, on this occasion.[40] However, in the same issue of the *Targum* that offers an account of this concert, the following article, under the title "Glee Club Notes," appears:

> On Monday evening [May 14, 1906] the college Glee Club unanimously requested the resignation of the leader, Mr. George Wilmot, of New Brunswick. The request was immediately complied with, said resignation to take effect immediately after the June concert.
>
> This action has long been looked for in certain circles of college activity, owing to the increasing unpopularity of the leader, due to his arbitrary manner and his general incompetence.
>
> The *Targum* and other well-wishers of the Club congratulate it upon its action, and sympathize with it in the widely expressed desire for the immediate resignation of the incumbent. The Club has too long been handicapped by inefficient leadership; but in spite of this it has attained an enviable reputation, and has probably more than any one other undergraduate organization, been the means of spreading the name and fame of Rutgers far and wide.
>
> The friends of the Club also offer their congratulations upon the choice of a successor, whose name we are not at liberty to disclose. We feel confident that he will prove all that could be desired, and that under his regime the Club will exhibit fresh life and vigor conducive to enlarged opportunities and influence.[41]

It should be noted that references to the "arbitrary manner" of Wilmot toward the Club members (or anyone else for that matter) are scarce, to say the least; the printed records do not seem to bear this assessment out. And the matter of incompetence is equally hard to substantiate, especially in light of the documented success of the Glee Club during Wilmot's ten-year reign as musical director; the author of the article himself acknowledges this success.

Contemporary accounts from New Brunswick newspapers shed a good deal of light on this matter. An article in the *Central New Jersey Home News* on May 22, 1906, announced Wilmot's resignation, attributing it to "fraternity politics." The article goes on to state that "Professor Wilmot has tendered his resignation every year for the past five years, but no notice has been taken of it. The announcement came as a surprise."[42]

The ascription of the motivations behind the campaign against Wilmot's directorship to "fraternity politics" seems to have had some basis in fact. The author of the *Targum* article was Maurice I. L. Kain, '06, who, at the time of the article's printing, was serving as editor-in-chief of that publication.[43] It was asserted at the time by a member of the college student body that Kain, along with the Glee Club's business manager, J. Harvey Murphy, '06, were motivated by their affiliation with the Delta Upsilon fraternity.[44] The student's case is laid out thus: "Mr. Murphy is ambitious and he desires that only fraternity men be enrolled as members of the Glee Club, and particularly men from the D.[elta] U.[psilon]: but Mr. Wilmot's experience of twenty-three years has taught him to require that the best singers of the College be in the Glee Club—therein lies the conflict."[45]

More directly personal reasons for instigating the movement against Wilmot and for writing the *Targum*

piece were assigned to Kain from other sources. In a letter to the editor published in the May 29, 1906, edition of the *Home News*, a "correspondent" who signs his letter "Quid" makes his views on this controversial matter known. After expressing his displeasure with Rutgers College officials for not offering "some official disavowal of this nasty editorial"—that is, the May 21 article by Kain—he goes on to offer his view of the motivations behind these events:

> Mr. Kain was the [r]eader on the Club for the season 1904–05. At the close of the season it was unanimously decided that the gentleman's services must be dispensed with. His resignation was forthwith demanded. Mr. Wilmot, being the leader of the club, sustained the opprobrium of the whole matter and immediately became the victim of Kain's ill-will.
>
> A new editor of the *Targum* was about to be elected—Kain is to graduate this year—and his time to "get even" was becoming short. The golden opportunity for revenge had arrived; it was an only opportunity—it was his opportunity and one not to be lost.[46]

The author of the letter goes on to impugn Kain's writing abilities, stating that "the whole [May 21] article might more properly have emanated from the pen of some puerile high school editor than stand as the literary production of a collegian" and concludes the missive with the question, "What do the faculty think about it?"[47]

The Glee Club itself takes issue with Kain's evaluation of the circumstances surrounding the call for Wilmot's resignation in the June 6, 1906, edition of the *Targum*, again under the title "Glee Club Notes":

> The members of the Rutgers College Glee Club desire to make [a] statement disclaiming any connection with the article published in the May 21st issue of the *Targum* under the heading "Glee Club Notes." While the author of that article undoubtedly spoke sincerely, yet the statements made by him do not express the sentiments of the Club. We felt and still feel that we acted properly in the matter of our leadership according to the constitution of the Club and fairly toward our former leader. We have no ill-will toward him; we are grateful for his long service and we recognize his musical ability and high character.
>
> We sincerely regret any unkind expressions by anyone and any unpleasantness resulting.
>
> The Rutgers College Glee Club.
> P. E. Brown, '06,
> R. A. Stout, '07,
> Committee.[48]

Percy Edgar Brown and Royal Arthur Stout both sang first bass in the ensemble; Stout also served as one of the auditors for the 1905–6 year. While some of the sentiments of this statement may be attributed to an effort at limiting unwanted notoriety for the Club, the overall attitude expressed in this rebuttal to the May 21 article should almost certainly be taken at face value, particularly in regard to the issue of competence. And these sentiments seem to be corroborated by the statements to the local press cited previously. Still, whatever problems had manifested themselves over the years between director and ensemble indeed resulted in the forced resignation of Mr. Wilmot.

It also appears that Wilmot himself engaged in a bit of pushing back on the allegations leveled by Kain. At one point, he was reported to have engaged a lawyer to investigate the possibility of filing libel charges against the young *Targum* editor-in-chief.[49] However, Wilmot appears to have thought better of this and ultimately backed away from legal action.[50]

Kain's May 21 article stated that Wilmot would leave the organization "immediately after the June concert," referring to the Glee Club's annual appearance at the commencement festivities. However, it would appear that Wilmot's departure was of a more immediate nature than that suggested in this article. The account that appeared in the *Home News* on the day following the May 21 *Targum* article stated that

Wilmot had "resigned his position, the resignation taking effect immediately." The *Home News* article also names Wilmot's successor:

> [Wilmot] has been succeeded by James Smith, of Newark, tenor in the Mendelssohn Quartet, of New York. Mr. Smith took charge last night.
>
> Mr. Wilmot will lose the annual Glee Club benefit proceeds.[51]

Accounts of the June 18, 1906, commencement concert state that the Glee Club was in fact led for this performance by Raymond W. Smith, who, despite the confusion regarding the first name, is clearly the man referenced in the *Home News* announcement.[52] These events marked the end of the term of George W. Wilmot as musical director of the Rutgers College Glee Club. As was the case with his predecessor, Loren Bragdon, his tenure came to a somewhat unceremonious resolution.

Raymond W. Smith
(Leader, 1906–11)

It would be fair to say that the directorship of the Rutgers College Glee Club fell somewhat abruptly on Raymond W. Smith. Indeed, a description of the June 18, 1906, commencement concert indicates that

Smith and the Club were still adjusting to the new circumstances engendered by Wilmot's resignation:

> The Rutgers Glee Club held its annual commencement concert in Ballantine Gymnasium last evening, having the misfortune of a stormy night, which resulted in a house only about two-thirds full, to welcome the club and its new leader, Raymond W. Smith, of Newark.
>
> The program rendered was of individual excellence, but its snap and swing was destroyed by long waits between the numbers, and tediousness was threatened by the too insistent encore-ists.[53]

But this is not to suggest that Smith was in any way unqualified to lead the Club. On the contrary, all indications are that he was an excellent choice to lead the group. In fact, he seems to have had solid instruction and substantial professional experience, both in performing and conducting, prior to his appointment to this position. He is reported to have been most thoroughly trained in conducting, having studied with such notable early twentieth-century masters as Edward MacDowell, Victor Harris, and Arthur Woodruff. A resident of Newark, New Jersey, Smith was active in the amateur theatrical circles of that town, staging productions of Gilbert and Sullivan's *H. M. S. Pinafore* and other like material. He maintained a prominent performance profile in New York.[54] For many years, he was a member of the Mendelssohn Glee Club of that city, a prestigious organization that claims to be the oldest male chorus in the United States; this group is still in existence today.[55] And at the time of his appointment as leader of the Rutgers Glee Club, he was a member of the New York Minnesingers, "a male quartette of

The *Central New Jersey Home News*,
September 15, 1906.

considerable reputation."[56] Both of these latter organizations were heavily influenced by the male chorus tradition described in chapter 1.

Smith was portrayed in contemporary accounts as "possessing a remarkably sweet as well as clear, tenor voice, and, though he has not a heavy volume, he has the art of placing the tones so that they are easily heard at a considerable distance."[57] He put his vocal talents to immediate use with the Club; for his first appearance, the commencement concert on June 18, 1906, Smith performed as a member of the quartet and as a soloist.[58] Also of note in Smith's inaugural concert was the fact that, unlike his predecessors as director, he employed the use of a baton in conducting the ensemble: "His method of conducting the club—making use of a baton—is an innovation, but the light and shade of tone rendered possible by this method alone, fully warrants the novelty of its appearance."[59]

Smith brought with him to the Club ideas for invigorating the repertory by including among the standards works ("On the Banks," "Bow-Wow-Wow," and so on) other pieces for the entire ensemble that would appeal to the latest fashions and tastes. By the end of the summer of 1906, Smith was prepared to announce some of the latest additions to the Club's future programming. The list includes the following categories and selections:

The Phantom Band—A part march and glee
   chorus, bringing in bits of well-known
   melodies; it is exceptionally funny.
   Composed by Thayer "and others."

"Dinah Doe," "I'se Comin'," "Kindlin'
   Wood"—A group of humorous
   and pathetic Southern songs, noted
   for their exquisite harmony.

"Jackie Horner" (Caldicott)—This is an
   alphabetical fugue, in which each part goes
   skipping all over the scale, and terminates
   in a harmony during the last four measures.

"The Boston Cats" (Newcomb)—A serio
   comic tale of a grafting feline club.

"Tom, the Piper's Son" (Smith)—The
   same old nursery rhyme, humorously
   set to interesting, new music.

"Annie Laurie" (Buck)—Probably the most
   musical arrangement on the program.

"Heavy Frost," "The Elfman," "Lullaby" (Archie
   Gibson)—Possibly the best productions
   of this young and talented composer.

"Courtship" (Thayer)—A short history of
   flirtation, with a sudden burst of the
   Mendelssohn wedding march.

New Medley—Containing snatches of
   the latest popular airs, arranged
   in true medley style.[60]

Thus the stage was set for Smith's inaugural year as director. The "History of the Glee Club" provided in the yearbook for 1906–7 handles the installation of the new regime in an understated manner. While bemoaning the loss of so many "valuable men" from the class of '06, the narrative goes on to say that "under our new leader, Raymond W. Smith, the club rapidly rounded into shape." The "History" goes on to reiterate the importance of the Club to the college and the fact that the Club is "perhaps the most representative of all [Rutgers College organizations], doing a great deal to spread the name of Rutgers around the country and to interest men for future classes in our college."[61]

The configuration of the Club remained more-or-less intact through this transitional period. The ensemble was still an all-student affair, with three singers on a part. The practice of maintaining permanent substitute performers was also carried over. Members are listed as such for the second tenors and the first and second basses (or *bassos* here); presumably, Smith would be available to fill in as a substitute first tenor should the need arise. Further, as mentioned in the discussion of the 1906 commencement concert, Smith adopted the practice of singing in the quartet, as had Wilmot before him.

The leadership structure for the group remained similar to that of the Wilmot group. Officers were chosen from the ensemble's ranks; these included a president and a vice president. Also listed among the leaders of the Club was the business manager, a position of vital importance to the group, as we have seen. This position was filled for Smith's initial season by Royal A. Stout, '07, who was on the committee that repudiated the derogatory statements concerning Wilmot in the *Targum*. The Club also maintained a historian. This tradition can trace its origin back to the Bragdon period; it was during the 1890–91 season that the Club first officially listed this position. It was customary for a member of the ensemble to fill this role. As mentioned earlier, a reader was utilized for recitations in performances; this position was occupied by a student, though not a member of the vocal forces.[62] The only positions filled by nonstudents were those of leader / musical director and accompanist; the latter position was occupied in 1906–7 by Clarence G. Rolfe, who also accompanied the Mandolin Club.[63]

By its own admission, some of the missteps and awkwardness that manifested themselves in the Club's first appearance under Smith in June of 1906 were still present when the 1906–7 season began. The group's historian characterized the first few concerts of that year as "trials, to cure the club of stage fright."[64] Some of these problems would soon vanish; however, a certain amount of turmoil would persist throughout this season. Notwithstanding these difficulties, the Club gave twenty-five concerts during the season, including the traditional commencement performance given on June 17, 1907. Venues were mostly within New Jersey, including South River, Harlingen, New Brunswick, Hackensack, Rahway, Newark, Ridgewood, Asbury Park, Pennington, Chrome, Plainfield, and Elizabeth. However, the group also performed in New York City, Brooklyn, Schenectady, Walden (New York), and Philadelphia. Programming for these events comports well with the aspirations set forth by Smith at the beginning of the year. Concerning the response to the concerts presented by the Club, the following was offered: "The audiences were always agreeably surprised to find that the club so small in numbers could furnish such a varied program as to include choruses, sextettes, quartettes, tenor and bass solos, piano and violin solos and recitations. . . . Many requests came from the audiences for our college song."[65] Indeed, the commencement concert of 1907 is an excellent example of the programming that Smith brought to the group. This event, held at the Ballantine Gymnasium on June 17, featured many of the works that Smith had promised to deliver. Offering the variety in selections that previous audiences had commented on, the commencement concert presented the Club "at its best."[66]

As was customary, the concert featured a guest artist; in this case, that role was filled by the well-known soprano Miss Ada Pierce. Miss Pierce offered several selections, including a popular operatic piece by Giacomo Puccini ("Vissi d'arte, vissi d'amore" from *Tosca*) as well as several English-language works. Not to be outdone, Smith performed a tenor solo from the opera *Cavalleria rusticana* by Pietro Mascagni. The Club accompanist, Clarence G. Rolfe, joined in the soloistic proceedings, offering a Franz Liszt *Polonaise*.[67]

As stated above, works that Smith had promised for the ensemble were presented in this performance. The chorus "Jack Horner," the so-called alphabetical fugue by Caldicott, was given, as were several other works for the chorus, including "A-lass" by the popular contemporary composer C. H. Tebbs. The Mandolin Club was also featured on this program, presenting popular standards such as "The Bullfrog and the Coon." And of course, as tradition demanded, the performance began with a rousing rendition of "Bow-Wow-Wow" and concluded with the sentimental favorite "On the Banks of the Old Raritan," "the audience rising and joining in the last verse."[68]

The description of this concert in the *Targum* noted the following: "Both clubs [the Glee Club and the Mandolin Club] are closing a very successful season and as each lose only a few members by graduation, they are looking forward to a prosperous season next year."[69] This statement would prove to be a foreshadowing of events that would transpire in the following academic year, events that would have great significance for both organizations.

Collaborative Efforts

The academic year 1907–8 opened amid rumors that the Glee Club and the Mandolin Club might merge and form a combined unit. On October 2, 1907, the *Targum* reported that "the union of the Glee Club with the Mandolin Club is practically assured."[70] This was quickly followed by another announcement in the October 30 edition of the *Targum*: "The outlook for a successful season for the Glee Club is very bright. Twelve engagements are being considered and will be accepted if the Faculty favor them. A new feature of the Glee Club is its combination with the Mandolin Club, thereby giving a larger and more varied program, which should be especially agreeable to the audiences. With the added feature of the Mandolin Club and the number of engagements on hand there is no apparent reason why this should not be the most successful season the Rutgers Glee Club has ever had."[71] The new entity that resulted from this amalgamation of forces was dubbed the Rutgers College Glee and Mandolin Club. In the "Glee and Mandolin Club History" provided in *The Scarlet Letter* for this season, the following explanation for this merger is offered:

In the autumn of 1907, there was a grand wedding at Rutgers. The Glee Club was married. Now, don't be misled by this statement, and

Rutgers College Glee and Mandolin Club,
The Scarlet Letter, 1907–8.

think that the individual members all went out of town and were married (they wouldn't be allowed to in town), but the organization as a unit was married. It happened in this way. There is a saying, "Een Dracht makt Macht," and as there was a Mandolin Club here, it was thought that the union of the two musical clubs would produce a combination that could not be beaten. So the Glee Club married the Mandolin Club, and both are living in the height of conjugal bliss.[72]

To be sure, this union—when viewed in the context of the times and considering the history of the two clubs—could not have been very surprising to the contemporary audiences that the new entity served. Such combined groups were very much in vogue during the late nineteenth and early twentieth centuries, both on and off college campuses. Cornell boasted a group that toured under the collective name of the Cornell Glee, Banjo, and Mandolin Clubs.[73]

Columbia maintained an amalgamated society of this sort, which was also comprised of the glee, banjo, and mandolin clubs; by 1891, this group was performing as the Columbia College Music Society.[74] These are but two of many such consolidated groups that flourished during this period.[75]

That other colleges were forming such consolidated associations was not lost on the men of Rutgers College. As early as 1895, the following sentiments encouraging the development of such an organization at the college were expressed:

It has become the custom with the musical organizations of the different colleges to make a more or less extensive holiday tour, and in this way the American college is kept before the American public during the interum [*sic*]

67

between foot-ball and base-ball. In the matter of her glee club, Rutgers has long felt a just pride and undoubtedly holds her own with institutions of greater numerical strength. But why should we content ourselves with a glee club? The representative clubs of other colleges combine generally a glee, banjo and mandolin club, and on account of the greater variety offered, an audience invariably pronounces in favor of the combined clubs, while in respect to the glee alone its performance may be far inferior to ours. There used to be a banjo club in college but without the incentive of an occasional tour it has disbanded. If our club wishes to retain its reputation among the first, there is a growing necessity for including a banjo and perhaps a mandolin club.[76]

The author of this article is correct to point out that a banjo club did, at one time, exist at Rutgers College. The Banjo and Guitar Club is first listed in *The Scarlet Letter* for the academic year 1888–89. It consisted of ten members, five playing guitar and five playing banjo; no officers or administrators for the club are named.[77] The Banjo Club continued in more or less the same configuration, with varying membership numbers, over the next three academic years, disappearing by the year 1892–93.[78] A loosely organized Banjo,

Mandolin, and Guitar Club was present on campus for the 1894–95 year but was also short-lived.[79]

An official mandolin club appears in the 1895–96 edition of *The Scarlet Letter*. This is a fully formed group consisting of mandolins, guitars, and other instruments (flute, violin, and violoncello). The club has officers (president, vice president, and secretary), a historian, and a business manager. Most of the group consists of current students, though there were some recent graduates filling out the ranks. For example, the president and designated leader, who also played first mandolin, was Herman C. Weber, '95. The club also listed a musical director who was not a member of the Rutgers College student body, H. L. "Pop" Sebastian, '67. The story of the club's evolution in its own view is provided in the "Mandolin and Guitar Club History" that accompanies the list of members.[80]

Thus, the alliance of the Glee Club with the Mandolin Club (or variations thereof) precedes their official merger in 1907 by more than a decade. Notices in the *Targum* from as early as the beginning of 1896 speak to the close association that these groups enjoyed even then, as well as to the fluidity of configurations for the instrumental group. For example, a reception for students was given by the college YMCA in the assembly room of Winant's Hall on January 13, 1896. The entertainment included a recitation by the college's instructor in elocution, Edward Livingston

Rutgers College Mandolin Club, *The Scarlet Letter*, 1895–96. Special Collections, Rutgers University Archives.

Barbour,[81] as well as an appearance by both the Glee Club and the Banjo and Mandolin Club. A report of the event states that during Professor Barbour's recitation of Dickens's "A Christmas Carol," which was divided into three sections, "music from the Glee Club and also from the Banjo and Mandolin Club intervened."[82]

Similar events took place in the immediately ensuing months. The Glee Club and the Mandolin Club took part jointly in a reading given at Kirkpatrick Chapel on February 12, 1896, for the benefit of the College Athletic Association "and won laurels for themselves by their excellent work."[83] Along the same lines, but exhibiting a somewhat different configuration, is a concert scheduled for May 8, 1896, that is identified as being given by the Mandolin Club, at which "they will also be assisted by the Glee Club."[84]

69

The clubs worked together amicably and profitably as the nineteenth century drew to a close. A concert was given on February 22, 1898, in Newark, New Jersey, by "the Glee and Mandolin Clubs," according to the *Targum*.[85] Similarly, the *Targum* reports that "the Glee and Mandolin Clubs gave a concert at Millbrook, N. Y. last Friday night [March 4, 1898]."[86] Both concerts are mentioned in the list of "Glee Club Engagements" for 1897–98 provided in the yearbook. However, there is no mention made there of participation by the Mandolin Club.[87] And at the annual commencement concert held at the Ballantine Gymnasium on June 17, 1898, "the Mandolin Club appeared with the Glee Club in the opening and closing selections and also in the vocal gavotte, 'Forget-Me-Not.'"[88] As this concert was a traditional showcase for the Glee Club, the joining of forces here, and in the other instances recounted previously, speaks to a level of practical cooperation that belies the distance that the official college yearbook implies between the clubs.

The following season would yield even more cooperation. During the Christmas holiday break of the 1898–99 year, the Glee Club again embarked on a southern trip. Participation of the Mandolin Club in this enterprise was hinted at in published reports as early as February of 1898.[89] That this collaboration did indeed occur is confirmed in *The Scarlet Letter* of that academic year. The Glee Club version of these events includes this excerpt:

[When] the Christmas holidays arrived, . . . we, imbued with the spirit of expansion and seeking new cities to conquer, started on our Southern trip.

The Glee Club, accompanied by the Mandolin Club, left New Brunswick on the morning of the 26th of December, and reached Washington that afternoon.[90]

The matter of which club played the role of the "accompanying" party is up for debate, however, and is dependent on one's point of view; consider the Mandolin Club's account of these events given in the same issue of *The Scarlet Letter* only six pages later: "Hurrying over our successful concerts at Neshanic, Orange, and Newark, we come to our famous 'Southern Trip,' which we took during the Christmas holidays, accompanied by the Glee Club."[91] This slight discrepancy in accounts of the southern excursion could be seen as an indication that some level of antagonism might still have remained between these two organizations. Indeed, collaborations involving both clubs in the following months and years were quite sporadic. A combined concert occurred on April 24, 1901, at Kirkpatrick Chapel for the benefit of the Rutgers football and track programs. The description of the concert, however, offers some insight into the position of the Mandolin Club at this time: "The Glee and Mandolin Clubs got a very hearty reception and acquitted themselves very creditably, especially the Mandolin Club, which has been rather neglected during the past two years."[92] Matters improved somewhat for the Mandolin Club over the next two years. The alliance with the Glee Club seems to have been at least partially restored; the 1901–2 yearbook lists four combined concerts with the Mandolin Club in the "Glee Club Engagements" section.[93] At this point, though, it seems that, even by its own admission, the Mandolin Club is subordinate and somewhat dependent upon the Glee Club for support, as an excerpt from that Club's "History" for that season demonstrated: "The concerts given by the Mandolin Club last season [1901–2] were all in connection with the Glee Club, because the patrons of our college Clubs know how complimentary [sic] are these two organizations."[94] The following year saw similar collaborations between the groups, with five combined concerts, including the commencement concert on June 15, 1903. These events are still noted as collaborations on the "Glee Club Engagements" page of The Scarlet Letter;[95] however, the Mandolin Club page makes no reference to them in its "History" for that year.[96]

During the season of 1903–4, matters for the Mandolin Club again begin to deteriorate. There are no combined concerts with the Glee Club mentioned in either club's section of that season's yearbook. Membership had declined; the group now listed only nine players, whereas the standard number for this group had been at least eleven in past years. And there is no "History" section provided in the yearbook.[97]

By the academic year 1904–5, the Mandolin Club seems to have been discontinued. No concerts of any sort are mentioned in any publications of the period. The only mention in that year's edition of The Scarlet Letter is a brief obituary for the group, which reads, "In Memoriam—Mandolin Club—June 20, 1904."[98] However, this demise was temporary. By October of the following academic year (1905–6), a movement to reinstitute the Mandolin Club was already in progress: "It is rumored that a project is on foot for the reorganization of the Mandolin Club. Such a movement should meet with much encouragement from the student body. We sincerely hope that every man in college who can 'pluck a string' will avail himself of the first opportunity to ally himself with the musical interests of our college."[99] By the following month, the Mandolin Club had been reconstituted, boasting twelve members, of which four officers were elected.[100] This reorganization of the group is also reflected in the yearbook for the academic year 1905–6; the Mandolin Club once again has its own section in that publication, as does, of course, the Glee Club. The Mandolin Club "History" for this season speaks of combined concerts featuring the Glee and Mandolin Clubs: "At Paterson [N.J.], we made a 'hit'; . . . we accompanied the Glee

71

Club when they sang 'Bow-Wow-Wow' and 'On the Banks.' The experiment proved worthy of repetition in the future."[101] The Glee Club "History" is silent on this matter, however. Though that group's list of engagements for the 1905–6 season does include a performance on March 30 at Paterson, participation by the Mandolin Club is not acknowledged therein.[102] However, it must be remembered that this is the period during which the turmoil that would lead to the resignation of George Wilmot as musical director of the Glee Club was in full force. The combined concert on May 8, 1906, at Elizabeth, New Jersey that is detailed above was, in fact, Wilmot's last appearance with the group. And the commencement concert on June 18, 1906, which again featured both groups, marked the debut of the Glee Club's new leader, Raymond W. Smith. Therefore, it seems that during this chaotic period for both groups, while combined performances clearly took place, some resistance to the idea of such events still remained, mostly emanating, it would appear, from the Glee Club. At this point, the Mandolin Club is still seen as an entirely separate entity, though one that held promise, as this brief summation of the newly reorganized group attests: "In the Mandolin Club better material was developed than in many previous years. A number of concerts were given which proved highly satisfactory."[103]

The groups are still discrete organizations during the 1906–7 season. The Glee Club, as previously stated, is now under the leadership of Raymond W. Smith and remains a vibrant and vital part of Rutgers College life.[104] The Mandolin Club section of *The Scarlet Letter* for this year presents possibly the most robust manifestation of that group since its inception. The Club boasts thirteen members and a full complement of officers and administrators, including a president, a secretary, and a business manager, all students and taken from the ranks of the ensemble. The leader of the group was Harold H. Febrey, '06. Febrey had been a member of the group since his freshman year, becoming leader and business manager during the 1905–6 season. He was also active in the Glee Club during this year.[105] He was retained in the leader position of the Mandolin Club following his graduation but relinquished his role as business manager to F. D. Halliwell, '06. He did, however, continue to perform with the ensemble; he is listed as playing first mandolin for the 1906–7 season.[106]

Cooperation between the clubs seems to have been reestablished during this year, at least in the accounts provided in *The Scarlet Letter*. Both organizations refer to collaborative performances in their respective histories; these narratives refer to combined concerts in Harlingen and Asbury Park during this season.[107] But while the Mandolin Club seems to have found its footing and solved the problems it had experienced a few years earlier, the Glee Club showed signs of instability. The joint concert at Asbury Park, which occurred on February 22, was described as being "well received by the large audience that filled Library Hall"; it was also mentioned that the Glee Club was "somewhat crippled by the absence of several men."[108] Indeed, it was reported at this time that "owing to the resignation of some of the old members of the Glee Club, new members have been taken on, and substitutes have been brought in from outside." This would seem to indicate that the Glee Club was still struggling to find an identity and a unified system of organization in the early years of the Smith regime.

Notwithstanding, the Glee Club pressed on with its commitments for the 1907 spring semester. In April, two concerts were given: one in Chrome, New Jersey, on April 3 and one at the Jersey City High School on April 5. On May 25, the Club appeared as entertainment for the interscholastic track and field meet, at which they "entertained the visiting schools with a short program in the Gymnasium."[109] And the season concluded, according to tradition, with the commencement concert on June 17, a joint concert with the Mandolin Club. At this point, the two clubs are still distinct and separate entities; the June 5, 1907, issue of the *Targum* offers individual histories for each group. Both clubs were said to be in good shape, despite troubles alluded to in the reports cited above concerning the Glee Club. Indeed, the Mandolin Club is described as being "in prosperous condition, which augers well for the future." But that future would look quite different for both clubs.

Merger

The 1907–8 academic year opened with an announcement that, as expected, Raymond Smith would again lead the Glee Club. But there was also an expectation within the college that structural changes were to be expected in the group:

> The trials for the Glee Club, held last Thursday, September 26, were very successful . . . The final list of the successful applicants will appear in about a week, the sifting process having not yet been completed.
>
> The prospects of the Club are very bright. The union of the Glee Club with the Mandolin Club is practically assured. This will enable our patrons to obtain a more varied program for a slightly additional expense, owing to the fact that the membership of the two clubs is nearly identical.[110]

Less than a month later, the *Targum* announced the official merger of the two clubs: "The outlook for a successful season for the Glee Club is very bright. Twelve engagements are being considered and will be accepted if the faculty favor them. A new feature of the Glee Club is its combination with the Mandolin Club, thereby giving a larger and more varied program, which should be agreeable to the audiences. With the added feature of the Mandolin Club and the number of engagements on hand there is no apparent reason why this should not be the most successful season the Rutgers Glee Club has ever had."[111]

Thus the consolidation of the two clubs was official. However, two important points should be noted from the above quotes. In the first quote, the article states that the membership of the two groups "is nearly identical." This is somewhat of an overstatement; the list of members and officers that is appended to the article from which the second quote is drawn shows that, of a total of nineteen ensemble members in the Glee Club and fourteen in the Mandolin Club, only six were members of both.[112] The second point to note is that both quotes, but especially the second, seem to privilege the Glee Club as the surviving entity. True, in that year's *Scarlet Letter*, the official title is the Rutgers College Glee and Mandolin Club. However, the phrasing in these quotes, and other published reports, would indicate that the Mandolin Club has been absorbed by the Glee Club as a "new feature"; the Glee Club is the dominant force in the consolidated enterprise.

The structure of the new Rutgers College Glee and Mandolin Club, as articulated in the yearbook for 1907–8, was indeed a hybrid format. This in many ways reflects the analogy of a "grand wedding" between the two groups, as the "Glee and Mandolin

Club History" for that year describes the pairing.[113] The club memberships are presented separately, each with its own leader, accompanists, and readers; however, both groups list the same members for the latter two positions. The leader for the Glee Club is, of course, Raymond W. Smith, who continues to serve as a first tenor. The Glee Club complement had grown somewhat, now boasting sixteen members: four first tenors (including Smith), four second tenors, five first basses (called *bass* on the yearbook page), and four second basses. There are also two permanent substitutes listed, one each on the two bass parts.

The leader of the Mandolin Club continued to be Harold Febrey. This group can also point to robust membership in this new configuration. The ensemble consists of thirteen members: five first mandolins (with Febrey serving as a sixth), three second mandolins, two banjos, two guitars, and one cello.

Subsuming these two entities was the leadership of the Rutgers College Glee and Mandolin Club. The president of the amalgamated group was Harry F. Brewer, '08. Other positions in the leadership included a vice president, a secretary, a business manager, an assistant business manager, a historian, and a librarian. All officers and administrators of the combined group served as members of both ensembles, with the exception of the librarian, J. Bishop Woolston, '11, who sang first tenor in the Glee Club but did not play in the Mandolin Club.[114]

The initial concert schedule for the group, announced in November, listed seven appearances, a somewhat low number in comparison to other years. Venues included Bound Brook, New Market, Jersey City, Union Hill, Rahway, Morristown, and Brooklyn (New York).[115] The opening concert was given at Voorhees Hall in Bound Brook on November 15, 1907, to an "attentive audience which crowded the hall [and] expressed their appreciation by repeatedly calling for encores." The program for the concert resembles those given as a combined effort by these clubs on previous occasions. The Glee Club is clearly the featured group, with intermittent pieces for the Mandolin Club scattered throughout the performance. The only collaborative works on the program are the "Nursery Rhyme Suite" and "On the Banks of the Old Raritan," which serve as the concert finale. The customary tenor solo by Glee Club leader Smith is also a feature of this program.

The season progressed well. The concert at Union City in December drew an audience of 1,500 who "showed their appreciation by encoring every number on the program."[116] To be sure, large audiences were reported for all of the concerts during the fall semester of 1907.[117] Credit for the good attendance must, at least in some measure, be given to the business manager for the consolidated group during this period, G. Condé Lawsing, '08. His aggressive advertising, highlighting the new, combined nature of the group

RUTGERS COLLEGE
Glee and Mandolin Club.

These two, formerly separate, musical clubs are now united into one organization and offer to their patrons

COLLEGE GLEES, POPULAR SONGS AND CHORUSES, CATCHY UP-TO-DATE STRING SELECTIONS, SOLOS, QUARTETTES AND RECITATIONS.

For particulars as to dates, terms, etc., address

G. CONDE LAWSING, '08, Manager,
NEW BRUNSWICK, N. J.

Advertisement in the *Targum*, October 2, 1907, for the combined clubs.

and the advantages thereof can be found in every issue of the *Targum*.

Print descriptions of these concerts consistently refer to the group as the Glee and Mandolin Club. However, Smith is always designated as the leader of the group, again a nod to the dominance of the Glee Club part of the combined ensemble. Indeed, even when Smith is not present, as occasionally happened, Harold Febrey, leader of the Mandolin Club contingent, did not lead the singing. At such an event at the Second Presbyterian Church in Trenton on February 24, 1908, "in the absence of Mr. Smith, the regular leader, Potter, '09 successfully lead [*sic*] the singing."[118] F. M. Potter is listed as a second tenor in the Glee Club

75

part of the group; he did not participate in the mandolin ensemble.[119]

In April, the group undertook a four-day limited excursion, described as the group's "Easter Trip," to upstate New York.[120] Concerts were given in Kingston, New Paltz, Albany, and Schenectady. The benefit of having such fine representatives of the college performing in venues outside of the immediate environs of New Brunswick was again noted in a contemporary account of this successful endeavor.[121]

The 1908–9 season got off to good start with the annual benefit concert for the YMCA on September 25. This event, featuring the combined club, was held in Winant's Hall, and as tradition dictated, all the college men were invited.[122] However, it seems, particularly regarding the Mandolin Club, that the course of events was not placid. In the annual announcement for trials for the clubs, the following news was made public: "The [Mandolin] Club this year will miss the excellent guidance and instruction of Mr. Febrey, '06, who was the organizer of the Mandolin Club and has directed it during the past two years. Owing to the demands of his business in New York he will be unable to give much of his time to the club but may conduct the preliminary rehearsals."[123] Febrey was as good as his word concerning the rehearsals; he was scheduled to conduct the October 1908 "drillings and rehearsals of the Mandolin Club" as was his usual practice. Notwithstanding

Febrey's efforts, the prospects for the Mandolin Club were rather grim at this point: "The rehearsals of the clubs have been regularly progressing although the outlook for the Mandolin club [sic] is not quite as good this year as in the past, because those who play the various instruments do not come out. At present there is not enough to compose a full club; there is an especial lack of guitar players."[124] This news was greeted with dismay from Mr. Febrey, whose considerable efforts in establishing and guiding the Mandolin Club over the past several years had been noted in many quarters. The announcement that the club was once again in jeopardy prompted him to write a letter to the editor of the *Targum*. He outlined his appraisal of the situation, providing historical context and offering advice on how to proceed in the club's best interests.[125]

This impassioned plea was effective in that the Mandolin Club component of the combined entity survived. However, the lack of interest bemoaned by Febrey in his *Targum* piece was only partially mitigated. Insufficient numbers for the Mandolin component forced a compromise, the details of which are set forth as follows: "Both [the Glee and Mandolin] clubs have been rehearsing although the prospects of the Mandolin club are not so promising as those of the Glee club. Instead of having a regular Mandolin club of sixteen instruments the club will be organized as a double quartet since there does not seem to be available material enough for a full club."[126]

Despite further delays and distractions,[127] the combined ensemble managed to launch its first full program on February 25. This event took place at the Central Branch of the YMCA in Brooklyn, New York, and received an excellent response from the audience: "Every number of the program was encored and the Mandolin Club was hailed with the wildest outbursts of enthusiasm."[128] By March, the combined club was presenting a concert every Friday evening, beginning on March 19 with an event at the Elks Lodge in Newark.

The structure of the group had solidified as well by this time. Though *The Scarlet Letter* lists only the officers for the 1908–9 season,[129] the *Targum* does provide a detailed personnel list for the group during the spring semester. The forces of the Glee Club were quite strong; four first tenors (including Smith, leader), five second tenors, four regular first basses with one permanent substitute, and four second basses, also with one permanent substitute.

The mandolin component did not, as may be expected when considering the information above, fare quite as well. The *Targum* lists three first mandolins, two second mandolins, one cello, one pianist, and one recitationist.[130] Still, the college community was pleased with the results of the season and held out hopes for improved circumstances. In early June, the following assessment was offered in the *Targum*: "The Glee and Mandolin Clubs in their combined form have all but ended a very successful season. . . . The trips have been to different localities and the clubs have been very favorably received. It is hoped that with the incoming class a full Mandolin Club may be conducted, but still the abbreviated form this season has succeeded well."[131]

The final concert of the season, as always, was the commencement concert at the Ballantine Gymnasium on June 21, 1909, with guest contralto soloist Dorothy Pollock. The program featured a good mix of the vocal and instrumental components; in addition to Miss Pollock, Raymond Smith performed his traditional tenor solo. The first half of the program concluded with a banjo duet and the entire concert concluded, again traditionally, with both ensembles performing "On the Banks." The academic year for the clubs was summarized as follows: "Although the season was not so successful as usual, measured by the number of concerts, yet the work done by the members under the leadership of Raymond W. Smith and H. H. Febrey was excellent, and their last concert was no exception."[132]

Moving into the ensuing season, the prospects for both clubs seemed bright. The Mandolin Club in particular experienced a resurgence in interest and in membership. As noted in the above quote, Harold Febrey had remained in his position as leader of the Mandolin Club throughout the 1908–9 season, though his intention had been to resign in the fall of 1908. He was replaced the following academic year (1909–10) by George Stannard of Trenton, said to be "one of the best leaders in the State." Stannard was a well-known mandolinist and banjoist in the northeastern United States and had several publications for mandolin duo and other forces to his credit.[133] His initial efforts at the helm of the Club are characterized as follows: "The Mandolin Club held its first regular rehearsal on Friday night [October 15, 1909], under the direction of Professor Stannard, with great success. The new leader proved himself exceedingly competent and led the rehearsal in a way that points towards a most successful season. A number of good mandolin and banjo players have been found in the freshman class who will develop into good material."[134] And indeed, the forces of the Mandolin Club were restored to their former glory during this season. With Stannard as leader and a member of the first mandolin section, the club offered five first mandolins (including Stannard), five second mandolins with one permanent substitute, one banjo (with Stannard frequently playing banjo solos in concerts), one guitar, one pianist, and one recitationist.

The Glee Club component was similarly well stocked, with a complement of nineteen members, including Smith as a first tenor. The configuration was four on a part, with a permanent substitute for all voices except second bass.[135]

The roster of officers also speaks to a greater degree of organization in the combined club at this

PART I.
(a) Bow! Wow! Wow!......
(b) In a Quaint Old Jersey Town...Rutgers Songs.
Glee Club.
A Tragic Story................ ...John W. Metcalf.
Glee Club.
The Gay Musician ....Edwards.
Mandolin Club.
Where the Crossroads Meet (Manuscript)....
....Ward Stephens.
Dorothy Pollock, Contralto.
The Owl and the Pussy Cat.............De Koven.
Glee Club.
Recitation .... Selected.
H. D. Leslie.
Banjo Duet.
Messrs. Stover and Savage.
PART II.
Campus Songs .... Rutgers.
Glee and Mandolin Club.
Tenor Solo .... Selected.
Raymond W. Smith.
Summer Lullaby .... Glee Club.
Solos—
(a) I Know of Two Bright Eyes........Clutsam.
(b) Boat Song....................Harriet Ware.
(c) Who'll Buy My Lavender?....Edward German.
Dorothy Pollock, Contralto.
Society Swing......................Mandolin Club.
Recitation .... Selected.
H. D. Leslie.
(a) Tom, Tom, the Piper's Son............Kendall.
(b) On the Banks of the Old Raritan......Rutgers.
Glee and Mandolin Club.

Program for the commencement concert, *Targum*, June 21, 1909.

point. In addition to the two respective club leaders, Smith and Stannard, the positions include president, vice president, secretary, librarian, and historian, all students serving in one or both ensembles. There was also a combined post of treasurer and manager filled by George W. Stout, '11. Stout became manager during the course of the 1908–9 season when the post went vacant.[136] He seems to have pursued his duties vigorously, particularly in the role of manager; he would regularly put forth the following proposal in the *Targum*: "Five dollars reward will be given to anyone securing a glee club concert. Now is the time to make arrangements. See Stout, '11."[137]

The combined club also retained the Glee Club tradition of an annual banquet. During this season, the event was held on February 18, 1910, at the Mansion House. This would appear to have been a less formal and decidedly more student-oriented affair, as both Smith and Stannard were absent. Manager Stout appears to have presided over the proceedings, calling for "impromptu speeches from the various [Club] members" and proposing toasts to the absent leaders.[138]

The year progressed smoothly; the only hint of trouble came from a letter to the *Targum* editor in April. Titled "Is Our Glee Club up to Standard" and signed by "Pytheus," the missive raises several objections to the quality of the group's performances. The letter suggests that on Club trips, "some of the members are objectionable because of their general loudness, and often rude in their actions." The author also finds it objectionable that both clubs utilize printed music in the performances. It is his contention that this practice "would indicate a paucity of rehearsals, and in time will spoil the organization," noting that "this is the only society of the kind I have ever seen us[ing] notes on scheduled concerts." He states that, in his opinion, "three good concerts have been lost" due to these practices; as "an ardent well wisher and supporter of all Rutgers activities," he asks the group to correct these flaws.[139]

But barring this somewhat subjective assessment of the Club's behavior, the 1909–10 season was very successful, particularly considering the difficulties of the previous year. The combined group gave approximately twenty concerts during this season, all of which were well received "and showed the excellent training of the clubs," according to the brief narrative of the season provided in that year's *Scarlet Letter*. It is also noted there that the Glee Club component of the combined group had reinstituted the quartet, which was a very popular feature of that Club going back to the Loren Bragdon years. This small ensemble featured Smith as first tenor and Manager Stout as first bass. Combined with the reinvigorated Mandolin Club, things looked extremely promising for the future of the combined unit.

One other matter concerning the personnel for the 1909–10 season should be noted. That year's Glee and Mandolin Club roster lists a freshman as the pianist for the Mandolin Club component. The name of this young man is Howard D. McKinney, '13. McKinney will have a great deal to do with guiding the trajectory of the Glee Club in the years to come;

it is interesting to note his background role here and the unobtrusive beginning to his long association with the Club (see chap. 5 sidebar, "Howard Decker McKinney [1889–1980]").

Change remained an essential element of the combined club as the years progressed. For the 1910–11 season, Raymond Smith remained as the leader of the Glee Club, but George Stannard had moved on. The *Targum* reported in October 1910 that he was to be replaced as "conductor" of the Mandolin Club component by Francis E. Weiss of Trenton.[140] But it would seem that the appointment of Weiss was more along the lines of a professional coach rather than the traditional leader of the group. Indeed, during this academic year, a groundswell of sentiment seemed to be forming against the notion of a professional leader for either of the component parts of the combined ensemble or, indeed, for the entire combined club. An editorial from the *Targum* in February of 1911 suggests that this custom is the proximate cause of a general decline in the quality of the clubs. The matter is detailed as follows:

> Musical clubs have a prominent place in the activities of most colleges, and some of them have become famous. There was once a time, not very long ago, when Rutgers Glee and Mandolin Clubs were known from Maine to Florida and as far west as Chicago, but now they do

not enjoy such a wide reputation. What are the reasons responsible for this state of affairs? . . .

> [One] reason is that the organization is not a paying proposition. In 1889 the Clubs made two trips to Florida and up until 1900 each man was clearing about forty dollars. In 1907, each man received *twelve cents*. And last year there was a deficit of $4.50 per man.

> And why are the clubs not paying? Mainly, we believe, because they are too expensively run. Professional coaching is a very good thing, but there is no reason why two coaches should be paid for time, services and traveling expenses, when the clubs should be able to get along without them. Other clubs have student leaders, and why cannot we? In the case of the Mandolin Club, this has been demonstrated and with considerable success, a coach having been retained for only about two months; but the Glee Club is still dependent on someone to beat time. If anything should happen so that Mr. Smith could not get to a concert the Glee Club would make a failure of it.[141]

This criticism, whatever its basis, seems to have gathered support from the college and from within the combined club itself. It does seem that, by the end of February 1911, the services of Mr. Weiss as coach of the Glee Club had been dispensed with; Fred A.

Briegs, '12, had assumed a prominent role in the mandolin component: "The Glee and Mandolin Clubs gave a very enjoyable concert at 3 o'clock on Friday afternoon [February 25] in Kirkpatrick Chapel . . . Mr. Smith, the leader of the Glee Club, was as popular as ever; and Briegs, '12 who did some solo work was greatly appreciated. The Spring Maid selection by the Mandolin Club took the house by storm."[142] Indeed, *The Scarlet Letter* for the 1910–11 season lists Briegs as leader of the Mandolin Club and president of the combined organization. Briegs also plays first mandolin in the ensemble and sings first bass in the Glee Club.

This criticism may also have led to the publication of a detailed report of the Glee and Mandolin Club's finances for the 1910–11 season in the September 27 issue of the *Targum*. Totals for receipts and expenditures are provided, including money allocated to Smith for each separate concert of the season; for nine concerts, including the commencement concert, Smith received a combined salary of $220.94, with $37.85 in unpaid expenses still owed to him at this point.[143]

Publication of this report was preceded, however, by an announcement that a new leader for the Glee Club would be taking over for Raymond Smith. In August 1911, it was reported that George W. Wilmot would return to the Rutgers Glee Club, now in its combined form, to direct once again the vocal component of the group. A contemporary newspaper account describes the prospects for the 1911–12 season as follows: "Under the able management of Prof. George W. Wilmot, who served the club for twenty years in the capacity of member and later as coach and leader, the music and rendition will be of a high order of excellence. Besides his experience with this club, Prof. Wilmot has had marked success with other glee clubs and choral societies, and it is with great pleasure that Manager [Leroy C.] Wilsey ['12] announces that he will again be Rutgers coach."[144] The terminology, as can be seen in this quote, can be somewhat confusing. In various published reports during the 1911–12 season, Wilmot and Briegs are referred to as coaches, directors, and/or leaders. Nonetheless, it is clear that they are in control of the respective parts of the combined ensemble, each bringing their own particular talents to bear on their part of the group. The following account speaks to the general configuration of the group at this time:

The clubs have put in a good many hours of faithful work rehearsing[;] under the direction of Prof. Wilmot, the program [for a concert at Kirkpatrick Chapel on February 17] is as well balanced as one could be. There is enough of the element of fun to satisfy anyone, and yet there is such of the more difficult music as to show what the club can do in ensemble work . . .

As leader and baritone soloist Mr. Briegs uses a naturally good voice with pleasing effect, and his rendering of "Grey Eyes," one of the latest of the English songs, is very capably done . . .

The Mandolin Club is larger than ever before and is playing better music with such snap and precision as should characterize an organization of its kind.

As for the Glee Club, not only have the numbers been increased, but the quality of the men's voices is much better than heretofore. This is a result of the fact that over fifty men tried out for twenty-four places.[145]

The official configuration, then, as reported in the 1911–12 edition of *The Scarlet Letter*, lists Fred Briegs as president and leader of the combined Glee and Mandolin Club. And the ranks of both component groups had indeed swelled. The Glee Club segment boasted twenty-six members; six on a part for first and second tenor and seven for first and second basses.[146] The difference between this number and that provided in the quote immediately above can be explained by a clause in the recently revised constitution, which states that substitute performers would be treated more as permanent members of the group and would therefore be so considered: "Under the new constitution 'subs' will have a much better time than heretofore, will be taken on all concerts where expenses can be procured and on all the short trips. They must attend rehearsals, however, just as the regulars."[147] And, as stated previously, the Mandolin Club had also grown. Its membership now included seven first mandolins, six second mandolins, three guitars, one cello, and a recitationist. Howard D. McKinney was now the accompanist for both groups.[148] The commentary on the season in the 1911–12 yearbook states the following: "The Glee and Mandolin Club is now up to its former excellence. With George W. Wilmot to coach and Fred A. Briegs, '12 to lead, it seems almost as if the palmy days of Loren Bragdon had returned."[149]

New Leadership

The 1912–13 season saw the emergence of Howard D. McKinney, accompanist for the Glee and Mandolin Club, as a driving force in this burgeoning organization. Having held no office or post in the administration of the Club prior to this, his senior year, McKinney is cited in the September 25, 1912, edition of the *Targum* as being the Club's manager.[150] By October, McKinney has been elected president of the combined club;[151] he is replaced in the role of manager by R. E. Cooper, '13. The January 22, 1913, edition of the *Targum* had praise for the work of this pair:

The Rutgers Glee and Mandolin Clubs, under the leadership of H. D. McKinney, '13 and R. E. Cooper, '13 have been singularly successful during the present season. The Clubs have given a series of concerts during the past two months and have not failed in any instance to make a profound impression upon the audience . . .

The college is to be congratulated upon the efficiency of its musical representatives.[152]

It is clear, however, that "leadership" in this quote refers to McKinney's role as president, and not to any role as leader of either component of the combined club or the entire club itself. The role of leader for the combined club, following the graduation of Fred A. Briegs, is now Harry K. Davies, '14. Davies is listed as a second bass in this year's *Scarlet Letter* and holds the post of assistant manager.[153]

Despite the shifting personnel, the structure of the group remained intact. Contemporary accounts state that "Prof. G. W. Wilmot is again coaching the members of the Rutgers College Glee Club."[154] And the general configuration of the clubs in terms of numbers compares well to those of the previous year; Glee Club forces were the same, while the Mandolin Club had lost three mandolins (one first and two second), one guitar, and did not have a cello for this year.[155] That the Club—and presumably its patrons—find this mode of

organization to be optimal is expressed in the yearbook narrative: "The hearty support and co-operation of the student body has resulted in many marked successes of the Glee and Mandolin Clubs during the past season. The services of Mr. George W. Wilmot as coach of the Glee Club made possible the rendering of the attractive and varied programme, while Harry K. Davies, '14 has again shown the practicability of a student leader."[156]

This season came to a rather inauspicious end, however, despite the cheerful outlook expressed in the above quote. On June 2, 1913, the local press carried the proposed schedule for the Rutgers College commencement activities. This notice contained the following information: "The Glee Club concert, which from time immemorial has been one of the events of commencement week, is to be omitted. The Junior Exhibition will be held Monday evening [the traditional night for the Glee Club concert] instead of Tuesday."[157] Indeed, the Glee Club concert had been a highlight of the commencement-week activities at Rutgers College since 1881. The official print media of the college were eerily silent on this matter, though some concern over the absence of the Glee Club at this important event was apparently expressed by at least one high-ranking school official and some members of the general public:

There is a possibility that the Glee Club concert, which has been a feature of Rutgers commencement week for many years, may still be held, contrary to general impression. Dr. Demarest has expressed the hope that the custom will be maintained, and has spoken of the appropriate character of the concert for this period of the year.

The matter is now under consideration, and the student body, as well as many townspeople, are anxious that the concert shall be given as usual.[158]

To be sure, there were many other changes instituted by the college for the commencement program in 1913. The exercises were held at the Second Reformed Church, on the corner of George and Albany Streets in New Brunswick, instead of the Ballantine Gymnasium, as had been the custom for several years. The time of the ceremonies was also changed, from the traditional 8:00 p.m. starting time to 11:30 a.m. All of this was apparently aimed at making the commencement ceremonies "[matter] more to the city than it has in some years."[159] Therefore, protestations notwithstanding, the Glee Club concert was removed as a featured part of the 1913 graduation ceremonies.

The 1913–14 season was relatively quiet for the clubs. With President Howard McKinney due to graduate in June 1913, the elections held the previous May installed Robert Dooling, '14, who sang second bass

in the Glee Club component, as president of the combined clubs. Harry Davies was moved from the post of assistant manager to manager, in addition to his duties as Glee Club leader.[160] George Wilmot was still coaching the Glee Club,[161] while leadership of the mandolin component had been given to A. G. Leeds, '14, who played first mandolin.[162] Davies and Leeds were frequent soloists for the group during this season.[163]

The 1914–15 season was equally sedate. The elections of May 1914 placed B. J. Folensbee, '15, in the post of president, with W. E. Schwanhausser, '15, elected to the post of manager.[164] Wilmot was again coach of the Glee Club; Leeds had returned, despite his graduation, as coach of the mandolin component.[165] The overall leadership of the clubs was given to Folensbee. The configuration of the individual groups had evolved somewhat. The mandolin group now contained only mandolins, seven on a part (first and second); all other instruments (guitar, banjo, and cello) that were present in earlier groups had been eliminated. The Glee Club group had grown considerably. There were now twenty-nine members of the ensemble; six first tenors, seven second tenors, and eight apiece of first and second basses.[166]

The 1914–15 season introduced some innovations, particularly within the Glee Club component. Two vocal quartets were formed, each with a specialized repertory.[167] One was dubbed the "Prickly Heat Quartette"; this group apparently catered to more modern, jazz/

ragtime-oriented sensibilities. There was another quartet, however, "with more serious intentions"; this ensemble "succeeded in interpreting negro lullabies to the satisfaction of its audiences." The Mandolin Club produced its own specialized group, a mandolin trio, which also proved popular with the group's audiences.[168]

The 1915–16 season began with the announcement that George Wilmot would no longer be serving as the coach for the Glee Club: "The executive council of the Rutgers Glee Club has decided to engage Allan Hall, Yale, 1914, who is the newly appointed chapel organist, as director of the club for the coming season."[169] There is a dearth of information regarding Hall and his involvement with the group. His name does not appear in the 1915–16 yearbook for the college except in the narrative describing his position with the Glee Club, which also describes the Club as being "under the direction of Mr. Hall, Yale, '14." But it seems clear that he is now filling the coaching position that Wilmot vacated. The leader of the Glee Club is William H. W. Komp, '16, while the Mandolin Club leader is listed as W. Phillips Thorp Jr., '17, who also did some arranging for the group.

Membership in both components of the Club continued to grow. The Glee Club now boasted thirty-two voices: seven first tenors, ten second tenors, seven first basses, and eight second basses. The Mandolin Club had also expanded, both in numbers and in the inclusion of instruments. It now consisted of sixteen

PART ONE.

1. Opening Medley ....Arranged by Thorp '17
   Canoeing Song
   Rutgers Cheering Song
   Song of Victory
   Combined Clubs
2. The Musical Trust ....Hadley
   Glee Club
3. Recitation .... Selected
   Mr. Scarr
4. Solo .... Selected
   Mr. Whisler
5. Ken Tuc Kee ....Weidt
   Mandolin Club
6. Quartette—A Summer Lullaby ....Gibson
   Mr. Whisler, Mr. Komp, Mr. Croker, Mr. Miller
7. Rockin' in de Win' ....Neidlinger
   Glee Club

PART TWO.

1. (a) The Dreamy Lake .... Schuman
   (b) Carry Me Back to Old Virginny.....Bland
   Glee Club
2. Banjo-Mandolin Quintette .... Selection
   Mr. Thorp, Mr. Jenkins, Mr. Herbert, Mr. Post,
   Mr. Taylor
3. But—They Didn't .... Rogers
   Glee Club
4. Recitations .... Selected
   Mr. Scarr
5. Prickley Heat Quartette ....Selected
   Mr. Conklin, Mr. Van Arsdale, Mr. Boes, Mr.
   Whisler
6. Illusion Waltz ....Carlo Neve
   Mandolin Club
7. Campus Songs ....Selected
   Glee Club
8. On the Banks of the Old Raritan........Fuller
   Combined Clubs

Program for the annual Junior Week concert, Brunswick Hall, *Targum*, February 18, 1916.

mandolins (parts not designated), four violins, a guitar, and a "Yukalale." A single accompanist served both sections of the group, as in past years.[170]

The programs for the season reflect a balance between the groups in performance. The program for the annual Junior Week concert, given at Brunswick Hall on February 18, 1916, is representative.[171] The concert opens with a medley for the combined clubs, arranged by Thorp. Selections by the full Glee Club ensemble are present, as are selections for the full mandolin component. The Glee Club quartets are featured, both the more serious quartet and that which was dubbed the "Prickly Heat Quartette." This latter group also attained the moniker of the "Scarlet Fever Quartette" during this season.[172] And a banjo-mandolin quintet earns a place on the program. Of course, the concert concluded with a rendition by the combined clubs of "On the Banks of the Old Raritan." The appearance of the Glee and Mandolin Club as the main attraction at the Junior Week festivities had now become an annual event, replacing the Glee Club's traditional role at the commencement proceedings.

The concert schedule once again kept mostly to New Jersey locales, though the group did provide preliminary entertainment for a meeting of the American Rights Committee at Carnegie Hall in March of 1916.[173] The calls for a more expansive scope for the travels of the clubs that arose at the conclusion of the 1914–15 season did not produce results, though the Hackettstown-and-Dover trip from that year was repeated, with similar excellent results.[174]

One point of interest during the conclusion of this year bears mentioning. In the May 24, 1916, edition of the *Targum*, an article titled "Student Organization and Scholarship" was presented. This piece was basically a compilation of the average grades of various student groups, looking back over the previous three semesters. These averages were then compared to the average grades of the entire student body. It seems that the Glee Club fared extremely well in this comparison. When examined against the student-body average of 73.3 percent, the Glee Club attained an average of 76.1 percent, trouncing the football squad (69.5 percent) and beating out all other groups save the gymnasium team (77.1 percent), the Ivy Club (78.7 percent), and the Queen's Players (76.9 percent). It would appear that the Glee Club could hold its own with the best of the academic field during this period.

3 THE MODERN ERA

RUTGERS AT 150

The first decade and a half of the twentieth century was a pivotal time in the development of the Rutgers College Glee Club. These years saw the consummation of the long flirtation with the Mandolin Club and its predecessors (to continue the wedding analogy put forth at the time of the clubs' official amalgamation), providing stability for both component groups. These years also saw the demise of certain cherished institutions, such as the prominent role of the Glee Club concert during commencement week. Included in the latter category would be the move toward student leadership for the groups, a controversial measure that seems to have been implemented more or less by popular demand from the students themselves. The efficacy of this mode of leadership may well be debated. The switch to professional coaches with student leaders rather than professional leaders (who also performed) may well have proved more economically efficient; however, this system had the built-in defect of inducing a quick turnover of group leaders due to their inevitable (one would hope) graduation. This aspect of the Glee Club's configuration would evolve quickly during the ensuing years. And of course, world events of a nature not previously contemplated would affect all facets of life in the early twentieth century, both within the college and without. It is within such parameters that the Glee Club would continue to develop into the modern organization that we know today.

It is perhaps fitting to draw attention to the 1916–17 season. This year marked the 150th anniversary of the college, and festivities at the school and in the town of New Brunswick were to be seen throughout the academic year. It is a convenient line of demarcation in the history of the Glee Club as well, for a variety of reasons. But among the most important of these reasons is again the question of the leadership of the Club and the unity and strength that derives from stability therein.

Howard D. McKinney, '13, as Director

The Rutgers sesquicentennial exposition that was held in the fall of 1916 was an elaborate affair to be sure. The *Central New Jersey Home News* ran an eight-page supplemental section on October 14, 1916, detailing the numerous and splendid events that had occurred during the prior week of celebrations. Honorary degrees were conferred on various world dignitaries, including Chevalier W. L. F. C. van Rappard, Minister Plenipotentiary and Envoy Extraordinary from the Netherlands to the United States, reflecting the original association of Rutgers College with the Dutch Reformed Church.[1] Indeed, Queen Wilhelmina of the Netherlands herself sent official word of congratulations to the college. Various college presidents and other dignitaries spoke of the importance of Rutgers as a model educational institution, including Baron Shiba of the Imperial University of Tokyo, demonstrating the close ties to that country that Rutgers College traditionally enjoyed. The city of New Brunswick issued a resolution welcoming all visitors to the college, "whose honor and prestige has always been so valuably reflected upon this town 'On the Banks of the Old Raritan.'"[2]

The centerpiece of the festivities was an anniversary pageant, a lavish outdoor spectacle rendering the history of the college through a series of stylized episodes, such as depictions of the "Seven Arts and Philosophy," the "English Settlers," and so on. Complete with singing, dancing, and instrumental music, these various tableaux were extremely well received. Naturally, an ambitious project of this type called for the best available artists and craftsmen from the local population, both within the college and from the city of New Brunswick. Front and center among the participants was Howard D. McKinney, '13, who was a member of the pageant committee as well as serving as the director of instrumental music for the overall event.[3] He also presided at the organ for the vesper service at the First Reformed Church that served as the closing ceremony for these celebrations.[4] McKinney had continued to be a well-known presence in the New Brunswick area following his graduation; he was, in fact, the regular organist at the aforementioned church and was also in charge of the choir at that establishment.[5]

McKinney had also retained an interest in the activities of the Rutgers College Glee Club. In March of 1916, he placed an announcement in the *Targum* outlining his plans for compiling a revised edition of the volume *Songs of Rutgers*, first edited by Frank S. Scudder and published in 1885 (see chap. 1 sidebar, "The Rutgers Songbook [*Songs of Rutgers*]").[6] Considering all of McKinney's recent activity in and around the college, it was, then, not surprising when the following announcement appeared in the local New Brunswick press on October 17, 1916:

The trials for the Rutgers Glee Club were held in Van Nest Hall yesterday afternoon under the supervision of Mr. McKinney and Professor [Harry Nelson] Lendall, assisted by Herbert Boes ['17, business manager of the combined clubs]. Fully thirty-five Sophomores and Freshmen turned out.

. . . The Junior and Senior trials are to be held this afternoon after which Mr. McKinney expects to put the fellows through a series of rehearsals in anticipation of the schedule for the coming winter. Mr. McKinney's reputation as a leader is well known in this vicinity and the Glee Club is to be congratulated on securing him as their coach.[7]

Thus the appointment of Allan Hall as coach of the Glee Club for the 1915–16 season was short-lived. McKinney would take over the role of coach for that unit, with William Thorp becoming president of the amalgamated Club and continuing in his role as leader of the mandolin component.

The call for student leadership in these ensembles had propagated the system of professional coaches to which McKinney now added his name. He had served as president of the combined clubs during the 1912–13 season, his senior year at the college, and in the course of that season had occasionally been referred to as the "leader" of the Glee Club. However, the coaching duties were at that time carried out by George Wilmot and the designated student leader for that year was Harry Davies, '14.[8] The 1916–17 season, therefore, is usually referenced as the starting date for McKinney's tenure as musical director of the Glee Club.[9] It seems that, right from that start, McKinney's vision for the consolidated group was bold and wide-ranging: "Howard D. McKinney has been engaged to coach the [Glee and Mandolin] Clubs and has several plans in view. Mr. McKinney has envisioned the organization of a triangle league with Stevens and N. Y. U., similar to that including the clubs of Harvard, Dartmouth, U. of P., and Penn State. . . . It is hoped that we can produce a club this year which will honor Rutgers as an institution of musical students."[10] The intercollegiate alliance, or "league," to which this article refers was the series of competitions initiated in 1914 by the Harvard Glee Club and its then student-director, Albert Pickernell, Harvard, '14. During that season, Pickernell and the Harvard ensemble issued a challenge to the Columbia University Glee Club, the Dartmouth College Glee Club, and the University of Pennsylvania Glee Club (though apparently not the Penn State group) to participate in a vocal competition. Pickernell's original idea was to raise singing standards among collegiate groups through competition in the way that football and track teams had been doing, on an intermural basis. Hence the notion of a "league" of glee clubs. The first such competition was organized in New York in 1914 with the assistance of the University Glee Club of New York City; three additional such events were held until the start of World War I forced the cancelation of this series. These events mark the birth of the institution that is known today as IMC: The Tenor-Bass Choral Consortium (formerly the Intercollegiate Men's Choruses), an organization to which the modern Rutgers University Glee Club belongs.[11]

By the end of the fall semester, it is clear from accounts in the contemporary press that McKinney's position involved more than just coaching the Glee and Mandolin clubs. On December 17, 1916, McKinney led "a choir of thirty mixed voices consisting of students and young ladies of the city" in a Christmas Vespers service at Kirkpatrick Chapel.[12] On January 22, 1917, a "Lecture-Recital" was given at the chapel by the well-known American composer and music critic Daniel Gregory Mason (1873–1953), at that time serving as an associate professor of music at Columbia University. An account of the event contains the following passage: "This [Lecture-Recital] was the first of the series of concerts to be given under the direction of Howard D. McKinney, [Rutgers College's] new musical director, and it was in every way a great success. More than seven hundred people attended the concert, and it was enjoyed by all."[13] In subsequent references to

McKinney's position in the local news outlets, he is usually identified as "musical director of Rutgers College."[14] Modern histories of Rutgers College confirm that he "assumed the recently created post of Musical Director in 1916."[15] As a function of this position, McKinney brought to Rutgers College some of the finest musical talent of the day. The third concert in the series mentioned in the previous quote occurred on February 16, 1917: "Music lovers flocked in large [numbers] to Ballantine Gymnasium last night to hear a recital given by Rudolph Ganz, the famous Swiss pianist and composer, brought here by Musical Director Howard D. McKinney of Rutgers College."[16] Ganz was indeed a well-known artist at the beginning of the twentieth century. He was highly regarded not only as a virtuoso pianist but also as a composer, conductor, and music educator who advocated for the acceptance of art-music works in the modern style. This was also a point of emphasis in the work of Professor Mason of Columbia and undoubtedly one of the reasons McKinney chose these artists to inaugurate this new concert series. McKinney would continue to work toward promoting an understanding and affirmation of modern musical idioms—whether arising from the European or from the new American compositional tradition—throughout his career.[17]

The Glee and Mandolin clubs that McKinney inherited were robust groups. But the groups continued to expand, both in size and scope, under McKinney's direction. W. Phillips Thorp Jr., '17, leader of the Mandolin Club component in the 1915–16 season, served as president of the combined clubs for the 1916–17 academic year. He continued as Mandolin Club leader, with McKinney serving as the coach of the Glee Club section. The Glee Club forces now stood at a total of thirty-three voices: seven first tenors, eleven second tenors, nine first basses, and six second basses. The Mandolin Club complement had changed again somewhat with regard to instrumentation and had slightly increased in number. The arrangement of forces was ten first mandolins, nine second mandolins, a return of banjos (two), one guitar, one "Ukalele," and an added performer on "Traps," or a drum set. The violins of the previous year had been discarded, and the clubs continued to share a single accompanist, C. Russell Gildersleeve, '18.[18] Since some members served in both club components—for example, John Henry Wallace, '20, played traps for the Mandolin Club and sang second tenor—this brought the total membership of the amalgamated group to approximately fifty performers.

There is a bit of a discrepancy concerning when the first concert under McKinney's administration of the combined clubs took place. *The Scarlet Letter* for the 1916–17 season states that this occurred on November 24, 1916, at South Bound Brook.[19] However,

1—Rutgers Songs—
   Bow-wow-wow .... Bragdon '76
   ▲ Rutgers March ..L. R Reed '11
   Steps Song ...... McKinney '13
   Hand Me Down My Bonnet
   Down Where the Raritan Flows.
   Glee and Mandoline Clubs
2—Swing Along .... W. R. Cooke
   Glee Club
3—"My Dreamy China Lady ......
   Van Alstyne
   Mandolin Club
4—Reading .... Selected
   Burch '20.
5—Selections ....
   Mandolin Club Sextette
6—On the Road to Mandalay ......
   O'ey Speaks
   Glee Club
7—The Cat With the Baritone Voice
   C. P. Scott
   Glee Club Quartette
8—Rosemary Waltzes .... Von Hagen
   Mandolin Club
9—Reading .... Selected.
   Bingham '20.
10—In Its Annual Breaking Out ....
   Prickly Heat Quartette
11—Hunting Song .... Fred F. Bullard
   Glee Club
12—Campus Songs .... Selected
13—On the Banks of the Old Raritan
   Fuller
   Glee and Mandolin Club

Howard D. McKinney's first program as director of the Rutgers College Glee Club, November 24, 1916, at South Bound Brook. As reported in the *Central New Jersey Home News* (November 27, 1916), 7.

the *Targum* reports that the first concert of the year occurred on December 13 at Middlebush, New Jersey.[20] The yearbook appears to have the correct information here; a local New Brunswick newspaper provided details of the November 24 performance. As might be expected with the changes taking place, some performance flaws were detected: "For the first concert, it was considered a success, although several of the parts were not up to mid-season form. The best feature was 'On the Road to Mandalay' sung by the Glee Club. The Rutgers songs and campus songs all went off with enthusiasm and were heartily encored."[21]

This iteration of the combined clubs, like many of its predecessors, strove for a balance between the two components of the group, as well as between solo and ensemble selections. The tradition of opening with Bragdon's "Bow-Wow-Wow" and closing with "On the Banks" was also upheld under the new regime. It should be noted that the Prickly Heat Quartette was still a featured act for the group; it was undoubtedly to accommodate such modern styles that the clubs added the drum kit, or "Traps," to the ensemble for this season.

The "triangular" competition for which McKinney had advocated was indeed established during this season. An article in the *Targum*'s March 28 edition, titled "Vocal Combat," announced a "Triangular Glee Club Concert between [*sic*] N. Y. U., Stevens, and Rutgers."[22] The event was scheduled for Friday, April 13

at the Proctor's Roof Theatre in Newark, under the auspices of the Newark Guild of the Homeopathic Hospital. The *Targum* printed bold-faced encouragement for the group in this competition along the lines of "Alumni, Hear your Glee Team in Action" and "Friday, the 13th, cannot phase our Gleemen."[23] The outcome of the battle was described as follows:

Last Friday evening, in a joint concert with the Glee Clubs of N. Y. U. and Stevens, the Rutgers Club were [*sic*] pronounced victorious. The competition was sharp and every member hotly contested for the supremacy . . .

The basis of judging the contest was as follows: Enunciation of words, quality of tone, choice of selections, spirit and enthusiasm, general impression and difficulty of selections.

Although the Rutgers Club was composed of the least number of men the judges awarded the silver cup to them by a vote of two for Rutgers and one for Stevens. The cup shall become the property of the club winning it three consecutive meets.[24]

The Glee Club was presented with a new anthem written especially for its use in May of 1917. Howard N. Fuller, '74, composed the lyrics for this new work and set them to music by Robert K. Quayle. The piece was composed in honor of the sesquicentennial of Rutgers College. Titled "The Flag of Scarlet Hue," Fuller's lyrics paint a stirring portrait of the dedication of the Rutgers College men to their alma mater.[25]

World War I

Such expressions of dedication to the institutions of home and country were sorely needed at this point in the history of the nation. On April 2, 1917, after a series of provocative incidents by Germany, including the sinking by that nation's submarines of seven U.S. merchant ships, President Woodrow Wilson called on Congress for a declaration of war. Congress issued that declaration four days later on April 6, 1917, paving the way for the United States to enter what had to that point been termed the European War. Though not officially a member of the Allied Powers, the United States, as an Associated Power, made major contributions to the Allied effort, supplying raw materials, monetary support, and perhaps most significantly, troops beginning in 1917.[26]

With the European War now a matter of immediate urgency to the American people, individuals and institutions alike prepared to assist in the war effort to the best of their capabilities. Rutgers College was no exception in this matter. In the same edition of the *Targum* that announced Fuller's new song—in fact, on the facing page to that which carried the announcement—the following brief article appeared:

> Arrangements are being rapidly completed to make the coming summer session at Rutgers meet the demands of this country in the present war situation. The authorities in charge are overlooking nothing in their efforts to make the courses as useful as possible to the individual and to the nation.
>
> Although nothing definite has yet been done it is very probable that the students will receive military instruction. However it is certain that even if drill is not included in the regular curriculum, participation in military activities will be encouraged.[27]

Naturally, with the entire country's attention turned to matters of global conflict, local matters were bound to suffer. Still, though recognizing the altered circumstances of their existence, at the start of the 1917–18 academic year, the Rutgers College Glee and Mandolin Clubs envisioned for themselves a season that was, while different from those of the recent past, in keeping with the goals and ideals of the organization as they had been in place for so many years. This perspective was articulated as follows:

There has been planned a radical change in the policy of the Glee and Mandolin Clubs for this year. The trips last year were made nearly every week-end from shortly after the opening of college until well into the spring. This year, however, the activity of the clubs will be limited to two extended trips—one during the Christmas and the other during the Easter recess. It is rumored that one of these will be out to the west and our warblers await anxiously the confirmation of this rumor. But no matter what the itinerary may be, it is generally agreed that this plan is superior to last year's.[28]

Considering the circumstances, it is not surprising that the 1917–18 season got off to a bit of a slow start. The official roster for the Glee Club group was not announced until mid-December, at which time the official picture of the combined clubs for that year's edition of *The Scarlet Letter* was taken.[29] The first concert of the season did not take place until January 18, 1918, at the Lafayette School Auditorium in Bound Brook. This concert had originally been scheduled for December 14, 1917, but inclement weather forced a postponement to this later date.

The roster for both clubs was cited in the *Targum* article describing this event,[30] and the numbers correspond to both the official Glee Club roster announced in December and to the combined rosters provided in *The Scarlet Letter* for this season.[31] Though neither roster designates precise instrumentation for the Mandolin Club, the *Targum* article does note that the drum set, or "Traps," was still being utilized as a part of this group; they were played by G. E. Pierce, '20. The pianist for the combined ensemble was also associated with the Mandolin Club; he is identified as Malcolm Slack Pitt, '19, who also sang second tenor in the Glee Club.

The January *Targum* article identifies McKinney as the coach of the Glee Club component, as he had been described in the preceding season. That article does not identify any corresponding leader for the mandolin group; however, in the roster provided in *The Scarlet Letter*, McKinney is identified as accompanist and musical director. Further, though Pitt is still singing second tenor, Pierce, and presumably the drum set, did not survive the entire season.

McKinney's position as musical director is confirmed in a *Targum* article reporting on a concert at Westfield, New Jersey, on March 22. This account states that vocalist Miss Helen Bessler of Plainfield, New Jersey, was a featured guest of the combined clubs, offering "four numbers composed by Howard D. McKinney, '13, director of the clubs."[32]

Despite the chaotic backdrop of a global war, the combined clubs strove to maintain the obligations that traditionally befell them in the course of the collegiate season. The annual concert for Junior Week took place as usual, with the Glee Club performing at Kirkpatrick Chapel on Saturday, April 20. McKinney also continued to encourage events along the lines of the "triangular competition" with NYU and Stevens that he had initiated in the 1916–17 season. For this year, however, it would seem that Stevens College demurred and was replaced by Columbia; further, the competitive nature of the affair was abandoned in favor of a more collaborative approach. The concert also featured a guest soloist of some notoriety:

> Music lovers are looking forward with pleasure to the concer[t] arranged by Musical Director Howard D. McKinney, of Rutgers College, for Saturday evening, May 18, when the Glee Clubs of Rutgers College, New York University and Columbia will combine. Each club will give two numbers as well as one special number in the form of a solo.
>
> Paul Robeson, the famous football, [sic] baseball player and trackman, of Rutgers, who possesses a magnificent voice, is to be one of the soloists. This will begin the commencement activities at Rutgers.[33]

Paul Robeson was, of course, an exceptional member of the Rutgers College student body, an outstanding athlete and scholar. In fact, he won the Junior Exhibition Prize for Oratory during this year, beating out the second-place winner, Malcolm Pitt, '19, a tenor in the Glee Club,[34] who remained a lifelong friend of Robeson's following their college days together. Only the third African American student to enroll in the college, and the only Black student on campus during the period in which he attended (1915–19), Robeson participated in Glee Club activities occasionally, but only on an informal basis. Full membership in the Glee Club would have meant that Robeson would have had to attend all-white events on campus and to perform at segregated venues while traveling, circumstances that the moral standards of this period would not have sanctioned. Nevertheless, his contributions to the Glee Club, such as this combined concert, were hailed and appreciated by most of his contemporaries, student and townsperson alike.

PAUL LEROY ROBESON

'19 (1898–1976)

He came in like a lamb. He was seventeen and full of innocence. Favorite child of a loving father, smiled upon by congregation and community, teacher's pet and most popular boy in high school—love had made him sweet and gentle.[35]

Thus the young Paul Robeson initially approached the adventures of his freshman year at Rutgers College in the fall of 1915. Robeson was born in Princeton, New Jersey, to the Reverend William D. Robeson, a Presbyterian minister who had been born a slave, and Anna Louisa (Bustill) Robeson.[36] The family left Princeton in 1907 and relocated to the central New Jersey town of Westfield,[37] a city that is said to have had a "more relaxed 'northern' racial climate" that did not enforce the "strict racial etiquette" of segregation characteristic of contemporary Princeton.[38] Reverend Robeson's efforts at restoring the struggling Westfield Presbyterian congregation, the Downing Street AME Zion Church, into a fairly well-established community earned him the chance to pastor another such troubled institution, the St. Thomas AMEZ in Somerville, New Jersey. Therefore, the family moved to that town in 1910.[39]

In June of 1915, Robeson participated in a competitive examination, open to all New Jersey students, that offered

Signed headshot of Paul Robeson, circa 1941. Special Collections, Rutgers University Libraries.

as a prize a four-year scholarship to Rutgers College. On July 15 of that year, it was announced that Robeson had won the $650 state scholarship, and he prepared for what he later described as a "decisive point in my life." Having won this scholarship, Robeson now strongly felt that "while equality might be denied, . . . I knew I was not inferior."[40]

Robeson arrived at Rutgers College on September 15, 1915, the third African American student to be admitted in the college's history. His achievements during his undergraduate years are well documented. As in high school, Robeson excelled in athletic endeavors, most prolifically in football; he was twice named a collegiate football all-American. Robeson was also a valuable member of the Rutgers baseball, basketball, and track teams. In addition to these activities, he was a member of the Mathematics Club and the Philoclean Society and was inducted in his senior year into the Cap and Skull, the Rutgers College honor society that recognizes superior achievement in the areas of academics, athletics, the arts, and public service. He was named a Phi Beta Kappa scholar in his junior year and, perhaps most impressively, gave the valedictory address, titled "The New Idealism," at his graduation ceremony for the class of 1919.[41]

To be sure, his situation as the only African American member of the student body during his years at the school proved in many ways to be a constraining factor. It is undeniable that he encountered blatant, and occasionally violent, racism at Rutgers, most famously on the football field, from both opponents and, especially early in his football career, from his own teammates.[42] The benign inclusion that he experienced in Westfield and Somerville, which did so much to mold his youthful character, failed in many respects to prepare him for the barrage of prejudice that would engulf him upon his arrival at Rutgers. Still, despite that inclusion during his high school days, Robeson was deeply cognizant of the social skills concerning the navigation of the general racial decorum of the period; those skills would prove invaluable at Rutgers College. At the college, he adopted a policy of avoiding social settings that could prove to be embarrassing for all parties, recognizing and accepting, rather than challenging, the unwritten societal rules. This proved to be a complicated dance, both for Robeson and for his classmates. He was, for example, not asked to join any Rutgers fraternity but was accorded house privileges at several of these; he instead joined Alpha Phi Alpha, the oldest intercollegiate Black fraternity in the country.[43]

As to Robeson's activities with the Glee Club at Rutgers College during his student days, there are conflicting accounts. It has been reported that he auditioned for the Glee Club but was rejected by the Club director, ostensibly on the grounds of problems with the singer's pitch.[44] But this seems an unlikely scenario. It is clear that, while Robeson was never officially invited to join the Glee Club, he frequently performed with them and was associated with the group both on campus and off. Indeed, most accounts of his experiences with the Club do not question his innate talent, nor do they contend that Rutgers was unaware of his musical abilities. It was, in fact, common knowledge that Robeson possessed a fine singing voice and had demonstrated this in many settings whenever the opportunity presented itself. He would frequently perform at informal gatherings, often accompanied by Glee Club member and lifelong friend Mal Pitt, '19. It was reported that he would sing with his football teammates at team suppers, and he often sang in local churches.[45]

The reasons for Robeson's official exclusion from the Club, therefore, fall mostly along racial lines, as might be expected. Most accounts of this time, in fact, report that the Glee Club actively encouraged Robeson's participation at their events; one such narrative describes Robeson's voice as "the chief adornment of the Rutgers Glee Club." But Robeson's son reported that "[while] the Rutgers Glee Club eagerly recruited him to sing with them, . . . Paul performed at home engagements only; they decided that it would be impossible to have a black member traveling with them. Nor was he welcome at social events after the Glee Club performances at home."[46]

Other accounts would seem to corroborate this version. The many racial barriers of the day placed insurmountable official restrictions on Robeson's interactions with the Club. In the manuscript version of Mary Seton's 1958 book *Paul Robeson*, she suggests that Robeson's presence at Glee Club performances, or perhaps even more so at the dances that were frequently held after concerts, would have violated the previously discussed unwritten rules of the college: "These rules were that no Negro student would be welcome because there were white girls present."[47] As a classmate of Robeson's would put it years later, "Social functions

were all-white, and Robey never forced himself in. As people used to say in those days, he 'knew his place.'"[48]

Indeed, any ties to the Glee Club were completely unofficial. The *Targum* does not mention Paul Robeson in connection with any Glee Club events during his time at the college, nor does it list the Club among Robeson's numerous extracurricular activities. *The Scarlet Letter* for the class of 1919 is similarly silent on Glee Club participation when listing Robeson's pursuits.[49] Apparently, Robeson himself did not consider his occasional participation with the Club to constitute official membership.[50] But evidence of such participation is not hard to unearth. Robeson is identified as "one of the soloists" at a prestigious concert in which the Rutgers Glee Club participated alongside similar groups from New York University and Columbia during his senior year (see chap. 3, "World War I"). It was, in fact, not uncommon to associate Robeson with the Club in media accounts. When he appeared as a singer at a memorial service in Washington, D.C., on June 1, 1919, he was described in the press account as "Paul Robeson, the Rutgers College football star and Glee Club star."[51] A similar account, again concerning an appearance by Robeson in Washington, D.C., states the following: "The colored citizens of Washington will have their first opportunity to see Paul Robeson, Rutgers College athlete and Glee Club soloist, tonight at Odd Fellows' Hall, M Street near 16th Street."[52] Thus it would appear that Robeson was an active, if occasional and unofficial, Glee

Club participant throughout his college days and that this participation was something of an open secret.

Robeson's ties to the musical offerings at Rutgers College remained strong following his graduation. He would return to campus periodically throughout the various phases of his post-Rutgers career, most visibly for featured appearances in Howard McKinney's concert series. Robeson participated as a soloist for series concerts during the 1927, 1929, and 1932 seasons; he also appeared at the silver anniversary concert of the series in 1940.[53] This latter event offered the opportunity for the Glee Club to assist Robeson in a performance of the patriotic cantata "The Ballad for Americans," a work that the singer had recorded for CBS earlier that year (see chap. 4, "World War II: An Unwelcome Detour," for details). By this time, Robeson had achieved international fame as a vocalist, stage and film actor, and political activist. And at this stage in the country's history, with European troubles looming significantly over world affairs, patriotic Americans were somewhat less inclined to indulge in the racial animus that had so characterized Robeson's undergraduate career.

Indeed, Robeson in his later years—and quite in spite of the unfortunate damage to his reputation that ensued following his blacklisting as a Communist sympathizer by Senator Joseph McCarthy and the aligned House Un-American Activities Committee in the 1950s—became a treasured favorite son of Rutgers University. His accomplishments had, of course, been recognized in previous years; Robeson was awarded an honorary master of arts degree from Rutgers in 1932. He was "the first person in the arts, black or white, and the youngest ever to be chosen for such an honor."[54] But in more recent times, Robeson's achievements have been recognized at Rutgers with further and greater, though mostly posthumous, honors. The Paul Robeson Campus Center at the Rutgers-Newark campus was dedicated in 1972,[55] and the Paul Robeson Library, which serves as the main library for the Camden campus of Rutgers University, was dedicated in 1991.[56] In the new millennium, the Paul Robeson Plaza, which features eight black granite panels detailing the story of Robeson's life, was dedicated on April 12, 2019, in honor of the one-hundredth anniversary of his graduation. Shortly thereafter, on June 24, 2019, the city of New Brunswick renamed Commercial Avenue, which abuts the present-day Douglass Campus, "Paul Robeson Boulevard." His legacy is preserved in the extensive compilation of materials of the Paul Robeson Collection, which is maintained at the Rutgers University Special Collections and University Archives division.

Paul Robeson died in Philadelphia on January 23, 1976, following complications from a stroke.[57] A memorial service was held in Kirkpatrick Chapel at Rutgers University on what would have been Robeson's seventy-eighth birthday, April 9 of that year. Fittingly, the Glee Club—of which Robeson, despite efforts toward racial camouflage, was very much a part during his storied undergraduate years—was a central feature of that service.

The 1917–18 academic year was, to be sure, a disconcerting one for the clubs. Despite the early optimism, an expansive schedule of performances never transpired. Not counting the intramural concerts cited previously, the appearances at Bound Brook and Westfield represented the only performances the clubs undertook during this season. Still, in the analysis of their efforts presented in that year's *Scarlet Letter*, the men of the clubs chose to look at the season as a qualified success, preferring to emphasize the positive aspects of a year that played out under such unprecedented constraints:

> The musical clubs of this year have done their best to maintain the high standards set by the organizations of previous years, and considering the rather difficult conditions under which the men have had to work, the result has been far from unsatisfactory. Here again the unsettled conditions caused by war activities have seriously hampered the work of the men, and have made it exceedingly difficult to secure satisfactory engagements . . .
>
> It soon became evident . . . that the [proposed] schedule [of concerts] could not be carried out as originally planned for the reason that many of the organizations under whose auspices the concerts are usually given, turned their attention to work of war service, and engagements for college musical clubs were not particularly sought after. Scarcity of concerts has not, however, prevented the men from obtaining the training and coaching which accompanies the rehearsals. . . . Mr. McKinney's varied experience in musical direction has shown itself to be of great value in coaching the clubs, and the only regret of the clubs is that greater opportunity has not been offered for exhibiting the results of his careful training.[58]

What was now, following the entrance of the United States, often termed the World War raged throughout the summer of 1918. The Hundred Days Offensive, a series of Allied attacks that would effectively end the conflict with the Central powers, began on August 8, 1918.[59] Rutgers College, like virtually all institutions of this period, remained on a war footing. The 1918–19 academic year began with an announcement that Rutgers College had officially been recognized as an army post and a participant, along with 350 other American colleges and universities, in the Students' Army Training Corps (SATC) program. This initiative was designed to prepare as many as 150,000 college-age men for immediate induction into the nation's armed services.[60] At Rutgers, this initiative was administered under the commandant of the local program, Infantry First Lieutenant James C. Torpey. Though the program itself received mixed reviews, all sides seemed to agree that, in terms of its primary objective of training college men to be military officers, it was for the most part successful.[61]

A major reason for the success of the program, paradoxically, was that this primary objective was soon to become a goal of considerably lesser importance. On November 7, 1918, news organizations from all over the world announced the end of hostilities and the conditions upon which the armistice with Germany had been reached, though the exact terms of this armistice would not be announced by President Wilson until November 11. At Rutgers, a spirit of celebration was palpable, as was a general sense of relief. An impromptu peace jubilee broke out at the announcement of the news, as reflected in this *Targum* account:

Such a rejoicing as that shown last Thursday [November 7, 1918] has seldom been witnessed at old Rutgers. After five minutes of tuning up by New Brunswick's sirens and whistles, the tension in class rooms became too great and work was hastily dismissed. The report was that the war was over. It was hard to realize, but soon cry after cry of rejoicing rang out. Pee-rades and pee-radelets sprang up on the campus with rather uncertain destinations . . .

After a few short speeches by the lieutenants and some cheering and singing, the formation broke up into groups of wildly discussing and conjecturing students.[62]

Thus relieved of the burden of preparing for a world conflict, Rutgers College immediately began the process of returning to its core educational mission. By December 14, the SATC had completely demobilized; rifles were turned in and certificates of honorable discharge were issued. With the winter recess imminent, many students left the campus early to spend a more serene holiday season with their families than had been possible the year prior.[63]

The academic year 1918–19 was further compromised by the outbreak of a deadly epidemic of influenza. So deadly was the (unfortunately characterized) Spanish Influenza that, by December of 1918, the death tolls from the disease were staggering: "The appalling ravages of Spanish Influenza are perhaps best realized by the statement recently made, that more deaths have resulted in little more than a month from this disease than through our whole eighteen months' participation in the battles of the European War."[64]

Again, these types of disruptions to the collegiate routine played havoc not only with the academic programs but with the various clubs and organizations on campus as well. In the face of such obstacles, the Glee and Mandolin Clubs announced in December that they would not attempt to organize for the 1918–19 season, citing "the many complications in which we find ourselves, due in large measure to the late military organization of the college."[65] However, the return from the holiday recess brought a different attitude and renewed enthusiasm; the January 8 edition of the *Targum* issued the following brief statement: "Howard D. McKinney, Director of Music, recently announced that plans are well under way for the reorganization of the Glee and Mandolin Clubs. Rehearsals and tryouts will be held in the very near future and it is hoped that the clubs will be well supported."[66] The reorganization proceeded swiftly. McKinney and the newly elected president of the combined clubs, Austin M. Rice, '19, held trials for the Glee Club on Monday, January 13. Tryouts for the mandolin contingent were held at the same time, with McKinney and H. G. "Griff" Parker, '21, a Mandolin Club member, adjudicating.[67]

This reorganization also dealt with the nature of the programs that the clubs intended to present for this season. Indeed, McKinney and the student leaders of the combined clubs contemplated radical revisions to the traditional program format: "In departure from the time-honored form of program, the Glee Club this year wishes to present many specialties made possible through the abundance of good material at the disposal of this year's club. These specialties consist of instrumental and vocal numbers, as well as readings. In order to accomplish this the Club offers the sum of ten dollars for the best original sketch presented to the manager on or before Wednesday, January 22. This sketch must present ample opportunities to work in these numbers."[68] This new program made its debut at the first concert of the season, which took place in Rahway, New Jersey, in

March of 1919. According to the account presented in the March 19 edition of the *Targum*, "The program differed from former years as the second half was arranged as a sketch." This sketch was titled "'Rehearsal Night in the Metropolis'—an Original Drama in One Act." The *Targum* account provides the following details:

> The scene is laid in the long wished for, and at present ethereal, Rutgers Club in New York. An alumnus is seated and greets an old friend. These characters in a sufficient, but not exceptional or humorous dialogue introduce the various numbers. This arrangement gives an informality to the concert which is desired, and the shocked expression of some of the maiden ladies of the audience evidenced their opinion of the use of cigarettes in the concert hall.
>
> However, this arrangement seems to be an improvement, and a little more life will insure its success.[69]

Thus the new program presented two distinct formats; a first half that very much resembled the traditional program design, opening with Rutgers songs such as "Bow-Wow-Wow" and continuing with an alternating mix of Glee Club and Mandolin Club selections, and the second part, the new sketch format. This program would be repeated two more times throughout the season, at Maplewood, New Jersey, on April 1 and again on April 4 at the auditorium of the Plainfield High School.[70] Both concerts received favorable commentary.

One other event of significance from this season should be noted. On September 18, 1918, the New Jersey College for Women opened its doors "with simple but impressive ceremonies." With an initial enrollment of fifty-four young women, the initiative was hailed as a "notable event in [the] educational life of New Jersey." In her opening address, Mrs. Mable Smith Douglass, dean of the college, "expressed her appreciation of the co-operation given by President W. H. S. Demarest of Rutgers College."[71] Opportunities for collaborative efforts between the new women's college and Rutgers College would present themselves almost immediately. Many of these early collaborations would involve the musical organizations of the respective colleges and would become important events in the development of both institutions.

Peacetime Pursuits: The Development of the Musical Clubs

A return to peacetime meant a more deliberate focus on Rutgers College as an institution dedicated to a student body that was rapidly growing; between the academic years 1906 and 1916, enrollment increased from 236 to 537.[72] Concomitantly, due to the implementation of certain structural changes to the liberal-arts curricula, many departments in the college experienced rapid expansion and new courses of study arose. Having assumed the post of musical director of Rutgers College in 1916, Howard McKinney was in the 1919–20 academic year recognized as an officer of instruction for the college; he is listed in that year's *Scarlet Letter* as "Howard Decker McKinney, Litt.B. (Rutgers); Instructor in Music," announcing that the college could now boast a legitimate department of music.[73]

The concert series that McKinney had inaugurated in the fall of 1916, shortly after his appointment as musical director of the college, was by the following year recognized both within the college and by the New Brunswick townspeople as the Annual Winter Concert Course.[74] For the 1919–20 season, McKinney put together an impressive array of guest artists:

> The welcome announcement that there will be a series of high class concerts in New Brunswick this winter under the direction of Howard D. McKinney, director of music at Rutgers College, is made with the accompaniment of more good news to the effect that Mme. Louise Homer will be the first artist to appear on the opening date . . .
>
> Other artists who will appear in the series are Lambert Murphy, tenor, and May Peterson, soprano, and there is one special feature coming in the New York Chamber Music Society, who will give a fine program under the direction of

Miss Carolyn Beebe, a woman of great musical ability who has formed the organization and leads it herself.[75]

These concerts were certainly in keeping with the college's emphasis on increasing the scope of available courses, while at the same time solidifying musical endeavors as an integral feature of that augmented curriculum.

Notwithstanding the increased duties that McKinney experienced during this period, his involvement with the Glee and Mandolin Clubs remained strong. It is without doubt a testament to his leadership of musical matters at the college that interest in the clubs among the members of the student body was intense. It was reported that trials for the Glee Club attracted no less than 137 hopeful songsters, from which a list of 87 finalists was drafted by McKinney. When paired down to the best available voices, the Glee Club component of the combined group stood at thirty-eight voices.[76]

The Mandolin Club also maintained a robust enrollment and again featured some interesting instrumental additions to its complement. The group consisted of thirty-two members; among the instruments utilized in addition to mandolins were banjos (three), violins (two), guitars (three), saxophones (three), the now customary traps, and a mando-cello, a mandolin tuned like a cello and designed to play in mandolin quartets.[77]

The emphasis on student leadership that was so much a facet of prior iterations of the clubs had returned

during this season. While McKinney is officially listed as "Coach" for the combined ensemble, each group has its own leaders. The Glee Club is led by Edward A. Willard, '21, who sings first tenor; the Mandolin Club leader is Harold C. Taylor, '20, a first mandolinist.

The opening concert of the season took place on November 14 in Freehold. The sketch element, a prominent feature of the previous year's program, had been dispensed with and replaced by a more traditional format. The Prickly Heat Quartette was back, and as the presence of the mando-cello would suggest, a mandolin quartet was also a highlight of the performance.

In addition to local concerts, a somewhat-extensive trip to the Hudson Valley, along the lines of those that were undertaken by earlier clubs, was incorporated into the schedule, including stops at White Plains, Tarrytown, Middletown, and Albany, all in New York. The clubs also appeared at the Steel Pier in Atlantic City, a performance that spotlighted a string quartet consisting of two mandolins, a guitar, and the mando-cello.[78]

McKinney also produced another revised edition of the collection *Songs of Rutgers* during this season. In preparation for its release, McKinney solicited contributions from all quarters: "Mr. McKinney is now editing a new edition of 'Songs of Rutgers' to be issued at Commencement. In connection with this new edition a prize of ten dollars is being offered for the best song submitted in competition. All compositions must be in Mr. McKinney's hands by March 1. Original words are wanted and original music should accompany them if possible."[79]

The Glee Club unit for the 1920–21 season carried thirty-three members, while the mandolin component had another twenty-one men. Some members participated in both units, as was customary; this brought the total number to around forty. The accompanist for this season was Robert Garlock, '24, indicating that McKinney had, at this point, abandoned that particular duty. Contemporary sources also mention an elocutionist; as seen above, recitations by a trained reader were an intermittent feature of the clubs for many years. Though no reader is listed on the roster provided in this year's *Scarlet Letter*,[80] the following season's list (1921–22) of participants does designate W. O. Allen, '25, in that role.[81]

The following account describes a typical Club concert: "The program usually consists of several numbers by the combined clubs and three selections by the Glee Club, three by the Mandolin Club and five specialties. While the group numbers possibly provide more 'music,' the specialties furnish the fun of the evening."[82]

Some of these "specialties" have been mentioned previously, particularly the Prickly Heat Quartette, which is still very much active during this period. The performance of this group is said to be "antagonistic to all forms of the Blues. You're just bound to laugh—that's all."[83] The group is further characterized as "a distinctly Rutgers creation": "[The Prickly Heat Quartette] always makes a big hit, without the 'get.' While their harmony is at times startling, to say the least, their performance is certainly musical, so they claim."[84] However, the 1920–21 season offered yet another of these novelty features. Dubbed the Jazz Bandits, this group consisted of three players. Harold "Scrappy" Lambert, '23, played piano, Garrett Irons "Johnny" Johnson, '22, performed on banjo, and Wilbert Baker "Babe" Hitchner Jr., '22, rounded out the group on saxophone, though another saxophone would be added the following year.[85] The performance of the three-man group is detailed in the following account:

A society syncopated hold up perpetrated by the three Jazz Bandits, Lambert, Hitchner and Johnson, kept the audience in a continual uproar. One minute you are listening to Rubenstein's Melody in F, rendered with a unique skill; the next minute you are stepping it out to some popular air. Soon after, a la Strand, you are taken to the bad lands, see the villain and the girl, and then the hero, springing up from nowhere, fixes everything so that they all live happily ever after. You even see them going to church. You hear the church bell pealing out its "dry" harmony. Such is the command of music in the clasp of these three "Jazz Bandits."[86]

The 1922–23 combined clubs maintained the same organizational structure as their immediate predecessors. The emphasis was on student leadership of the individual clubs under the general direction of Howard McKinney. Thus the list of officers of the consolidated clubs for this season is quite brief: Harold Lambert, '23, serves as president and leader of the Glee Club; Treadwell K. Berg, '24, is listed as leader of the Mandolin Club; Noel T. W. Kane, '23, who also serves as the accompanist for the Glee Club, fills the position of manager; and McKinney is listed as the director.[87]

In addition to the standard local concerts at the college and in nearby towns, a brief excursion during the Christmas holidays to the Hudson Valley was again on the schedule. However, the most notable event of this season was a concert given on December 11, 1922, at the broadcasting station WEAF in New York. The local New Brunswick press reported the event as follows:

> Tonight will be a big night for Rutgers College because its Glee Club, composed of forty men, will sing to 500,000 people, the students having been requested to give a concert from the American Telegraph and Telephone Station, the largest of its kind in New York City, and known as the W.E.A.F. Station.
>
> The Glee Club is composed of singers and musicians. Harold Lambert of this city will be the soloist and Noel Kane of Beverly, N.J., will be the accompanist. The program will begin at 7:30 o'clock and local radio fans are requested to tune in.[88]

WEAF, which would become WNBC in 1946, had only been in existence since March of 1922; it was, in fact, one of the earliest commercial radio stations in the country. An appearance by the clubs on this impressive new medium was indeed an accomplishment. Local reaction to the concert was favorable; a knowledgeable fan wrote to a local New Brunswick newspaper to say that "as far as [similar] radio concerts have given him the opportunity to judge, Rutgers is the best musical society in the East," surpassing, in his opinion, the clubs of Yale, NYU, and Princeton.[89] This was apparently not an isolated assessment; the same news outlet reports in a later account that the radio performance "received wide and deserved acclaim."[90]

Also of note this season was a combined concert undertaken by the Glee Club of the New Jersey College for Women and the Rutgers Glee Club. As mentioned earlier, combined performances employing these groups can be traced to the very beginnings of the former institution's history. However, the collaboration of the groups on the Frederic H. Cowen cantata *The Rose Maiden* presented on May 11, 1923, in the Ballantine Gymnasium was said to have eclipsed their previous efforts. Praised as "probably the greatest feature of the local musical season," this concert was the final performance of the year for both groups. The concert featured three well-known soloists imported from New York. Miss Dicie Howell sang soprano, Miss Frieda Klink took the contralto part, and William Fischer was the tenor soloist; Club president Harold Lambert served as baritone soloist for this performance. But special praise was reserved for the combined male and female glee clubs: "Fifty-four members of the Glee Club of the New Jersey College for Women and twenty-three of the Rutgers Glee Club took part in the chorus. Their work was magnificent, showing the result of the fine training given by Musical Director McKinney, . . . who deserves great credit for the success of the enterprise. Local lovers of music are indeed grateful to him for his magnificent work in directing last night's production."[91] McKinney was perfectly positioned to lead such combined efforts; he is officially listed as an instructor of music in both colleges.[92] As previously noted, some of the finest moments in the history of the Rutgers Glee Club resulted from collaborations such as this one.

It would appear that McKinney's involvement with the musical activities at the College for Women became his primary focus during the 1923–24 academic year. Local newspaper accounts mention his performances with the glee and mandolin clubs of the women's college, such as the concert that took place on March 1, 1924, at the Ballantine Gymnasium.[93] These concerts frequently featured the Weeping Willows, an ancillary offshoot of the clubs of the women's college. The *Quair*, the yearbook for the New Jersey College for Women from the 1921–22 season, describes this small group as follows: "The 'Weepies' are a small band of clever musicians whose '*raison d'etre*' is to amuse people. Whenever the Glee Club's more serious numbers begin to lag a little or an entertainment or social gathering grows dull this little group may always be found ready with their ukuleles and a few sprightly songs. In all the many calls made upon them they have been most obliging and have never failed to win enthusiastic applause."[94]

Concerts such as the March 1, 1924, event were described as being the result of "splendid instruction by Directors of Music Howard D. McKinney and Miss Mary Schenck." Mary Elizabeth Schenck, listed in the *Quair* as the assistant director for the glee and mandolin clubs of the women's college under director McKinney,[95] was a graduate of the New England Conservatory of Music in Boston and, like McKinney, is listed as an instructor of music for the women's college.[96] It would seem that the two worked together closely, both in the actual performances of the clubs of the women's college and in designing and implementing the course of instruction for the musical curriculum therein. Also lending a hand in these efforts was Wilbert Hitchner, '22; the women's college Mandolin Club during this period is said to be under his direction.[97] Hitchner, who, with the Rutgers College Glee Club, distinguished himself as a member of the Jazz Bandits, seems to have played an active role in the development of the glee and mandolin clubs for both the women's college and Rutgers College at this time.

THE JAZZ BANDITS

Success after Rutgers

Beginning with the 1920–21 season, the Rutgers College combined clubs began to offer at their concerts something a bit different from the standard Glee and Mandolin Club fare that had dominated Club performances in the past. This was the dawning of the Jazz Age, and the Rutgers men were clearly not to be left in the sizable artistic wake that the developing art form was producing. Their main response to the current trends came in the form of a small, featured ensemble that was "the leading attraction at the musical clubs' concerts."

The group was initially a three-man ensemble: "Scrappy" Lambert, '23, piano; "Johnny" Johnson, '22, banjo; and "Babe" Hitchner, '22, saxophone, a lineup that remained intact for the first two years of the group's existence. During this period, the Jazz Bandits were said to be a remarkable recruiting tool through which "new performers were added to the college's musical ranks year by year."[98] All three men had strong ties to the Glee and Mandolin Club; Johnson and Lambert each served as president of the combined clubs while students (Johnson, 1921–22; Lambert, 1922–23) and Hitchner returned following his graduation to serve as the clubs' director during the 1923–24 season. Lambert and Hitchner also sang in the Club's Prickly Heat Quartette, an offshoot of the Glee Club component that, like the Jazz Bandits, tended toward more modern musical tastes. An additional saxophonist,

C. L. Stanwood, '25, was added to the Bandits for the 1921–22 season, making the group more popular than ever.[99]

The Jazz Bandits ensemble also performed outside the scope of its function as an ancillary feature of the Glee and Mandolin Clubs; they were reportedly "in great demand for dances in New York, Newark, New Brunswick and the surrounding towns." For such affairs, they would augment their forces by adding a drum set; Pete Van Clefe was their usual choice for this position in these early years. The group accepted an engagement at Schlitz's Boardwalk Cafe in Atlantic City and proved so popular as to draw patrons away from a competing act a few doors away—that of Sophie Tucker and her band.[100]

With the graduation in 1922 of Johnson and Hitchner, the prospects for continuing the ensemble seemed grim. However, William "Billy" Hillpot, '25, a Metuchen native, was recruited to replace Johnson on banjo, and "Ted" Couse, '26, filled Hitchner's saxophone position. Combined with Lambert and Stanwood, the new Jazz Bandits took part in all the Glee and Mandolin Club concerts. This configuration of the group was very highly regarded in contemporary accounts:

Needless to say, the Jazz Bandits are now at their best and are reputed to be among the best college orchestras in the country. They have several times broadcasted from Newark [station WOR] and have always been well received by those who have been fortunate enough to hear them.[101]

HAROLD RODMAN LAMBERT
Liberal
New Brunswick, N. J.
Κ Σ

"A fellow of infinite jest"
Cheer Leader (3, 4); Song Leader (3, 4); Junior Prom Committee; Junior Banquet Committee; Senior Banquet Committee; Musical Clubs (1, 2, 3), President (4); Jazz Bandits; Band (1, 2, 3, 4).

Senior photo and précis from *The Scarlet Letter*, Harold "Scrappy" Lambert, '23. Special Collections and University Archives, Rutgers University Libraries.

As popular as the Jazz Bandits were during their student days at Rutgers College, many of the early members of the group went on to significantly greater fame. Lambert and Hillpot were particularly successful entertainers, performing together under a variety of names. They worked for a time for WEAF Radio in New York, billed as the Smith Brothers, an advertising scheme for the well-known cough drops. Broadcast appearances such as this, as well as live engagements in Atlantic City and other local venues, brought the duo to the attention of the jazz violinist and bandleader Ben Bernie (1891–1943), who signed the singers as a specialty act with his orchestra; the two appeared frequently with Bernie from 1926 to 1928.[102] An account of the duo's activities in a New Brunswick newspaper stated that "although they graduated several years ago, they are still doing the same sort of thing. . . . They are singing the same type of duets [as with the Glee Club] for the greatest audience of all time: the air."[103]

Exposure through Bernie's group led to great opportunities for Lambert. Since Bernie had a recording contract with Brunswick Records, this led to Lambert being utilized on many recordings featuring the cornetist and bandleader Red Nichols, who also recorded for Brunswick. Throughout the 1920s, "Scrappy" Lambert sang on numerous Nichols recordings and worked for many other record labels, often uncredited. In the course of his career, he recorded with Benny Goodman, the Dorsey brothers, Glenn Miller, Gene Krupa, and many other top artists of the day. He is regarded as one of the most recorded singers of the period.[104]

Lambert was also featured on many of the early radio shows of the 1930s. He appeared on the *Texaco Star Theater* (known originally as *Ed Wynn, the Fire Chief*), Fred Allen's *Town Hall Tonight*, and *The Firestone Hour*. However, his performing career came to an end in 1943, when he was offered a position with the Music Corporation of America (MCA) packaging radio shows to be sold to networks. Among the shows that he developed were staples such as *The Dinah Shore Show*, *Father Knows Best*, and *Queen for a Day*. He worked for MCA for five years and later went into the real estate business. He died in Riverside, California, on November 30, 1987.[105]

A successor to "Scrappy" as director of the Jazz Bandits in the 1928–29 season was Hawley Ades, '29. The Jazz Bandits duty came within the scope of his role as student leader of the Instrumental Club component of the combined clubs. In addition to being a fine pianist, Ades would often prepare arrangements for the Instrumental Club, including the Jazz Bandits. These were said to be in the style of the popular bandleader, composer, and arranger Hal Kemp.[106]

Following his graduation, Ades was hired as a staff arranger for the publishing company of Irving Berlin. He held that position until 1936. In 1937, he was hired as an arranger for Fred Waring's choral ensemble, *The Pennsylvanians*. He continued to work with that group for the next thirty-eight years. He is also the author of a highly regarded textbook in the field, *Choral Arranging* (Shawnee Press, 1966).[107]

Wilbert "Babe" Hitchens also went on to have an excellent career in music after graduation. He became a music educator, teaching initially in Pennsauken, New Jersey; later, he was the band director in Merchantville. From 1946 to his retirement in 1967, he was the chairman of the Music Education Department at Temple University in Philadelphia.[108]

The Jazz Bandits continued to exist as an affiliate of the Rutgers Musical Clubs until the demise of the Instrumental Club component in 1933. The last leader of the Jazz Bandits was Daniel H. "Eddie" Lipman, '33. At that point, the title of the band passed to "Gil" Horner, who retained it into the 1940s, "entirely separated from its original connection with the college."[109] A separate ensemble, led by Rutgers student Jeff Jefferay, often played for the dances that followed Glee Club concerts and was therefore occasionally identified as being affiliated with the college.[110] Horner continued to play engagements under the name Jazz Bandits in the local New Brunswick area for many years. However, the original Jazz Bandits of Rutgers College are among the brightest stars that the school has ever produced.

Rutgers University

The 1923–24 academic year was, to be sure, a dynamic and historic one in the history of Rutgers College. A variety of circumstances—not the least of which being the proper integration of the affiliated women's college into a broader and more unified Rutgers curriculum—culminated at this time to produce the long-awaited conversion of Rutgers College to Rutgers University. In reassessing its commitment both to women's education and to the state of New Jersey, college officials decided to initiate the processes of internal reorganization and campus planning necessary to bring this venture to a successful conclusion. These processes, if lacking in a clear overarching view of how such a university might best be constituted, nonetheless maintained an admirable practical nature: "No clear-cut philosophy guided the reforms, which tended to be piecemeal in nature and represented responses to various stimuli. On the whole, however, there was a discernable effort to adjust the educational offerings [of the newly constituted university] to a student body that was not only growing in number but was also displaying different interests, aptitudes, and degrees of preparation from the prewar generation."[111]

It is against this backdrop that the Rutgers University Glee and Mandolin Club—that is, the male version at what is still called Rutgers College—continued its activities. In general, the constitution of the combined clubs appeared unchanged. *The Scarlet Letter* for the 1923–24 season lists McKinney as director, and student leaders are also named. Dana B. Scudder, '24, is the designated leader of the Glee Club and serves as president; Franklin J. Maryott, '25, is listed as the leader of the Mandolin Club. But Wilbert Hitchner appears on the roster of officers for this season as coach. The yearbook describes the makeup of the combined ensemble in this way: "Early in the season Mr. McKinney, last year's director, turned over his work with the clubs to Wilbert Hitchner of the class of '22. Mr. Hitchner has proved a success both in training the Glee Club and in developing the Mandolin Club along original, novel lines."[112]

Again, to outward appearances, McKinney was still acting as director of the combined clubs. A local account of a concert on December 12, 1923, at the Roosevelt Junior High School in West Orange, New Jersey, names McKinney as director of the group and further states that he served as accompanist for the solos.[113] Another account similarly describes the combined clubs' appearance at the Rutgers College Junior Prom on February 21, 1924. The concert program that is outlined in this report is the standard one for the clubs at this time; ensemble works from both components, selections by the Prickly Heat Quartette and the Jazz Bandits, and so on. And this evaluation is also offered: "The concert last evening brought a climax to a most successful season by the combined Musical Clubs of the college. Under the careful instruction of Howard D. McKinney, professor of music at Rutgers, great progress was made, and music lovers throughout New Jersey have enjoyed the musical treats given in different parts of the state by the clubs."[114] So while McKinney remained in nominal control of the combined clubs, it seems that, undoubtedly as a result of the increased responsibilities that the creation of the university system placed upon him, he withdrew at least to some degree from the everyday coaching and directing of the organization. This approach would manifest itself throughout the remainder of McKinney's tenure as the clubs' director.

4 CHANGE IN FOCUS

The Demise of the Mandolin Club and the Rise of the Musical Clubs

Clearly, the spirit of reorganization was afoot in the newly conceived university system. This general, large-scale atmosphere of progress and change was also experienced within the Glee and Mandolin Clubs. For one thing, the collaborations between the Glee and Mandolin Clubs of Rutgers College and those of the New Jersey College for Women became officially consolidated under a recognized designation in the new university system. By 1925, combined concerts of this sort occurred several times per season and were an annual attraction on campus. The following account previewing an April 1925 concert provides commentary on the nascent tradition of the University Choral Club:

> The University Choral Club, composed of the glee clubs of Rutgers and the New Jersey College for Women will give its third annual concert in Ballantine Gymnasium tomorrow evening. Professor Howard D. McKinney will direct.
>
> This year's program contains many interesting features which have proven exceptionally interesting to audiences in Trenton and Maplewood thus far this season. The central feature is Alfred Noyes' famous poem, "The Highwayman," by one of America's most prominent composers, Deems Taylor. The composition is difficult and its performance reflects great credit on the ability of the clubs. The accompaniment for the number is played by a string quintet, two violins, viola, 'cello and double bass, and piano . . .
>
> The program is one selected with infinite care and good taste, and is being given for the benefit of the music department of the University.[1]

Further, the terminology utilized in discussing the activities of the Rutgers College Glee and Mandolin Clubs began to shift a bit during this period as

113

well. In *The Scarlet Letter* for the 1923–24 season, the appellations of Rutgers College Glee and Mandolin Clubs and Rutgers College Musical Clubs are used interchangeably.[2] Indeed, the term *Musical Clubs* can be found with increasing frequency in many newspaper accounts throughout the late 1920s. By the 1925–26 academic year, it was clear that the terminology used to describe this amalgamated group had officially changed, and with it the overall composition of the clubs:

> One of the many excellent features of the first appearance of the Rutgers University Combined Musical Clubs, at their concert tomorrow night at the Community Building of the Highland Park Reformed Church, will be the thirteen[-]piece orchestra of the Instrumental Club.
>
> This is the second year of the new form of instrumental club, which supersedes the old Mandolin Club. The instruments used are three violins, three saxophones, two trumpets, a trombone, a tenor banjo, a bass horn, a piano and a set of drums. Each of the men who play these instruments is a finished artist.
>
> Under the able direction of T. E. Couse, '26, who has been with the Instrumental Club for the past four years, and who was the leader of the club last year, some excellent programs

are being prepared. The orchestra will play a number of popular selections at its first appearance on Thursday night.[3]

Thus the Rutgers College Mandolin Club—in its various iterations so much a part of the collegiate landscape for nearly thirty years at this point—had by the 1925–26 season, for all intents and purposes, ceased to exist.

The 1926–27 yearbook reinforces the changes alluded to in the above article and confirms that these adjustments are of a permanent nature. The heading for this section of *The Scarlet Letter* is "The Musical Clubs," and that is how they are referenced throughout. The thirteen-member configuration of what is now the Instrumental Club from the 1925–26 season remains intact for this year; though the instrumentation is not designated in the yearbook, it is likely the same or very similar to that listed in the preceding quote. And Theodore E. "Ted" Couse, '26, has remained in his position as coach of the Instrumental Club following his graduation the previous year.[4] As mentioned in the article, Couse was an active member of the combined Glee and Mandolin Clubs since his freshman year, at which time he joined the mandolin component as a saxophonist.[5] In later years, he also sang with the first basses in the Glee Club section.[6] Couse's position as coach of the newly formed Instrumental Club is a continuation of McKinney's tradition of delegating some of the directorial duties of the combined clubs to others.

McKinney's work in establishing the music curricula at both Rutgers College and the New Jersey College for Women was spotlighted in an early 1927 interview in the *Central New Jersey Home News*. The highlights of his efforts to date, as well as some commentary on his accomplishments, are included in the article:

> Since ten years ago, with the appointment of the present incumbent as director of music at Rutgers University, the growth of the Musical Department has been slow but consistent. Before this appointment no regularly organized working music course had been undertaken at Rutgers. With the establishment of the Women's College came an opportunity for class instruction, and in 1919 the first class in harmony was started with five members. Today the enrollment is more than 200. The man who has done all this is Howard D. McKinney.
>
> Speaking of the advancement of music [within the university], he said: "Gradually work in history and appreciation, more advanced work in theory, instruction in practical music with credit counting toward a degree and courses in public school music have been added to the Women's College and courses in music history and elementary theory have been established at Rutgers [College]. Actual student participation in music has been fostered in every way, and as many opportunities as possible provided the undergraduates for hearing the best music."[7]

The expansion of the "Musical Department" that the article describes was to be greatly aided by the prospective addition of two new facilities. McKinney goes on to describe how the Voorhees Memorial Chapel "will contain one of the best and largest organs in the state and is being especially built, not only for church but for concert purposes." Further, the new music building "will be equipped with practice studios available for teaching, classrooms and an auditorium for chamber music with small groups of instruments."[8] These additions to the music program at Rutgers, both curricular and physical, may in no small measure be credited to McKinney's efforts on behalf of the program.

By the 1926–27 season, McKinney's work had been recognized in the form of his elevation to the rank of associate professor of music.[9] The 1927–28 yearbook's roster of Club officers is the first to recognize him as "Professor Howard D. McKinney, Director," however. The list of officers is small, with a president—Rodney P. Gibson, '28—a manager, and two assistant managers, all students. The need for a substantial contingent of managerial personnel can be seen from the still-growing ranks of the Musical Clubs' rosters. The Glee Club component this season has forty-eight singers: fourteen first tenors, nine second tenors, sixteen first basses, and nine second basses (the bass parts now designated *bassos*). The Instrumental Club also boasts a robust complement, with fifteen members.

A typical concert program during this season consisted of a combination of Rutgers songs—including "Down Where the Raritan Flows" and "Men of Rutgers"—and vocal pieces of a more serious nature. The latter category included musical settings of popular poems, such as "I Must Down to the Seas Again," based on the well-known John Masefield poem "Sea Fever," and "The Rouge Bouquet," based on a Joyce Kilmer, '08, poem. The effect that these settings, with their weightier musical connotations, had on "the harmonic and dramatic technique of the club" was emphasized by McKinney during this season. The yearbook narrative states that "Professor McKinney has stressed these qualities in an effort to get away from the typical 'rah-rah' songs by which many college musical clubs have identified themselves."

The quartet was still a featured part of the performances, as were vocal solos by individual Glee Club members. Also featured were piano solos, including Gershwin's "Rhapsody in Blue," performed by student

leader Hawley Ades, '29. And there was another prominent feature of the standard program during this season: "Maintaining the custom established several years ago of having a one-act play to make the programs complete, Robert R. Blunt, '29, assisted by Perry H. Murdick, Jr., '31, and John H. Hasbrouck, '31, produced 'The Green Chartreuse,' a modern murder mystery play which created a sensation whenever it was given."[10] The one-act play, then, is a descendent of the "sketch" that first appeared in the 1918–19 season and remained a part of the clubs' programs intermittently moving forward.

The clubs' season concluded with a weekend trip on April 13 and 14, with concerts at Port Jervis and Middletown, New York. Shortly after these performances, the following announcement appeared in the New Brunswick press:

Professor Howard D. McKinney of Highland Park, director of music at Rutgers University, will leave this afternoon [May 25, 1928] for Quebec, and will sail Saturday on the Mont Royal, Canadian Pacific Line, for Hamburg.

Professor McKinney, who has been granted a year's leave of absence from Rutgers, will spend the summer in study abroad and in attending musical festivals in Europe . . .

He will return to New Brunswick in October and spend the greater part of the winter here, but expects to sail for Europe again in the spring and remain until September, 1929. While in Europe this summer [he] will act as publisher's representative of J. Fischer and Bro., well known book publishing concern of New York City.

During his leave of absence from University duties, Professor McKinney will work upon the preparation of a book on music in Europe for eventual publication by one of New York's largest publishing houses.[11]

McKinney would, of course, become a well-known composer, editor, and author in addition to his activities in the educational field. The prospective book mentioned in the above account would almost certainly have been *Discovering Music* (1934), though perhaps the research that he garnered during this sabbatical played a role in future volumes as well (see chap. 5 sidebar, "Howard Decker McKinney [1889–1980]").

McKinney's leave of absence necessitated the appointment of replacements. For his duties at the women's college, Cleveland Bohnet, who had previously taught at the American Conservatory of Music in Chicago, was assigned. A well-known pianist and accompanist,[12] Bohnet, who spent ten years at the American Conservatory, had specific goals and aspirations for the groups at the women's college; concerning the repertory,

he was quoted as "wish[ing] to introduce a more serious type of music into the concert work and to specialize on artistic interpretation."[13]

At Rutgers College, the replacement for McKinney was Robert MacArthur Crawford, Princeton, '25 (1899–1961). While at Princeton, Crawford was the director of the Glee Club and the University Orchestra. He continued his studies at the Juilliard School of Music in New York and at the American School of Music in Fontainebleau, France. Crawford is perhaps best known today for composing the official song of the U.S. Army Air Corps.[14] His appointment as visiting instructor in music was announced in local New Brunswick newspapers on September 8, 1928.[15]

Crawford continued with the series of winter concerts that McKinney had instituted, which remained extremely popular. His first such event featured the renowned French flutist George Barrere, who was at that time a member of the Philharmonic-Symphony Society of New York (later the New York Philharmonic). Barrere performed with his ensemble, the Little Symphony Orchestra, at the Ballantine Gymnasium on November 12, 1928.[16] Crawford, of course, served as the director of the combined Musical Clubs as well, although he is identified in the 1928–29 yearbook as "Robert D. Crawford."[17]

A combined concert was given with the Musical Clubs of the women's college on December 9; this program was repeated on December 12 on a radio broadcast over station WOR. On December 14, the Rutgers College Musical Clubs opened their season with a concert at Perth Amboy: "The Glee Club has been practicing for the past two months under the direction of Robert M. Crawford, director of music at Rutgers and the Instrumental Club has been rehearsing for the same period under Hawley M. Ades, '29, who will direct the concert Friday."[18]

This description indicates that, while Crawford was nominally the director of the clubs, the actual administration of the performances was left to the young assistant and designated student director of the Musical Clubs, Hawley Ades.[19] Accounts of later performances, such as the one given in East Orange on January 18, 1929,[20] suggest that Crawford directed the Glee Club while Ades directed the Instrumental Club, but the above account, positing Ades in the overall directorial role, seems more likely under the circumstances.

In McKinney's absence—that is to say, under the direction of Hawley Ades—the program for this season reverted to a more traditional form. Songs of Rutgers—"Hail Mother," "Dear Old College," "Down Among the Dead Men," and "Loyal Sons"—opened the concerts. This was followed by the Instrumental Club's rendering of a three-part suite ("Nautch Dance," "From a Dance," and "The Fakir") by the American composer, painter, and writer Lily

Anderson Strickland. Songs by the clubs' manager, John M. Carney, '29, who accompanied himself on guitar, and piano selections by Ades followed. Selections by the now restored Prickly Heat Quartette were then offered, followed by a "One-Act Comedy" of a humorous nature entitled "Something Different" by William E. Allen, '31, of the Glee Club. The concerts ended with Glee Club selections: "Maiden Fair, O Deign to Tell" by Joseph Haydn and "Dance of the Gnomes" by Edward McDowell.[21]

Leadership from Within

McKinney returned to his duties at Rutgers for the 1929–30 season. That year's *Scarlet Letter* lists McKinney's position as musical director of the Glee Club. McKinney was reported to have conducted trials for the Glee Club as was his usual custom.[22] W. Clark Peck, '30, is named as student director and coach of the Instrumental Club, continuing the emphasis under McKinney on the role of student directors.[23] The opening concert for the year was broadcast on the evening of December 9 over station WOR in Newark. The program included the Rutgers songs "Alma Mater" and "Hail Mother," "Landsighting" by Grieg, and two numbers from *Songs of the Fleet* by Charles Villiers Stanford, "The Little Admiral" and "Farewell."[24]

The musical highlight of the fall semester at Rutgers College, however, was the presentation on December 15 of an original composition by McKinney titled "A Mystery for Christmas." Billed as a "pageant," the work unfolded as a series of costumed scenes depicting the various musical subjects. This performance was a condensed version of McKinney's original work, which was published by J. Fischer and Brothers of New York "for congregational use in connection with choral performances."[25] McKinney claimed to have drawn his inspiration for the work from art forms of the Middle Ages and of the Renaissance, forms that, according to him, communicated "a strong religious conviction that was peculiar to that epoch and has never been equaled. . . . We need only remind ourselves of such examples of this art as Amiens or Chartres Cathedrals, the liturgical music of the Catholic Church or the naively beautiful Christmas carol to realize the truth of this."[26] It seems clear that McKinney's experiences abroad during the previous year influenced the creation of this work greatly.

Indeed, McKinney continued to offer new and innovative approaches to the appreciation of Western art music for his students and for the general public. He instituted a series of "phonograph concerts," really "lectures on music illustrated by phonograph records," in the spring of 1930.[27] And his winter series of concerts continued; the final such event of this season featured the English cellist Felix Salmond (1888–1952).[28]

The Rutgers College Glee Club, with McKinney as the designated musical director, flourished as well. The 1929–30 contingent of the combined clubs boasted a membership of forty-two voices: ten first tenors, eleven second tenors, thirteen first bassos, and eight second bassos. The Instrumental Club, on the other hand, could not make a similar claim to robust membership. The numbers for this component had dropped to a mere eight members during this season.[29] And at this point, it would be fair to say that participation in the concerts of the combined clubs by the Instrumental Club had been to some extent minimized. A performance on April 11, 1930, is representative. The Glee Club component was prominent in the performance. It presented many of the pieces that were part of the December 9, 1929, performance: Rutgers songs, the Grieg "Landsighting," the Stanford works, and so on. A double quartet was also featured. The now routine skit or sketch was presented, and the concert concluded with baritone solos followed by folk songs from the Glee Club and "On the Banks." The Instrumental Club's contribution was restricted to "selected popular tunes." True, the Jazz Bandits were still associated with the combined clubs, but they seem to have performed only for the dances that often followed Glee Club concerts.[30] The Instrumental Club also made appearances apart from the Glee Club as well, but of a rather informal nature: "The Rutgers Glee Club Orchestra [i.e., the Instrumental Club] furnished syncopation for 250 dancers at the St. Patrick Day dance that was sponsored by the local council, Knights of Columbus, Monday evening in the auditorium of the clubhouse."[31]

Thus McKinney's return seems to have placed the emphasis on the Glee Club component of the clubs. This is evident in the relative numbers of the two groups, the program format, and McKinney's explicit leadership of the Glee Club contingent. These trends would continue as the 1930s progressed.

The 1929–30 season should also be noted for the fact that it marks the first appearance of an important figure in the history of the Rutgers Glee Club. Making his debut with the clubs as a first tenor is a young sophomore named F. Austin Walter.[32]

The Assistant Director:
F. Austin "Soup" Walter, '32

The 1930–31 season saw more of the trend toward the bifurcation of emphasis between the two Musical Clubs. McKinney seems to be guiding the Glee Club component in the direction of more serious, "classical" music. This is evident in the employment of the Glee Club in one of this season's concert series events. For

the final concert of the winter series, which took place on March 5, 1931, at the Roosevelt Junior High School in West Orange, McKinney obtained the services of the renowned baritone William Simmons. Simmons offered solo songs for most of the concert but was joined in the final segment by the Rutgers Glee Club in the Stanford *Songs of the Fleet* selections that the Club had performed at previous concerts.

The Instrumental Club, on the other hand, with its dwindling membership, was faced with performing opportunities that were becoming even more limited than the previous year: "The Rutgers Glee Club orchestra [that is, the Instrumental Club] will provide dance music for the balloon dance to be held at the Maple Meade Fire Company No 2 headquarters, Georges Road, North Brunswick Township, on Wednesday night, December 10. A door prize of $2.50 in gold will be awarded."[33]

The clubs were still, at this point, performing as a single unit. The now annual home concert in April, which had replaced the clubs' appearance at the junior prom, offered a program that was heavy on Rutgers school songs by the Glee Club unit and, again, a few "Popular Tunes" by the Instrumental Club. The Jazz Bandits were once more relegated to providing music for the dance that followed the concert.[34]

The combined clubs of the 1931–32 academic year are, as was now customary, heavy on student leadership. In the yearbook for this season, senior Francis A.

The Glee Club at Atlantic City, April 1932. Director McKinney is front row center, with student director Walter to his immediate left. Special Collections, Rutgers University Libraries.

(F. Austin) Walter is designated as the student director of the Glee Club while his classmate, John E. Hannan is listed as the student director of the Instrumental Club; McKinney is still designated as the director of the amalgamated organization. However, press accounts from this period indicate that the student director of the Glee Club took an active role in the performances, as had been the case in previous years. This was apparently true even in the most prestigious performances involving the Glee Club. The Club had entered an intercollegiate contest with several other such organizations, which was held at Carnegie Hall on February 27, 1932: "F. Austin Walter '32 will lead thirty picked Rutgers singers against the glee clubs of four universities. New York University, last year's winner, will enter along with Princeton, Yale and Columbia. Fordham, entered last year, will not compete."[35] This, then, was the first concert in which F. Austin Walter

121

conducted the Rutgers Glee Club, indeed his first public appearance as a conductor of any group. That it took place at such a prestigious location was a matter of pride and some little amusement to the conductor in his later years.[36]

Walter continued in the role of conductor of the group throughout the remainder of the season. At a special concert celebrating the bicentennial of the birth of George Washington, the Rutgers Glee Club appeared alongside the New Brunswick Symphony Orchestra. The Glee Club's portion of the program was described as follows: "The Rutgers University Glee Club, led by the student conductor, F. Austin Walter, sang the 'Scottish War Song' by Max Bruch, with Philip V. D. McLaughlin as soloist . . . [Additionally, Arthur] Sullivan's 'The Lost Chord' was sung."[37] Walter was also at the helm of the Glee Club when a new president of Rutgers University, Dr. Robert Clarkson Clothier, was inaugurated on June 11, 1932. Walter led the Club in a rendition of "On the Banks" following the new president's inaugural address.[38]

This directorial arrangement should be viewed in the context of McKinney's continually expanding duties. To those already enumerated, during this season, he added the position of director of the Rutgers Preparatory School Glee Club, replacing Edward J. McCloskey, who left to pursue graduate studies at Boston University.[39]

In October of 1932, it was reported that, for the first time in the history of the university, the Glee Club and the Jazz Bandits attended what we today would call an outdoor pep rally in preparation for the football game against NYU: "The Glee Club members sang several songs over the amplifying set between selections by the Jazz Bandits."[40] An account from later that month reports on the membership and tentative schedule for the Glee Club for this season, which would include an appearance in April of 1933 in Atlantic City at the Hotel Chalfonte-Haddon Hall. Forty-nine men were chosen for the Glee Club; the students are listed by class. However, there is no mention of the Instrumental Club in this announcement.[41]

Since F. Austin Walter had graduated in 1932, he was forced to relinquish his role for the 1932–33 season as student director. This was taken up by Ewald H. Bergmann, '33, a first bass with the Glee Club in previous seasons. Bergmann led the group in many performances during this academic year, including a return to the IMC competition, this time at Town Hall in Manhattan, competing against Yale, Princeton, Columbia, NYU, and Barnard.[42] Walter's talents had caught McKinney's eye by this time, however; he was approached by McKinney to return to the Club as assistant director, a position that Walter readily accepted.[43]

By the spring semester of 1933, the detachment of the Instrumental Club from the combined clubs seemed complete. The last remnant of the Instrumental Club, the Jazz Bandits, was now employed exclusively for the after-concert dances that frequently followed a Glee Club performance. In fact, Glee Club performances during this season often featured the student Glee Club, led by Assistant Director Walter, and the faculty Glee Club, another project of McKinney's, which he would direct himself in performance.[44]

By the 1933–34 season, a level of stability regarding the constitution of the Glee Club had been reached. The list of officers for this season now includes a president, George A. Kramer, '34, as well as a manager, two assistant managers, and an accompanist, all from the student ranks. Also listed are Professor Howard D. McKinney, '13, as director and Francis A. Walters, '32 (really F. Austin Walter), as assistant to the director. The Glee Club has a membership of forty-five men: twelve first tenors, ten second tenors, fourteen first basses, and nine second basses (the term *bassos* again having been discarded). As outlined above, the Instrumental Club has ceased to exist; no mention of the group can be found in this season's yearbook.[45] Concerts for this season are described as containing "ballades, spirituelles and college songs as well as a one-act play."[46] A complete program for a concert at the College Avenue Gymnasium (which replaced the Ballantine Gymnasium after that facility burned down in 1930) on April 14, 1934, manifests the aforementioned description.

I.
Rutgers College Songs,
The Glee Club

II.
My Heart is Victorious.....Carissimi
By Bonnie Lass ....Morley
A Border Ballad ....Willan
The Glee Club

III.
Piano Solos ......Howard West '35

IV.
"A Girl to Order"..One-Act Comedy

V.
Negro Spirituals:
(a) Ezekiel Saw de Wheel
(b) Ol' Man River
(c) Po' Ol' Lazarus
The Glee Club.

VI.
Selections ....Quintet

VII.
Chorale ....Bach
The Autumn Sea..From the German
Land-Sighting ....Grieg
Faculty, Alumni, and Glee Club .
Solo by William B. Swayze '33
Baritone.

VIII.
Musical Trust ....Clokey
Schnitzelbank, German student song
The Glee Club.

IX.
On the Banks,
Faculty, Alumni, and Glee Club.

Program for the concert at the College Avenue Gymnasium ("The Barn") on April 14, 1934.

The circumstances of F. Austin Walter's appointment at the university at this time are a bit nebulous. Newspaper accounts suggest that, by the 1934–35 season, he is engaged with activities other than those associated with the Glee Club. For example, he is reported to have been appointed to assist Charles Cook, instructor in military science and bandmaster at Rutgers, in the administration of a four-year course in band practice and instruction beginning with the 1935–36 season. In this account, Walter is referred to as "assistant director of music" at Rutgers;[47] on another occasion, he is identified as an "assistant in the music department of the university,"[48] which seems more in keeping with his official title of assistant to the director of the Glee Club. Whatever the case, Walter continued to lead that group in concerts, as he did for a concert on May 4, 1935, at the College Avenue Gymnasium.[49] He would eventually be appointed as a full-time faculty member at Rutgers in 1938.

Travel to venues outside the immediate environs of New Brunswick was a concept that was also being revived during this period. The 1935–36 season was to include an extended tour to the island of Bermuda:

> Rutgers University's glee club will give five concerts in Bermuda this year, Professor Howard D. McKinney, director of music, announced today.

> The group of approximately 27 students will leave New York City on February 1, on the Furness liner Monarch of Bermuda, and will return a week and a half later on the Queen of Bermuda.

> Three concerts will be given in Hamilton, one in St. George, and one in Somerset. Donald K. Moore, '32, soloist, F. Austin Walter, assistant in music, and Prof. McKinney will accompany the group.[50]

However, the death of King George V of England on January 20, 1936, forced the postponement and eventual cancelation of this event.[51] This proposed excursion would have been the first time that the Rutgers Glee Club had taken an engagement outside of the United States. The Glee Club's initial involvement with international travel is usually associated with the tenure of Walter as the Club's director (see chap. 5 sidebar, "Francis Austin 'Soup' Walter [1910–2000]").[52] This earlier effort to engage with international travel may be seen as an indication of the extent of Walter's influence on and involvement with the group during what is still, technically, McKinney's tenure as director.

The Glee Club had grown significantly since the loss of the Instrumental Club component in 1933. By the 1936–37 season, the membership had swelled to sixty men: twelve first tenors, sixteen second tenors, seventeen first basses, and fifteen second basses. This may be in response to the fact that it had become customary for the Rutgers College Glee Club to perform under the title of the Rutgers University Choir or the Kirkpatrick Chapel Choir. In previous seasons, nominal distinctions were often made between these groups. For example, the 1922 issue of *The Scarlet Letter* lists the members of the Glee and Mandolin Clubs on pages 238–39. Immediately following is a listing and group photo of the Kirkpatrick Chapel Choir (p. 240). A comparison of names between the two listings shows that all of what are termed "undergraduate members" in the Kirkpatrick Chapel Choir are also members of the Glee Club. But the Chapel Choir also has "faculty members," three in all, including Howard McKinney. Though they always existed as interchangeable entities, according to contemporary press accounts, the groups were officially united in 1933, following the separation of the Glee Club from the Instrumental Club, for the purpose of furnishing all music for services in Kirkpatrick Chapel.[53] Thereafter, the group designations were used synonymously. Concerning a concert at Kirkpatrick Chapel on December 6, 1936, the following description is provided:

> The Kirkpatrick Chapel Choir of Rutgers University will sing Sunday evening at 7:45 o'clock in the First Methodist Church . . .
>
> F. Austin Walter will conduct the group.

The choir, which is also the Rutgers University Glee Club, has given concerts in White Plains, Buck Hill Falls, Pa., Atlantic City, Jersey City, Elizabeth and Glen Ridge.[54]

The photograph of the group that is included with this story is the same as that which is provided on the Glee Club page of this season's *Scarlet Letter*.[55] Further photographic evidence of the conflation of titles present here can be seen in the 1940 edition of *The Scarlet Letter*. In the Glee Club section, two photographs are provided: the first is the ensemble, standing and dressed in white tie and tails, directed by Walter with McKinney accompanying on the piano; the second shows the group seated in robes in Kirkpatrick Chapel, with McKinney prominently positioned, front row center.[56] This combining of forces and interests would account for the increased size of the ensemble. Another announcement from two weeks later tells the same story with regard to the designation of "University Choir": "The Rutgers University Choir and Glee Club, composed of 50 undergraduates, will present the third and last of the community Christmas carol programs on the steps of the courthouse on Bayard [S]treet at 7:30 tonight. F. Austin Walters [*sic*] will direct."[57]

The program for the December 6 concert at Kirkpatrick Chapel reflects the trend toward more serious art-music works that the Club had been exhibiting since the beginning of McKinney's involvement in 1916. Works included "Brothers, Sing On," Edvard Grieg; "Lo, How a Rose E're Blooming," Praetorius; "Grant Us to Do With Zeal," J. S. Bach; and "Praise to God," Beethoven. Indeed, the Grieg song would become a staple of the Rutgers Glee Club performances, eventually becoming the traditional opening chorus at concerts.[58] Such works could certainly benefit from a more robust ensemble.

By the 1939–40 season, many of the components of the post-Mandolin/Instrumental Club configuration had stabilized. The levels of leadership are now clearly defined as being dual in nature; Howard D. McKinney holds the position of director of the Glee Club, while F. Austin Walter is designated as the conductor of the group.[59] This would imply what previous and current accounts of performances indicated; Walter was the primary leader of the group at most events. The size of the group has likewise stabilized at approximately sixty members. Many of the events at which the Club appeared were annual, or at least recurring, occasions. The Glee Club began making appearances at what would become known as the Winter Sports Weekend in 1933. Held at a Buck Hill Falls, Pennsylvania, lodge between the fall and winter semesters, the two-day affair offered winter sports such as tobogganing, skating, and skiing to all Rutgers undergraduates, faculty, alumni, and their guests. The Glee Club concert followed by a dance/dinner was

the premiere attraction. This tradition remained in place during the 1939–40 season.

Further, McKinney's winter concert series was still a highlight of each academic year at Rutgers. The quality of artists that McKinney drew in the latter part of the 1930s was impressive. The 1938–39 season brought the famed violinist Yehudi Menuhin, Metropolitan Opera coloratura soprano Josephine Antoine, and the Boston Symphony Orchestra (BSO) under Serge Koussevitzky. Ms. Antoine performed with a combined vocal unit made up of the glee clubs of Rutgers, Princeton, and NYU.[60] For the 1939–40 season, McKinney procured the Philadelphia Orchestra under Eugene Ormandy, Metropolitan Opera artists Elizabeth Rethberg (soprano) and Ezio Pinza (bass), and a return of the BSO under Koussevitzky. The fourth concert in the series this year, presented on March 13, showcased the Rutgers Glee Club combined with those of NYU and Columbia and featured Metropolitan Opera contralto Anna Kaskas. This concert was repeated on March 16 at Town Hall in Manhattan.[61]

Thus the Rutgers University Glee Club found itself in excellent shape—organizationally as well as artistically—as it headed into the decade of the 1940s. McKinney's talents and artistic vision, combined with the institutional and musical support of F. Austin Walter, had placed musical activities at Rutgers at the forefront of collegiate endeavors. And the Glee Club

THE UNIVERSITY SINGERS

FIRST NEW YORK APPEARANCE

RUTGERS, COLUMBIA, NEW YORK UNIVERSITY
GLEE CLUBS
and THE HALL OF FAME SINGERS

F. AUSTIN WALTER
JAMES GIDDINGS
ALFRED M. GREENFIELD

Directors

Soloist

ANNA KASKAS

Leading Contralto
Metropolitan Opera Association

THE TOWN HALL

123 WEST 43rd STREET, NEW YORK CITY

SATURDAY, MARCH 16, 1940, 8:15 P.M.

Tickets $1.00 to $2.50 — Loges (seating six) $18.00 tax exempt

May be procured from

Manager, New York University Glee Club, Box 109, University Heights, N. Y. C.
Manager, Columbia University Glee Club, Columbia University, N. Y. C.
Manager, Rutgers University Glee Club, New Brunswick, N. J.
The Town Hall Box Office, 123 West 43rd Street, N. Y. C.

Make checks payable to THE UNIVERSITY SINGERS

JOHN RAHE, Graduate Manager

Flyer announcing the concert at Town Hall in Manhattan featuring Metropolitan Opera contralto Anna Kaskas, March 16, 1940. Special Collections, Rutgers University Libraries.

was the showpiece of this creative environment, representing the best that student-oriented groups could offer.

World War II: An Unwelcome Detour

The winter concert series did experience a problem related to its schedule, however, during the 1939–40 season. The third concert in the series was to have featured Myra Hess (in 1941, Dame Myra, DBE), the renowned British pianist. However, certain contemporary events conspired to make that appearance impossible. With World War II already raging in Europe, Ms. Hess felt it necessary to defer her travels abroad: "Miss Hess announced recently that she would cancel her American tour this winter to remain in England to aid in the musical program being used to strengthen morale in her war-torn nation."[62] Ms. Hess had performed at Rutgers some years before, when Robert Crawford had secured her appearance during McKinney's leave of absence in 1929.[63] Her inability to join the concert series for this particular season, no matter how admirable, was a loss keenly felt nonetheless.

In the spirit of making the best of a disappointing situation, McKinney decided to keep the name, or names, of the replacement performer(s) a "mystery" until the concert itself began. "Professor Howard

127

McKinney, head of the [music] department, has long wanted to present a concert by an unidentified artist," the *Central New Jersey Home News* reported, "but not until this concert did the opportunity present itself." The only hint as to who might be performing was a vague indication of the repertory, which was announced to include "Handel, Bach, Brahms, Milhaud, Strauss, Moussorgsky, and contemporary Americans."[64] When the crowd of 2,700 had assembled on January 8 for the event, they found that "they were keeping a musical rendezvous with two old favorites, Ethel Bartlett and Rae Robertson, the distinguished piano duo."[65] The performers had been part of McKinney's series previously, appearing in November of 1937.[66]

Though this is a minor disturbance in the context of world events during this period, still, this episode can be seen as a precursor to the disruptions to normal activities that World War II would entail. For Rutgers, these disturbances would, in many ways, be significant. Unlike other periods in the university's recent past, the focus of the institution during the early 1940s was not on the rapid development of facilities and curricula but rather on the struggle to adapt to the extremely adverse circumstances that the onset of the American involvement in the global conflict would necessitate.[67]

Indeed, most of the undergraduate institutions that had grown up over the previous 175 years of the college's history dissolved during the wartime years.

A mid-twentieth-century account states the matter as follows: "By the end of 1943, virtually all student organizations, including the Student Council, had been disbanded for the duration and even *Targum*, which had been published continuously since 1869, went into eclipse in February 1944, after a dispute over editorial policies. All but a handful of the fraternities suspended operations. . . . The Gymnasium was converted into a mess hall. The athletic program survived only on an extremely limited basis, and intercollegiate competition was confined chiefly to contests with nearby colleges and military installations in football, basketball, baseball, track, and swimming."[68] The situation was, in fact, so dire as to cause the suspension of the publication of the university yearbook, *The Scarlet Letter*, for the years 1944 through 1946. But at the outset of the 1940s, things were only slowly beginning to unravel.

Glee Club activities remained mostly unchanged; in fact, some rather prestigious engagements came their way prior to America's entrance into the war. The opening event of the winter concert series for the 1940–41 season featured Rutgers alumnus Paul Robeson. Appearing before an enthusiastic crowd of approximately 3,600 music lovers, Robeson performed signature works including "Go Down, Moses" and "Shortnin' Bread" as well as more serious fare, such as Mussorgsky's "The Orphan" in the original Russian. An original composition by F. Austin Walter, "Old

Paul Robeson rehearses with F. Austin Walter and the Glee Club for the 1940 performance of *The Ballad for Americans*. Special Collections, Rutgers University Libraries.

Queens Bell," was also given at this concert, as was a "novelty act" by Miss Clara Rockmore, who performed works by Bach, Brahms, and Ravel on the theremin.[69]

The main attraction of the performance, however, was the presentation of *The Ballad for Americans*. Originally titled *The Ballad for Uncle Sam*, this work is a patriotic cantata written in 1939 by composer and folk singer Earl Hawley Robinson, with lyrics by John La Touche. A product of the Federal Theater Project, a Roosevelt New Deal program, the work was performed over sixty times under the latter title.[70] In November 1939, CBS hired Robeson to perform the work on the radio show *The Pursuit of Happiness*. Robeson subsequently recorded it with the American People's Chorus in 1940.[71] For the October 9 performance, a select group from the Rutgers Glee Club was

129

chosen to provide the choral parts; Walter conducted the work.

A good deal of preparation went into this concert. In fact, the amount of work necessary seemed to require special measures. To that end, McKinney and Walter removed the contingent of Glee Club members who would participate in the *Ballad* for eight days in September to the town of East Milford, Pennsylvania, where "the group underwent the unusual training in preparation for [the] performance with Paul Robeson in the gymnasium on October 9."[72] This excursion, albeit at a different venue, would become an annual event for the Club for the next several decades.

The spring semester of 1941 was highlighted by the appearance of the Rutgers Glee Club with the Boston Symphony Orchestra, again under Koussevitzky, as part of McKinney's winter concert series. A performance of the *Faust Symphony* by Franz Liszt was presented at the Rutgers Gymnasium on Wednesday, April 2, with repeat performances at Carnegie Hall on April 3 and 5.[73] F. Austin Walter would subsequently have ample opportunity to engage with the BSO during the summer of 1941, when he would attend the summer school at the Berkshire Music Center at Tanglewood and the Berkshire Symphonic Festival of the BSO.[74]

Despite increasing tensions abroad, the Rutgers Glee Club continued along its usual course in the fall term of 1941. To begin the season, certain members of

the group again left the environs of New Brunswick for preliminary training, as was reported in September of 1941:

The Rutgers University Glee Club has left on its second annual pre-season training jaunt, according to its conductor, F. Austin Walter of Highland Park.

Walter, Director Howard D. McKinney, also of Highland Park, and a nineteen-man squad, are making the eight-day stay at Lake Minnewaska, N.Y.

Preparing for what Walter terms "a tough season," the club is currently undergoing a conditioning schedule of daily practices and nightly concerts. "We may even book a scrimmage or two, if the squad brushes up on its fundamentals fast enough," Walter said.[75]

Thus prepared, the Club embarked on its usual schedule of events. On Saturday, December 6, the group was the featured attraction at the annual scholarship concert of the New Brunswick Borough Improvement League at the Franklin School. All seemed well in the town and in the university.

On Sunday evening, December 7, the Glee Club gave a performance at the New Jersey State Museum in Trenton. The program was a preview of what the group would present for its December 14 Christmas program at Kirkpatrick Chapel. Included in what was described as a lengthy program were traditional carols such as "Bring a Torch, Jeanette, Isabella" and "Ding, Dong, Merrily on High." Also offered were Glee Club standards such as "Lo, How a Rose E're Blooming" and "Brothers, Sing On."[76]

This event in Trenton turned somber at the conclusion, however. A description in a local newspaper some days later recounts the following scene:

> The Rutgers University Glee Club sang an encore to an encore when it appeared in Trenton at the New Jersey State Museum this week.
>
> The program had been completed and the encores given by the famed campus musical organization when a messenger approached director F. Austin Walter of Highland Park, and handed him a note.
>
> "Japan has declared war upon the United States," Walter read to the capacity audience.
>
> The Glee Club delivered one more full-throated encore—The Star Spangled Banner.[77]

Christmas program at Kirkpatrick Chapel, December 14, 1941. Rutgers University Glee Club Archives.

In a 1983 interview, Walter would recall, "This [singing of the anthem] sounded like our defiant answer to the 'act of infamy' and the Glee Club sang the anthem as never before."[78]

Concert

by the

Rutgers University Glee Club

at the

NEW JERSEY STATE MUSEUM

Sunday Afternoon, December 7, 1941

4:00 o'clock

GEORGE H. PULLAN................President
HOWARD D. MCKINNEY.............Director
F. AUSTIN WALTER...............Conductor
STEPHEN DUNTON................Manager

Program

I. SLEEPERS AWAKE ....J. S. Bach

    WHATE'ER GOD WILLS ....J. S. Bach

II. PEOPLE LOOK EAST ....Besancon

    A LITTLE CHILD IS BORN...............German

    BRING A TORCH, JEANETTE ISABELLA.......French

    DING DONG MERRILY ON HIGH..........French

III. SOLO—

    Richard Ziegler

IV. THE SHEPHERD'S STORY ....C. Dickinson

    LO, HOW A ROSE E'ER BLOOMING .... M. Praetorius

    WASN'T THAT A MIGHTY DAY......Negro Spiritual

    RICHARD DE CASTRE'S PRAYER TO JESUS

INTERMISSION

V. BROTHERS, SING ON! ....E. Grieg

    MY LORD WHAT A MORNIN' ....Negro Spiritual

    TORCHBEARERS ....Pomona College Song

    STENKA RAZIN ....Russian Folk Song

VI. SONGS OF RUTGERS—

    LOYAL SONS

    A HYMN TO QUEENS

    HAIL MOTHER

Program for the Glee Club concert on the afternoon of December 7, 1941.
Rutgers University Glee Club Archives.

With the announcement of war, the sense of normalcy and order that had come to be taken for granted would disappear for quite some time. The Japanese attack on Pearl Harbor on December 7 placed America in the midst of the ongoing global conflict. Franklin Roosevelt asked Congress on December 8 to recognize that, as a result of the Japanese attack, a state of war now existed between that nation and the United States. Germany declared war on the United States on December 11, 1941, and Roosevelt immediately reciprocated.

The spring semester of 1942 offered a somewhat curtailed schedule. Opening at the Millburn High School on February 6, the Glee Club also presented concerts in East Orange on March 6 and in Garden City, New York, on March 20. The latter event featured a combined performance with the glee club of the Adelphi College for Women.[79]

The standard program for this season also featured solos by Leonard Hansen, '43, who is described as "a football-playing yodeler."[80] A member of the Glee Club and lifelong friend of both Howard McKinney and F. Austin Walter,[81] Hansen's role in the program for this season was to "sing cowboy songs accompanying himself on guitar." The Glee Club, with Hansen in this role, performed at a combined event with the Rutgers Band on April 15, 1942, at the College Avenue Gymnasium. Walter led the Glee Club in selections such as the (so-called) Negro spiritual "Po' Ol'

Lazarus" and "Tutti venite armati" by the Italian composer Giovanni Giacomo Gastoldi.

This concert was remarkable on several counts, not the least of which were Hansen's songs. The event marked the first band concert at Rutgers that came under the supervision of the Music Department. That being the case, the role of band director was filled by a Glee Club—and, more importantly, Jazz Bandits—alumnus, Wilbert Hitchner. The audience for the affair was impressive at 1,400 attendees, all the more so for the fact that the concert took place during a blackout. But not to be daunted by wartime conditions, Walter came prepared for the occasion, "conduct[ing] the glee club in college songs using an illuminated baton."[82]

The spring semester of 1943 saw the Club continuing to perform in as normal a fashion as possible. However, the vicissitudes of war were becoming manifest at the university. The drain of students and funds was as devastating to the Glee Club as it was to every other organization on campus. Still, striving for excellence as always, the group made use of what resources it had left and decided to memorialize its accomplishments for posterity. In February of 1943, it was announced that "the Rutgers Glee Club's album of famous Rutgers songs" could be ordered for the amount of $3.50. Test recordings for the album, the group's first such effort, were played for interested parties at the Music House on College Avenue by F. Austin Walter. The release of the album, while an exceedingly positive step, was not without certain somber overtones:

> More than a little sentiment is attached to the recordings made by the Glee Club, for not only do they consist of Rutgers songs famous throughout the country for many generations, but they mark probably the final performance of the widely-known 55-man singing group.

The exigencies of war have already whittled the group to almost 50 percent of its original membership, it was learned yesterday. Since the Christmas holidays at least 20 members have left the university to serve Uncle Sam. Glee Club officials would not hazard a guess as to how small the group will be after March 1, when students in the Air Corps Enlisted Reserve are scheduled to leave.

Glee Club performs at the College Avenue Gymnasium during the 1942–43 season. Special Collections, Rutgers University Libraries.

F. Austin Walter leads the Glee Club during a recording session in the mid-1940s. Special Collections, Rutgers University Libraries.

The *Targum*, undergraduate weekly, said in an editorial this morning, "Included among the campus extra-curricular activities which are slowly but surely coming to an end is an organization which has brought pleasure to many—students and outsiders alike—and fame to the university. We mean the Rutgers Glee Club.

The pre-1943 Glee Club of 55 men, however, has left a permanent record—not only for the duration of the war, but also for future generations. This record, as announced recently, consists of an album of eight recordings of favorite Rutgers songs.

These recordings are the last performance of the ensemble as we know it for the duration. But they are not only the presentations of a highly-talented group; they are also remembrances through which many men of Rutgers will recall the scenes of their undergraduate days in the long future to come."[83]

Much of what this article suggests would indeed come to pass. As the spring semester of 1943 progressed, more and more signs proclaiming "Gone for the Duration" sprang up on campus, attesting to the dormancy of many organizations, the Glee Club included. Finally, shortly after the announcement of the recording, the following article appeared in a local newspaper:

Chalk up Rutgers' nationally-famous glee club as another casualty of war. The 63-year-old musical aggregation, which has appeared at Carnegie Hall and Radio City Music Hall, has lost nearly half its members to the service, according to Prof. F. Austin Walter, director. For the duration it will be heard only as the choir in the Rutgers Kirkpatrick Chapel on Sunday mornings at 11a.m.

Averaging more than 60 students in normal years, the organization now has about thirty members. Those "remaining do not compose a group large enough to complete a well-balanced musical group capable of continuing the extensive program the club has undertaken in past years," Walter said . . .

"[T]he club can only hope to survive as a small choir. It will try to keep up a high standard of quality in harmony with the organization's traditions until the war is over."[84]

The Glee Club would not need to sit out the entire duration of the war, however. The determination and mettle of the Rutgers students had, by the summer of 1943, enabled many of the inactive organizations to resume at least partial activity:

The "gone for the duration" signs hung up by nearly all Rutgers University organizations early this year are on their way down.

With the *Targum*, undergraduate newspaper, the Winants Club, chief civilian dormitory group, and the Rutgers Glee Club already resuming activity, the Student Council has recommended of Dean of Men Fraser Metzger that departmental and dormitory clubs be reinstated as soon as possible . . .

Through a combination of soldier and student talent, the Rutgers Glee Club is being reorganized under the direction of F. Austin Walter, music instructor. When the initial tryouts were held, Walter reported, about 25 civilians and an equal number of Army trainees were accepted.

The Glee Club, Walter said, is participating in the Sunday afternoon vesper services, which are held weekly in Kirkpatrick Chapel at

4:30p.m. Solos by civilians and soldiers, organ playing by Walter, and reading of the Scriptures by Dean Metzger are features of these services which are open to the public.[85]

Walter also pointed out that soldiers as well as civilians could visit the Music House on College Avenue and listen to recordings or play the piano, and that, at the time the article was written, a great many soldiers were already doing so.

Naturally, wartime contingencies limited the Glee Club to very few activities beyond the Kirkpatrick Chapel vespers. The Club made a brief appearance at a fundraising event at the Roosevelt Junior High School in New Brunswick on January 17, 1944. The featured guest was Eleanor Roosevelt, who spoke of the role of the United States regarding postwar responsibilities. Sponsored by the B'nai B'rith Hillel Foundation of Rutgers University, the primary focus of the event was to call attention to the "fate of the Jewish people in Europe" and the question of open immigration to Palestine. The Glee Club joined a few other performers, including a Coast Guard quartet from the Third Naval District, in the entertainment portion of the program.[86]

Such appearances were quite rare, however. The group was mostly confined during this period to the duties of the Kirkpatrick Chapel Choir at the Sunday services mentioned above. The toll of the war on the student body only increased as the conflict continued. By the time hostilities ended in August of 1945, 1,700 undergraduate men from Rutgers had seen their college careers interrupted by service to their country. The efforts to keep the spirit—if not the fully functional formats—of the student organizations alive should be seen as heroic in nature when viewed in the context of the upheaval in which they occurred:

In almost every sense, the war represented a disaster for the University. Its students, and many of its staff, were scattered to every corner of the globe. Its academic program, built up over the course of decades, was changed beyond recognition. The traditional humanistic values that gave it meaning were discarded in favor of courses designed to give men the technical training needed to win a war. Freedom of inquiry became irrelevant when the practical task of survival assumed uppermost importance. . . . Fortunately, the damages proved not to be irreparable. Fortunately, too, the ultimate victory, to which Rutgers and all other institutions of higher education had contributed so much in terms of men and knowledge, more than redeemed the losses that had been incurred.[87]

GLEE CLUB DISCOGRAPHY

From the Vicissitudes of War
to European Tours

At the beginning of 1943, in the midst of a global conflict, normal societal processes had deteriorated to a large degree in the United States. Many, if not most, organizations were depleted of a sizable portion of their workforce in order to serve the ever-growing needs of the various battlefronts of World War II. Institutions of higher learning were no exception to this, and Rutgers University was as affected by this drain as any like establishment. This, of course, meant the curtailment or outright demise, at least on a temporary basis, of many of the school's organizations, the Glee Club included. By February 1943, the Glee Club had lost at least twenty of its fifty-five man complement, and many more absences were expected in the months to come. The Club would maintain a very limited existence for the duration of the war but would not resume its usual robust schedule of performances until the close of the conflict (see chap. 4, "World War II: An Unwelcome Detour").

Recognizing this inevitable chain of events, F. Austin Walter determined to act with expedience to preserve the essence of what he and Howard McKinney had built together over the past ten years. Assembling the entire

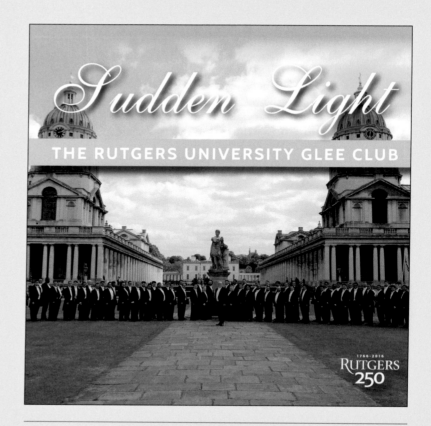

Cover for the Glee Club CD *Sudden Light*, 2016.

fifty-five-man Club of the 1942–43 season for the final time in the winter months of 1942, Walter engineered a recording session designed to preserve "the last performance of the ensemble as we know it." The resulting album, released in 1943 under the title *Songs of Rutgers*, contained eleven traditional Rutgers selections, including "Brothers, Sing On," "Down Where the Raritan Flows," and "On the Banks of the Old Raritan."

Following the resumption of normal Glee Club activities during the 1946–47 season, Walter would go on to supervise a series of recordings over the next four decades. He would produce nine more involving the Glee Club and several others with the combined unit known as the Rutgers University Choir, of which the Glee Club was an integral component. Subsequent directors would also avail themselves of the opportunity that recordings provided to widen the scope of exposure for the Club. Timothy McDonald, Club director from 1986 to 1987, produced during that period the long-playing album titled *We Sing Thy Praise, Old Rutgers*, which, according to the label, was "dedicated to F. Austin 'Soup' Walter"; the album was not released, however, until 1989.

During Patrick Gardner's time as director of the Club beginning in 1993, he also enthusiastically pursued opportunities for recording the ensemble. Many of these projects during Gardner's regime focused on the repertory and performances from the Club's frequent European tours. Now released as compact discs rather than the 33 1/3 record albums from Walter's time, these sleek vehicles presented a different, more cosmopolitan, face of the Club and greatly enhanced its reputation outside the confines of the university's walls.

A list of recordings in which the Glee Club has participated since 1943 is presented, including those that the Club appeared on as part of the University Choir.

It is an impressive catalog of achievement by any measure.

DISCOGRAPHY OF THE RUTGERS UNIVERSITY GLEE CLUB

Title of Recording	Date of Release	Producer	Performing Group(s)
Songs of Rutgers	1943	New Jersey: Nelson Cornell Custom Records	Rutgers Glee Club
Christmas Music: An Album of Traditional Carols	1950s (†)	New Jersey: Nelson Cornell Custom Records	Rutgers Glee Club
Rutgers Glee Club	1950s (†)	Recorded publications Company	Rutgers Glee Club
Yale Wind Symphony and Rutgers Male Chorus	1962	New York: RCA Custom Records	Yale University Wind Symphony and Rutgers Glee Club
Songs Our Alma Mater Taught Us (American College Songs)	1960s (†/##)	New York: F.T.P. Records	Rutgers Glee Club
American Colleges Sing Stephen Foster	1966 (†)	Hollywood, Florida: Request Records	Rutgers Glee Club

Title of Recording	Date of Release	Producer	Performing Group(s)
Christmas in Carol and Song	1970s (⁺)	New Jersey: Cinematape Productions	Rutgers Glee Club and Kirkpatrick Chapel Choir
100 Years of Football	1970	David E. Politziner, Producer	Rutgers Glee Club
His Master's Voice	1976	Victor S. Garber, Producer	Rutgers Glee Club
Horatio Parker, *Hora Novisima*	1976	Reel-to-reel tape, Douglass Library, Rutgers University	Rutgers University Choir
Three Whale Songs	1983	Newark, N.J.: Rutgers University Studios	Rutgers Glee Club
We Sing Thy Praise, Old Rutgers	1989	Newark, N.J.: Rutgers University Studios	Rutgers Glee Club
Let Thy Good Spirit	1996	New York: Ethereal Recordings	Rutgers Glee Club
The Bells Must Ring	1998	New York: Ethereal Recordings	Rutgers Glee Club
1999 European Tour	1999	New York: Ethereal Recordings	Rutgers Glee Club
The Miracle	2002	New York: Ethereal Recordings	Rutgers Glee Club
Rejoice!	2003	New York: Ethereal Recordings	Rutgers Glee Club
Back to the Banks	2004	New Jersey: Mason Gross School of the Arts	Rutgers Glee Club and Rutgers Wind Ensemble
Hear the Voice	2007	New York: Ethereal Recordings	Rutgers Glee Club
Travels	2012	New York: Ethereal Recordings	Rutgers Glee Club
Sudden Light	2016	New York: Ethereal Recordings	Rutgers Glee Club
The Rutgers University Glee Club at Utrecht University (DVD)	2016	John Baker, Producer	Rutgers Glee Club

(+)—The exact publication years for these recordings could not be determined from the record sleeves, but the liner notes indicated they were completed during the decades noted above.

(##)—This recording was commissioned by General Electric for the television show *GE College Bowl* to introduce college teams competing on the show.

The following recordings were originally issued as LPs and have been rereleased as CDs. The original publication information shown below is taken from the liner notes on the reissued CDs.

Title of Recording	Date of Release	Producer	Performing Group(s)
Carl Orff, *Carmina Burana* Winner—*Gran Prix du Disque*	1960	New York: Columbia Records	Philadelphia Orchestra, Eugene Ormandy, conductor and the Rutgers University Choir
William Walton, *Belshazzar's Feast* Nominated for Grammy Award: Best Choral Recording, 1962	1961	New York: Columbia Records	Philadelphia Orchestra, Eugene Ormandy, conductor and the Rutgers University Choir
George Frideric Handel, *Ode for St. Cecelia's Day*	1961	New York: Columbia Records	New York Philharmonic, Leonard Bernstein, conductor and the Rutgers University Choir

Postwar

Disruptions of the magnitude described previously are not easily resolved. The 1945–46 academic year was dubbed the "Reconversion Year" within the college and efforts were undertaken to resume normal activities that had been disrupted by the war.[88] By the winter of 1945, these efforts were beginning to manifest themselves throughout the campus. For the musical organizations, the logical place to begin was with the Christmas program that had always been so much a part of the university holiday atmosphere:

> All the old-time Yuletide favorites will be sung by the Rutgers University choir of 22 voices during a special vesper service which will be held in Kirkpatrick Chapel tonight at 7 o'clock. . . .
>
> Carol selections on the program include: "God Rest You Merry Gentlemen," "What Child Is This?" "Joy to the World," "It Came Upon a Midnight Clear," and "Oh Little Town of Bethlehem." . . .
>
> The program will also include a vocal solo by Donald R. Moore '32; instrumental selections by Girair M. Nazarian, '47, violinist; and Harold H. Zilch, '48, cellist. Dr. Howard D. McKinney, professor of music, will play several organ selections . . .

> This program is, in modified form, a revival of the Christmas Services which were given annually in Kirkpatrick Chapel before the war.
>
> The vesper service will be continued on a monthly basis.[89]

It should be noted that credit for the direction of the Rutgers University Choir during the Reconversion Year was shared between McKinney and Wilbert Hitchner, with assistance from Donald K. Moore, '32, "who sang frequently as a baritone soloist."[90]

The Glee Club would not be truly reorganized along the lines of its former iterations until the following year, however. The university was generally interested in returning to its core educational goals and in continuing the expansion that so characterized its nature before the war. The Music Department was no exception. In May of 1946, McKinney announced ambitious plans for such an expansion, plans "that would make New Brunswick one of the state's foremost music centers." In an interview, McKinney stated that he intended to revive the Buck Hill Falls festival that had been popular before the war and, indeed, to expand the festival concept. He also prioritized reconstituting the student organizations that played such a large role in the music program and that had "crumbled during the war because of decreased enrollment":

In the past years Rutgers prided itself on a large glee club, band, and symphony orchestra. All these organizations are scheduled to be rejuvenated and expanded next fall, when the present student enrollment is expected to double. Under a new system, students will receive college credits for participating in these activities.

"Everything will have to be rebuilt from the ground up," Dr. McKinney [added].[91]

These plans clearly necessitated the directed attention of McKinney. Appointed as the first director of the Music Department at Rutgers in 1946, McKinney's focus began to shift away from direct involvement with the Glee Club to his new administrative role. By the spring of 1947, McKinney was heavily involved with moving the Music Department to its new home on the corner of College Avenue and Bishop Place in New Brunswick. Though the building would be shared with other departments, such as the English department, McKinney viewed the move as a definite upgrade, offering freedom from the "inadequate facilities" of the previous building and providing the space necessary for the proposed expansion of the department.[92]

Thus beginning with the 1946–47 season, the leadership of the Rutgers University Glee Club fell exclusively to F. Austin Walter. The narrative for the Glee Club in *The Scarlet Letter* for this season—its first year of

publication since the forced shutdown in 1944—offers a brief synopsis of the group's history. However, the account inaccurately states that 1874 was the year of its inception. The Glee Club was first organized in 1872 by the members of the class of 1874, hence the confusion. The narrative also emphasizes the group's transition in terms of repertory, stating that, whereas once the Glee Club sang only college songs, "the repertoire now includes both college songs and the classical works of Wagner, Bach, and Sibelius."

In addition to his Glee Club duties, the yearbook names Walter as director of the Kirkpatrick Chapel Choir. The link between the two groups is made explicit in the yearbook narrative: "The Choir, which sings in Kirkpatrick Chapel on Sundays, is composed of members of the Glee Club. F. Austin Walter '32, who is director and conductor of the Glee Club also directs the Choir."[93]

The Glee Club had by this time reconstituted itself to a semblance of its former vigor. The group had fifty-two men in its complement for this season and began once again appearing at events involving the most important functions on campus. In a ceremony announcing the university's plans to expand its campuses across the Raritan River on February 4, 1947, the Club performed and indeed stood as an example of President Robert C. Clothier's promise in his address that day to adhere to the traditions of the school through this process of expansion.[94]

McKinney's winter concert series, now most often simply referred to as the concert series, remained in place as well. For the 1946–47 season, the list of performers included renowned cellist Gregor Piatigorsky as well as the Boston Symphony Orchestra under Koussevitzky, the Cleveland Orchestra under George Szell, and the San Francisco Orchestra conducted by Pierre Monteaux. The initial concert this season featured Paul Robeson, who was a regular series participant.[95] Robeson appeared in concerts for the series in 1927, 1929, 1932, and in the silver anniversary series in 1940, demonstrating his continuing commitment to the musical organizations at Rutgers.[96]

By the 1947–48 season, the Glee Club's ranks had swelled to seventy-four men. Interest in the group had also increased; the annual Christmas concert, usually presented in Kirkpatrick Chapel, was moved this year to the College Avenue Gymnasium "in order to accommodate a larger audience than in the past."[97] Following the winter recess, the Club regrouped for a series of spring concerts, beginning with a performance at the Highland Park High School auditorium on February 27, 1948. The program for the concert unfolded as follows:

Paul Robeson (center) with Howard McKinney (to his immediate left) and F. Austin Walter (far left) at the first performance in McKinney's concert series for 1946–47. Special Collections, Rutgers University Libraries.

Opening the program will be a group of five selections by the entire Glee Club, under the direction of F. Austin Walter, assistant professor of music at the University. These numbers, "A Toast to Rutgers Men," "Brothers, Sing Out!" [sic], "Sleepers Awake," "Fain Would I Change That Note," and "Feasting I Watch"—will be followed by a group of baritone solos by David Bray, who will be accompanied at the piano by his wife. The first half of the program will be concluded by four Glee Club offerings: "Stenka Razin," "A Smuggler's Song," "Carol of the Bells," and "When Johnny Comes Down to Hilo."

Three Negro spirituals, "Po' Ol' Lazarus," "Water Boy," and "Ezekiel Saw the Wheel," will open the second portion of the concert and will be followed by the Glee Club Octet. Concluding the program will be an American folk song, "Casey Jones," and a medley of college songs.[98]

The highlight of the Glee Club season, at least in terms of artistic endeavor, was a concert given by the Rochester Philharmonic at the College Avenue Gymnasium on March 15, 1948, as the final performance of the concert series for that season. Under the direction of Erich Leinsdorf, the orchestra presented Beethoven's *Symphony No. 6 in F major*, two scenes from Wagner's *Götterdämmerung*, and a relatively new, but immediately successful, work by American composer Randall Thompson (1899–1984), *The Testament of Freedom*, in which the Glee Club served as the chorus. The composer was present at the performance and was introduced to the audience at the conclusion of the piece, along with Walter, as conductor of the Glee Club, and Leinsdorf.[99]

During the 1948–49 season, the number of concerts given by the Club continued to increase. In addition to the (once-again traditional) Christmas, Easter, and spring concerts, the Club appeared early in the season again with the Rochester Philharmonic. Also included in this year's schedule were engagements in Freehold, Chatham, Asbury Park, Trenton, and Newark. The spring concert on May 18, 1949, at the College Avenue Gymnasium, the final performance of the season, was attended by over 2,000 enthusiastic patrons. In December of 1949, the Club announced that it would undertake no less than seventeen concerts during the 1949–50 season, comparing favorably to the most productive years of the organization. This would include the reappearance of a Christmas classic; McKinney's "A Mystery for Christmas" was again presented as the traditional holiday concert and returned to Kirkpatrick Chapel, which was deemed a more appropriate site for this work to be performed than the gymnasium. To accommodate an expected large turnout, three performances were scheduled for one day, December 18, at 5:00, 7:00, and 9:00 p.m.[100]

145

Erich Leinsdorf conducts the Rochester Philharmonic and the Rutgers Glee Club in a performance of Randall Thompson's *Testament of Freedom* at the College Avenue Gymnasium, March 15, 1948. Rutgers University Glee Club Archives.

LAKE MINNEWASKA

An Idyllic Location for Work and Recreation

For the opening event of the 1940–41 concert series at Rutgers, Howard McKinney had planned a patriotic extravaganza. McKinney had invited Rutgers's favorite son and unofficial Glee Club alumnus Paul Robeson to be the featured performer at this event. Robeson offered several of his contemporarily famous songs as an appetizer in the first half of the concert. This was followed in the second half by the highlight of the event, the performance of the patriotic cantata *The Ballad for Americans* by composer-arranger Earl Hawley Robinson (1910–91; see the narrative, chap. 4, "World War II: An Unwelcome Detour"). Considering the deteriorating wartime situation in Europe during the fall of 1940, such expressions of nationalistic pride were looked upon with favor in an America that sensed a growing danger to its own security.

For the choral parts in Robinson's cantata, a select contingent of the Glee Club was utilized, with Walter conducting. These parts were challenging, as were other ensemble sections of this prestigious event. Therefore, it was decided by McKinney—who was still nominally the director of the Glee Club, with F. Austin Walter serving in the role of conductor[101]—that a more robust schedule of preparation should be undertaken to ensure good results for this performance. In early September of 1940, the group was removed to a hotel along the Delaware River in East Milford, Pennsylvania,[102] for what was described as "eight days of pre-season training in regular football team fashion." Walter is designated as the leader of this expedition in contemporary accounts.[103]

The immediate outcome of this unprecedented rehearsal regimen was that the resulting concert with Paul Robeson was a resounding success. But in the long term, this excursion to East Milford would have tangible consequences. The early September retreat was once again undertaken at the beginning of the 1941–42 academic year. Now described in local accounts as the Club's "annual pre-season training jaunt," the group again prepared for a "tough season" by sojourning this time to the recreational areas of Lake Minnewaska near the town of New Paltz, New York. Walter and McKinney were joined on this outing by nineteen Glee Club members, who were subjected to "a conditioning schedule of daily practices and nightly concerts," though Walter allowed that "we may even book a scrimmage or two, if the squad brushes up on its fundamentals fast enough."[104]

And to be sure, these two early presemester expeditions would form the basis for an annual rite that would continue for four decades, settling permanently after the first year at Lake Minnewaska. World War II interrupted all Glee Club activities for a brief period, and even when normal musical pursuits were restored, it was some time before these annual outings were reinstituted. However, by the 1960s, this tradition had once again become ingrained in the routine of the Club. The students and faculty members would customarily stay at the Wildmere Hotel, one of the two so-called Mountain Houses, along with Cliff House, that had passed out of the hands of their private owners in 1955 and came under the care of a general manager for the entity that is today known as the Lake Minnewaska State Park Preserve.[105] The primary focus of these trips was rehearsal for the upcoming Glee Club season. Practices were usually held in a small, shingled wooden cabin known for housing a bust of George Washington; this structure is reportedly still standing. Still, ample time was provided to the students for such activities as sailing, horseback riding, swimming, long walks in the

Wildmere Hotel, Lake Minnewaska, New York, circa 1941. Rutgers University Glee Club Archives.

beautifully wooded areas, and, apparently, visits to the very popular Emil's Tavern.[106]

A typical outing began on September 5, 1969, when thirty members of the Club descended on Lake Minnewaska for the purpose of what had become known by then as "taking the cure." Upon arrival, rehearsal was the first order of business, followed by an early trip to the bar and the traditional Lake Minnewaska marathon dinner, and then further rehearsal. The remainder of the stay consisted of a fairly rigorous agenda of rehearsals and meals in alternating periods, though, as usual, time was made for Emil's and also for the traditional cartwheels by Professor Walter that often followed these visits to the tavern. Golfing was on the agenda for the scheduled free time as well as "the ceremonial jump off the big rock into the lake," this year performed by the Club's tour manager.[107]

The Minnewaska tradition continued into the 1970s. In 1974, the Club was in attendance at the resort from September 4 through September 8. During this period, it was not unusual for alumni members to be invited to participate in these outings. For this year's expedition, arrangements were made for the former members to arrive on Friday, September 6, and stay through the weekend, thus affording them a chance to share their past experiences with the current members and to preview the musical bill of fare for the upcoming Glee Club season.[108]

F. Austin Walter, the longtime director of the Club who was so instrumental in the founding and development of this tradition, announced his retirement from teaching in 1978, though he remained active with the Glee Club until 1983. In the spirit of Club continuity, the 1978 trip to the lake was attended by Walter's new assistant conductor and putative eventual replacement, Richard Alan Bower. Bower, whose duties under Walter would include conducting sectional rehearsals and accompanying full rehearsals, also used the time at the lake resort to work with smaller ensemble units, such as quartets and octets.[109]

Unfortunately, conditions at the Lake Minnewaska resort began to deteriorate in the early 1980s. This was particularly true of the Club's preferred hotel, the Wildmere, which fell into disrepair and was forced to close,[110] signaling an end to this particular chapter in Club history. Notwithstanding, the spirit of the Lake Minnewaska excursions was resurrected in the 1990s when Patrick Gardner took over as Club director. Gardner introduced a series of rehearsal retreats, one each for the fall and spring semesters, during which the Club members would engage in an intensive rehearsal schedule. A favorite location for these retreats was and remains the Engleside Inn in the town of Beach Haven on Long Beach Island, New Jersey. Though the Club has traded the Catskill Mountains for the Jersey shore as the venue for these activities, it is a common sentiment among Club members that these rehearsal retreats share "the same eternal bonds and traditions" that McKinney and Walter sought to foster with the original preseason excursions.[111]

5 PRESTIGE AND TRAVEL

The 1950s: The University Choir

The year 1950 marked the two hundredth anniversary of the death of the great German composer Johann Sebastian Bach (1685–1750). To celebrate this event, Howard McKinney—now designated chairman of the Music Department—and Glee Club director F. Austin Walter, in collaboration with the chair of the New Jersey College for Women's Music Department and Erich Leinsdorf of the Rochester Philharmonic Orchestra, planned a three-day Bach festival to take place on Easter weekend, April 7, 8, and 9, 1950. The festival included a concert of orchestral works by the Rochester ensemble and "two illustrated lectures" by McKinney on the music performed at the festival.[1]

The focal point of the weekend, however, was the two performances of the *St. Matthew Passion*, BWV 244, given on April 7 and 8 at the College Avenue Gymnasium. Leinsdorf's orchestra shared the stage with the members of both the Rutgers Glee Club and the New Jersey College for Women's Chapel Choir, along with several soloists. Leinsdorf worked with the combined choral group for over a year, taking great pains in the preparation of the work. The results were judged as follows:

> Neither the clarity nor the emotional impact of the Bach Passion are lacking, nor in any case is one element sacrificed for the other . . .
>
> The choral group, consisting of approximately 185 well-trained voices, sings with sincerity, and gives a fresh and vibrant interpretation of this epic work.[2]

This festival was technically part of McKinney's concert series, considered to be the fifth and final event of the season. But the impact of these performances, particularly the *Passion*, would have implications for the structure of the Glee Club as the decade progressed.

In October of 1950, it was announced that a new choral group, to be designated the Rutgers University Choir, was to be formed. This group would consist of

St. Matthew Passion by J. S. Bach performed by the Rochester Philharmonic and members of the Rutgers Glee Club and New Jersey College for Women's Chapel Choir, April 8, 1950. Special Collections, Rutgers University Libraries.

"the combined glee clubs of the men's colleges in New Brunswick and the Voorhees Chapel Choir of the New Jersey College for Women."[3] The initiative to form this group was undertaken by a committee consisting of two members from the Voorhees Choir and representatives from the Glee Club. A constitution was drafted and subsequently approved by the dean of the university, Albert E. Meder Jr. The constitution was endorsed by heads of the music departments from both Rutgers and the New Jersey College. Said to be modeled on similarly constituted collegiate organizations, such as the Harvard-Radcliffe choir, this new entity would have F. Austin Walter as its director.

It seems clear from contemporary press accounts that the impetus for the formation of this group was at least partially initiated by the performance in the previous semester of the Bach *Passion*. Indeed, there were plans already underway for a repeat performance of the *Passion* on Good Friday of 1951. Further, it was felt that an organization such as this was necessary to "extend cultural and educational musical activities and to pass on the benefits thus derived through public performances." It was stated that, going forward, the new combined group would only be employed in the performance of "serious works difficult enough to warrant the resources of so large an organization."

The new constitution stated that "there will be two classifications of membership, active, open to full-time students of Rutgers, and associate, open to faculty, alumni, and members of the Rutgers family." However, the "total active membership" of the group would consist of the Rutgers Glee Club and the Voorhees Choir.[4]

Certainly, precedents for this amalgamation existed in the history of both Rutgers College and New Jersey College. Perhaps the closest comparison to the University Choir was the University Choral Club of the mid-1920s, which combined the forces of the Rutgers College Glee Club and the glee club of the New Jersey College for Women under Howard McKinney's direction (see chap. 4, "The Demise of the Mandolin Club and the Rise of the Musical Clubs"). But this new, officially constituted combination of groups was significant for future large-scale musical endeavors involving the musical ensembles at Rutgers.

It should be noted that the decade of the 1950s saw significant changes to the procedures and practices of the Glee Club in addition to its enhanced participation in the newly formed University Choir.

In previous decades, the Glee Club had traditionally rehearsed on Monday and Wednesday evenings at Kirkpatrick Chapel. During this period, however, the site for these rehearsals changed to Suydam Hall, now demolished, which was located on Holy Hill, the current site of the New Brunswick Theological Seminary. Later in this decade, the rehearsals once again shifted to the Parish House of the Second Reformed Church on College Avenue. It was not until the mid-1960s that the former St. James Methodist Church, located at the corner of Easton Avenue and Hamilton Street in New Brunswick, was purchased by the university and converted into the current Glee Club facility known as McKinney Hall.

The advent of the University Choir had a further, more direct, impact on the Club's routine during this period. The new group claimed Monday evenings as their rehearsal time, thereby leaving the Glee Club with only Wednesdays for practice sessions. Fortunately, this problem was eliminated in 1955, when the university schedule removed Saturday as an official day for class sessions. The Glee Club immediately seized on Saturday mornings as a replacement for the Monday night sessions, instituting a tradition of providing coffee and doughnuts for all at these weekend rehearsals.[5]

The proposed repeat performance of the *St. Matthew Passion* was indeed undertaken utilizing the

153

newly formed Rutgers University Choir. Accounts of this event state that the "175-voice [Rutgers University] Choir consists of students from New Jersey College for Women, the Men's Colleges and the Newark Colleges of Rutgers, the State University of New Jersey."[6] Choir rehearsals were initially conducted separately; Walter took charge of the Glee Club component while Duncan McKenzie, chairman of the New Jersey College Music Department, rehearsed the women's choir. Leinsdorf conducted a joint rehearsal on January 31, 1951. Thereafter, joint rehearsals were held every Wednesday, Leinsdorf attending approximately twice per month;[7] on those occasions when Leinsdorf was not present, Walter conducted the combined groups.[8]

The orchestral ensemble that Leinsdorf conducted this year, however, was the Philadelphia Orchestra rather than the Rochester Philharmonic, though he continued as the latter's music director until 1955.[9] As planned, the concert took place on Good Friday, March 23, in what was at this point generally referred to as the Rutgers Gymnasium on College Avenue.[10] The work was sung in English, Leinsdorf having furnished his own translation of the original German text by Christian Friedrich Henrici (pen name, Picander), one of Bach's preferred librettists. The performance was generally well received; observers cited the "clarity, the dramatic power, and the depth of feeling" that the combined choir produced.[11]

Erich Leinsdorf rehearsing the University Choir in Schare Recital Hall, February 1951. Special Collections, Rutgers University Libraries.

The 1950–51 season ended for the Glee Club with the annual home concert on May 9 at the Rutgers Gymnasium. In addition to this concert and the Bach *Passion* conducted by Leinsdorf, the group gave ten performances during this season, including a southern tour that took the Club to two Virginia colleges. The usual Glee Club program for this season consisted of Club standards "Brothers, Sing On" and "Feasting I Watch" combined with spirituals like "Wasn't That a Mighty Day" and the traditional Rutgers college songs.[12] Included in the last category during this period were selections such as "A Toast—Down among the Dead Men," "We Sing Thy Praise Old Rutgers," "Down Where the Raritan Flows," and "A Hymn to Queens." Tradition also dictated that, at a final home event such as this one, members of the graduating class stood in front of the Club during the last selection, and the group was led by the outgoing (i.e., graduating) manager of the group. Walter would then lead the audience in "On the Banks" and close the concert with "Vive Les Rutgers' Sons."[13] These final selections were presented without pause, so that the latter was performed *attacca*, for maximum effect.

The University Choir continued its exploration of the works of J. S. Bach during the 1952–53 season.

Group photo, Glee Club, 1950–51 season. Director Walter is seated in the front row, on the far right of the picture. Special Collections, Rutgers University Libraries.

Billed as "the University Choir of Rutgers Glee Club," the combined group performed selections from Bach's *Mass in B Minor*, BWV 232, on May 3, 1953, at the First Presbyterian Church in Newark, with Walter directing.[14]

The 1953–54 season reunited Erich Leinsdorf and the University Choir, this time for a series of three performances. Presented, as was the custom, as part of the concert series, the program featured two choruses from the opera *Boris Godunov* by Mussorgsky and the *Symphony No. 9 in D Minor*, op. 125, by Beethoven. Leinsdorf once again led his home ensemble, the

Rochester Philharmonic Orchestra for this trio of concerts, with assistance from Irene Jordan, soprano; Nell Rankin, contralto; and Mack Harrell, bass, all members of the Metropolitan Opera Company; and Walter Fredericks, tenor, of the New York City Center Opera Company.[15] Performances were given at the Rutgers Gymnasium on March 25, Carnegie Hall in Manhattan on March 26, and the Brooklyn Academy of Music on March 27. Tumultuous applause was said to greet the performers following the Rutgers concert. The crowd was particularly receptive to the choir—reported to be

Rutgers University Choir at Carnegie Hall, March 26, 1954. Behind the podium are F. Austin Walter, Metropolitan Opera bass Mack Harrell, New York City Center Opera Company tenor Walter Fredericks, and Erich Leinsdorf. Rutgers University Glee Club Archives.

two hundred voices—and its director, F. Austin Walter, "the man responsible for the excellent training the young men and women received."[16]

For the 1954–55 season, the Glee Club had a very robust contingent of voices—sixty-one in its entirety: fourteen first tenors, thirteen second tenors, eighteen first basses, and sixteen second basses. F. Austin Walter reportedly "struggled, sweated, and strained" to produce the highly professional qualities for which the Club was so well regarded. There were hopes at the beginning of the year for a trip to Italy to participate in the Florence Music Festival, but this excursion did not occur. Still, the usual events of the season were all in place, and the Club "concert[ed] its collective force in many and varied places throughout New Jersey and neighboring states." The season was capped by a banquet at the Martinsville Inn and, for members who would return the following year, the now traditional reunion at Lake Minnewaska during the summer of 1955.[17]

The Glee Club continued its traditional activities throughout the decade of the 1950s. To be sure, modifications and adjustments were made to accommodate changing circumstances. The annual Winter Weekend festival, usually held at Buck Hill Falls, was moved during the 1955–56 season to the Pocono Manor Inn in Pennsylvania and held during the weekend of January 27–29.[18] The traditional Christmas program at Kirkpatrick Chapel took place on December 18 and consisted of three performances throughout the day (10:45 a.m., 7:30 p.m., and 9:00 p.m.). An additional Christmas concert was presented via television from the WATV (Channel 13) studios in Newark on December 19.[19] And of course, the Glee Club was still called on for important intramural events, such as performing at the thirtieth annual conference of the New Jersey Association of High School Councils, which took place on November 18, 1955, on the Rutgers campus. Dr. Mason W. Gross, provost of the university, greeted the guests; the Glee Club, under Walter's direction, provided a few selections for the occasion.[20]

But certainly, the highlight of the 1955–56 season for the Glee Club was its participation, again via the University Choir, in the concert series. Two performances of *Symphony No. 2* (*Resurrection*) by Gustav Mahler were given in which the choir collaborated with the Philadelphia Orchestra under Eugene Ormandy. The first concert was presented at the Academy of Music in Philadelphia; this was followed up with a performance at the Rutgers Gymnasium on February 27, 1956. Local accounts of this latter event emphasized the fact that the first concert of the newly established Rutgers University Choir, the performance of Bach's *St. Matthew Passion* on March 23, 1951, was undertaken in partnership with the Philadelphia Orchestra. Five years later, the cycle of collaboration was completed with this new joint venture.[21]

It should also be noted that the University Choir, as of 1955, now officially consisted of "the glee clubs from the men's colleges [in New Brunswick] and the Newark Colleges and the Douglass College Choir,"[22] reflecting the conversion of the New Jersey College for Women to the Douglass Residential College in that year.

The presentation of the Mahler symphony was not the only significant event that the University Choir participated in during this season. The choir also appeared with the Baltimore Symphony, under the baton of the Italian American conductor Massimo Freccia, in a performance of Giuseppe Verdi's *Requiem* on March 14. The University Choir—and by extension, the Glee Club—gained even greater public exposure through this concert. The following account appeared in the *Central New Jersey Home News* on March 24, 1956:

Plans of the Voice of America to use recordings of a concert by the 230-voice Rutgers University Choir were revealed today by the United States Information Agency.

Joseph L. Newman of the agency staff said excerpts of a concert in Baltimore, March 14 will be broadcast on the English language "Panorama, USA" program beaming daily to Europe. . . . The series is designed to provide overseas listeners with examples of music by

American symphony orchestras and college bands and glee clubs.[23]

Verdi's *Requiem* would be reprised in the following season (1956–57), this time with an extremely distinguished group of soloists. Verdi's work—at this time often referred to as the *Manzoni Requiem*, as it was dedicated by the composer to the memory of the Italian poet and novelist Alessandro Manzoni (1785–1873)—was performed at the Rutgers Gymnasium on February 18, 1957. The University Choir this time joined the Philadelphia Orchestra under Eugene Ormandy to present this work as part of the concert series. The cast of soloists was truly extraordinary, including Leontyne Price, soprano; Nan Merriman, mezzo-soprano; Richard Tucker, tenor; and Giorgi Tozzi, bass. The *Requiem* had been given the previous evening for Philadelphia audiences and would be repeated the following evening, February 19, 1957, at Carnegie Hall.

Reaction to the performance of the University Choir was once again favorable: "The choir, with F. Austin Walter, director, was widely admired throughout the audience, not only for its excellent singing but for its usual dignity, that bespeaks many months of training and planning. This group is certainly the type of which the university can be proud, knowing that no matter where the young singers appear they will be a credit to the school they represent."[24]

F. Austin Walter conducts the Glee Club in 1957. Special Collections, Rutgers University Libraries.

The annual spring concert was given by the Club on May 6, 1957, at the gymnasium. The program that was presented varied only slightly from those that were employed earlier in the decade. The first part of the concert offered the familiar "Brothers, Sing On" by Grieg and "Fain Would I Change That Note" by Vaughn Williams along with newer additions, such as "To Music" by Schubert and "The Broken Melody" by Sibelius. A series of baritone solos, also customary during this period, followed. The ensuing segment of the program, featuring a series of contemporary works,

offered the greatest departure from earlier presentations: "Sam Was a Man" by Vincent Persichetti, "Here is thy Footstool" by Paul Creston, and "Father William" by Irving Fine. Four Negro spirituals followed: "My Lord, What a Morning," "Water Boy," "I'm a Rollin'," and "Let Us Break Bread Together." Longtime favorite "When Johnny Came Down to Hilo" led into a Trinidadian calypso number, "Marry a Woman Uglier Than You." The evening concluded with selections by the latest iteration of a four-man ensemble, "The Queensmen," who apparently sang in the style of a barbershop quartet, and traditional college songs by the complete Club.[25]

In the 1957–58 season, Erich Leinsdorf returned to Rutgers to again lead a distinguished instrumental ensemble and the Rutgers University Choir in a performance of Bach's *St. Matthew Passion*. The orchestra that Leinsdorf led for this occasion, however, had something of an air of notoriety about it. Known as the Symphony of the Air, it had enjoyed a previous life as the NBC Symphony Orchestra under the eminent Italian conductor Arturo Toscanini. The *Passion* was performed three times. The first concert was given at the Rutgers Gymnasium on March 25, 1958. This was followed by performances at Newark's Mosque Theater on March 27 and at Carnegie Hall on March 28. As in previous concert series productions, these performances employed an impressive array of highly regarded soloists: Maria Stader, soprano; Blanche Thebom, Metropolitan Opera mezzo-soprano; Swedish tenor Nicolai Gedda; and famed Bach interpreters Kenneth Smith (bass-baritone) and Norman Farrow (bass). Daphne Powell was the harpsichordist for the work, with David Drinkwater playing the organ.[26]

The 1958–59 season was a busy and eventful one. With a robust complement of sixty-five voices for this season, the Club performed their regular program for twelve regional engagements at venues in New Jersey, New York, and Pennsylvania.[27] The winter house party event at the Pocono Manor Inn took place, as usual, during the semester break, this year during the weekend of January 23 to 25; the Glee Club's firelight concert on Friday evening was a featured attraction.[28] And in their role as the quintessential performing group at the university, the Club was front and center at the 150th-anniversary celebration for the Old Queens Building that took place on April 27. Speeches by university president Mason Gross and university historian Richard Patrick McCormick were followed by selections from the Club.[29]

Fittingly, what might be considered the climax of the season, and perhaps the decade, occurred in late April and early May. At that time, the University Choir presented a series of four concerts, from April 30 through May 3, at Carnegie Hall with the New York Philharmonic Orchestra under Leonard Bernstein. In commemoration of the two hundredth anniversary of

the death of the German composer and longtime resident of England George Frideric Handel (1685–1759), the University Choir joined with the Philharmonic in performing Handel's *Ode for St. Cecilia's Day*, HWV 76, a cantata set to a text by the English poet John Dryden. Soloists for the performances included soprano Adele Addison and tenor John McCollum. It was also announced at this time that the University Choir would offer for commercial release a recording of these performances.[30] The choir's participation in prestigious events such as outlined here is indicative of the level of achievement that was in evidence since the initial unification of the various choral units. Credit for this impressive list of achievements throughout the decade of the 1950s goes first, of course, to the students, whose enthusiasm, dedication, and inherent talent were necessary to the proper realization of the complex works performed during this period. But credit must also be given to the University Choir's director, F. Austin Walter, whose clear vision for this combined entity made possible the impressive collaborations that brought prestige and honor to the university and enhanced the reputation of Rutgers as an artistically adept, progressive educational institution throughout the country.

But as the University Choir (and by extension, the Glee Club) continued to thrive, another aspect of the vibrant musical scene at Rutgers was eclipsing. At the final concert series performance of the 1958–59 season, a concert on April 7 that featured Eugene Ormandy and the Philadelphia Orchestra, university president Mason Gross announced that the forty-three-year career of Howard D. McKinney at Rutgers—College and University—would end when he stepped down from all duties in the Music Department at the end of the academic year. McKinney, class of '13, whose career at Rutgers began in 1916, would leave the university with a Music Department that offered thriving ensembles and vibrant programs in music history, theory, and appreciation. The concert series, though, might be the crowning achievement associated with McKinney's legacy. Having initiated the series in 1916, by the time of this announcement, it had grown to be recognized as a vehicle through which the best musical talent of the day could be offered to both university students and the local townspeople in an effort to allow them, as McKinney put it, "to understand music's role as an important part of everyday life."[31]

At the ceremony following the concert, which had been secretly arranged by Gross with the cooperation of Ormandy, McKinney was presented with a gift of great significance to him:

> McKinney, who has long had a strong liking for the music of Wagner, was given two first editions of that composer's operas. He received the engraved full score of "Die Meistersinger,"

printed in German in Mainz in 1868, and the lithographed full score of "Lohengrin" published in Leipzig in 1852. It is thought that this edition consisted of only 60 copies when first printed.

> Both volumes contained a specially designed bookplate, noting their presentation to McKinney . . .

> After the presentation ceremonies, Ormandy conducted the Philadelphia Orchestra in the prelude to the third act of Lohengrin. This unexpected addition to the program of the concert was also in tribute to McKinney.[32]

To be sure, the concert series would continue. The program for the following season, which would again include an appearance by the Philadelphia Orchestra, was announced at the same time as McKinney's retirement. However, for the first time in decades, McKinney would not be in direct control of the series events, though he would occasionally participate by way of preconcert lectures and other ancillary activities as the years passed.[33] Administration of the series would fall to Julius Bloom, '33, a former teacher of philosophy at Rutgers and longtime director of the Brooklyn Academy of Arts and Sciences. In 1959, Bloom was appointed director of concerts and lectures at Rutgers, placing the series under his control.[34] He would also serve as the executive director of Carnegie Hall beginning in 1960.[35]

HOWARD DECKER MCKINNEY

(1889–1980)

It is incontestable that the Music Department at Rutgers University as it exists today—a highly regarded and vibrant entity situated within an equally well-known School of the Arts—was, to a large extent, the creation of Howard Decker McKinney. Musing about the development of the music program at Rutgers on the occasion of his retirement in 1959, McKinney recalled that "in 1916 [when he first took up his position at Rutgers] there was an informal singing group which would perform in the [Kirkpatrick] Chapel on Sunday, but that was about the extent of the program."[36] Over the ensuing several decades, McKinney would systematically add courses to and develop ensembles for the nascent music programs at Rutgers College as well as its sister institution, the New Jersey College for Women, while simultaneously initiating a series of concerts at the men's college that would bring students, faculty, and New Brunswick citizens into close contact with some of the major musical artists of the early and mid-twentieth century.

McKinney was born in Pine Bush, New York, on May 29, 1889, to John L. and Marianna McKinney. He attended Middletown High School in Middletown, New York, before enrolling at Rutgers College in the fall of 1909. As stated in the accompanying narrative, McKinney's involvement in the

Howard Decker McKinney, Glee Club director 1916–46.
Special Collections, Rutgers University Libraries.

combined Glee and Mandolin Clubs began during his freshman year at the college, when he joined the group as their pianist; in his senior year, he was elected president of the combined clubs. McKinney was also a member of the Delta Upsilon fraternity and was inducted into the honor society Phi Beta Kappa during his undergraduate years. On completion of his bachelor of letters (B Litt) degree in 1913, McKinney undertook graduate studies in New York, enrolling at Columbia University under the tutelage of the American composer and music critic Daniel Gregory Mason (1873–1953). For a short period, he held a position as professor of music at St. Paul's School in Garden City, New York, but he left this post in 1915 to continue his musical studies in New York.[37] He took private instruction during this time in organ from T. Tertius Nobel (1867–1953) and in composition from the famed American composer Ernest Bloch (1880–1959).[38]

McKinney returned to the New Brunswick area in 1916 and immediately renewed his association with the Rutgers College Glee Club. His efforts in producing a new edition of the *Songs of Rutgers* in 1916 led to him being named as the new coach of the combined Musical Clubs. Though hardly his only duty as the newly appointed musical director at the college, McKinney's efforts with the Rutgers Glee (and Mandolin) Club over the next decades went far in establishing that group as the premier performing organization of the college/university.

As part of his extensive duties, McKinney immediately instituted a tradition of concerts that came eventually to be known as the Rutgers winter concert series. Early press notices concerning these events described them as "a series of high-class concerts . . . under the direction of H. McKinney, director of music at Rutgers College."[39] This series would become a cherished tradition at Rutgers for decades, providing an opportunity for members of the Rutgers student performing ensembles, including the Glee Club, to work with some of the greatest musical talents of the period on masterworks from the vocal/instrumental repertory.

McKinney was an accomplished organist and pianist, serving as an instructor of those instruments for generations of Rutgers students. He published several editions of organ works, including *Preludes for Fifty-Five Well-Known Hymn Tunes* (New York: J. Fischer, 1968), the subtitle of which states that these works are "modeled after the free organ accompaniments of T. Tertius Noble." He was also the composer of *A Mystery for Christmas*, a Yule play/cantata based on art forms of the Middle Ages and Renaissance periods, also published by Fischer. Though trained as a performer and composer in the works of the great masters of Western art music, McKinney was an avid proponent of the new musical styles that were emerging in the early twentieth century, both art music and popular.

McKinney was a well-known and highly regarded author. His first book, *Discovering Music: A Course in Music Appreciation* (New York: American Book Company, 1934) was written in collaboration with W. R. Anderson, a music critic and lecturer at Morley College in London. The pair subsequently produced the volume *Music in History: The Evolution of an Art* (New York: American Book Company, 1940), followed by *The Challenge of Listening* (New Brunswick, N.J.: Rutgers University Press, 1943) and *How to Listen to Good Music* (New York: Blue Ribbon, 1947). These works, like many of the lectures that McKinney presented at Rutgers College, sought to introduce the reader to the art of critical listening through engagement with various aspects of music history, tradition, and performance practice. Working alone, McKinney produced *Music and Man: A General Outline of a Course in Music Appreciation* (New York: American Book Company, 1948), which sought to expand on the concepts of his previous books by extending the reference points of the listener to diverse yet connected ideas in seemingly dissimilar art forms.

For his years of dedicated service, McKinney received three of the highest honors that Rutgers can bestow. In 1940, he was awarded the honorary degree of doctor of letters; in 1953, he was presented with the Rutgers University Medal; and in 1954, he was among the first recipients of the distinguished research awards given by the Rutgers Research Council Advisory Board.[40]

McKinney retired from his university duties in 1959 at the age of seventy after forty-three years of distinguished service as a music professor, composer, author, and concert impresario. Upon retirement, he was granted the title of professor emeritus of Rutgers College. The class of 1963 honored McKinney's myriad achievements by dedicating that year's issue of *The Scarlet Letter* to him, noting that "his career as a composer, pianist, and lecturer enabled him to bring a world of song to Rutgers."[41] He was further honored by the university in 1970 by having the musical activities building at the corner of Hamilton Street and Easton Avenue on the College Avenue Campus named McKinney Hall.[42]

Howard D. McKinney died on September 26, 1980, at the age of ninety-one at his residence in the Francis E. Parker Memorial Home in Piscataway, New Jersey, after what was described as a long illness. A memorial service was held in his honor on Sunday, October 19, 1980, at 1:00 p.m. at Kirkpatrick Chapel. He was interred at the Bruynswick Rural Cemetery in Wallkill, New York.[43]

The 1960s: International Travel

McKinney's replacement as chairman of the Music Department was Dr. Alfred B. Mann, who had come to Rutgers in 1947 following his studies at Columbia University. Mann was trained as a musicologist; his field of specialization was in the history of music theory, particularly the writings of the Austrian theorist and pedagogue Johann Joseph Fux (1660–1741). Mann was an ardent supporter of the performing musician, encouraging students in these endeavors through his writings for collected editions of Fux, Handel, Mozart, and Schubert.[44] Mann also organized early music concerts in the department, featuring works by Handel, Telemann, and Mozart.[45] Thus the oversight of the Music Department performing groups was in capable hands.

The Glee Club continued under the direction of Walter into the new decade. Collaborations with other choral groups were still part of the group's procedures. On October 23, 1959, the Club joined with the glee club of Princeton to present a concert at the Trenton War Memorial Building. Each group offered independent selections but joined for a performance of a TTBB arrangement of "Stomp Your Foot," an accompanied choral work extracted from the opera *The Tender Land* by Aaron Copland. More traditional programs were given in local venues such as Metuchen (March 2, 1960) and East Brunswick (March 18, 1960). However, the Club was fortunate enough to receive an opportunity to greatly expand its operational ambitus when the Rutgers Club of Southern California extended an invitation for the group to perform in that state.[46] The proposed tour would be the longest in the history of the Glee Club to date, taking place during the spring recess in March of 1960.

The excursion was largely underwritten by the Southern California organization, but the effort was also aided by contributions from the university, other alumni groups, student groups, and the Rutgers Parents Association. Five concerts were planned for the Club, which had fifty-five members during the 1959–60 season. Venues included an initial performance at Disneyland, followed by stops at Chapman College in Orange, the Civic Auditorium in Pasadena, Royce Hall on the campus of the University of California at Los Angeles (UCLA), and the Civic Auditorium in Santa Monica. Accompanying the group were Walter, director; Ernest T. Gardner, director of alumni relations at Rutgers; and Edgar G. Curtin, associate dean of men. The trip lasted eight days; the group boarded an American Airlines 707, nicknamed the "Flagship California," at Idlewild Airport on Saturday, March 26, and was back in New Brunswick on Sunday, April 3.[47]

There is an interesting anecdote associated with this trip concerning a disappointed Glee Club aspirant. In May of 1960, renowned bandleader and star of radio and television Oswald George "Ozzie" Nelson, '27, was in New Brunswick to serve as master of ceremonies at the Cap and Skull Society reunion. Also

The Glee Club departs from Idlewild Airport in New York for their California tour, March 26, 1960. Special Collections, Rutgers University Libraries.

performing at the ceremony was the Glee Club quartet "The Queensmen." Ozzie took the opportunity to tell the tale of how, after having heard the Glee Club perform at a concert in Hackensack in 1925, he had decided to try out for the group. He was, however, unceremoniously turned away. Ozzie related that, despite this rebuff, he went away feeling that the Club's decision had been hasty and that he indeed should have been welcomed into the group. However, as Ozzie related to the audience that evening, when he heard the Glee Club in California a few weeks prior to this occasion, he understood that their evaluation in 1925 had been

correct. "I didn't realize until a couple of weeks ago I was wrong all along," Nelson joked. After hearing the Club during its California trip, Nelson said, "that's when I knew the Glee Club director 30 years ago knew what he was doing when he turned me down."[48]

During the 1960–61 season, the group stayed closer to home, giving thirteen concerts at local venues.[49] But that did not deter the Club from continuing in its efforts to enhance its profile. On January 25, 1961, the group received what was termed "a signal honor" when they were chosen to be the first group to appear on a new radio show on WCBS dedicated to presenting collegiate musical offerings.[50] And the annual visit to the Pocono Manor Inn was again part of the Club's January agenda.

The season ended with the spring concert (known in earlier years as the "home concert") at the Rutgers Gymnasium on Friday, May 5. In addition to the usual fare of college songs and spirituals, this year's program, as exhibited at this performance, included works from composers such as Brahms, Bach, Handel, and Sibelius. Also featured on the program was a series of solo folk songs and the Queensmen, who performed in their usual barbershop style.

It should also be mentioned that the Kirkpatrick Chapel Choir presented an hour-long concert of sacred music on May 7, 1961. The choir of forty voices offered the Fauré *Requiem* and a motet by Johannes Brahms, "Create in Me a Clean Heart," op. 27, no. 2. Led by David A. Drinkwater, organist and choirmaster of Kirkpatrick Chapel, this event marked the first independent performance in the choir's history; prior to this, the group had only performed with the Glee Club, notably at the annual Christmas concerts.[51]

On February 26, 1962, the male members of the Rutgers Glee Club and the University Choir appeared with

The Glee Club performs at the Pocono Manor Inn, January 1961. Special Collections, Rutgers University Libraries.

the Yale Concert Band, conducted by Keith Wilson, at the Rutgers Gymnasium. The band was staffed by seventy-five instrumentalists, while the chorus numbered seventy participants. The program consisted of works by twentieth-century composers, including Wallingford Riegger, Jacques Ibert, Paul Hindemith, Robert Ward, and Randall Thompson. Thompson's *The Testament of Freedom*, which the Glee Club had performed in 1948 with Erich Leinsdorf and the Rochester Philharmonic, was a good example of the modern ethos invoked at this concert. The work is set in four passages, which are adapted from the writings of Thomas Jefferson.

The direction of the ensemble for this performance passed between Wilson and F. Austin Walter. Walter presided over both ensembles in the Thompson piece, while Wilson led many of the purely instrumental works, such as Hindemith's *Symphonic Metamorphosis on Themes by Carl Maria von Weber* and Riegger's *Dance Rhythms*. Encores included several Yale college songs arranged for the band, and "On the Banks" was rendered by the Rutgers chorus.[52]

At the intermission of this concert, Julius Bloom, director of concerts and lectures for Rutgers, made an announcement of great significance for the Rutgers choral groups. He disclosed that selected members of the two organizations represented at this performance—the Yale Concert Band and the Rutgers contingent of singers—would be sent to Norway during the summer of 1962 to attend the Bergen International Festival on June 6. This festival, a major annual European event, was founded by the Norwegian composer Edvard Grieg and perpetuated in his honor. Both groups would send approximately sixty members on the trip; initial plans called for them to leave for Norway on June 4. Wilson was tasked with leading the Yale contingent (which was listed as the Yale Wind Symphony for the Norway event), while Walter, as in this concert, would lead the ensemble in joint performances of the combined groups. Also accompanying the groups were Howard J. Crosby, the associate dean of men at Rutgers who served as the student counselor, and Peter Pastrich, a Yale graduate and manager of the Greenwich Village Symphony who acted as the tour manager.[53]

This was, by far, the most extensive excursion in the history of the Glee Club; though it must be said, this was an expanded form of the Club, to be sure, with the inclusion of the Yale component. Further, it represented the first international trip in the Club's history, the planned 1936 excursion to Bermuda having been canceled due to the death of King George V. And by all accounts, it was extremely successful. The tour lasted nearly a month, with the Rutgers group returning to the New Brunswick area on June 29. The first stop of the journey was for the festival at Bergen, but concerts were also given at Voss and Oslo, Norway; Copenhagen, Denmark; Hamburg, Germany; and, finally, Amsterdam, Heerlen, and Hengelo, the Netherlands to close the tour. The local news outlets were favorably impressed

The Rutgers Glee Club and the Yale Wind Symphony perform during the Club's first European excursion, 1962. Special Collections, Rutgers University Libraries.

with the groups, particularly so in the Netherlands and Norway. There was also ample free time, during which many of the students engaged in side trips to Paris and Rome. All concerned considered the experience to be a rewarding educational experience as well as an exciting adventure.[54]

The 1962–63 concert series had included performances of the Philadelphia Orchestra under Ormandy combined with the University Choir, this time in a performance of Beethoven's *Symphony No. 9* on November 27, 1962.[55] It was, then, no surprise when the schedule announced for the following season of

the concert series again included the Philadelphia ensemble. In collaboration with the choir, a series of six performances of two works by Johannes Brahms—*Ein deutsches Requiem*, op. 45, and *Schicksalslied*, op. 54—was slated. Included in these performances was a concert scheduled for November 25, 1963, at the Rutgers Gymnasium and one at Carnegie Hall the following evening.[56] Performances at the Philadelphia Academy of Music on November 18 and the Lyric Theater in Baltimore on November 20 were also to be presented.[57]

Tragic events, however, would necessitate an addition to this already ambitious schedule. On

F. Austin Walter conducts the Glee Club in a concert given at the Heerlen City Hall, June 21, 1962. Special Collections, Rutgers University Libraries.

November 22, 1963, President John F. Kennedy was shot in Dallas, Texas, and taken to the Parkland Hospital in that city, where he passed away. Shortly after news of the president's death was announced, Ormandy contacted Walter and made a request: "[Ormandy] asked if [Walter] could bring the choir to Philadelphia the next day to make a video tape for telecasting on CBS that night. Walter and his talented charges complied and performed admirably."[58]

The resulting performance was broadcast from 9:00 to 10:30 p.m. on the evening of November 23, 1963, and included both of the Brahms works. As a further tribute to the fallen president, the November 25 concert at the Rutgers Gymnasium was given as scheduled. The audience of over 3,000 visibly distraught people marked the occasion as a solemn one by refraining from applause at any time during the event. University president Mason Gross dedicated the performance "as an expression of our deep sorrow on the death of John F. Kennedy." Indeed, the November 25 concert took on a decidedly reverential tone. All involved remarked on the extraordinary efforts of the choir; Ormandy described the group as "ready to drop from exhaustion, . . . but they kept on giving their all."[59]

During the ensuing spring semester, the University Choir would have a major role in a concert series performance featuring the American Symphony Orchestra under Leopold Stokowski. The program of the February 26, 1964, event at the Rutgers Gymnasium included a variety of orchestral works, including *Symphony No. 88* by Joseph Haydn. The featured performer, however, was Metropolitan Opera mezzo-soprano Nell Rankin. Ms. Rankin sang the aria "Es is vollbracht" from J. S. Bach's *St. John Passion* and was the soloist for the highlight of the concert, the cantata *Alexander Nevsky*, op. 78, by the Russian composer Sergei Prokofiev, derived from the music composed for the film of the same name.

This concert marked the first appearance by Stokowski and his orchestra at Rutgers.[60]

By the 1965–66 season, the Rutgers Glee Club was enjoying robust growth and an excellent reputation. A seventy-five-man group at the beginning of this academic year, the Club had earned the admiration of audiences throughout the country as well as within the university community. This reputation was certainly enhanced through its association with the University Choir and the series of impressive concerts that the Club experienced as part of that group during the 1950s and early 1960s. But on its own, the Glee Club was achieving equally impressive results through its customary activities and beyond. The Club got an early start this season, presenting concerts at Columbia University, at Rutgers with the Columbia Glee Club, and in Wayne, New Jersey, all in the months of October and November.[61] A traditional schedule of local concerts followed, such as the performance at the Madison Township, New Jersey, high school on November 20, 1965. There, and during other such concerts this season, the Club performed a mixture of traditional spirituals, Rutgers college songs, and in keeping with the practice of recent years, a good amount of more serious art-music works, including pieces by Schubert, Poulenc, Sibelius, Handel, and Bach. Announcements for concerts during this period could boast of the group's recent successes, including the California excursion as well as its European tour with the Yale Wind Symphony. They could also call attention to the latest record album, which had recently been released on the Imperial label with the help of Rutgers alumnus and friend of the Club Ozzie Nelson, '27.[62] The relationship with Nelson had been reinforced during the 1963–64 season. Nelson was chosen Rutgers Alumnus of the Year and received that honor at the All-Rutgers Alumni Dinner at the Far Hills Inn in Somerville, New Jersey, on April 4, 1964.[63] As might be expected, the Glee Club performed for this occasion.[64]

But perhaps the most excitement that was generated during the 1965–66 season concerned the Glee Club's plans for the bicentennial celebration at Rutgers the following year. Discussions were already underway as to the best way to procure funding for a projected European tour during the summer of 1966. The proposed trip would last from June 2 to June 26, 1966. The announced objectives of the trip were as follows: "The Glee Club's Bicentennial European Tour [seeks] first, to bring recognition to the University in New Jersey and the United States, and second to raise funds for the extension and recognition of the college in its bicentennial year throughout the states and Europe."[65] To that end, the group actively sought support from students, alumni, and friends of the Glee Club, as well as from the university, and indeed, contributions from the members themselves, in order to make this dream a reality.[66] This effort included a benefit concert on May 1, 1966, at Symphony Hall in Newark. May 1 was declared by New Jersey governor Richard J. Hughes as "America Sings Day" in honor of the Glee Club's upcoming European tour. Hughes hosted the benefit event and Senators Clifford P. Case and Harrison A. Williams were its cochairs. At this concert, the sixty-man group slated to make the trip previewed the program that would be presented, which included "representative American songs, ranging from 'The Star-Spangled Banner' and 'America' to spirituals and folk music."[67]

The Glee Club left for its bicentennial concert tour of Europe on May 30, 1966, from Kennedy Airport. The actual on-departure count of the Club membership for the trip was sixty-three men. Accompanying the group was Barry M. Millett, associate dean of men at Rutgers. Walter, who would, of course, serve as the Club's director, left for Europe two days later, on June 1.[68] The first stop on the tour was at Amsterdam on June 2, where the Club sang at the auditorium of the Heineken Brewery. Following the concert, a dance was held; the Heineken company had arranged for eighty young women from the American Institute to attend.

The second concert was given in Utrecht. This performance was significant for several of the Club members. Having left the country before the commencement ceremonies for the 1965–66 academic year, eight members of the graduating class had not been able to accept their diplomas. Walter had stayed behind, not only to collect these diplomas for the men but to properly acknowledge his own receipt of

an honorary degree from Rutgers as well. At a formal reception following the concert given at the University of Utrecht, the diplomas of the seniors were distributed to their recipients by the *Rector Magnificus* of that university, Dr. H. M. J. Scheffer.[69]

Two additional concerts were given in the Netherlands, one at the United States Air Force Base at Soesterberg. The Club then proceeded to Munich, Germany, via rail, a journey of approximately twelve hours duration. The Munich concert took place at the Technological University on June 10; this performance was followed by concerts at Lüneburg and Hamburg. There were also programs given at Echternach, Luxembourg, where the group performed on the steps of the town hall, and Paris on the evening of June 16 at the American Students' and Artists' Foundation. The final concert of the tour took place the following evening at the opera house in Orleans, for "perhaps the most enthusiastic [audience] of the entire tour. The sold[-]out house's rhythmic clapping thundered through the hall at the concert's end." At the expedition's conclusion, the Rutgers students were given six days in which to tour the continent as they liked. Popular destinations for the men were London, Copenhagen, Vienna, and return trips to Amsterdam.[70]

Glee Club life resumed its usual routine following the return of the group from their European excursion. The annual Christmas concert with the

University Hall at Utrecht University, 1966. Special Collections, Rutgers University Libraries.

Kirkpatrick Chapel Choir was a two-night event this season (1966); two performances were given on Sunday evening, December 18, as well as one on the following evening, all at the chapel.[71] This concert was preceded by a similar event at the Second Reformed Church in Somerville, New Jersey, on December 4, also featuring both groups.[72] Glee Club personnel were again employed in the University Choir for a concert on March 2, 1967, at the Rutgers Gymnasium. Erich Leinsdorf returned, this time directing the Boston Symphony Orchestra. The Choir joined with the Orchestra for the first half of the program, in which they presented the *Mass in Bb Major* (*Harmoniemesse*) of Joseph Haydn. Soloists for this performance were, as usual, of the highest caliber: Beverly Sills, soprano; Beverly Wolff, contralto; Placido Domingo, tenor; and Ara Berberian, bass. This concert was the fourth in a series of five that presented this program. The fifth and final concert in the series took place at Carnegie Hall on March 4.[73]

The University Choir was also invited to participate in the opening ceremonies for the Expo '67 World Festival in Montreal. The group performed Beethoven's *Symphony No. 9* with the Montreal Symphony Orchestra directed by Wilfred Peletier. Two performances were to be given at the Place des Arts in Montreal, on April 30 and May 1.[74]

Though the Montreal event was, to be sure, a prestigious one, the University Choir was slated to be part of an even more illustrious ceremony in

173

the following semester. In October of 1967, it was announced that the Russian composer and conductor Igor Stravinsky would be awarded an honorary doctor of music degree from Rutgers on October 21. The award was to be presented during a concert that evening with the French National Orchestra. Stravinsky himself was to conduct the concert, with assistance from his close associate, the American conductor and author Robert Craft. Scheduled as the highlight of a ten-day music-lecture series on Stravinsky's music held at the university, the program consisted of the composer's *Le Sacre du Printemps*, *Symphony of Psalms*, and a new work completed less than a year earlier, *Requiem Canticles*.[75]

However, it was announced on October 17 that Stravinsky had fallen ill and would not be able to accept his honorary degree nor conduct the concert on October 21.[76] A replacement was subsequently found that allowed the performance to continue. Jean Martinon, at the time music director of the Chicago Symphony Orchestra, was available. As a well-known exponent of Stravinsky's works, Martinon was able to step in with minimal preparation. By all accounts, the concert was a great success, attended by 3,000 enthusiastic supporters of the musical efforts of the University Choir.[77]

Prestigious events were to be found everywhere for the choir during the fall of 1967. On October 24, 1967, the University Choir performed in the Assembly Hall of the United Nations in Manhattan as part of the annual United Nations Day celebrations. The Vienna Symphony Orchestra was the guest ensemble for this year. The choir was to assist them in a performance of Beethoven's *Choral Fantasy*, op. 80, for piano, vocal soloists, chorus, and orchestra, with the Cuban American virtuoso Jorge Bolet as piano soloist. U.N. Secretary-General U Thant spoke during the intermission of the concert, which was attended by Rutgers University president Mason Gross.[78]

In April of 1968, the Glee Club held an event that was often referred to as "Fun Night." This occasion had become somewhat of a tradition over the past several years. It was essentially a concert; a traditional program was presented. The first half of the performance consisted of English glees, music of a sacred nature, some Romantic works, and a few contemporary American pieces. After a brief intermission, the second half found the men singing folk songs, spirituals, and songs of Rutgers.

The highlight of the evening, however, came at the conclusion of the program, "when the Glee Club members gleefully toss[ed] their officers into the [gymnasium] swimming pool" (hence, the "fun" part). But this year, there was also an important announcement to be made. The proceeds of this concert would be put toward funding the group's third trip to Europe during this decade. This tour would begin immediately after commencement exercises on May 29 and would include stops at the Netherlands, Luxembourg, Germany, Sweden, and Denmark.[79] The challenges faced on this tour, including long train rides and what were contemporarily described as "sometimes strange conditions" were all happily endured, "earn[ing] the praises of audiences everywhere."[80]

The Glee Club continued the traveling tradition during the following academic year (1968–69) by embarking on a nine-day tour of the Virgin Islands on March 21, 1969. The fifty-seven-man Club, who were lauded as "ambassadors of good will and culture," gave a series of performances that were aimed primarily at student audiences, from the elementary level to college. The group performed at St. Thomas, Tortola, and St. Croix. The men were also treated to a free day in Puerto Rico at the end of the tour.[81]

The season, and the decade, ended with the annual spring concert at the Rutgers Gymnasium on April 18, 1969. The program contained "a wide-ranging selection of works, classical and contemporary, serious and humorous." Two Glee Club quartets, "The Dutchmen" and "The Quarter Tones," appeared on this program. Selections by the entire Club included the spiritual "Water Boy" and a calypso number, "Man Piaba."[82]

Glee Club group photo 1968–69 season. Director Walter and Tosci, Walter's faithful dog, are front row center. Special Collections, Rutgers University Libraries.

GLEE CLUB ON THE ROAD
Sixty Years of International Travel

The Rutgers Glee Club has always been a peripatetic organization. From the earliest years, particularly under the direction of Loren Bragdon, the Club's first professional leader, a core objective of the group was to showcase the best that Rutgers had to offer to the world at large. During the 1880s under Bragdon, the Club embraced this ideal by engaging in extended excursions to a variety of locations within the United States. These trips included visits to Maine, Virginia, and St. Augustine, Florida. It was also during this period that a series of tours of the Hudson River area of upstate New York was instituted, a tradition that would continue for several decades under a variety of Club leaders. Bragdon also commenced a series of tours of the southern United States, giving performances at locations in Virginia as well as North and South Carolina, a practice that was continued by his successor, George Wilmot. And of course, travel within the New York / New Jersey / Pennsylvania region was always a main feature of the Club's schedule.

In the 1930s, with Howard McKinney as director and his protégé F. Austin Walter serving as conductor, the value of travel in displaying the talents and virtues of the burgeoning college/university was equally evident. To that end, in addition to the Club's continued schedule of tours within the United

States, a few forays into international travel were scheduled but abandoned; a planned trip to Bermuda in 1936, for example, had to be canceled due to the death of King George V in January of that year. But the idea of international travel remained tantalizing, especially for F. Austin Walter.

An invitation to tour Southern California in 1960 resulted in the longest and most geographically far-reaching excursion in Club history to that point. The success of this effort demonstrated to Walter, now Club director, the practicality and, indeed, utility, of such extended trips in achieving the goal of exhibiting the considerable capabilities of his organization. When an opportunity arose in 1962 for the Glee Club to attend the Bergen International Music Festival together with the Yale Wind Symphony, Walter immediately agreed. This highly successful tour paved the way for a series of such events over the ensuing decades.

Walter presided over a total of ten such trips between 1962 and 1982. Patrick Gardner has continued the tradition; he has facilitated what he refers to as "once-in-a-college-lifetime" tours every four years, with minor variances to accommodate certain circumstances, during his time as Club director (1993–present). The list provides dates and other information about these international excursions. A separate list for extended tours within the United States and its territories has also been provided. Further information on each of these events can be found in the general narrative.

International Tours

Year	General area of travel	Miscellaneous (other participants, venues, comments, etc.)
1962	Bergen Music Festival, Norway. Also Denmark, Germany, and the Netherlands	With the Yale Wind Symphony. Concerts at the Aula at the University of Oslo and the *Grosse Musikhalle* in Hamburg.
1966	The Netherlands (Holland), Germany, Luxembourg, and France	1966 bicentennial tour. Concerts at Amsterdam, Utrecht, Hamburg, Lüneburg.
1968	The Netherlands (Holland), Germany, Luxembourg, Sweden, and Denmark	Travel by train from Stockholm to Copenhagen. Concert at the *Amerika Haus* in Frankfurt canceled due to the assassination of Robert F. Kennedy.
1970	The Netherlands (Holland), France, Luxembourg, Italy	High Mass at the Cathedral of St. Gatien.
1971	Czechoslovakia	First tour behind the Iron Curtain. Prague, Brno, Bratislava.
1973	Germany, Austria, Hungary, Italy, the Netherlands (Holland)	Glee Club is joined by a chamber ensemble from the Kirkpatrick Chapel Choir.
1975	Romania	Bucharest and other locations.
1978	Italy, Germany, the Netherlands (Holland), Denmark, France, and Belgium	Final program of the tour, at High Mass celebrating the Feast of St. John, given at the Duomo in Florence.
1980	Morocco, Spain, and Portugal	First tour to Africa.
1982	France, Germany, Italy, the Netherlands (Holland)	Final tour for F. Austin Walter.
1989	Hungary	Arranged through the Friendship Ambassadors Foundation, New York.
1991	Mexico	Performances at the *Iglesia de San Francisco* in Mexico City and the Church of Santa Prisca in Taxco de Alarcón.
1996	Poland, Lithuania, Estonia, Russia, Finland (brief stopover in London, England)	First overseas tour under the direction of Patrick Gardner.
1999	Hungary, Austria, Slovakia	Recording session at the Berlin *Heilig-Kreuz-Kirche*.
2003	Germany and France	Concert at Notre Dame Cathedral, Paris.
2007	The Netherlands, Germany,	Concerts at the *Dreikönigskirche* in Dresden and the *Thomaskirche* in Leipzig.
2011	Italy	Performance at St. Mark's Basilica in Venice
2015	United Kingdom and the Netherlands	Concerts at Gloucester Cathedral and University Hall in the *Academiegebouw* at Utrecht.
2018	Estonia	Concerts in the cities of Tartu and Tallinn.

Tours within the United States and Its Territories

Year	General area of travel	Miscellaneous
1960	Southern California	First West Coast tour.
1969	U.S. Virgin Islands	St. Thomas, St. Croix, etc.
1976	U.S. Virgin Islands	Full concert at the St. Croix Island Center.
1985	Domestic tour	Washington, D.C., Los Angeles, San Francisco, Dallas, etc.
1986	Puerto Rico	Frederic Ford, director. Concerts at the University of Mayagüez and the Inter American University in San Juan.
1993	Southeast United States	Bruce Kolb, director

GLEE CLUB AND THE GRIDIRON

Early Involvement and a Continuing Tradition

Rutgers College/University has always had strong connections to the development and popularization of the game of American football. The first intercollegiate football game took place at Rutgers College; on November 6, 1869, the Rutgers squad defeated the team from Princeton by a score of six goals to four. Such contests quickly became a staple of college life at Rutgers, providing the students with an exciting and invigorating diversion from the routine of their studies.

So prominent was Rutgers in the evolution of the game that its football team members were sought out for a developmental conference in New York City in 1873, the purpose of which was to "to organize the first intercollegiate football association and define a uniform game."[83] Among the Rutgers participants chosen to serve on this committee was Howard Newton Fuller, at that time the sitting president of the Rutgers College Foot Ball Association. Fuller is also renowned in Rutgers lore as the author of the lyrics for "On the Banks of the Old Raritan," which were set to music in the same year as this conference (see chap. 1 sidebar, "Howard Newton Fuller [1854–1931]").

When the Glee Club came into existence in 1872, one of its main functions was to help popularize the songs that were routinely sung at these football contests. Indeed, much of its early repertory consisted of school spirit and football songs sung at college events and local performances.[84] However, by the early decades of the twentieth century, there arose a recognition within Rutgers College that the Club, which by this time had grown in both size and prestige, should become a more visible and permanent component of the football culture at the college.

This sentiment was expressed in a brief article that appeared in the *Targum* at the beginning of the fall semester in 1913. The piece reads as follows:

In commending the improved quality of college spirit which [recent] events seem to have called into being, it is well to say a good word for the Wednesday evening song practice instituted by the Y.M.C.A.

About 7:30 every Wednesday evening the "crowd" gathers on the steps of Winants [Hall] and runs through the college songs. The practice contains the germ of a mighty college institution. The song practice is led by glee club men and affords a great big stepping-stone to college spirit. Perhaps every one [*sic*] doesn't know of it; for some reason not as many as ought are seen out to support it. It is too good an opportunity to let pass.[85]

It would appear that this call for support of a nascent tradition met with a favorable reaction, for, during the following fall term, student officials sought to codify the Glee Club's role in the football culture. The following notice appeared in an October issue of the *Targum*:

> At the last regular meeting of the Senior Council a short time ago two resolutions were passed:
>
> *Resolved*, That the first and last stanzas of "On the Banks," . . . be recommended to the student body for use at [football] games . . .
>
> *Resolved*, That this council recommend to the Glee Club that it attend games in a body and lead the singing. The meeting then adjourned.[86]

The extent to which the Glee Club complied with this resolution over the ensuing years is unclear. However, it does seem that the Club was perceived as not only an active participant on game day, providing a rendition of "On the Banks" to show support for the school, but also as a force in the ancillary activities that came to surround each week's football game. On October 7, 1932, for example, the Glee Club participated in a rally held on the Old Queens campus designed as a sendoff for the team as they departed for their game against New York University the following day. This marked the first time in the history of the college that the Club participated in such an activity; accompanied by the Jazz Bandits, an instrumental offshoot of the Mandolin Club, they sang college songs over an electronic amplifying system, greatly enhancing the crowd's enthusiasm.[87]

World War II severely restricted the activities of the Glee Club; only the barest semblance of a performing schedule was maintained during those turbulent years. However, by 1947, the Club was again participating in what were now officially termed *pep rallies* held in advance of featured football games on the season's schedule. The game with Columbia University was often the object of these rallies, as was the case in both 1947 and 1948. The rallies would frequently feature, in addition to the Glee Club, a speech from the head coach of the Rutgers squad and a performance by the college's cheerleading team.[88] This tradition would extend into the 1950s as well; a "Beat Princeton" rally, for example, was held behind the College Avenue Gymnasium on October 3, 1952, featuring selections from the Club as well as an exhibition of baton twirling.[89]

In the 1960s, participation by the Club at Rutgers home games increased. By the end of the decade, it was not uncommon for the Glee Club to be present at many, if not all, of the Rutgers home games. 1969—dubbed the centennial year in football in honor of the 1869 Rutgers versus Princeton contest mentioned above—saw attendance by the Club at nearly every game. The Centennial Game on September 27 also marked the official release of the Club's newest recording, *100 Years of Football*.[90]

The football program at Rutgers took a turn for the big time during the mid-1970s. When Edward J. Bloustein took over as president of Rutgers University in 1971, he actively promoted an expansion of the sports program at the school. Over the objections of the university administration and faculty members, who Bloustein characterized as "patronizing intellectuals," the new president, with the blessing of the Rutgers board of governors, moved ahead during this period with the development of a major sports program that included the construction of a modern field house and the awarding of athletic scholarships.[91]

Much of this was accomplished with the support of Madison Square Garden president David A. (Sonny) Werblin, '31, onetime part owner of the American Football League's New York franchise, the New York Titans; shortly after purchasing a share in the team in 1963, Werblin changed the team's name to the New York Jets. Werblin envisioned his alma mater attaining the status of a big-time athletic power, with Bloustein's backing, by the early 1980s. Bloustein was a bit more circumspect, however, anticipating a more modest rise to prominence. "I don't expect Rutgers football will reach the stage Sonny Werblin says it will," Bloustein remarked in 1978.

Nonetheless, Bloustein was able to see the enormous advantages of offering football schedules that pitted the Rutgers Scarlet Knights against powerhouses such as Penn State and the University of Alabama. The primary goal for Bloustein was to see "moderate growth" in the program while featuring "competition with some major football powers, and some games at the 76,000-seat Meadowlands Stadium" in East Rutherford, New Jersey.[92]

This meant that the Glee Club had the opportunity in the late 1970s and the 1980s to attend the games that were scheduled at Meadowlands Stadium, later renamed Giants Stadium and today known as MetLife Stadium. As this would count as a Rutgers home game, the Club was expected to be on hand to sing the national anthem. The group would rehearse in the morning and then board a bus for the brief journey up the New Jersey Turnpike to the stadium.

Commencing home games with the national anthem was the normal procedure under Club director F. Austin Walter at this time. Members of the Club from this period recall that Walter always scoffed at renditions of the anthem that were too ornate or that proceeded in a dirge-like fashion. Walter always presented the anthem in a quick and urgent manner. Though the Glee Club was not required to stay for the entire game, many members did so, allowing them the opportunity to participate in the singing of the Rutgers song "Loyal Sons" with the Rutgers Marching Band at the end of the game. Often, the Club would also join the fans in the Rutgers Rah Chant at pertinent points throughout the contest.

The homecoming game was usually the major event of each football season. Pregame events were a significant part of the Glee Club's schedule for all home games, but this was especially so for homecoming. During this period, the official site for the homecoming pregame festivities was the President's Lawn at 1245 River Road. These activities would include festive tailgating, usually consisting of groups organized according to family ties, class years, or similar classifications. The Club would always make an appearance, sing a few Rutgers songs, and then lead the revelers to the stadium for the game.[93]

Many of these decades-old traditions were eagerly embraced by Patrick Gardner when he took over the directorship of the Club in 1993. By necessity, the visits to Giants Stadium were a fact of life for the Club in Gardner's inaugural year. Having joined the Big East Conference two seasons prior, it was decided by the Rutgers administration that a new stadium would be necessary to accommodate the expansion of the football program. The groundbreaking ceremony for this new building, which would be constructed on the site of the old stadium, took place on March 9, 1993, with work commencing shortly after. It was, however, not until September 3, 1994, that the first game, against Kent State, was played. Thus the football team and the Glee Club once again made their way to the Meadowlands for home games during the 1993 season.

As the new millennium dawned, many of the customs and practices associated with the Rutgers home football games continued as in previous decades. The annual homecoming game was certainly a large part of this ongoing tradition. As stated above, homecoming is considered one of the most exciting events in which the Club takes part during its season; this is due in no small measure to the fact that these events place a strong emphasis on the participation

of alumni and their families. The activities surrounding the 2003 homecoming contest against the University of Pittsburgh Panthers on October 18 of that year provide a glimpse into the typical structure of events surrounding these games. Alumni and their families were invited to attend the game and encouraged to participate in the entertainment and diversions that were part of the pregame festivities, now held at the Ronald N. Yurcak Memorial Field on Busch Campus. The tent that was erected on this field provided shelter for these activities as well as for the group singing led by members of the Club. The various entertainments commenced around 10:00 a.m. At 11:30 a.m., the Club met behind the tent for a rehearsal with Gardner. Alumni members of the Club were encouraged to attend this rehearsal, as it was customary for them to participate in the singing of the national anthem with the Club at these homecoming games.[94]

During Gardner's tenure, there have been many opportunities, in addition to the 1993 Giants Stadium excursions, for the Club to perform outside the confines of the home stadium of the Scarlet Knights. One such event had the Club traveling to the Bronx, New York, on November 12, 2011. Yankee Stadium would be the site for the football contest that day between the Rutgers squad and the team from the U.S. Military Academy at West Point. For this occasion, the Club joined with its analogue organization from West Point and the marching bands from both institutions to present a series of musical offerings.

The combined glee clubs performed the national anthem prior to the game, led by the West Point director, Constance Chase. They then had the opportunity to listen to the combined bands perform the traditional West Point march and the Rutgers fight song "The Bells Must Ring." The halftime show concluded with the combined glee clubs singing a medley of songs encompassing the five branches of the U.S. military. As a special treat for the student performers, they were provided with a private tour of Monument Park, where memorials to Yankee greats such as Lou Gehrig, Joe DiMaggio, and Babe Ruth can be contemplated. One Club member remarked that "singing in this historic space while performing with my friends is a dream come true."[95]

Participation by the Club at the Rutgers home football games continued in the 2010s much as it had for decades. Rutgers officially joined the Big Ten Conference in 2014 and subsequently instituted a major renovation of Rutgers Stadium to accommodate this new reality. The refurbished facility was renamed High Points Solutions Stadium in 2011 (and subsequently renamed SHI Stadium in 2019). The presence of Rutgers in the most prestigious American collegiate football conference meant greater and more extensive national exposure for the team and all concerned, including the Glee Club, which still performed at the majority of the home contests, particularly the homecoming games.

The homecoming game, for example, on October 20, 2018, against Northwestern featured all the usual activities: an early morning tailgate, Rutgers songs led by the Club, and the national anthem sung by current members and alumni at the game. But as with all activities at Rutgers and elsewhere, the COVID-19 pandemic would preclude the participation of the Glee Club in all such endeavors—football-related and otherwise—beginning in the spring of 2020. With vaccines being distributed at a record pace as of this writing, however, it seems likely that the Glee Club will once again be on hand in the fall of 2021—the start of their sesquicentennial year—to urge their football squad on, as has been the case for so many decades.

Soup Bowl

A Modern Glee Club Tradition, 1967–Present

One of the most cherished traditions of the modern Rutgers Glee Club involves an athletic competition between that group and the Rutgers University Marching Band. This annual event—dubbed the "Soup Bowl" in honor (apparently) of the originator of the contest, longtime Club director F. Austin "Soup" Walter, '32—manifests itself in the form of a full-contact flag football game consisting of four twelve-minute quarters with eight men to a side.[96]

The origins of this competition appear to be somewhat in doubt. It has been reported in numerous sources that the event began in 1971 (or, in some sources, 1970) as a way of settling a dispute between the two musical organizations as to which group would lead the pregame shows that accompanied each Rutgers football game.[97] However, this account is disputed in several more recent sources. According to this alternate version, which is derived mainly from eyewitness accounts from early participants in these contests, the event that sparked controversy took place in 1967. When Dr. Scott Whitener first arrived in the Rutgers Music Department and took over control of the Marching Band in 1966, the group was in a state of disorganization. This disarray was

quickly righted by Dr. Whitener, so much so that the Marching Band's growing reputation as a polished and respected organization, which they had crafted by 1967, began to rival the position of Walter's Glee Club, which had long enjoyed the status of being the premiere performing ensemble of the university. This turn of events was, it seems, a source of some friction between the groups.

The precipitating incident that led to the competition apparently involved alterations to the groups' shared rehearsal and office space in McKinney Hall on the College Avenue campus. During the summer of 1967, the Glee Club undertook to paint their offices on the top floor of the hall. When Dr. Whitener learned of this, he thought it was a good idea and sought permission from the Rutgers administration to do the same for the Marching Band office. To his surprise, he was told that to have students perform this type of work was prohibited and was reprimanded for suggesting this course of action. The Glee Club, however, received no such reprimand. This perceived slight toward the band, along with the friction caused by the band's rapid rise to prominence within the university community, is cited in the eyewitness accounts referenced above as the direct instigator of the athletic competition.[98] It should also be mentioned that this version of events does not attribute the designation "Soup Bowl" as a reference to the Glee Club director. Rather, this account states that the appellation was derived from the National Football League's terminology for their newly minted AFL-NFL

Members of the 1997–98 Marching Band and Glee Club face off across the line of scrimmage in that year's Soup Bowl contest. Special Collections, Rutgers University Libraries.

championship game, which was designated the Super Bowl. As Glee Club alumnus Peter Jensen, '71, relates, "I think it was a short linguistic jump from that name (Super Bowl) to calling our more important contest the 'Soup Bowl.'"[99]

Thus by the timeline of this version of events, the first Soup Bowl was played in the fall of 1967 at Buccleuch Park in New Brunswick, a convenient location within easy walking distance of McKinney Hall. As recalled by a participant, the Glee Club won this inaugural game four touchdowns to three. Since these humble beginnings, the game has evolved considerably over the last fifty-plus years. The modern version

of the Soup Bowl is played on a regulation-sized football field with game officials provided by Rutgers Recreation. The game is still basically the same: eight on eight, full-contact football with a large degree of physicality involved. However, all participants are now required to wear flag belts, the object being to remove opponents' flags as opposed to tackling them.[100] No pads are worn and all applicable NCAA rules governing play are enforced by the officials. Though these new adjustments have changed some of the outward aspects of the event, it nonetheless retains its flavor as a spirited competition between two (mostly) friendly collegiate rivals. The winner is awarded the coveted Soup Bowl Cup and receives bragging rights for the year.

As might be expected, there are numerous traditions, great and small, related to this contest that have developed over the years. One that is frequently commented on by Club alumni is the ritual of the team Pasta Party. This usually takes place the night before a game at a chosen player's home. All team members and an unlimited number of associates are invited for an athletically supportive meal of high-carb pasta and bread, with ample supplies of Gatorade on hand as well. After viewing the game film from the previous year's contest, graduating seniors are given the opportunity to address the assemblage with any final thoughts they might have.[101] In another such tradition, at the next Club rehearsal following the event, the game's most valuable players are selected and their names are written on the "Big Stick," which is quite literally a wooden plank set aside for this purpose.[102]

For the fiftieth anniversary of this competition, Gardner secured the use of the main Rutgers football facility, High Point Solutions Stadium (now SHI Stadium). This required a good deal of negotiating by Gardner with the relevant administration officials. The opportunity to play the game on a regulation football field of the Big Ten conference, however, was seen by all, including Gardner, as recompense for the myriad issues that the Club director was forced to negotiate in order to secure the use of the facility.

For this event, as had been the case for many years prior, players and attendees were encouraged to bring canned food for the less fortunate members of the community, yet another expression of the Rutgers Glee Club's commitment to fostering the best possible presence as high-profile representatives of the university community to the outside world, even as they engaged in a bit of brotherly competition.

The 1970s: The Centennial Year (1972)

As the decade of the 1960s came to a close, the Rutgers University Glee Club, which had been described in some accounts as "peripatetic" during those years,[103] looked to extend its itinerant ways into the new decade. While the 1960s had been a tumultuous period socially and politically, the Club had cultivated a cultural equilibrium, primarily through the maintenance of a schedule that was so intense as to, at least partially, preclude any intrusions from the chaos of the decade into the traditions of the Club. Certainly, outward affectations of the times—longer hair styles, facial hair, bell-bottom jeans, and so on—were to be found among the members at the early part of the new decade. But under the continued guidance of F. Austin Walter, the traditional mission of the group—to advance the argument for the special nature of the university—and the means and methods of presenting the ideals contained within that mission remained intact.

Centennial celebrations of all sorts were prominent features during the decade of the 1970s. The first intercollegiate football game in history took place between Rutgers and Princeton at approximately 3:00 p.m. on November 6, 1869. Played at the site of the current Rutgers Gymnasium on College Avenue, Rutgers defeated the Princeton squad by a score of six to four.[104] To commemorate this event, the Rutgers University Glee Club released an album of football songs, *100 Years of Football*, in early 1970.[105] Side one of the album contains the alma maters of various colleges, including Princeton, Columbia, Cornell, Navy, and Army, along with what are described as collegiate "drinking songs." Side two presents Rutgers college songs, including "A Rutgers Toast," "Down Where the Raritan Flows," "Vive Les Rutgers' Sons," and other favorites.[106] The recording, their eighth to date, was made in June of 1969 at St. Michael's Chapel in Piscataway, New Jersey (see chap. 4 sidebar, "Glee Club Discography: From the Vicissitudes of War to European Tours").[107]

The University Choir tradition remained vigorous during this decade. The 1970–71 semester saw a return to form in this regard for the choir when it was employed in a performance of a newly composed work by the Polish composer and conductor Krzysztof Penderecki (1933–2020). The program presented at the Rutgers Gymnasium on October 27, 1970, featured Zubin Mehta conducting the Los Angeles Philharmonic Orchestra in Beethoven's *Symphony No. 9* and Penderecki's cantata *Cosmogony*. This latter work was commissioned for the Silver Jubilee celebrations at the United Nations; it utilizes a variety of special techniques—glissandi, tone clusters, breathing effects from the chorus—juxtaposed with more conventional aspects of tonal music. Though the concert was generally well received, there were some comments in the press regarding balance problems with the choir. It was also stated that the scoreboard in the gymnasium—which was situated directly behind the choir and read "Rutgers . . . Guest . . . Bonus"—was a bit incongruous with the materials on the program.[108]

It should be pointed out that, since its inception, the Rutgers University Choir had been inextricably linked to the Glee Club. This had a good deal to do with the involvement of F. Austin Walter, who was the driving force behind both groups almost from the beginning of his tenure at Rutgers. The fact that the Glee Club, under Howard McKinney and later Walter, took great pains to include serious, art-music repertory in their programs also reinforced the link between the groups. It was therefore not unusual, both within the university and among the general public, for statements conflating the organizations in terms of personnel and purpose to be made.

Further, it is certainly the case among Glee Club alumni and supporters from all periods that this conflation of organizations exists in their minds as well. It is often the case that when a former Glee Club member is asked about the most memorable moment in their experiences with the group, the tale that is related concerns a reminiscence from a University Choir concert, such as the videotaped performance of the Brahms *Requiem* on the occasion of President Kennedy's

assassination or appearing with Leonard Bernstein at Carnegie Hall. The link is clearly a strong one. It should be further stressed, however, that the unifying factor for these groups—as well as other musical organizations at Rutgers during the four decades preceding the 1970s—was the presence of F. Austin Walter.

The ethos of collaboration with other ensembles on works from art-music literature can be seen in concerts given in 1970 and 1971 with the women's glee club of Beaver College in Pennsylvania. The earlier performance took place at Beaver College, but the latter occurred on February 26, 1971, at Kirkpatrick Chapel. The combined group was well over one hundred voices. The major work on the 1971 program was *Mass No. 2*, D. 167, by Franz Schubert, though other sacred and secular vocal works were also presented.[109]

The opening years of the decade provided more opportunities for international excursions by the Club. In June of 1970, the group embarked on its fourth tour of Europe. The Club departed the country from Kennedy International Airport on June 7, arriving at Schipol Airport in Amsterdam at 10:30 a.m. on June 8. After two days in that city, the group traveled by bus to the town of Heerenveen, in the northern provinces of the Netherlands. Following a brief stop in Paris, the Club continued to Tours, France, where a concert of sacred vocal works was presented at the Cathedral of St. Gatien. The Club also visited Luxembourg and the Italian cities of

Members of the 1970–71
Glee Club with F. Austin
Walter at Voorhees
Mall. Rutgers University
Glee Club Archives.

Merano and Florence, and ample free time for sight-seeing was provided at the end of the excursion before leaving Europe for home on July 5, 1970.[110]

A similar tour took place in 1971, though this trip would have the added excitement of placing the Glee Club behind the Iron Curtain, the political boundary that delineated the sides in the post–World War II Cold War. The specific destination was the Soviet-controlled Eastern Bloc nation-state of Czechoslovakia. This trip extended over more than three weeks and brought the Club to many of the major metropolitan areas of the country, including Brno, Bratislava, and Prague.[111] Club members were also afforded a chance to interact with their youthful Czech counterparts at a variety of summer camps that were visited as part of the tour.[112]

The 1971–72 season was, of course, a historic one for the Glee Club. First, it marked the fortieth anniversary of F. Austin Walter as director of the group. He was appointed student director in his senior year at Rutgers, 1931–32, and continued with a string of unbroken appointments, all of which made him de facto, if not immediately de jure, leader of the Club (see chap. 5 sidebar, "Francis Austin 'Soup' Walter [1910–2000]"). To mark the occasion, a dinner was held in Walter's honor at the Ramada Inn in East Brunswick on February 27, 1972. The toastmaster of the event, which had over four hundred attendees, was Mason Gross, who had retired the previous year as president of Rutgers and had been an influential supporter of the Music Department and of Walter throughout his tenure.[113]

However, this year also marked the one-hundredth anniversary of the Glee Club itself. Though there had been confusion over the years as to the exact date of inception of the Club, by the 1970s, conventional wisdom had settled on 1872 as the birth year, and quite accurately at that. The first Rutgers College Glee Club was organized by the sophomore class in 1872; a Glee Club of some configuration was launched—some more successfully than others, to be sure—every year thereafter.

The centennial was duly marked by the one-hundredth anniversary spring concert at the Rutgers Gymnasium on April 21. The traditional climax of the Glee Club's season—the spring concert, as it was often called—had become quite a popular event in recent times, and so made for a fitting tribute to the Club. Also sometimes termed "Fun Night," the highlights of the event, outside of the musical features, were the appearance of Tosci (full name Toscanini), a canine companion to Walter that had been given to him by the Club some years earlier, and the unceremonious depositing of the Club officers into the gymnasium swimming pool at the conclusion of the festivities.

Both traditions were in full effect on this hallowed occasion.[114]

The following year's annual spring concert on May 5, 1973, represented the final appearance that season for the Club before it embarked yet again on a summer sojourn to European destinations, its sixth such venture; this concert was, in fact, a benefit event for this upcoming tour.[115] Continuing in its efforts to support the cause of Hungarian freedom, the group included that country on its itinerary for this trip. The Club would also give performances in Belgium, Germany, Austria, Switzerland, and northern Italy. The Glee Club was joined by members of the Kirkpatrick Chapel Choir; ten women from that group supplemented the thirty-four men from the Glee Club. Again, there was considerable crossover between organizations as eight of the Glee Club members were also members of the choir. After a free week during which the ensemble's members traveled the continent at will, they reassembled in Amsterdam for a final performance. The Amsterdam concert had become a traditional concluding feature of the Glee Club's European tours.[116]

The spring concert on May 4, 1974, provides a glimpse into the standard repertory for the group during this period. As has been commented on previously, the move toward more serious art music was, by this time, firmly established. The program included works by the great Franco-Flemish Renaissance composer Josquin des Prez (d. 1521), "Night Song" by Schubert, and "And Now 'Tis Time to Go" from the *Peasant Cantata*, BWV 212 by J. S. Bach. More contemporary works included selections from Randall Thompson's *The Testament of Freedom* and "In taberna" from the cantata *Carmina Burana* by Carl Orff (1895–1982). However, the concert also made room for traditional favorites like the Rutgers college and drinking songs. The evening concluded with the Club's rendition of "On the Banks," eliciting the following commentary: "The performance came to an appropriate conclusion with the college's Alma Mater ['On the Banks']. When the Glee Club sings this simple music it takes on a sound filled with fire and conviction. It was a sound that brought the evening to a stirring close."[117]

The Glee Club got to reprise the Thompson work later that month. The group was featured at a Memorial Day celebration marking the opening of a spring series of concerts at the Garden State Arts Center. This represented the first appearance of the Glee Club at the Arts Center. The Thompson work, which had been in the group's repertory since they performed it in 1948 with Erich Leinsdorf and the Rochester Philharmonic Orchestra, was followed by a program of patriotic band music.[118]

The Club joined in the spirit of the United States Bicentennial in 1976 by opening its spring schedule with a concert at the United Methodist Church in New Brunswick on February 8. This was the first in a series of concerts presented by the church to honor the American Bicentennial as well as the one-hundredth anniversary of its sanctuary.[119] The Club was also asked to sing at an even more auspicious, if sadder, event later in the semester. On April 9, the Club performed at a memorial service at Kirkpatrick Chapel for the seventy-eighth anniversary of the birth of Paul Robeson. Robeson, who had died on January 23 in a Philadelphia hospital, was a Rutgers alumnus of great renown and a participant, however tangential, in the early days of the Rutgers Glee Club (see chap. 3 sidebar, "Paul Leroy Robeson, '19 [1898–1976]"). The Club's presence at this event served to recognize the contributions of Robeson to the university, the town of New Brunswick, and to the Glee Club itself.[120]

The Glee Club made a return trip to the Virgin Islands during this semester. The fifty-member group mounted what was referred to as their bicentennial concert tour, leaving on March 19, 1976, from New York and arriving in St. Croix, USVI, later that day. During the tour, they presented twenty-nine concerts in a wide variety of venues, including churches, schools, historic sites, and vacation resorts.[121] On their return, the Club wrapped up their season with the annual spring concert on May 1, 1976, at the Rutgers Gymnasium.[122]

On October 27, 1977, the Milwaukee Symphony Orchestra, under the direction of Kenneth Schermerhorn, appeared at the Rutgers Gymnasium as the opening event for the 1977–78 university concert series. The symphony offered an ambitious program. Among the works presented were the song cycle *Shéhérazade* and the *Concerto for Piano (Left Hand Alone) and Orchestra* by Maurice Ravel and *Symphony No. 7* by Sergei Prokofiev. The Rutgers University Choir would join the Milwaukee ensemble for two works: Samuel Barber's *The Prayers for Kierkegaard* for soprano, chorus, and orchestra and the *Choral Fantasy*, op. 80, by Ludwig van Beethoven. Soloists included the French pianist Michel Block and soprano Evelyn Lear.[123]

The concert had a greater significance to the university and, in particular, the musical organizations

thereof, since this event was dedicated to F. Austin Walter in recognition of his fiftieth year of association with Rutgers. Entering the college as a freshman in 1928, Walter rose through the ranks of the Glee Club to become its student leader before his graduation in 1932. Naturally, he was actively involved in the performance; the Barber and Beethoven works were conducted by him, with "his well-known vibrations, gesticulations and vibrant physical style . . . abundantly in evidence." It was also emphasized in local press accounts that Walter's beloved Glee Club was part of the two-hundred-voice University Choir.[124]

On October 11, 1977, Mason Welch Gross, sixteenth president of Rutgers University, died in Red Bank, New

The Rutgers Glee Club, 1977–78. Special Collections, Rutgers University Libraries.

Jersey, at the age of sixty-six. Gross's role as an avid supporter of the university's musical organizations earned him the distinction of having a new unit within the university, the School of Creative and Performing Arts, named in his honor. At a service that was held to commemorate his passing on November 3, 1977, over two hundred attendees heard the eulogy given by university president Edward J. Bloustein, followed by excerpts from Gross's speeches. The Glee Club and the Kirkpatrick Chapel Choir were on hand, attired in scarlet and white robes, to provide hymns, including "Thou Knowest Lord," "A Hymn to Queens," "Ein feste Burg," and the Rutgers fight song, "Loyal Sons."[125]

The spring semester of 1978 began as usual, with a variety of local performances on the schedule. The Glee Club performed at a celebration of the 350th anniversary of the Reformed Church in America at the First Reformed Church in New Brunswick on February 26.[126] A joint concert with the Wellesley College Women's Choir and the Glee Club took place at Kirkpatrick Chapel on March 5. Plans were also set in motion regarding the upcoming European tour during the summer of 1978. This time, the Club panned to perform at venues in Germany, the Netherlands, Italy, and Belgium.[127]

In early April, it was announced that a weekend of festivities honoring F. Austin Walter on the occasion of his retirement would begin on April 29 at the Glee Club's annual spring concert. Walter had decided to officially retire from his teaching activities; however, he would stay on to direct the Glee Club and the University Choir.

The program that the Club presented that evening was quite eclectic, offering works from virtually all the genres utilized by the Club in its past performances. The evening got off to a dramatic start, with Walter entering the spotlight to conduct empty bleachers. The Club was concealed offstage in the side balconies and rendered "O magnum mysterium" from those positions. Once reassembled on stage, the group performed works by Josquin des Prez (the "Gloria" from the *Missa Mater Patris*, though some modern scholars dispute attribution to this composer), Francis Poulenc (*Four Small Prayers of St. Francis of Assisi*), and Leonard Kastle (*Three Whale Songs*) on the first half of the program.

The second half of the evening's festivities was performed "according to strict glee club tradition." Attired in red blazers with white carnations, the Club offered renditions of favorites such as "A Rutgers Toast." "Bow-Wow-Wow" accompanied the now traditional appearance onstage of Tosci, Walter's canine companion. There were also selections by "The Highwaymen," a barbershop quartet, and another group described as specialists in the music of P. D. Q. Bach (1807–1742?), the fictional musician created by the American composer and educator Peter Schickele. Selections from this latter group included "Imperial Sons of the Dowager

Princess" and "Good King Kong," a Christmas carol in celebration of spring. The standard college and drinking songs were, of course, included.[128] Proceeds from this performance were put toward funding the Club's proposed trip to Europe in June.[129]

This celebratory event was followed up the next day, April 30, with a banquet in honor of Walter. Held at the Martinsville Inn and hosted by the Club and its alumni association, the testimonial affair began at 2:00 p.m. and was open to the public.[130]

In keeping with his plan to retire but stay active in the direction of the musical organizations with which he had been so long associated, Walter was present at the commencement ceremonies for the university on May 25, 1978. There, as was now Rutgers tradition, he led the Glee Club in their performance for the graduation exercises.[131]

Exactly how this retirement arrangement would work was clarified during the summer of 1978. It was announced at that time that Richard Alan Bower, '68, a conductor, pianist, and vocal coach, would take over Walter's classroom-teaching duties. He would also be serving as assistant conductor for the Glee Club as well as the University Choir. During Bower's academic career at Rutgers, he had performed in the Glee Club and the University Choir and studied conducting under Walter. He was eventually named student leader of the Glee Club and served as the student conductor

for the Kirkpatrick Chapel Choir under David Drinkwater. In addition to his musical duties, Bower served as manager for both ensembles. His later studies took him to the University of Wisconsin-Madison, where he earned master's degrees in musicology and piano accompaniment.

His duties as a member of the Rutgers faculty included teaching courses for music majors and non-majors alike; he was also expected to teach piano students, occasionally assist Professor Scott Whitener with his Collegium Musicum ensemble, and help with Whitener's conducting course. His main tasks, however, involved the vocal groups. For the Glee Club and the choir, Bower conducted sectional rehearsals and accompanied the Club at full rehearsals. It was anticipated at the time of his appointment to this full-time position that Bower would eventually conduct several Glee Club concerts throughout the year and be involved in choosing repertory, much in the same way Walter assisted Howard McKinney in the early 1930s. This would have seemed a natural progression, especially considering that Bower had firsthand experience with the practices and traditions of the Rutgers vocal ensembles.[132] However, initially, Walter was retained by the university to pursue his usual directorial duties on what he would later describe as "an unpaid basis."[133]

Therefore, to all outward appearances, things remained as they had been for many years with the

Glee Club. The Club made a surprise visit to a concert by the piano soloists Richard ('32) and Frances Hadden, at which the well-known duo performed a variety of works from different periods and genres. Hadden had been a classmate of Walter's, so the choral conductor decided to appear on stage with the Club, offering a rendition of a Hadden composition, "The Bells Must Ring," as well as performing "On the Banks" to conclude the performance.[134] The Glee Club joined with the Wind Ensemble and the Queens Chorale to present Christmas music on December 8, 1978, at the Rutgers Student Center and then appeared at Kirkpatrick Chapel with the Chapel Choir over the weekend of December 9–10 for four holiday performances.[135] In the spring, the Club once again joined forces with the Wellesley College Choir to perform works by the British composer Benjamin Britten.[136] And of course, the Glee Club season ended with the annual spring concert, featuring its usual mixture of art-music offerings (Bruckner, Orff, Elgar, etc.) followed by spirituals and college songs.[137] Walter was the conductor for all these events and more during the 1978–79 season.

Walter was also at the helm of the two-hundred-voice University Choir when it appeared with the New Jersey Symphony in a performance of the Verdi *Requiem* on May 2, 1979, at the College Avenue Gymnasium. This was the final concert of the university concert series for that season.

The 1980s: Walter's Retirement—New Directors and Directions

As part of the New Brunswick tercentennial celebrations in 1980, a gala concert was presented on January 26 at the State Theater in that city. The program included Sousa marches and Broadway tunes rendered by the New Jersey Symphony Orchestra directed by George Marriner Maull, the ensemble's assistant conductor. There was also a musical revue titled "They Knew New Brunswick" performed by the Halfpenny Players of Kearny, New Jersey. The Glee Club was on hand as well; with Walter conducting, the group opened the celebration with "an energetic version of 'The Star-Spangled Banner.'"[138]

The University Choir was active as usual during the 1979–80 season. They appeared in a concert on April 13, 1980, that presented two works for chorus and orchestra: *Carmina Burana* by Carl Orff and a secular cantata, *The Rio Grande*, by the British composer and conductor Leonard Constant Lambert (1905–51). However, beginning with this academic year, for the first time since the formation of the University Choir in 1950, the group was under the official direction of someone other than F. Austin Walter. The choir was instead conducted by the newly appointed director of the group, Frederic Hugh Ford. Walter, though now

195

officially retired from teaching, remained available to Ford, offering valuable assistance and allowing the latter "to become acquainted with the choir's distinguished performing tradition." But the directorial duties had passed to Ford by the time of this concert.[139]

Indeed, Ford was appointed as an assistant professor in the Music Department after an extensive national search for a full-time, tenure-track professor who would handle the University Choir and, with the expectation of Walter's imminent retirement, the Glee Club. Ford had already made several appearances as a conductor in the months prior to this performance. A concert titled "The Jewel of the Adriatic: Music in Renaissance Venice," given by Scott Whitener's Collegium Musicum on November 30, 1979, featured a group of sixteen instrumentalists and ten singers "specializing in the historical interpretation of Renaissance music." Ford led the singers in madrigals and other works from this repertory.[140] Ford also conducted the University Choir in two performances of the *Messe di Minuit pour Noël* (*Midnight Mass for Christmas*) by the French Baroque composer Marc-Antoine Charpentier (1643–1704) on December 8 and 9 at Kirkpatrick Chapel.[141]

The April 1980 concert, which featured the Orff and Lambert works, was Ford's first major performance with the University Choir. The long tradition of the choir performing with renowned symphony orchestras, which had been the organization's hallmark since its founding, was reportedly in some existential jeopardy, a circumstance attributed in some measure to financial considerations. On accepting the appointment as director of the choir, Ford had announced that his ambitions for the group included presenting "different kinds of concerts" and an avoidance of what he described as "the major work syndrome."[142] Therefore, the somewhat unusual paring of the Orff—a familiar but not, perhaps, "major" work—with the Lambert would seem to fit into this paradigm. Further, the concert did not employ an established symphony orchestra; rather, the instrumental ensemble was made up of "university faculty, students, and area professionals." Highly regarded vocalists were employed for the solo parts, including Metropolitan Opera tenor Michael Best and baritone Julius Eastman. The Lambert work included a rather prominent and demanding piano part, which was "expertly played" by Wanda Maximilien, a Rutgers Music Department faculty member. Despite these deviations from past traditions, the concert was very well received; concerning the Orff work, the following commentary was offered in the local press:

> The Rutgers choir captured the mood of the varied poetry on which the work is based, presenting the text with splendid diction and intonation and full understanding of the quality of

poetic statement, and the hypnotic and repetitive musical motives . . .

The choir responded to Ford's demand for dynamic and tonal variety, and the orchestra was clearly in command of the score's colorful and brilliant instrumental contrasts.[143]

Still, all the traditional performances of the Glee Club that delineated in many ways the timeline of a typical Rutgers semester remained in place, and Walter continued to direct the group as he had for decades. The annual spring concert was given on May 3, 1980, at the Rutgers Gymnasium on College Avenue. The following semester, the Club again united with the Kirkpatrick Chapel Choir for the annual Christmas in Carol and Song concerts, which were presented this season in Kirkpatrick Chapel four times over the weekend of December 14 and 15, 1980. The Glee Club, with Walter, was still a cherished institution of the university.

The summer of 1980 brought yet another international excursion. The itinerary for this trip, however, was somewhat more exotic than previous expeditions. This tour began with a performance in Casablanca, Morocco. From there, the group took a ferry through the Strait of Gibraltar to the Spanish tourist center of Fuengirola, where they enjoyed some relaxation time before resuming their performance schedule. Several concerts were given in Spain, notably in Madrid, before

the group pushed on to Lisbon, Portugal. Performances in Portugal were received with enthusiasm, and on the evening of the Club's departure for home, a dinner party was given in their honor by the city of Lisbon.[144]

The University Choir maintained its tradition of high-profile concerts in 1981. On April 26, the group appeared with the American Symphony Orchestra at Carnegie Hall in a performance of the cantata *Belshazzar's Feast* by the British composer William Walton.[145] And on the Rutgers campus, Ford led the choir in the Béla Bartók work *Cantata Profana* for double mixed chorus and orchestra. The soloists for this concert included tenor Michael Best and baritone John Powell, a Rutgers Music Department faculty member. The concert took place at Voorhees Chapel on December 6, 1981.[146]

On May 8, 1982, the Glee Club presented its annual spring concert. The venue, however, was not the venerable Rutgers Gymnasium on College Avenue but the newly opened Nicholas Music Center on Douglass Campus, adjacent to the Maryott Music Building. The need for a new performing venue had been discussed for many years. Indeed, F. Austin Walter was active in the debate that took place during the early 1980s on whether the State Theater in New Brunswick might make a more suitable location for many of the performances than the gymnasium, particularly those involving large orchestral and/or vocal forces. Walter had come down heavily on the side of retaining the gymnasium—often referred to on campus as "The Barn"—as the preferred concert site, largely on the grounds that "there is something special and unique about having a famous musician or a great orchestra come directly to the campus," as opposed to holding such concerts at "an outworn, off-campus movie house" like the State Theater.[147] The new Nicholas Music Center, which was officially inaugurated on November 5, 1982, but had been in use for some months prior, was only a 750-seat facility, accommodating considerably fewer people than the gymnasium, or the State Theater for that matter,[148] something that Walter saw as a drawback. Nonetheless, it would become the center of musical activities at Rutgers for decades to come.

The final international concert tour of F. Austin Walter's career, the tenth such excursion for the Glee Club since 1962, took place during the summer of 1982. This tour focused on presenting concerts at three European universities at which Rutgers had junior-year-abroad programs. These venues included Tours, France; Konstanz, Germany; and Florence, Italy. Additional concerts on this trip were presented at Westminster Abbey and the ancient Anglican church All Hallows by the Tower in London. In France, half-hour concerts were performed from the high altars of the Cathedral of Notre Dame and the Cathedral of Our Lady of Chartres. The acoustics encountered in

these sacred venues left a lasting impression on the participants in these performances.[149]

The following season saw the Glee Club's annual spring concert on April 23, 1983, returned to the Rutgers Gymnasium, at which the Club presented "Classical, spiritual, and whimsical selections from composers including Bach, Williams, Grieg and Foster."[150] This performance, however, marked the final formal appearance of Francis Austin Walter, '32, as director of the Rutgers Glee Club. Walter had announced earlier in the year that he planned to retire from this post in June of 1983. A contemporary written account of his retirement remarked on his long association with the Glee Club, his "ebullient" character, and his role in shaping the Club into the highly effective "roving musical ambassadors" for Rutgers that they had become. His importance to campus life was also referenced: "Walter's rhythmic gyrations at the podium have become as much a part of Rutgers lore as the venerable buildings of the Queens campus and the school's alma mater, 'On the Banks of the Old Raritan.'"[151]

Walter's retirement meant that Ford would now officially step into the role of director of the Glee Club, as had been the plan at the time of his hiring in 1979. Again, the traditional duties of the Club were not interrupted during this period. They made an appearance at the annual homecoming ceremonies on October 15, 1983, and once again combined with the Kirkpatrick

The Glee Club performs the final formal concert under the direction of F. Austin Walter at the College Avenue Gymnasium on April 23, 1983. Glee Club alumni join the current Club members for the concert's finale. Special Collections, Rutgers University Libraries.

Chapel Choir to offer four performances of the annual Christmas in Carol and Song program on December 10 and 11 at 7:00 and 9:00 p.m. There was also a combined concert with the Georgian Court College Women's Chorus on April 7, 1984, at Kirkpatrick Chapel.[152]

The annual spring concert on May 4, 1985, was again a mixture of light and serious as well as ancient and modern. Jacob Handl's "O magnum mysterium" and the brief "Adoramus te" by the French Renaissance composer Jacques Clément—better known as Clemens non Papa (1510–55)—were interspersed with works by the twentieth-century American composer Vincent Persichetti during the first half, which was presented by the group in white tie and tails. The second half of the program replaced the formal wear with red sweaters. The selections were decidedly more popular, with quartets offering works in both the barbershop as well as 1950s doo-wop styles. The full ensemble concluded the evening with drinking songs and spirituals, followed by the traditional college

199

songs. The concert was praised in local accounts as "a professional-level rendering of the program chosen by conductor Frederic H. Ford" and was, as usual, well received by an enthusiastic audience at the Nicholas Music Center.[153]

The Club eschewed its customary European expeditions in the summer of 1985 and opted instead for a tour of the United States. The group traveled extensively, presenting performances in Washington, D.C.; Houston; Dallas; Fort Worth; Los Angeles; Disneyland in Anaheim, California; and San Francisco.[154]

In 1986, the city of New Brunswick celebrated more than one hundred years of cultural ties with the Japanese cities of Fukui and Tsuruoka through the Sister Cities program. As part of these festivities, the Rutgers Glee Club played host to and performed with the Kwansei Gakuin University Glee Club. The event that was deemed to be the highlight of the "Celebrate Japan" ceremonies was a concert given at Voorhees Chapel on March 7, 1986. Titled "Japan and America: Voices of Friendship," the performance included the Kwansei Gakuin Glee Club, the Rutgers Glee Club, and the Vocal Dynamics, the glee club of New Brunswick High School. Proceeds from this event were to be put toward the high school group's three-week trip to Japan in May of 1986 and toward the July trip to New Brunswick of the Fukui Junior Orchestra.[155]

The spring concert on April 12, 1986, at the Nicholas Music Center marked Frederic Ford's final appearance as director of the Glee Club, as he had decided to leave the university to take up a position as director for the New Jersey Teen Arts program. In the fall of 1986, the University Choir would merge with the group Musica Sacra, the Rutgers vocal ensemble previously conducted by Barbara Lingelbach, who died in November of 1986. The new combined ensemble would perform the *Requiem*, K. 626, of W. A. Mozart under the direction of Richard Westenburg, who joined the faculty of the Rutgers Music Department during this semester, having been appointed as a visiting professor and choral conductor in the wake of the departure of Frederic Ford. Westenburg was a full-time faculty member and head of the choral department at the Juilliard School in New York at the time of his visiting appointment at Rutgers. Soloists for the concert included Judith Nicosia-Civitano and Gloria Clingerman, sopranos; Mary Ann Hart, alto; Frederick Urrey, tenor; and Robert Quehn, bass.[156]

With the departure of Ford, the Glee Club also underwent a change of leadership. In this case, the new director was a familiar face for the Club members. Timothy L. MacDonald, who had served for several years as the assistant director for the Glee Club under Ford, now stepped in as the new leader of the ensemble. The Club continued with its traditional appearances throughout the academic year. On December 5, 1986, the Club participated in a holiday concert with the Queens Chorale and the Rutgers Wind Ensemble. The finale of this event was a combined performance of Leroy Anderson's "A Christmas Festival," with audience participation encouraged. And of course, the academic year ended with the annual spring concert on April 25, 1987, at the Nicholas Music Center.[157] However, the Club extended its schedule beyond this performance, combining with the Voorhees Chapel Choir for a concert with the Westfield (N.J.) Symphony Orchestra in a program of works by Mozart on May 1.[158]

The 1987–88 academic year brought yet another change in directorship for the Glee Club. Timothy MacDonald's departure opened the door for Robert Kapilow to take charge of the group. Kapilow had been a student of the French conductor and organist Nadia Boulanger in the early 1970s. He received his undergraduate degree from Yale University in 1975, and upon completion of his graduate studies at the Eastman School of Music, he returned to Yale, where he served as an assistant professor and conducted the Yale Symphony Orchestra for six years.[159] At the time of his appointment to the faculty of the Rutgers Music Department, Kapilow was an established conductor, having directed over three hundred performances of the Broadway musical *Nine*.[160] Kapilow continued with the traditional Glee Club events, such as the joint holiday concerts; one of these featured both the Rutgers Wind Ensemble and the Queens Chorale

Robert Kapilow, director of the Glee Club, 1987–88.
Photo credit: Conductor Robert Kapilow, 2016.

on December 11, and another on the following day had the Club combining with the Kirkpatrick Chapel Choir.[161] Yet another joint event took place the following semester when the Club presented a program with the Smith College Choir on February 20, 1988.[162] And the annual spring concert took place on April 30, 1988, at the Nicholas Music Center on Douglass Campus.[163]

Kapilow was also keenly interested in the direction of other ensembles at Rutgers and elsewhere during this period. He was heavily involved in the new summer series of concerts at Rutgers, called Summerfest. Many performances of the orchestral ensemble for this series, the Rutgers Festival Orchestra, were given under his baton. Nonetheless, after an eventful summer of 1988 in which he was deeply engaged with the Summerfest events, Kapilow returned to his duties as Glee Club director for a second season, again directing the holiday concerts at Kirkpatrick on December 10 and 11, 1988.

Kapilow was, however, very much in demand as a conductor and composer. He would go on to have a highly successful career as a music commentator, garnering initial recognition in this capacity from his appearances on the radio program *What Makes It Great?*, part of the series *Performance Today* on National Public Radio.[164] These interests ultimately led to his relinquishing his position at Rutgers University, leaving the direction of the Glee Club in other hands.

The varied musical interests of the Glee Club directors who assumed that role in the wake of the retirement of F. Austin Walter—Ford, MacDonald, and Kapilow—along with the plethora of additional duties imposed on them within the Rutgers Music Department led to a situation in which their subsequent lack of attention to the group began to take a toll. A decrease in funding for the Club from the university also had an adverse effect on the group. Membership had dropped to well under forty men by the spring of 1989. Further, high-profile concerts that were once taken for granted for Club members now came only rarely. And indeed, the level of artistic consistency had suffered as well.

These facts were all readily apparent to the new Club director who appeared on the scene in 1989.[165]

Stephen Barton was the replacement for Kapilow chosen by the Music Department. A doctoral candidate in choral music at the State University of New York at the time of his appointment, Barton quickly went to work to remedy the many ills that had beset the Club over the previous several years. Barton and the student leaders were able to bring the membership of the Club back up to approximately forty members in the spring of 1989. Additionally, they planned a high-profile tour to Austria and Communist-controlled Hungary during the summer of 1989. This tour, which took place between May 31 and June 14, was arranged through the Friendship Ambassadors Foundation, a nonprofit division of UNESCO specializing in cultural exchanges of this sort. Notwithstanding that organization's support, the tour still required partial self-funding. One method that the Club employed to raise these funds was to offer the services of tuxedo-clad vocal quartets who would deliver roses and sing love songs to lucky Rutgers student-recipients during the Valentine's Day season, a service that was apparently utilized by both men and women scholars at the university.[166]

Barton, like his immediate predecessors, maintained Glee Club participation in all the traditional events, both on campus and elsewhere, during the 1989–90 academic year. The annual spring concert

The Rutgers Glee Club, 1989–90 season, Stephen Barton, director. Special Collections, Rutgers University Libraries.

was, of course, one of the high points of the season. The Club traveled down the road to the performing arts center at neighboring Middlesex Community College in Edison, New Jersey, for this event. The concert, which took place on March 31, was a benefit affair for the restoration and renovation of the Metuchen Memorial Park. The Club engaged the audience with selections that included the works of Antonio Lotti, John Dowland, Felix Mendelssohn, and Franz Schubert along with the traditional college songs.[167] The following semester, the Christmas Carol and Song concerts, performed jointly with the David Drinkwater's Kirkpatrick Chapel Choir, were held as usual on December 8 and 9, 1990, at Kirkpatrick Chapel under Barton's direction.[168]

The academic year 1991–92 marked the 120th anniversary of the Glee Club. But this season also marked the appearance of yet another new director for the group: Bruce Kolb, who had recently joined the Rutgers Music Department faculty. Kolb had graduated from Louisiana State University with a doctor of musical arts degree in vocal performance and put those skills to work in a variety of capacities at Rutgers. He instituted a new vocal ensemble within the Music Department, the Rutgers Concert Choir. Promising "to explore Western Choral Music of the last five centuries and to provide experience to Rutgers students majoring in vocal music and music education," this group had its premiere concert on November 19, 1991.[169] And he assumed the post of director of the Glee Club upon the departure of Stephen Barton, who left the university following the 1990–91 season.

Once again, a change in leadership did not deter the Glee Club from its duty as the university's representative at prestigious events. The Club was called upon to perform at a memorial service on November 25, 1991, in honor of Rutgers graduate David "Sonny" Werblin, '31. Following his graduation, Werblin had established a lengthy and extremely successful career as a talent agent to film and television personalities. He was, however, perhaps most remembered (particularly in the Greater New York metropolitan area) as the one-time owner of the NFL's New York Jets. Werblin also served as president of the Madison Square Garden Corporation and as chairman of the New Jersey Sports and Exposition Authority. At the time of his death,

Werblin had been on the Rutgers board of trustees for over twenty-five years and had been a member of the Rutgers board of governors since 1971.

The service was held at Kirkpatrick Chapel. Among the attendees were former Jets quarterback Joe Namath, broadcaster Howard Cosell, sportswriter Red Barber, and Wellington Mara, owner of one of the other New York NFL franchises, the New York Giants. According to press accounts, the Glee Club "performed 'Loyal Sons,' a song urging the Rutgers football team to 'Score once more, Oh, score once more.'"[170]

The 120th anniversary was noted at the annual spring concert, which took place this season at Kirkpatrick Chapel on April 25, 1992. The emphasis of the event was on the history of the Club and, particularly, its directors. In honor of the occasion, the Club had commissioned a new work by Rutgers Music Department faculty member Noel DaCosta and presented its premiere at this concert. This work, titled *Celestial Earth-Songs in Melodious Sound Tones* and scored for tenor/narrator, male chorus, percussion, and organ, was dedicated by the composer to F. Austin Walter, who led the group for over fifty years. Kolb also included on the program a work by recently departed Club director Robert Kapilow, "The Pasture," based on the setting of a Robert Frost poem. Other works on the program included "Loch Lomond" by Ralph Vaughn Williams, "Behold Man" by Ron Nelson,

"Sometimes I Feel like a Motherless Child" by Fenno Heath, and "Stouthearted Men" by Sigmund Romberg. The traditional Rutgers college songs were, of course, included.

Speaking of the well-established reverence for the culture that surrounded the Glee Club that Kolb inherited, the new director stated the following: "[Anniversary celebrations of this sort are] exciting because there is a feeling of tradition and continuity that is very important. There is a tangible feeling of history and spirit present in the daily goings on that is very important and nourishing."[171]

Rutgers Glee Club 1992–93. Bruce Kolb, director, 1991–93, is front row center. Rutgers University Glee Club Archives.

FRANCIS AUSTIN "SOUP" WALTER
(1910–2000)

To say that "Soup" Walter, '32, was important to the history of the Rutgers University Glee Club would be a considerable understatement. The contributions of Walter to the Club, to the university as a whole, and perhaps most importantly, to the individual students whose lives he changed for the better are such that they go beyond the praise from distinguished colleagues and alumni or the simple enumeration of his achievements and awards that follows.

Walter was born in Philadelphia, Pennsylvania, on December 28, 1910. He was the younger of two children of the Reverend Andrew Judson Walter, Rutgers College class of 1897.[172] The family resided in Hackensack, New Jersey; the elder Walter held a position as pastor at the North Hackensack Reformed Church.[173] Walter came by his nickname early in life. At the age of ten, he acquired a friend who had difficulty pronouncing the name "Austin"; it apparently sounded more like "Oyster." This led other children to refer to Walter as "Oyster Soup," later amended to just plain "Soup." The name stuck, though Walter admitted that there were times in his life when it caused some confusion. "I'm called 'Soup' by so many people that there are actually

F. Austin "Soup" Walter and his beloved Tosci at the statue of William the Silent, Voorhees Mall, College Avenue Campus, Rutgers University, 1971. Rutgers University Glee Club Archives.

those who think my last name is Campbell," he remarked in a 1977 interview.[174]

Walter enrolled at Rutgers College in 1928, following in the footsteps of his father as well as his elder brother, Robert, who was admitted to Rutgers in 1925 and went on to become the head of the mathematics department at Douglass College. Walter himself was not a music major during his undergraduate years; no such program existed at the time. In fact, there were only two music courses offered at the college during this period: harmony and music appreciation.[175] He therefore pursued a course of study in history and political science. Nonetheless, by his sophomore year, Walter had found his way to the organization that would so influence the remainder of his life, joining the Glee Club, as Francis A. Walter, for the 1929–30 season as a first tenor.[176]

Walter quickly rose to the position of student director of the Glee Club. Howard D. McKinney, '13, who had become Glee Club director in 1916, was still actively conducting the Club during Walter's junior year.[177] Walter's chance at the podium would not come until the following season, when he was called upon to direct the group during an intercollegiate choral competition at Carnegie Hall on February 27, 1932. His first public appearance as a conductor at this event marked the realization of a boyhood dream; when he was in high school, he had attended a performance of the New York Philharmonic and decided to become a conductor. "Few people can say that they started out at Carnegie Hall," Walter would remark later in his career.[178]

Following his graduation, McKinney approached Walter to join the university staff and remain with the Glee Club as his assistant director, to which Walter agreed. While serving in this capacity, Walter continued his musical studies at the Juilliard School and Columbia University. At the latter institution, Walter received lessons in music theory under Hadley Richard and voice culture under Robert Elmyn. Throughout the 1930s, Walter would continue to expand the compass of his musical training. Having studied organ with McKinney at Rutgers, he now undertook piano lessons from Chester B. Searle. He began formal training in conducting under the Austrian master Fritz Mahler and continued this course of instruction with the Belgian-American conductor Léon Barzin.[179] He would refine his training in conducting in 1941 as a student at the Berkshire Music Festival at Tanglewood.[180] Though Walter would not officially become director of the Glee Club until McKinney stepped down in 1946, his tenure as primary conductor of the group dates from the 1932 Carnegie Hall performance mentioned above. In 1945, when wartime exigencies forced the temporary cessation of activities of the Glee Club, Walter accepted a visiting professor post at Rollins College in Florida. However, barring that absence and one other for a similar post at the University of Michigan in 1964, he could always be seen on the podium at Glee Club concerts.[181]

Walter was appointed to the full-time faculty at Rutgers in 1938. Initially working closely with McKinney, but then later on his own, he oversaw an expansion of the musical opportunities made available to the students of the university over the next forty-five years. He served as a classroom instructor and, in 1940, organized and served as the first director of the Rutgers University Orchestra.[182] Regarding the Glee Club, McKinney and Walter both felt strongly that the group would do well to include more serious art-music selections in its repertory. They further felt that an expansion of the opportunities of the Club, as well as other vocal ensembles at the university, was needed in order to engage with large-scale performances of great masterworks of the choral literature at Rutgers and elsewhere. In 1939, as part of McKinney's winter concert series, the Rutgers Glee Club joined with the Glee clubs of Princeton and New York University to perform with the Metropolitan Opera coloratura soprano Josephine Antoinne for the final concert of that season's series. The biggest stride in this direction, however, came in 1941, when the Glee Club appeared with the Boston Symphony Orchestra under its longtime music director Serge Koussevitzky in a performance of Franz Liszt's *Faust Symphony*. Also part of McKinney's concert series, this program was initially presented at Rutgers and subsequently given twice at Carnegie Hall.[183]

Walter was leading a Glee Club concert in Trenton, New Jersey, on December 7, 1941, when, just before the finale of the performance, he was handed a note stating that the Japanese had attacked the American fleet at Pearl Harbor. As Walter would remember it years later, "I announced this to the audience and said: 'We will now sing *The Star-Spangled Banner.*' This sounded like our defiant answer to the act of infamy and the Glee Club sang the anthem as never before."[184]

In April of 1950, the Glee Club combined with the New Jersey College for Women's Voorhees Chapel Choir to perform J. S. Bach's *St. Matthew Passion* with Eric Leinsdorf and the Rochester Philharmonic Orchestra. So well received was this collaboration that it led to the formation of the Rutgers University Choir, a "town and gown" ensemble that included a significant number of members from the Glee Club, the Kirkpatrick Chapel Choir, and the Voorhees Chapel Choir under the direction of Walter.[185] It is true that the Kirkpatrick Chapel Choir and the Glee Club had been officially united since 1933 and, indeed, unofficially affiliated long before that date (see chap. 4, note 53); in fact, when combined during this early period, the groups were often referred to as the Rutgers University Choir as well.[186] The entity that was formed under that name in 1950, however, provided for the permanent presence of the female voices necessary for the performance of the major choral works that Walter envisioned undertaking.

For the next three decades, major symphonic ensembles engaged with the Rutgers University Choir under Walter's direction to present such performances. Concerts with the Philadelphia Orchestra under Eugene Ormandy, the New York Philharmonic Orchestra conducted by Leonard Bernstein, and the Rochester Philharmonic under the direction of Erich Leinsdorf were presented. Often mounted as part of the concert series at Rutgers, these collaborations were also given at various venues outside of the university, including Carnegie Hall and the Philadelphia Academy of Music. Perhaps the most famous of these performances was the presentation of Johannes Brahms's *Requiem* with the Philadelphia Orchestra that was telecast on CBS the day following the assassination of President John F. Kennedy in November 1963. According to Ormandy, the University Choir "performed admirably."[187]

Walter was also responsible for raising the profile of the Glee Club through extensive national, and eventually international, travel. A trip to the West Coast at the invitation of the Rutgers Club of Southern California in 1960 gave the group and its leader the confidence to further broaden the scope of their travels. A successful excursion to the Bergen Music Festival in Norway in 1962 led to further European tours, which included concerts in the Netherlands, Germany, Belgium, and France as well as trips to Communist-controlled areas such as Czechoslovakia, Hungary, and Romania. By the end of Walter's career, the Glee Club had participated in ten such European tours, greatly expanding the international profile of the university through its most able representatives.

Also contributing to the Glee Club's notoriety during the years in which Walter led the group was the series of recordings produced featuring both the Glee Club and the University Choir. Beginning with the 1943 *Songs of Rutgers*, undertaken just prior to the Glee Club's temporary cessation of activities during World War II, the Club produced several recordings that consisted of standard college songs of Rutgers as well as those of other schools. Recordings with the University Choir produced under Walter's direction include Handel's *Ode for St. Cecilia's Day* with Bernstein and the New York Philharmonic (1959), Carl Orff's *Carmina Burana* with the Philadelphia Orchestra under Ormandy (1960), and William Walton's *Belshazzar's Feast*, also with Ormandy and the Philadelphia Orchestra (1961; see chapter 4 sidebar: Glee Club Discography).

Walter's role as director of the Glee Club did not begin and end according to the academic calendar. His dedication to the excellence of both the Glee Club and the University Choir led him to explore and implement innovative methods by which to instruct the groups in the intricacies of the complex literature that they performed. Perhaps the most successful, and fondly remembered, of these deviations from a conventional rehearsal schedule was the annual group excursion to the shores of Lake Minnewaska in Ulster County, New York. Instituted in 1940 as an intensive presemester training session in the town of East Milford, Pennsylvania, the site was moved to Ulster County the following year and became a standard feature of the Club's season for decades.[188] Prior to the beginning of each academic year, a small contingent of Glee Club members would assemble at the lake. While the primary purpose of this outing was preparation for the upcoming concert season, plenty of time was built into the schedule for swimming, horseback riding, hiking, sailing, and a wide variety of other outdoor activities.[189] As much about building camaraderie among Club members as preparing musical details, these excursions are among the most fondly remembered events of Glee Club alumni.

In addition to his conducting activities with the Glee Club and the University Choir, Walter was an accomplished pedagogue, designing and presenting a variety of courses for the nascent Rutgers Music Department. Generations of students fondly remember classroom offerings such as "Opera and Music Drama," "Symphonic Music," "Chamber Music," and "Music Appreciation." He also provided private instruction in conducting for music majors and offered more focused directorial training for student leaders of the Glee Club, much in the way he had been mentored early on by Howard McKinney.

Walter announced his retirement from his full-time teaching position in the Music Department in 1978 and relinquished his role as conductor of the University Choir during the following season, handing the reins of that ensemble to Frederic Ford. Walter would continue, however, to serve as the Glee Club's director until 1983. For his final appearance at the annual spring concert on April 23, 1983, over one hundred Glee Club alumni joined contemporary Club members in a series of Rutgers songs, concluding with the Rutgers alma mater, "On the Banks of the Old Raritan."

Walter was a highly regarded conductor in his own right, considered to be eminently qualified to prepare the Glee Club and choir for performances with the likes of Ormandy, Bernstein, Leinsdorf, and other eminent masters. For Walter, the act of conducting was a strenuous one, both mentally and physically. A contemporary newspaper account of his rehearsal technique stated, "Drama, both visual and aural, has always been Walter's forte. Conducting and rehearsing for him are energetic acts into which he throws himself, body and soul."[190] Glee Club alumni tell of the dynamic yet frenetic style of directing that Walter employed: "[Walter] used to stand at the edge of the stage . . . at Carnegie Hall, with only his toes on the stage, and conduct furiously."[191] Clearly, this was a man focused on embracing the music that he was presenting to his fullest capacity.

Following his retirement in 1983, Walter remained an enthusiastic and dedicated participant in Rutgers events, attending concerts on campus and staying in touch with his colleagues and former students, many of whom had developed distinguished careers in music and other fields. Several Glee Club directors succeeded him, each adding their unique talents and visions for the group to the enormous legacy of brilliant performances of choral repertory that Walter left in his wake.

Walter was the recipient of many honors throughout his career. He was awarded honorary degrees—a master of arts degree in 1949 and a doctor of music degree in 1966—from Rutgers University.[192] He served as president of the Intercollegiate Musical Council (now known as IMC: The Tenor-Bass Choral Consortium) from 1962 to 1964 and was a member of the board of directors of the Friendship Ambassadors

F. Austin Walter conducts a vigorous rehearsal, 1971. Rutgers University Glee Club Archives.

Foundation. In recognition of the accomplishments that Walter had produced over his impressive career, he was elected to the Rutgers University Hall of Distinguished Alumni in 2015, garnering letters of support for his nomination from the likes of the internationally renowned conductors Zubin Mehta and Kazuyoshi Akiyama as well as his longtime Rutgers colleagues and former students.

On April 29, 2000, Patrick Gardner, the current director of the Glee Club, visited an ailing F. Austin Walter in his room at the Robert Wood Johnson Hospital in New Brunswick. Gardner delivered cards and flowers from concerned Glee Club alumni to the conductor and later reported that he had left Walter sleeping peacefully. Two nights later, on May 1, 2000, Francis Austin "Soup" Walter passed away at the age of eighty-nine. A memorial service, organized by David Drinkwater and Patrick Gardner with the assistance of members of the Glee Club, took place at Kirkpatrick Chapel on May 21, 2000. With approximately 250 family members and friends of Walter's in attendance, including former Club directors Stephen Barton and Frederic Ford, the service offered a series of eulogies from Club alumni interspersed with selections from the Club, including "Brothers, Sing On," "Salvation Is Created," and "A Rutgers Prayer." It was, as one Club alumni phrased it, "a fitting memorial service for a man who touched all our lives."[193]

FREDERIC HUGH FORD

(b. 1939)

As noted in the narrative, the impact of F. Austin Walter on the Glee Club, as well as the university itself, was considerable. When Walter announced that he intended to retire at the end of the 1977–78 season, the Rutgers Music Department felt an obligation to provide the best possible replacement for this legendary figure.

Throughout the evolution of Rutgers College/University, the various affiliated entities—Rutgers College; the New Jersey College for Women, which later became Douglass College; and so on—all produced a variety of vocal ensembles, many, if not most, organized under different programs and directors. However, the formation of the Mason Gross School of the Arts in 1976 as the arts conservatory of Rutgers University—and the Music Department's inclusion therein—provided an opportunity to reorganize and consolidate the various vocal groups. Such a restructuring necessitated the establishment of a permanent, full-time tenure track position in choral conducting for the purpose of instituting a unified pedagogical and artistic approach to the various choral groups in the Music Department, including the Glee Club.

After a far-reaching and thorough national search, the person selected for this position was Frederic Hugh Ford.

A native of Woonsocket, Rhode Island, Ford came to Rutgers with impressive credentials. He entered Harvard University in 1956 as a music major; during his undergraduate career, he sang in the Harvard Glee Club under the American conductor and Beethoven scholar Elliott Forbes and later Wallace Woodward. In his senior year, Ford served as the director of the Harvard Krokodiloes, a small a cappella male ensemble that featured elements of jazz and swing in their performances. Following graduation, Ford served as assistant conductor for the Harvard Glee Club on their 1961 tour of the Far East, with stops in Los Angeles, Hawaii, Japan, Korea, and Greece. During the 1961–62 academic year, while enrolled in a master's program in education at Harvard, Ford directed the Radcliffe Women's Choir.

Upon receiving his master of arts degree in 1962, Ford enlisted in the U.S. Navy, serving in Japan from 1962 to 1965. In 1965, Ford was enrolled at the Longy School of Music in Cambridge, Massachusetts. During the 1966–67 academic year, Ford conducted the University of Virginia Glee Club, filling in for their regular director, Donald Glenn Loach. In 1969, Ford received a master of arts degree in music history from the State University of New York at Buffalo, where he also conducted that school's glee club. From 1972 to 1979, Ford was on the faculty at Wabash College in Crawfordsville, Indiana, where he conducted the glee club, a TTBB organization. In addition to that responsibility, he also taught courses in music history and music theory and served as a piano instructor. Ford took the Wabash Glee Club on tours of Europe in 1975 and 1979.[194]

In the fall of 1979, Ford was appointed as assistant professor of choral conducting in the Music Department of Rutgers University. Though directing the Glee Club was originally to have been part of his assigned duties, F. Austin Walter's decision in 1979 to retire only from classroom teaching and remain as director of the Glee Club meant that Ford concentrated his activities on the Rutgers University Choir and the SSAA (soprano/soprano/alto/alto) ensemble, the Queens Chorale. During this period at Rutgers, he also taught courses in music theory and ear training. With Walter's final retirement in 1983, however, the responsibility for Glee Club performances then fell to Ford.

Ford made excellent use of his training and past associations in service of raising the level of performance, as well as the profile, of the Glee Club. During his first year at the helm of that organization, he brought his erstwhile ensemble, the Harvard Glee Club, to Rutgers for a joint performance at the Nicholas Music Center. Throughout his time as director of the Club, Ford continued the long tradition of including contemporary popular music in Glee Club performances, echoing his days with the Krokodiloes. The Club's performances during this time were well received; a review of the 1985 annual spring concert remarked on the "professional-level" quality of the performance (see the chap. 5, note 154). Ford also accompanied the Club on its extensive tour of the United States in 1985, which included stops in Washington, D.C., Los Angeles, and many points between. In 1986, Ford's final year at the university, he organized a joint concert with the Kwansei Gakuin University Glee Club of Japan.

Following his service at Rutgers, Ford spent several seasons as the program director for the New Jersey Teen Arts Festival. In 1990, he was hired to direct vocal music ensembles at Bridgewater-Raritan High School in Bridgewater, New Jersey. During his years of employment there, Ford maintained an active schedule of outside activities in the world of choral music. He served as the Eastern Division president for the American Choral Directors Association (ACDA) from 1998 to 2000, during which time he chaired that organization's 2000 convention in Baltimore. Ford served twice as president of the New Jersey chapter of the ACDA; he subsequently served as treasurer and webmaster for that group. In 1996, 1998, and 2009, Ford directed concerts of the Harvard Alumni Glee Club in Tokyo, Kyoto, New York, Cambridge (Massachusetts), and Nagasaki. At various points in Ford's career, he has directed concerts with the New York Choral Society, the New Jersey Chamber Singers, and the New Brunswick Chamber Orchestra.

Ford retired from his position at Bridgewater-Raritan High School in 2006 but remained active, directing the New Jersey Music Educators Association All-State Honor Chorus in 2007. Ford still lives with his family in New Jersey.

6

INTO THE NEW MILLENNIUM

The 1990s: Patrick Gardner, 1993–Present

As noted previously, the role of director of the Glee Club following the final departure of Austin Walter in 1983—and certainly with the departure of Frederic Ford in 1986—had been greatly in flux. In many ways, the men who followed Walter and Ford in this role were little more than part-time agents for the Club, with a variety of other duties both within and outside of the Rutgers Music Department. By the early 1990s, with the Club in a good deal of organizational disarray and membership reaching the midtwenties at some points during this period, the members of the Glee Club decided to take a more affirmative and proactive approach to their future.

In 1991, the position of faculty advisor to the Glee Club, held since the 1983–84 academic year by Rutgers professor Roger Locandro, '73, PhD[1]—who served the Club with dedication and distinction in that role

and who still maintains a close association with the group—was turned over to a former Glee Club member, Matthew J. Weismantel, '85. Weismantel, who had served as Club president from 1983 to 1985,[2] was at this time working in the office of the Rutgers vice president for student affairs as the coordinator of the Student Information and Assistance Center (later renamed the Campus Information Services). After several conversations, it was decided in the fall of 1991 that Weismantel would serve as the Club's official advisor.[3]

Further discussions between Advisor Weismantel and the Glee Club officers in the spring of 1992 led to the formation of the Rutgers Glee Club Advisory Committee. This group's goals of professionalization of the Club along with stronger ties to the various Rutgers administrative levels and to the greater Glee Club community were evident in its makeup. Alumni from different eras as well as administrators, including the chairman of the Music Department and the dean of the Mason Gross School of the Arts (MGSA), were invited to join the committee, as was the Rutgers

University development officer in charge of liaising with alumni and student groups. While the chairman of the Music Department never attended and the MGSA dean only attended once or twice, the interaction of alumni and the development office proved to be of some help for a few years. As Advisor Weismantel puts it, "The idea was to create a group of interested individuals to hear presentations from the Glee Club on directions, plans, and issues and provide feedback, advice, and, perhaps, support."[4] This approach led to immediate involvement in Club affairs from a variety of sources. One of the most impactful was that of Robert Mortensen, '63, who attended some of the first meetings of the advisory committee. Mortensen would become intimately involved in the affairs of the Club from this point on. At the request of Patrick Gardner, who would be appointed director of the Glee Club in 1993, Mortensen would go on to serve as the chairman of the 1996 Tour Campaign Committee, assisting in the planning of the Club's European tour of Poland, the Baltic States, Russia, and particularly Finland, as well as becoming involved in the development of Gardner's new long-term goals for touring in general.[5] Mortensen would have an important role in the Club's international tours over the next two decades and would also develop a close relationship with Gardner during this period.

In the spring of 1993, the Mason Gross School of the Arts, in keeping with the organizational design of other significant arts schools in the country, decided to hire a director of choral activities, a post that would likely include directing the Glee Club as well as the flagship mixed-choral group of the Music Department. The director would also teach graduate and undergraduate choral conducting and provide leadership to the entirety of the Mason Gross choral ensembles. To that end, a national search for a full-time tenure track choral position was approved by the university and subsequently undertaken. A search committee from the Music Department was set up; Weismantel and Glee Club president Kevin Pirelli, '93, were invited to attend some of the subsequent meetings of the committee related to this issue. Additionally, current Glee Club members were encouraged to attend special meetings with each of the prospective candidates for the director's position prior to their rehearsal audition. In the end, Patrick Gardner was the committee's choice to fill the role of director of choral activities. Gardner thus became the new director of the Glee Club and, in so doing, added stability to that position and the others that he would assume. Gardner, who had previously served on the faculties of the University of Texas at Austin and the University of Michigan, brought with him the skills, training, and experience necessary for this post (see "Patrick Gardner [b. 1953]" sidebar on the following page).

PATRICK GARDNER

(b. 1953)

With the establishment of the Mason Gross School of the Arts as the fine and performing arts conservatory of Rutgers University in 1976, the need to develop ensembles focused on professional training for performers and educators became a priority for this new entity. Most large state schools had long since organized their choral programs under the leadership of a director of choral activities. Such a faculty member would lead several significant choral ensembles, serve as the head of a graduate choral conducting program, and provide direction for the choral area as a whole.

However, the reality of the situation was that, while Rutgers had developed several ensembles of distinction prior to the 1980s, these groups were, for the most part, independently administrated. Such were the conditions that led in 1979 to the hiring of Frederic Hugh Ford as an assistant professor in the Music Department. Ford was engaged to conduct the Rutgers University Choir and, notably, to act as a replacement for the retiring F. Austin "Soup" Walter as director of the Glee Club. However, Ford himself departed from the Music Department of the Mason Gross School in 1986, leaving the direction of the various choral groups within the department to a variety of occasional employees, whose part-time status and outside commitments often made the type of dedication of time and energy to their respective organizations necessary to achieve optimal results difficult to implement. Therefore, by the 1990s, there was a perceived need for a director of broad experience and distinctive achievement to unify the school's approach to these matters.

This set of circumstances led to the formation of an ad hoc committee within the Mason Gross Music Department, the primary focus of which was to determine the future organization of the choral department at Rutgers. As a result of the deliberations by the Music Department's committee, the dean of the Mason Gross School and the department faculty created a new position. A subsequent nationwide search for a suitable candidate resulted in the appointment of Dr. Patrick Gardner to the post of director of choral activities. Gardner's

Glee Club director Patrick Gardner conducts at Lincoln Center, April 2016. ©Jody Somers, 2016.

prior experience as an assistant professor of conducting at the University of Michigan, which included a serious involvement with the performing of major works for chorus and orchestra, as well as his ability to administer a viable program in choral conducting brought his candidacy to the fore. And it was certainly a plus that Gardner had had the opportunity to direct the University of Michigan Men's Glee Club, as that duty would fall to him in his new position at Rutgers as well.

Gardner leaped into his duties at his new university with great vigor. Upon undertaking the position as Glee Club director, Gardner immediately instituted many of the procedures he had initiated at Michigan, procedures that continue in the Rutgers Club to this day. Gardner's time with the Michigan Club had taught him the importance of a commitment to building student leadership within such a group. To achieve this leadership structure in his new post, bound volumes of handbooks from the University of Michigan Club detailing the role of the student business leaders of that organization were shared with the members of the Rutgers Club as well as with the committee that had appointed him to this role. Further, the tradition of having Club officers maintain a carefully documented file listing all projects, contacts, and procedures for the year was brought to an already active Glee Club executive council. He set to work revising the recently established methods of the yearly officer's retreat weekend. He also initiated a late-summer follow-up retreat and reach-out to administrators and faculty, including Dr. Marie Logue, '83, PhD, at that time the

dean of students for the Mason Gross School and later a vice president in the Rutgers administration, who would go on to become the Glee Club advisor in 1998. Also included in this initiative was business school faculty member Dr. Peter Gillett, who would take over Dr. Logue's role as club advisor in 2002. Gardner felt it was important to emphasize the crucial role that the position of club advisor played within the organizational structure of the group. The positive effects of these new processes and procedures were immediately felt, and as a result of their implementation over a period of several years, the Rutgers Glee Club gradually coalesced as an exceptional performing organization recognized for its excellence throughout the United States and, indeed, the world.

Patrick Gardner was born in Visalia, California, in the San Joaquin Valley. He was one of five siblings—three brothers and one sister—born to parents Amos and Janis Gardner. Early in Gardner's life, the family moved to the midwestern United States, settling for a time in Dayton, Ohio. It was there that Gardner began to sing in the boys' choir at his school and to develop his musical interests.

In the fall of 1971, Gardner began his studies at Cal State East Bay. He commuted to the Cal State campus daily from a residence in the town of Alamo that he shared with members of the high school rock band of which he was a member, Labyrinth. His curriculum for that year included performing with the University Singers under the direction of Dr. Harry Carter as well as taking courses in music history and choral literature with David Stein. He remembers being in a particularly exciting composition course taught by Janice Giteck, a student of the French composer Darius Milhaud. His choral director, Dr. Carter, regularly programmed major works by living composers as well as canonical works from the early twentieth century. Gardner was thus afforded the opportunity to perform major repertory, such as Igor Stravinsky's *Les Noces* and Schoenberg's *Friede auf Erden*, alongside newly composed works by the American bassoonist, composer, and conductor Robert Hughes, American composers Fred Fox and Robert Basart, and many others. Carter's programming importantly included the second major performance of Lou Harrison's *La Koro Sutro* (1970), a work with which Gardner would be associated for many years. During this period, Professor Carter was forced to miss a number of rehearsals for the Harrison work, and Gardner was chosen to fill in for his teacher, his first significant experience on the podium.

An exciting professional opportunity arose in Gardner's senior year. A relatively new organization, the Oakland Youth Chorus (OYC), was advertising for a conductor. Gardner's work the previous summer conducting a summer youth musical program had come to the attention of a member of the search committee, and after several interviews and a podium audition, Gardner was hired for this position. Throwing himself into the program with abandon, Gardner quickly coached the youth chorus to an extremely high level of artistic achievement. Word of his excellent work with this ensemble soon became known locally, garnering him attention from a noted Bay Area music critic, who reviewed Gardner's second concert with the group in highly laudatory terms. Following this public praise, recruitment and development for the OYC took off: "If it were not for the Oakland Youth Chorus, I am not sure if I would have ended up on my career path. At the age of 20," Gardner recalls, "I was able to develop a group that could sing challenging contemporary works by William Schuman and Paul Creston and had conducted my first choral/orchestral work—the Schubert *Magnificat*. It was an exciting time."[6]

Gardner's tenure with the Oakland Youth Chorus afforded him the chance to conduct significant repertory at an early age; further, it provided an opportunity to develop skills in the areas of group development and organization, equipping him with the critical expertise necessary for administering any such ensemble. Gardner raised money to hire orchestras and fund tours of California and Oregon. He directed the youth chorus as well as a gospel ensemble, a chamber choir, and a women's chorus, and he added a chamber choir to the already existing SATB structure of the Oakland organization. His engagement with this group was a success for all involved.

Academically, the time had arrived to consider candidates for appropriate graduate programs in choral conducting. As his most influential professors, Carter and Stein, had both received their doctor of musical arts degrees at the University of Illinois, Gardner thought that he might follow in their footsteps and decided to visit the Illinois campus. He also thought it prudent, however, to visit several other schools. Therefore, in the summer of 1976, Gardner embarked on a series of interviews throughout the United States, financing this excursion by transporting vehicles across the country. In the course of this collegiate tour, Gardner visited the University of Southern California, which had another powerhouse graduate choral program, and then headed to the University of Texas at Austin (UT Austin) on the recommendation of his voice teacher before visiting the Illinois campus at Champaign-Urbana. He then proceeded east, intending to visit Westminster Choir College in New Jersey and then move on to the New England Conservatory of Music in Boston, Massachusetts.

Though all the institutions that he visited offered excellent programs, the surprise of the trip was the high level of the conducting class of Dr. Morris Beachy in Austin, Texas. Impressed by the remarkable standards of performance and classroom instruction at the University of Texas and feeling that this institution would be the best fit for his needs, Gardner submitted his application to the Austin program. He was therefore thrilled when, on returning to the Bay Area at the conclusion of the trip, he was greeted with a letter inviting him to join Beachy's conducting studio and an offer of full tuition remission. This offer also included an appointment to conduct his own group in his first year in the program and a salary beyond the tuition remission, an offer he eagerly accepted.

While at the University of Texas, a recruitment program instituted by Gardner led to record-high membership in the UT Austin University Choir. This enabled the group to perform major works such as the *Stabat Mater* by the Italian baroque composer Antonio Caldara and, perhaps most significantly, Lou Harrison's *La Koro Sutro*. Gardner had obtained funding for Harrison to lecture at the UT Austin campus and to be in attendance at the performance. This enterprise marked the beginning of a long collaboration between composer and conductor. Earlier, during his time at Cal State Hayward (East Bay), Gardner had had the opportunity to meet Harrison when the former sang in the second performance ever of *La Koro Sutro*. Harrison's work is a setting in Esperanto of the Heart Sutra from ancient Hindu texts. The work is scored for chorus and percussionists, the latter playing what Harrison described as "the American Gamelan," a set of instruments built by the composer to sound like a Javanese gamelan but modified to play in a historical nontempered tuning. During his career, Gardner would conduct this piece over a dozen times, to great acclaim, culminating in a performance of the work at Trinity Church Wall Street in Manhattan with the Rutgers University Kirkpatrick Choir. This performance earned a mention on the *New York Times*'s list of the "Best Classical Music Performances of 2017."[7]

As a result of his early encounters with Harrison and his works, Gardner decided to make this the topic for his doctoral dissertation. That project, undertaken in 1980 and 1981, was titled "*La Koro Sutro* by Lou Harrison: Historical Perspective, Analysis and Performance Considerations." The dissertation is cited in most major books and articles on Lou

Harrison since that time. Author and UC Santa Cruz professor of music Leta Miller, an expert in the field of mid-twentieth-century experimental music, later communicated to Gardner that his work was the most accurate and substantive discussion of Lou Harrison's music and life prior to the publication of her book on that subject in 1990.[8]

In 1981, Gardner accepted a position as assistant professor of conducting at the University of Michigan's School of Music, one of the most prestigious collegiate positions to become available during that year. While at Michigan, he conducted the University Choir, a large mixed ensemble of approximately eighty music majors. He also directed one of the oldest TTBB choruses in the nation, the University of Michigan Men's Glee Club. In addition to these duties, Gardner taught all the undergraduate choral conducting classes at the university.

During his time at Michigan, Gardner oversaw several prestigious projects involving the vocal groups of the school. This impressive string of successful productions began almost immediately upon his arrival. In 1982, Gardner was responsible for preparing the University Choir for several performances as the chorus in Igor Stravinsky's 1951 English-language opera, *The Rake's Progress*. The project was directed by the noted producer, screenwriter, and director Robert Altman, whose screen credits include the films *M*A*S*H* and *Gosford Park*. This production at Ann Arbor coincided with the annual meeting of the American Musicological Society at the University of Michigan, which had as its focus for that year the works of Stravinsky.

The Michigan performance garnered national attention and excellent reviews; many of these commented favorably on the choir's participation. The *New Yorker* cited the choral singing as "splendidly accurate and intelligible,"[9] while *Newsweek* noted that "the chorus had been rehearsed until it glowed."[10] The *Ann Arbor News* review was especially complimentary, offering the following commentary on the choir's role in the production:

> The chorus was thoughtful, thoroughly engrossed, establishing and maintaining individual characterizations while singing intelligently. I don't remember remarking such coherence in any opera chorus, amateur or professional.[11]

On the heels of this successful venture, Altman subsequently restaged the Stravinsky work later that year for the *Opera de Lille* in northern France. Having recognized the value of Gardner's exemplary work with the singers, Altman requested that Gardner engage twenty-four singers from the original production to perform in this new presentation. Gardner spent six weeks in France preparing the choir for a performance that was once again reviewed extensively and enthusiastically, notably in the French newspaper *Le Monde*.

In 1984, the University Choir was once again instrumental in the presentation of an impressive composition. This time, Gardner worked with that group in preparation for the premiere of William Bolcom's monumental *Songs of Innocence and Experience*, after William Blake's eponymous poems. Bolcom's piece is an ambitious one, scored for soloists, a huge chorus, and an orchestra. It was Gardner's task to prepare the choir and to conduct the a cappella movements of the work at the performance in April of that year.

In 1985, the University Choir was chosen to sing at the national conference of the American Choral Directors Association, an honor for any collegiate choral group. It was also at this time that Gardner organized a Lou Harrison festival at Ann Arbor. And under Gardner's direction, the University of Michigan Men's Glee Club was invited to sing the national anthem at the 1984 World Series between the Detroit Tigers and the San Diego Padres. The legendary sportscaster Vin Scully, who was calling the game that day, remarked at the conclusion of the club's performance, "What a magnificent rendition of our national anthem!"[12]

And in a foreshadowing of similar activities that Gardner would undertake in his Rutgers days, he organized an intensive five-week European tour for the Men's Glee Club. Performance venues for this excursion included Rome, Naples, Bari (Italy); Patras, Pireaus, Athens, Thessaloniki (Greece); Belgrade, Bled, Ljubljana (former Yugoslavia); Linz, Graz, Vienna, Salzburg (Austria); Munich, Freiburg, Neustadt im Wald (Germany); Strassburg, Nancy, Paris (France); London, Ham (England); and Cardiff and Llangollen (Wales).

In 1987, Gardner left his position at the University of Michigan to return to the University of Texas at Austin as associate professor of conducting and associate director of choral activities. The primary responsibility connected to this position was conducting the most celebrated UT Austin ensemble, the Chamber Singers.

While at Austin, Gardner again utilized his expertise in the music of Lou Harrison to organize a music festival featuring that composer's works. In 1989, he directed the U.S. premiere of Claude Debussy's *Printemps* (1887) for choir and orchestra at a conference of the American Musicological Society held at his university; this performance was broadcast on National Public Radio.

In 1990, Gardner accepted a position at Wagner College on Staten Island in New York as director of choral activities. While at Wagner, he also served as chairman of the Music Department. During this period, Gardner was very active in the Greater New York musical scene. He served for a time as the conductor for the Brooklyn opera company *Il Piccolo Teatro dell'Opera*. His credits with this group include performances of Benjamin Britten's *Noye's Fludde* and Gian Carlo Menotti's *Amahl and the Night Visitors*.

Gardner also became the director of the Riverside Choral Society, a position he holds to this day. In the early 1990s, he began reshaping this group into a significant choral ensemble, and since that time, it has been so considered by the musical establishment in New York.

As stated previously, in 1993, Gardner was hired as director of choral activities at Rutgers University in New Brunswick, New Jersey. Details of his reorganization and professionalization of the choral groups at Rutgers and their achievements under his direction—with a special emphasis on the Rutgers Glee Club—can be found in the section "The 1990s: Patrick Gardner, 1993–Present" in this chapter.

However, it should be made clear the extent to which Gardner's work with the Rutgers Glee Club has influenced the world of TTBB clubs and the choral world in general since his arrival at Rutgers. Among his colleagues in the choral field, he is held in the highest esteem. Frank Albinder, conductor of the University of Virginia Glee Club and current director of the Washington Men's Camerata, states that Gardner's work "is in the upper echelon—the stratosphere—of collegiate men's ensembles." In a world where once-dominant men's choruses have become far less prominent than in the late-nineteenth and early twentieth centuries, "Pat's [Rutgers Glee] Club is a model." Albinder compares the Rutgers Glee Club not only to its direct counterparts at American universities but, indeed, to the best choral groups in the world, stating that Gardner's ensemble is on a similar level to such well-known performing organizations as the Ylioppilaskunnan Laulajat (the Helsinki University Chorus), often referred to as the YL Male Choir.[13]

One of the reasons that Gardner's ensemble receives this level of acclaim from members of the choral community is its engagement with difficult but artistically significant repertory.

In that regard, according to Albinder and others, Gardner's Glee Club excels. Rutgers has twice played host to the Intercollegiate Men's Choruses (now known as IMC: The Tenor-Bass Consortium) conferences, with Gardner at the helm of these events. Albinder considers these meetings "the gold standard" of such conferences. As an example of the type of serious and challenging repertory in which Gardner's Club engages, Albinder points to a performance of Stravinsky's opera-oratorio *Oedipus Rex* at the IMC conference held at Rutgers in 2014. This performance—which featured the Glee Club as the chorus, with major professional soloists—represented for Albinder "a breathtaking achievement for a collegiate men's chorus." And it should be remembered that the Rutgers Glee Club is composed almost entirely of nonmusic majors, a highly unusual group for a performance of works exhibiting this degree of difficulty. "Most (university) Clubs don't tackle literature at such a high level," remarks Jo-Michael Scheibe, a recent past president of the American Choral Directors Association who currently serves as chair of the University of Southern California Thornton School of Music's Department of Choral and Sacred Music. "To hear them perform is quite remarkable. I really admire what Pat has done with this group."[14]

Gardner's commitment to important and serious repertory also extends to the commissioning of works on behalf of the Rutgers Glee Club from renowned composers across the globe. These commissions include William Bolcom's *The Miracle: 9 Madrigals after Giovanni Pascoli* for men's

223

chorus, percussion, and woodwind quintet and *Travels* for male chorus and four-hand piano by composer and musical pedagogue Lewis Spratlan. In 2005, Gardner also commissioned, on behalf of the Glee Club, *Voice of the Bard* for male chorus by Jennifer Higdon, the renowned American composer. It should be noted that all three of these composers are Pulitzer Prize–winning artists who have composed works for some of the most prestigious musical ensembles in the world. It should further be noted that major funding for all of these works was made possible through the generosity of Robert Mortensen, '63, a dedicated friend and generous benefactor of the Glee Club as well as an alumnus of the group. Gardner has also supported the compositions of his colleagues on the Rutgers Music Department faculty, staging vibrant and effective performances of works by noted faculty composers Scott Ordway, Robert Aldridge, Melissa Dunphy, and Gerald Chenowith, as well as performing numerous compositions by Rutgers students.

This engagement with the compositional process speaks to Gardner's remarkable breadth of knowledge and experience. He is at home with the works of composers from the likes of Josquin des Prez of the Renaissance period to contemporary artists like Jennifer Higdon. He is also extremely well-versed in the principles and practices of the historically informed performance movement, allowing him to slip seamlessly between modern and early music–oriented interpretations of music from a variety of eras. And according to his colleagues, he approaches each performance from a position of confidence that stems from the extensive training that his career has afforded him, along with intense preparation for every event. This enables him to make choices that might seem intimidating to other musicians in his role. "There is no fear with Patrick," Scheibe says. "I've never seen him shy away from anything."

This accumulated knowledge and experience now serves as a resource not only for his students and faculty colleagues but for choral composers and fellow music directors as well. When matters of repertory, historical accuracy, or programming arise in the course of planning a musical season, many of these musicians will turn to Gardner for advice and guidance. "We often go to Pat as an expert in the [choral conducting] field," says Scheibe. "[Gardner] is, first and foremost, a consummate musician and teacher." Albinder seconds that sentiment, stating that "[Gardner] has done yeoman's work in the field [of choral directing]."

Gardner's work with the Rutgers Glee Club is far from finished. Though the pandemic of 2020 slowed the momentum of the Club's trajectory momentarily, Gardner engaged with many innovative performance media in order to keep the spirit of the Club intact during this period. With the resumption of in-person instruction at Rutgers imminent at the time of this writing, it seems certain that the Rutgers Glee Club, with Gardner securely at the helm, will resume its traditionally active schedule of impressive and challenging events during its 150th anniversary year and beyond.

It should be noted that Gardner was hired as the director of choral activities largely on the basis of his extensive experience at the previously-mentioned institutions with directing large choral ensembles in the performance of major works for chorus and orchestra. Thus upon his arrival at Rutgers, Gardner saw an opportunity to reproduce, in a contemporary manner, the success of the Rutgers University Choir of the 1950s and ensuing decades under F. Austin Walter. During that period, the choir, incorporating many members of the Rutgers Glee Club, made numerous appearances with major American orchestras under a variety of acclaimed conductors (see chap. 5, "The 1950s: The University Choir"). Gardner sought to capitalize on the connections he had already made in the greater New York area to similarly provide quality performing experiences—often now for the entire Glee Club—with renowned area ensembles.

Prior to his being hired at Rutgers in 1993, Gardner had spent several years as chair of the Music Department at Wagner College on Staten Island, New York. During that period, he had established himself as a respected conductor of large-scale choral works. His appointment as director of the Riverside Choral Society in New York in 1990 placed him in a position to work with a variety of high-level instrumentalists in the area. For selected engagements, Gardner would supplement the Choral Society's ranks with members of the Glee Club in the performance of major choral/orchestral repertory.

Such opportunities were frequent. In 1998, Gardner served as chorus master for the Richard Strauss version of Mozart's opera *Idomeneo*, K 366, that was presented at Avery Fisher Hall at Lincoln Center. This event was part of that season's Mostly Mozart Festival, with Gerald Schwarz conducting the Mostly Mozart Festival Orchestra. Gardner was able to invite several Glee Club members to supplement his Riverside Choral Society, which was serving as the chorus for this presentation. Similarly, a Mostly Mozart event in 2000—which featured the *Great Mass in C Minor*, K 427, and two choruses from Carl Maria von Weber's 1821 opera *Der Freischütz*, a concert that garnered extremely favorable reviews in the *New York Times*[15]—afforded an even greater contingent of Glee Club members the chance to perform with high-level singers and instrumentalists. This was true as well for the August 2001 Mostly Mozart presentation of Robert Schumann's secular oratorio *Das Paradies und die Peri*.[16] All of these events—as well as many others detailed in the narrative following—enabled Gardner to provide noteworthy performing experiences for his Glee Club members, experiences that would, like those of Club members from the mid-twentieth century who performed under the likes of Bernstein, Ormandy, and Leinsdorf, remain with them for a lifetime.

On a more day-to-day level, Gardner set to work reestablishing the Glee Club to its former status as a premiere performing institution at Rutgers; these efforts began immediately in the fall of 1993. On September 13, a celebration of the signing of a peace treaty between Israel and the Palestine Liberation Organization took place at the Cathedral of St. John the Divine in Manhattan. Speakers representing delegations from both parties to the treaty as well as from the United Nations addressed the assembly. Gardner—who had been responsible for organizing and providing the chorus for the yearly "Concert for Peace," established by Leonard Bernstein and then run by the noted composer and conductor Lukas Foss—was invited by the organizers of this event to provide a chorus for the ceremonies and brought the Glee Club, a prestigious commencement to his association with the group. The Club was given little time for preparation for this performance. The event organizers phoned Gardner on the Friday before the Monday concert, leaving scarcely four days in which to learn the repertory, which included works in Hebrew and Russian. As Club president Eric Chrol, '95, remarked at the time, "It was quite a nerve-wracking weekend."[17]

The customary Glee Club engagements continued to be featured during Gardner's initial season. The traditional Christmas in Carol and Song performances at Kirkpatrick Chapel, with the combined forces of the Kirkpatrick Choir and the Glee Club, took place on consecutive evenings, December 10 and 11, with performances at 7:00 and 9:00 p.m. on both nights.[18] The spring semester saw the Club present two separate performances at the First Congregational Church in Westfield, New Jersey, on February 18 and March 9. The Rutgers men traveled to Northampton, Massachusetts, to join forces with the Smith College Women's Glee Club on February 26. An interesting historical footnote concerning this event: at this concert, Gardner's first major performance with the Club beyond the confines of Rutgers, several women from the audience sought Gardner out to complain about the single-gender nature of the alma mater.[19] The annual spring concert was held on April 23, this year at Voorhees Chapel, and featured a presentation of John David Earnest's *Only in the Dream* for brass, harp, and percussion. Also presented were works by Beethoven and Randall Thompson along with the traditional spirituals, folk songs, and Rutgers songs. As a finale to Gardner's first academic year, the Club combined with the Voorhees Choir at Voorhees Chapel on May 1 to present performances of *Kiddush* for tenor solo, mixed chorus, and organ by Kurt Weill and *Sacred Service* (*Avodath ha-kodesh*) by Ernest Bloch.[20]

The 125th anniversary of the first intercollegiate football game in America, which occurred on November 6, 1869, provided an excellent opportunity early in Gardner's tenure to showcase the revitalized Club. The concert commemorating this event was held at the State Theater in New Brunswick on November 5, 1994. The event was a joint performance that also featured the Rutgers University Marching Band (all 180 members) as well as the women of the Voorhees Choir. The program included favorites from the Glee Club's football-game repertory, including "Loyal Sons" and "Colonel Henry Rutgers."

The concert opened with choreography conceived by Gardner for "The Rutgers History Lesson." A small group from the Glee Club re-created the famous pose of the Glee Club of 1897, attired in academic gowns and mortarboards, and then morphed into a re-creation of the signing of the Rutgers Charter as depicted in the large stained glass window of Kirkpatrick Chapel. At the words "the Revolution came," the Club kicked over the table on which the charter was placed and morphed into Revolutionary-era Jersey soldiers. In the subsequent verse, a reenactment of the first Rutgers College/Princeton football game was presented, complete with the tackling of the "Princetonian."[21] Gardner's above-outlined presentation from this concert retains a prominent place in the Rutgers University Glee Club's many performances of "The Rutgers History Lesson" to this day. The "Princetonian" is a coveted "hand-me-down" position passed on to a new actor at the Senior Banquet.

Following this, the Glee Club joined with the Voorhees Choir and a brass ensemble from the Marching Band in a performance of Daniel Pinkham's *Christmas Cantata*.[22] F. Austin Walter also joined the Glee Club on stage that evening to conduct "Nobody Ever Died for Dear Old Rutgers," a piece by Jule Styne and Sammy Kahn that was written for the 1947 Broadway musical *High Button Shoes*; Walter arranged the piece for the Club. Apparently, Gardner paid homage to Walter by turning cartwheels across the front of the stage, as was the latter's custom, during this number.[23]

The Glee Club was quite active in the spring of 1995 as well. On April 1, the Club held a joint concert at Voorhees Chapel with the Smith College Alpha and Omega Choirs; the program for this event included the *Te Deum* by Joseph Haydn. The annual spring concert was held at the Nicholas Music Center on April 22; the program offered Franz Schubert's *Nachtgesang im Walde* for four French horns and chorus as well as the traditional Glee Club fare. And on the following evening, the Glee Club joined with the Rutgers University Orchestra, the University Choir, and the Voorhees Choir under the direction of Peter Rubardt, resident conductor of the New Jersey Symphony, for a performance of Beethoven's *Symphony No. 9*, also at the Nicholas Music Center.

One of the most important early initiatives launched by Gardner was the institution of a stable program for international touring. He envisioned a once-in-a-college-generation experience—that is, once every four years—for international excursions. One of the negatives of the touring procedure that he had encountered while teaching at the University of Michigan was that only about one-half of the group was taken on tour. Gardner was committed to making the experience available to the entire group; this schedule would provide ample time for proper fundraising efforts to support the trips while ensuring that every student would experience at least one international tour during their college years.[24]

The first international tour of Gardner's tenure was scheduled to begin immediately following the end of the spring semester in 1996.[25] The Tour '96 Campaign Committee was formed in the spring of 1995 to facilitate the fundraising efforts and manage other logistical affairs of this proposed excursion. Robert Mortensen, '63, volunteered his assistance to this project, requesting to be assigned chairman of the committee. He offered his motivations for his involvement in a brief article in the summer 1995 issue of *Glee Gab*: "I asked to be assigned as the Chairman of the Tour '96 Campaign Committee because I wanted to help ensure that today's students can have the same experiences through music, travel and fellowship that I cherish so fondly after more than thirty years. Give me the opportunity, I said, to help raise the necessary funds so that the Rutgers Glee Club can tour Eastern Europe and Russia next year."[26]

This proposed tour was an extensive one and required a great deal of preparation. Cities to which the Club traveled in the spring of 1996 included Warsaw (with a brief stopover in London); Vilnius and Kaunas, Lithuania; Tallinn, Estonia; St. Petersburg, Russia; Espoo, Finland, where the Rutgers contingent was hosted for a meal by the Espoo Male Choir, whom the Club had hosted at Rutgers in the fall of 1995; and

Helsinki.[27] Remembered as a highlight of this tour was the performance at the Glinka Cappella in St. Petersburg, where the Club was made to feel especially welcome. According to one Club member, the performance was called "a miracle" by a noted Russian choral director who was in the audience.[28]

Gardner recalls that the performances on this tour rose to previously unrealized levels of excellence. In his view and in the view of other interested parties such as Bob Mortensen, the results of a five-year plan, implemented on his arrival at Rutgers in 1993, to professionalize the Glee Club regarding its performance standards were beginning to take shape. Struck by the transformation of the group's abilities even at this early stage in its progress, Gardner off-handedly suggested to Mortensen during the tour that it would be extremely beneficial to have a recording of the tour program. As Gardner remembers it, Mortensen replied, "Let's do it," and the two men proceeded to put in place the logistical (mainly the efforts of Gardner) and financial (primarily Mortensen's contributions) necessities of undertaking such a project on short notice and far from home.

The exigencies of the situation were overcome, and a CD of the program, the Club's first recording in this format, was recorded in Finland on the last day of the tour (see chap. 4 sidebar, "Glee Club Discography: From the Vicissitudes of War to European Tours"). According to the liner notes for this recording, the choice of repertory for the tour—which included works by the celebrated Polish composer Krzysztof Penderecki and Russian a cappella works sung in Church Slavonic as well as American spirituals, folk songs, and jazz arrangements—was "intended to show the intersection of the spirits of tradition and change, of American and Eastern European traditions."[29]

The success of this tour set the stage for the next high-profile undertaking by the Club. The year 1997 marked the 125th anniversary of the establishment of the Rutgers Glee Club. There was, therefore, little time for the Club to relax after their European excursion came to a close; preparations for the next important set of performances marking this occasion needed immediate attention. Several events were scheduled for both the fall and spring semesters of the 1996–97 academic year, including a Black Tie 125th Anniversary Banquet and an exchange concert with the State University of New York at Geneseo.[30]

However, the most ambitious undertaking for this celebration was the proposal to hold the annual spring concert in Alice Tully Hall at Lincoln Center in Manhattan. To be sure, there was an element of financial risk that accompanied this ambitious project. The rental of Alice Tully Hall came with a hefty $7,000 price tag. Removing the annual spring concert to a Manhattan venue carried uncertainty as well, in that the local university (and New Brunswick) audiences might find

The Glee Club performs at Alice Tully Hall at Lincoln Center, May 5, 1997. Rutgers University Glee Club Archives.

it difficult to make such a trip.[31] Despite these obstacles, sufficient funding was obtained, and Gardner supplied the musical vision and artistic realization.

The concert took place on Monday, May 5, 1997. The highlight of the program was the Messe "Cum jubilo" of Maurice Duruflé, with accompaniment by the Rutgers University Orchestra. Also featured that evening was a presentation of the cantata Festgesang an die Künstler by Felix Mendelssohn, in which some attending alumni participated in the performance. The alumni also joined in the singing of many of the traditional Rutgers songs that appeared on the program.[32] The concert served as a fitting tribute to the 125 years of excellence that the Glee Club had attained.

It should be noted that this performance generated many positive consequences. The initial fears over financial issues did not come to fruition; Alice Tully Hall was filled to capacity, and the Club had done an excellent job of fundraising. This served as proof that such undertakings were not only possible but desirable. The concert had demonstrated to the university and to the Mason Gross School of the Arts how invaluable a commodity the Glee Club, when properly managed and directed, could be. It also demonstrated to the members of the Club the level of excellence that could be achieved through a renewed commitment to musical discipline and went some way toward fostering a strong link between the governing administration officials and the Club membership.

The following semester, the Club joined with the glee clubs of Yale University and Princeton University for a joint performance in Richardson Auditorium at Princeton on November 14, 1997. Featured on the program were Spasyeniye sodyelal by the twentieth-century Russian composer Pavel Chesnokov and a movement from Kurt Weill's Das Berliner Requiem. This marked the first joint appearance by the Rutgers Club with either of these counterpart organizations since the late 1950s, a testament to the ensemble's high level of achievement and recognition and to Gardner's extensive level of contact with the choral world at large.

The work of the Club continued as the decade of the 1990s came to a close. The group's second CD, The Bells Must Ring, featuring the songs of Rutgers, was produced in October of 1998, and the Club took great pains to promote this effort. This included a lunchtime concert at Ferrin Mall in downtown New Brunswick on October 9, 1998, led by assistant director David Kimock. This CD included Estonian, English, and Irish selections along with the traditional Rutgers school songs. Proceeds for the CD would be put toward the Club's upcoming tour to Central Europe, which would take place the following May.[33]

In April of 1999, the Glee Club was featured as a special artist on a program given by Gardner's

Riverside Choral Society. The program offered the *Alto Rhapsody*, op. 53, for contralto, male chorus, and orchestra by Johannes Brahms.[34] The solo part was performed by American mezzo-soprano Jane Shaulis, a veteran vocalist with the Metropolitan Opera with over sixty roles to her credit with that organization.[35] This event is very much in keeping with Gardner's vision of providing high-quality performing experiences for the members of the Glee Club. And in an event such as this, the Club—on its own and in its entirety—was spotlighted in a high-profile New York appearance.

The spring 1999 tour of Central Europe was intended to include stops in Gödöllő, Pécs, Sopron, Budapest, Vienna, and the Slovak capital of Bratislava.[36] However, the bombing of Serbia by NATO led to the university administration canceling parts of the tour to neighboring Hungary and a rerouting of the second half of the trip to Dresden and Berlin. During this last stop, the Glee Club's next CD was recorded in the acoustically beautiful Heilig-Kreuz-Kirche in Berlin (see chap. 4 sidebar, "Glee Club Discography: From the Vicissitudes of War to European Tours").

The decade closed out on notes of nostalgia and connections to past traditions. During Senior Week of 1999, the full complement of Glee Club members—a number that had risen during Gardner's short time at the helm back to a healthy sixty men—availed themselves of an opportunity to serenade the much-admired F. Austin "Soup" Walter at his home. Gardner had invited "Soup" to conduct at a Club rehearsal or two each fall during the former's time as director, focusing such sessions on Walter's beloved Rutgers songs. Gardner, having scheduled this event with the aging Walter's caretakers, marshaled the group at Walter's home. With the appearance of Walter and his faithful dog Tanzi, who had replaced the deceased Tosci, on his porch, the assemblage immediately burst into a few Rutgers songs. According to an account by one of the Club members, the energetic eighty-seven-year-old conductor was still eager to get back into the game: "[Walter] informed us proudly that the Glee Club had been the most important part of his university career. When asked if he felt up to conducting, 'Soup' flashed a quick smile and said, 'I think I remember a few!' As [a title was suggested] he would rattle off the first several lines, give a quick pick-up and off we would sing!"[37]

The final event of the 1990s was the traditional holiday concert series at Kirkpatrick Chapel. This took place on Saturday and Sunday, December 11 and 12, 1999.[38] Two performances on each evening, at 6:00 p.m. and 9:00 p.m. as was customary, were given, providing a time-honored link to the past through the medium of a much-revered Rutgers institution.

The following spring semester saw the Glee Club playing host to the biennial conference of the Intercollegiate Men's Choruses on March 4 and 5, 2000. Concerts by many of the best male glee clubs in the nation were presented during this conference; workshops and other events were also included, providing an excellent educational and artistic experience for all involved.

This IMC event was a watershed moment in the history of the Glee Club for a number of reasons. First, the Glee Club, under Gardner's supervision, had commissioned Pulitzer Prize–winning American composer William Bolcom to write a major work for the ensemble. The result of that commission—Bolcom's *The Miracle: 9 Madrigals after Giovanni Pascoli*, for men's chorus, percussion, and woodwind quintet—received its premiere performance at this conference. Gardner had worked closely with William Bolcom during his time at the University of Michigan, premiering the composer's magnum opus, a two-and-a-half-hour setting of British poet and painter William Blake's complete *Songs of Innocence and Experience*. *The Miracle*, which lasts approximately twenty-five minutes in performance, is one of the most challenging and beautiful pieces in the contemporary repertoire for TTBB chorus; conductors from throughout the United States were in the audience, and with their rendering of the piece, the Glee Club had made its mark musically. Indeed, the Club's appearance at this conference signaled the beginning of a two-decade period in which the Rutgers University Glee Club established a national reputation far beyond anything in its previous history.

The spring semester of 2000 ended on a more somber note, however, with the announcement of the passing of F. Austin Walter on May 1, 2000. Kirkpatrick Chapel Choir director David Drinkwater as well as a close circle of the aging director's friends had maintained close ties with Walter after his retirement and had been at his side during the last months of his life. Gardner was with "Soup" in his room at the Robert Wood Johnson University Hospital in New Brunswick two nights before he passed away, at which time Gardner had found Walter "sleeping peacefully."[39]

A memorial service was held for Walter on May 21 at Kirkpatrick Chapel. Organized by David Drinkwater and Gardner, with assistance from the students of the Kirkpatrick Choir and the Glee Club, the service was attended by approximately 250 family members and friends of the deceased. The eulogy on behalf of the Rutgers Glee Club was given by James P. Moore, '75. Other speakers included the Reverend Donald Stager, '76; Dr. Scott Whitener; Virginia Moravek, DC '64, GSE '77; William and Robert Walter; and the Reverend Harry W. Morgan, '60. The Glee Club, led by Gardner, provided selections including "Brothers, Sing On" and "A Rutgers Prayer."[40] It is perhaps fitting that the twentieth century, a century in which F. Austin Walter flourished both personally and professionally while bringing great acclaim to the institution that he cherished, should end with his passing.

The New Millennium

The year 2001 began the new millennium in good fashion. The Club was selected to perform at the 2001 American Choral Directors Association National Convention, which was held in San Antonio, Texas, from March 14 through March 17. Selection to perform at these events represents a major achievement; hundreds of choirs from around the country audition, but only twelve are chosen to perform.[41] The groups are selected through blind auditions—that is, the groups and conductors are not known to the evaluating committee and thus are chosen purely on their level of performance. The Club presented four concerts during the course of the convention, each with an audience of over two thousand.[42]

The Club followed up on this event by making an appearance at Lincoln Center's Avery Fisher Hall on April 18, 2001. This concert—a combined event in which the Glee Club performed with the Rutgers University Orchestra, the Kirkpatrick Choir, the University Choir, the Raritan Winds, and the well-known American pianist Ruth Laredo—was given as part of the Rutgers in New York series sponsored by the Mason Gross School.[43] Featured on this program were Bolcom's *The Miracle* and *Choral Fantasy*, op. 80, for piano, vocal soloists, chorus, and orchestra by Beethoven, with Laredo as soloist.[44] Indeed, this concert was in many ways reminiscent of the combined events

that F. Austin Walter had initiated and developed over the years as part of the University Choir performances in Howard McKinney's concert series, of which the Glee Club had been such an integral component. A review of the concert in the *Home News Tribune* cited the "beautifully prepared chorus of 50" in the Bolcom work, which was itself described as "a great delight in both the music and its wonderful performance."[45] The *New Jersey Star-Ledger* similarly lauded Gardner's "superb direction" and the Glee Club's "honeyed blend and sense of ticking rhythm."[46]

A more explicit homage to former Club director Walter was undertaken at the annual spring concert of 2001. Though billed in the local press as being a concert of "20th century music," the event was more internally described as the Soup Memorial Concert, featuring "Soup's favorites plus alumni involvement."[47]

The traditional Christmas in Carol and Song program, long a staple of the Rutgers calendar year, was given its customary multiple performances during December of 2001. The event, which during this period featured the Glee Club combined with the Kirkpatrick Choir, was held in Kirkpatrick Chapel on Saturday, December 8 at 6:00 and 9:00 p.m. and Sunday, December 9 at 5:00 and 7:30 p.m.[48] These concerts would mark the last performances of the academic year for director Gardner, who was scheduled for sabbatical during the spring semester of 2002. Gardner's plans for this period away from Rutgers included a five-week tour through the United States, conducting and lecturing at concerts and festivals.[49]

Standing in for Gardner as conductor during his absence was David Kimock. Kimock had received a master of music degree in choral conducting from the Mason Gross School of the Arts in 1999; as part of that course of study, he had served as assistant director of both the Glee Club and the Kirkpatrick Choir. On completion of his master's program, Kimock left the New Jersey area to take up various positions, mostly as a director of church ensembles. He subsequently returned to New Jersey to pursue other teaching and performing opportunities.[50] Among the highlights of the spring 2002 semester was a joint concert featuring the Glee Club from Mount Holyoke College. Both clubs presented separate works at the concert, which was given on March 3, 2002, but the centerpiece of the program was the combined performance of *Nänie*, op. 82, by Johannes Brahms, a setting of a poem by Friedrich Schiller. Kimock led the combined clubs in what was described as a "spirited performance."[51]

It was also during this semester that plans began to take shape for the proposed summer 2003 European tour. Gardner, utilizing the flexibility of his sabbatical schedule during this semester, visited several European locations in France and the Netherlands in preparation for the tour. He was accompanied on this site-inspection mission by Robert Mortensen, chair of the

Rutgers Glee Club advisory board. Mortensen, in his advisory board capacity, also organized the fundraising activities necessary for the implementation of the tour.[52]

The on-site inspection tour did much to solidify the relationship that had developed between Gardner and Mortensen as a result of their shared interests, in the Club as well as in other areas. This period marked the beginning of an extraordinary two-decade partnership during which the director and the donor would combine to produce excellent outcomes for the Rutgers Glee Club.

This is, perhaps, a point at which a bit more can be said of Robert Mortensen, since his impact on the modern Glee Club is so tangible. Mortensen, a Glee Club alumnus, graduated from Rutgers with a bachelor of science degree in education in 1963. Following his graduation, Mortensen joined the air force and served four years on active duty in Vietnam, many of those years acting as an intelligence-briefing officer for General William Westmoreland. His postmilitary career was impressive, serving as the CEO for two railroads.[53] But his role as a philanthropist and patron of the arts is certainly what binds him most directly to the Rutgers Glee Club as it exists today.

Many of the philanthropic projects that have been undertaken by and on behalf of the Glee Club over the last several decades would not have been possible without input, in one form or another, from Bob Mortensen. An early effort along these lines

Robert Mortensen, '63 (right), and Gregory Moore, baritone, arrive at the Nicholas Music Center for a Glee Club event in 2016. ©Jody Somers, 2016.

assist in the underwriting of the Glee Club director's salary. The donors requested that the Nicholas Music Center Green Room be named in honor of their mentor, former Club director Walter.

In 2001, Mortensen fully funded the Robert Mortensen Graduate Endowment Fund, which provides yearly stipends to Gardner's graduate students. In that same year, Mortensen endowed the Mortensen International Tour Fund, supporting Gardner's vision of consistently providing undergraduates with the experience of performing abroad with the Club.

Further, Mortensen has encouraged his peers to join him in supporting the Club, with significant outreach to the alumni community that has been extremely successful, particularly regarding raising money for the international tours. Mortensen has funded three different commissions from composers of original works for the Rutgers Glee Club, some of which have found their place in the modern repertory for TTBB organizations across the country and, indeed, around the world. And Mortensen has made (and, as of this writing, continues to make) significant yearly personal contributions to the Club. Mortensen's generosity led him to become the principal benefactor behind the construction of the new Robert E. Mortensen Hall, adjacent to the Nicholas Music Center on Douglass Campus in New Brunswick. This new building, which features practice rooms, offices, a small food court, and most significantly, the

involved Mortensen as a donor to the F. Austin Walter Director's Fund in the late 1980s. Other major donors for this effort included Richard Shindell and Richard Hale. The interest from this fund can only be used to

235

Shindell Performance Hall for choral groups, was a welcome addition to the Music Department facilities upon its completion in 2015. Notably, the three major donors involved with this effort—Mortensen, Richard Shindell, and John Bauer—are all Glee Club alumni. Shindell has also established a major fund for Glee Club performance and touring, while Bauer, for whom the Glee Club director's office and a major rehearsal space in the new building have been named, has also joined other alumni in supporting the choral arts at Rutgers.

It should be noted that Mortensen's level of philanthropy is more than matched by his significant accomplishments in business activities and community leadership. It is in acknowledgment of these latter efforts that Rutgers in 2005 inducted Mortensen into their Hall of Distinguished Alumni.

In the fall of 2002, the role of Glee Club advisor fell to a new faculty member. This position had been vacated in 1998 by Matthew Weismantel. His dedicated service to the Club was acknowledged at that

Robert E. Mortensen Hall on the Douglass Campus at Rutgers University. Work on this building was completed in 2015. ©Jody Somers, 2016.

Shindell Performance
Hall for Choral Groups
in Mortensen Hall.
©Jody Somers, 2016.

time by bestowing on him the Rutgers College Student Organization Advising Lifetime Achievement Award, which was presented to Weismantel at the 1998 Student Activities Banquet. Taking his place as advisor was Marie Logue, at that time associate dean of students and an honorary member of the Glee Club.[54] Though dedicated to the well-being of the Club, Professor Logue's tenure as advisor lasted but a few years. Following her in 2002 was Dr. Peter Gillett, a tenured professor in the Rutgers School of Business. A strong advocate for a successful arts program at the university, Gillett himself is an avid performer, singing with the Riverside Choral Society in New York, which Gardner conducts. He subsequently joined the Kirkpatrick Choir as their advisor and often performed with that ensemble. Gillett would also at this time regularly attend Glee Club concerts. At a private celebration of Gillett receiving tenure at Rutgers, Gardner declared,

"Well, now it is time for you to come on board as the advisor for the Glee Club!" Gillett's profound business acumen combined with his musical talents made him an ideal candidate for the position of advisor, and he was heartily welcomed by the Club into this role.[55]

Gillett's capabilities were immediately put to use; he played a pivotal role in organizing and otherwise facilitating the initial business arrangements for the 2003 European tour. By his own account, he was further involved throughout 2003 in such matters as negotiations with the tour company, reconciling their ultimate compensation, and monitoring the movements of the U.S. dollar in relation to the Euro in order to maximize the existing financial resources.[56] Gillett continues to provide guidance in such matters for the Club today.

The tour itself—which ran from March 25 to June 9—was, in Gillett's words, "triumphant." Armed with a repertory of European church music, American classics and spirituals, and the traditional Rutgers songs, the touring group included Gardner, Justin Bischof (organist and accompanist), Robert Mortensen, and Gillett. After arriving in Amsterdam, the Club presented concerts in Weert and Kerkrade before setting off for further engagements in Germany. Local families around the city of Köln provided much of the housing during this leg of the tour, with a hostel at Altenburg Haus taking up the remainder of those needs. Two performances were given at the Altenburg

Cathedral, the last of these with the *Kölner Kantorei*, an a cappella chorus based in Cologne, Germany, that specializes in choral works of the nineteenth and twentieth centuries. The group continued on to perform in the magnificent cathedral in Strasbourg.

The tour then proceeded to Paris; after checking in at the hotel in that city, an excursion to neighboring areas included concerts at Chartres Cathedral. There was ample time for the students to experience the magnificence of that building's famed stained glass windows. It was at the venerable Notre Dame Cathedral that the Club had the opportunity to perform the mass for Pentecost. The concert at Notre Dame takes particular pride of place in Glee Club touring history. While many choirs are presented at Notre Dame at their Friday morning concerts, to which tourists are admitted, Concepts Tours Paris representative Andrea Rose Rosseaux had excellent contacts at the highest levels within the cathedral's administration. She was able to provide recordings to the music director and the clergy, who were quite taken with the high level of the Glee Club's singing. They were also surprised to see that the Glee Club included movements of Jean Langlais's *Messe solennelle* and Maurice Duruflé's *Messe "Cum jubilo"* in their repertory. The Club was invited to sing one of the most important masses of the year, taking the place of the customary professional choir at the service on the eve of Pentecost. Over three thousand people were in attendance at the mass and during the service. The celebrant sent word that the Glee Club should process with the worshippers at the end of the service, an extraordinary honor according to Ms. Rose Rosseaux.[57]

The final concert of the tour took place at the Church of Saint-Sulpice in Paris, at which an audience member was heard to remark to the local organizer of the event that the Club could not possibly be an American choir, as it was far too well-behaved.[58]

The fall semester of 2003 began with earnest preparation by the Club for a scheduled November performance of the *Grande messe des morts*, op. 5 (also known as the *Requiem*), by Hector Berlioz. The Club combined for this event with the Philadelphia Singers, the official chorus of the Philadelphia Orchestra, and the orchestra from the Mannes School of Music in Manhattan.[59] There were two performances of this program presented: the first was given at Carnegie Hall on November 10, followed by a performance at the Kimmel Center for the Performing Arts in Philadelphia on November 16.[60] Both concerts were deemed "an absolute success."[61]

In the spring semester of 2004, the Club journeyed to Harvard University for an appearance at the national seminar of the Intercollegiate Men's Choruses. This seminar brought together some of the oldest and most distinguished men's glee clubs from all over the country. The Rutgers contingent performed six selections on their program, including "Sangerhilsen,"

Norwegian composer Edvard Grieg's original work that became an American favorite in English translation as "Brothers, Sing On" by the Rutgers Glee Club's own Howard D. McKinney. This was a bit of tongue-in-cheek programming of the high-brow sort on the part of Gardner. "Brothers, Sing On" had long been a traditional favorite of TTBB choruses. But almost no one was aware of the original Grieg version. The Glee Club purposefully left the translation off the printed program, marched onto the stage, and opened their set with the music that everyone knew—in the original Norwegian.

McKinney's translation of the Grieg work had been part of the Rutgers Glee Club's repertory since his early days as director of the group. Following its publication in the early twentieth century, McKinney's English-language version became an enormous favorite of men's choruses throughout the world. It has found its way into the repertory of virtually every college TTBB organization in the United States and, indeed, is a popular work for high school TTBB ensembles as well. The royalties that still accrue from "Brothers, Sing On" go to the Howard D. McKinney Fund at Rutgers University, which supports, in part, activities such as this tour by the Rutgers Glee Club.[62]

The Club's performance at the IMC seminar continued with an impressive program including Darius Milhaud's "Psalm 121," Volker Wangenheim's "O quam pulchri," and as a finale, "Girls! Girls! Girls!"

from the Franz Lehár operetta *The Merry Widow*, which featured elaborate choreography designed by New York City Opera director Jay Lesenger.[63] This appearance on March 11 was followed by the annual spring concert on April 24 at the Nicholas Music Center.[64]

In a late spring effort, the University of Michigan Men's Glee Club was hosted by their Rutgers counterparts for a joint performance on May 13 at Kirkpatrick Chapel. Fears concerning low attendance for this concert due to its placement after the end of classes and exams proved unfounded; a robust audience attended the event, which was followed by a reception at a popular New Brunswick watering hole.[65] Gardner notes that the conductor of the Michigan Glee Club during this period was Stephen Lusmann. Lusmann had studied conducting with Gardner at Rutgers and sung, by special arrangement as a postundergraduate student, with the Kirkpatrick Choir. Lusmann had been working in German opera houses and wanted to obtain conducting experience and worked with Gardner to that end. This course of action paid dividends for Lusmann; he subsequently secured an appointment to the voice faculty at the University of Michigan and was additionally engaged to conduct the Glee Club as part of his tenure track position.[66]

The fall of 2005 saw the Glee Club playing host to some old friends. On October 20, the Club welcomed the Limburg Male Chamber Choir, directed by Dion Ritten.

This group, consisting of singers from seven different choirs from the Limburg province of the Netherlands, joined with the members of the Glee Club—seventy members strong this year—for a combined performance at Kirkpatrick Chapel. Several of the choirs represented in Ritten's ensemble had played host to the Rutgers men during the 2003 European tour, and the New Jersey group was happy to be able to reciprocate their hospitality. The Club had, in fact, accommodated Ritten the previous fall, when his group Cantate Venlo, a women's choir from the Netherlands, visited Rutgers.[67]

On January 16, 2006, the Glee Club combined with the Cornell University Glee Club for a joint concert at Kirkpatrick Chapel. The program featured works by Franz Schubert, Estonian composer Veljo Tormis, and Grammy Award–winning American composer Jennifer Higdon. Later that semester, as it had done many times in the past, the Club had the sad duty of being featured at a memorial service for an outstanding figure in Rutgers history. In this case, the service at which they appeared was for a man who embodied that history: Richard P. McCormick. McCormick was the university's premiere historian; he was, in fact, often referred to as "Mr. Rutgers." He was also, at the time of his death on January 16, 2006, at the age of 89, the father of the sitting university president, Richard L. McCormick. The Glee Club, together with the Kirkpatrick Choir, performed "None Shall Part Us" from the Gilbert and Sullivan comic opera *Iolanthe*, which was sung at the elder McCormick's wedding in 1945. The singing groups closed out the service, which was held at Kirkpatrick Chapel on March 9, with a rendition of "On the Banks."[68] The semester ended with the annual spring concert on April 29 at the Nicholas Music Center, which included works by Higdon and Randall Thompson.

The fall semester of 2006 saw the Glee Club combining with the men of the Riverside Choral Society and the Kirkpatrick Choir for an interesting program presented at the Museum of Jewish Heritage in Manhattan. The concert was a commemoration of the sixty-fifth anniversary of the Jewish massacre at the ravine known as Babi Yar in Kyiv. The program featured a reading of several poems by the Soviet and Russian dramatist, essayist, and poet Yevgeny Yevtushenko (1933–2017), including what was described as "an impassioned, animated version of [his 1961 poem] 'Babi Yar' in which he moved seamlessly between Russian and English." The musical portion of this event was an all-Shostakovich affair, opening with that composer's *Concertino for Two Pianos*, op. 94, performed by the renowned duo of Misha and Cipa Dichter. The highlight of the night, however, was the first public performance of the first movement of the two-piano reduction of Shostakovich's *Symphony No. 13* (*Babi Yar*). Prepared by the composer to play for the Soviet censors before the first performance of the fully orchestrated work, this version is naturally limited by the constraints of the keyboard. Nonetheless, *New York Times* critic Allan Kozinn was highly complementary of the performance, stating that "Patrick Gardner conducted an illuminating performance in which the Dichters gave a muscular and sometimes fiery reading" of the transcription, which was "robustly supported" by the vocal forces listed above.[69]

For the choral groups under Gardner's direction, this concert, as impressive as it was, also served as excellent preparation for a repeat performance of the Shostakovich symphony under different circumstances. On October 29, the Kirov Orchestra of the Mariinsky Theatre, under the direction of Valery Gergiev, presented its own all-Shostakovich program at Avery Fisher Hall. The program featured *Symphony No. 8* and concluded with the powerful *Babi Yar* symphony, now in its full orchestral form. The *New York Times* reported, "The men of the Riverside Choral Society and the Kirkpatrick Choir and Glee Club of Rutgers University provided vigorous support."[70]

The spring semester of 2007 saw the Club joining forces with the Rutgers University Wind Ensemble for a performance of *The Ramparts* by American composer Clifton Williams. Scored for concert band and men's chorus, this concert took place at the Nicholas Music Center on March 27, 2007, with Gardner conducting the combined group. On April 27, the annual spring concert was presented at the same venue. This concert, the 135th in the series, served primarily to showcase the repertory that would be utilized for the Club's upcoming three-week European tour, which was scheduled for May. The program included works by Jennifer Higdon, Darius Milhaud, Krzysztof Penderecki, and Felix Mendelssohn.

This tour was undertaken in accordance with Gardner's vision of providing a once-in-a-college-generation experience for international tours and included stops in the Netherlands and Germany. Among the venues in which the Club performed were the Berlin Cathedral, the Dreikönigskirche in Dresden, and the Thomaskirche in Leipzig, the last of which served as the main venue of employment for the final twenty-seven years in the life of Johann Sebastian Bach. One of the highlights of the tour was a performance in front of an audience of nearly one thousand hosted by the choral group Cantabile Limburg and their conductor Jürgen Fassbender. A contemporary review from a major Frankfurt newspaper, which noted the Glee Club's "gripping and imposing sound" under the direction of its "excellent conductor, Patrick Gardner," speaks to the success of this concert.[71] A CD featuring repertory from performances given on this tour was subsequently released under the title *Hear the Voice* (see chap. 4 sidebar, "Glee Club Discography: From the Vicissitudes of War to European Tours").

As previously mentioned (see chap. 6, "The New Millennium"), one of the many honors bestowed on

F. Austin Walter at the time of his retirement as director of the Glee Club in 1983 was the dedication of the greenroom adjacent to the Nicholas Music Center Auditorium to his memory. The ensuing twenty-plus years had taken their toll on this facility, however, and it became painfully obvious to all interested parties—including university president Richard McCormick and dean of the Mason Gross School of the Arts George B. Stauffer—that major renovations needed to be undertaken. To that end, Rutgers administration officials reached out to Glee Club alumni to raise the funds necessary for a first-class restoration of the greenroom. The assistance of Robert Mortensen was once again enlisted to spearhead the fundraising campaign, an assignment he accepted readily. The donors recruited by Mortensen expressed vigorous support for this project and contributed handsomely. Their only stipulation, according to Mortensen's own account, was "that the Green Room would remain dedicated to the memory of Soup Walter." Mortensen himself contributed to this project generously, as did more than a dozen Glee Club alumni and friends, including Richard Shindell, '57, and the classes of 1932 (F. Austin Walter's class) and 1947.[72]

The rededication of the F. Austin Walter Green Room was marked by a Glee Club concert on November 11, 2007, at the Nicholas Music Center. This event was attended by more than fifty Glee Club alumni, who joined current members in song and celebration, as well as many of the donors to the renovation project and an assortment of Rutgers dignitaries. Dean Stauffer offered introductory remarks before the performance, which, along with the Club, featured the Voorhees Choir and several instrumentalists from the Mason Gross Music Department. A reception in the rehearsal hall adjacent to the newly rededicated greenroom followed the concert.[73]

The European tour of 2007, like all its predecessors, offered the Glee Club many opportunities to interact with a variety of continental counterparts. One such encounter was with the aforementioned Cantabile Limburg, a twenty-four-man ensemble under the direction of Jürgen Fassbender, one of Europe's most notable choral conductors. While visiting Limburg during this tour, the Club was hosted by the Cantabile, and the groups presented a joint concert. Selections on the program included *Quatre petites prières de Saint François d'Assise* by Francis Poulenc, which was performed by the Cantabile, and a joint performance of Franz Biebl's *Ave Maria*.[74]

The Club had a chance to reciprocate Cantabile's hospitality when that ensemble visited the United States during the spring semester of 2008. Over the course of one week in March, the ensembles united for a series of performances that included concerts at Kirkpatrick Chapel at Rutgers, the Riverside Church in Manhattan, and a performance at the Intercollegiate Men's Choruses National Seminar in Vienna, Virginia.

Selections performed jointly on these concerts included *The Last Words of David* by Randall Thompson and the Biebl *Ave Maria*.[75] The performance of the Biebl in Virginia created a special moment for the hundreds of singers and audience members in the Vienna church in which it was performed. The Biebl is perhaps one of the best-known works in the TTBB repertory. As Gardner led the second verse of the work, the IMC board of directors started singing quietly along. Within a minute, hundreds of singers stood and sang the work from memory, literally bringing tears to the eyes of many in the crowd. Those in attendance from the University of Michigan, the U.S. Army Chorus, the University of Pittsburgh, the University of Virginia, the Washington Men's Camerata, Bowling Green State University, the Miami University Men's Glee Club, and the Penn State contingent all went home with a very special memory.[76]

This semester offered the Club yet another opportunity for a joint event, this time with the Mount Holyoke Glee Club. That group, under the direction of Kimberly Dunn Adams, hosted the Rutgers men at South Hadley, Massachusetts, where the clubs presented a concert on April 11. That event featured the combined clubs performing *Five Mystical Songs* by Ralph Vaugh Williams with accompaniment from a twenty-one-member orchestral ensemble, all under the skillful direction of Ms. Adams. The groups had performed together earlier in the decade, and in many ways, this performance was meant to strengthen the bonds between the two clubs and encourage future joint efforts.[77]

While international tours and prestigious competitions may account for a large share of Glee Club activities in any given academic year, equal or occasionally greater satisfaction can be gained from performances of a more local variety. Such events are frequently of no less importance socially, institutionally, or often, artistically than their flashier, sexier counterparts. The spring semester of 2009 provided notable examples of such experiences. On March 1, the Glee Club combined with the three other choral groups in the Rutgers Music Department: the Voorhees Choir, the Kirkpatrick Choir, and the University Choir. The third in what had become an annual event, this concert, dubbed the Rutgers Choral Extravaganza, was seen as a vehicle by which "the combined talents of all the Rutgers choirs are brilliantly showcased."[78]

Also on the schedule for this semester was a benefit concert, organized by Director Gardner's wife, Susan, at the North Brunswick Township High School auditorium on March 29. The program for this concert featured a wide range of musical styles, from jazz to gospel to classical standards and, of course, Rutgers college songs, providing the Club with an opportunity to demonstrate its versatility. Members of the Rutgers football team were on hand to sign autographs.[79] And an event of historical importance to the university

also called for representation from one of the oldest student organizations of the school. On April 26, the Glee Club was on hand to commemorate the two hundredth anniversary of the Old Queens building, the oldest surviving structure on the campus. The building's bell was rung two hundred times by students, staff, and other members of the Rutgers community in celebration. The accompanying ceremony included brief remarks from President Richard McCormick and two other faculty members.[80] The Glee Club's subsequent performance indeed seemed appropriate.

In the spring of 2010, an opportunity to display their talents to a larger audience once again emerged. The Club was selected through a blind-audition process to perform at an ACDA event, this time Eastern Division Convention, which was held in Philadelphia from February 10 through 13. As noted at the time, such an invitation "is one of the brass rings in the choral world."[81] An appearance at such a prestigious event was a fitting highlight to the final season of the new millennium's first decade.

The 2010s

The most recent decade of the Club's existence began with a tribute to one of the most influential leaders in the group's long and distinguished history. On

October 23, 2010, at the Nicholas Music Center auditorium, an alumni concert was presented in memory of the late F. Austin "Soup" Walter. All Glee Club alumni were invited to attend the performance on the occasion of what would have been Walter's hundredth birthday. For repertory, Club favorites from Walter's time were included. The centerpiece of the program, however, was the performance of *The Testament of Freedom* by the American composer Randall Thompson, one of the best-known works of the men's chorus repertory. Originally written in 1943 to celebrate the bicentenary of the birth of Thomas Jefferson, this work had been performed several times throughout the Club's history.[82] The earliest performance occurred in 1948, with Erich Leinsdorf conducting the Rochester Philharmonic at the College Avenue Gymnasium; Walter, of course, prepared the Glee Club for its role in that performance in his capacity as director. The work, originally scored for piano and men's chorus, was subsequently scored for orchestra, and later for wind ensemble, by Thompson. It is the wind ensemble version that the Club performed at the alumni event.

Foremost on the minds of the Club during this academic year, however, were the preparations that were already underway for the proposed European tour of 2011. This time, the Club planned to travel to various cities in Italy, all with rich musical histories, including Rome, Florence, Venice, and Pisa.[83] Though the eventual itinerary would be somewhat adjusted

and expanded, the trip itself took place as scheduled. The Club—which numbered seventy members, including assistant conductors Daniel Spratlin (GS '13), Stephen Caldwell (GS '12), Mark Boyle (GS '10), and John Guarente (GS '11), as well as accompanist Paul Conrad, '14—departed from Newark Liberty Airport on May 18, 2011, and arrived the following morning in Milan. From there, the group proceeded to Padua, where they performed at the Chiesa di Santa Maria Assunta in the *comune* of San Doná di Piave. They then proceeded to nearby Venice, performing at the historic St. Mark's Basilica, before participating in a walking tour that included stops at the Doge's Palace and the Piazza San Marco. Concerts were subsequently given at the Chiesa di San Michele in Arezzo, the Chiesa dell'Addolorata in Salerno, and the Basilica di Sant'Agostino in Vatican City. The Club also had an opportunity to sing at St. Peter's Basilica, believed by Catholics worldwide to be the burial place of the eponymous saint. Following a guided tour of Rome on June 1, the Club departed the next evening from Fiumicino International Airport in Rome and arrived in New Jersey on the morning of June 2.[84]

The highlight of the ensuing semester (fall 2011), however, was undoubtedly the combined performance with the Kirkpatrick Choir that took place on November 4 at the Kirkpatrick Chapel. The Glee Club continued to build its reputation for presenting some

The Glee Club at St. Peter's Basilica in Rome, 2011.
Rutgers University Glee Club Archives.

of the most challenging works in the TTBB repertory by performing Giovanni Bonato's *O lilium convalium* for two men's choruses and two violoncellos; this work features extended string techniques as well as unusual sonorities for the antiphonal choruses. The Kirkpatrick Choir program featured the chorale-based motet *O Heiland, reiß die Himmel auf*, op. 74, no. 2, by Johannes Brahms and other a cappella works, including *Carols of Death*, short settings of Walt Whitman poems by American composer William Schuman.

The annual spring concert of 2012 was used to mark the 140th anniversary of the Club. For this occasion, alumni members were invited to join the current contingent to perform such works as "Rain, Beautiful Rain" by Joseph Shabalala of the isicathamiya group Ladysmith Black Mambazo and Giuseppe Verdi's "Evviva! Beviam!" The concert also showcased a work titled *Travels* by Pulitzer Prize–winning composer Lewis Spratlan.[85] *Travels*, commissioned by Gardner on behalf of the Glee Club, was given its premiere at a concert at Mount Holyoke College on March 31, 2012. At the Mount Holyoke event, the performance of this work was conducted by Glee Club assistant conductor Daniel Spratlin, GS '13, the composer's son.[86]

The Glee Club and Kirkpatrick Choir joined once again in the fall of 2012 to present a concert at the Nicholas Music Center on November 11. Presented under the title "Masterworks of the Jewish Tradition," the program included the rarely performed *Berliner Requiem* of Kurt Weill, scored for solo tenor, solo baritone, and TTBB choir with wind orchestra. Also offered at this concert were *Romancero Gitano*, op. 152, by the Italian composer and pianist Mario Castel-Nuovo Tedesco and the world premiere of "Jerusalem," an a cappella work for mixed voices by the American composer Kenneth Lampl.

The 2013–14 academic year marked the twentieth anniversary of Patrick Gardner as director of the Rutgers Glee Club and as a professor at the university. This kind of stability had been sorely lacking in the years immediately following the departure of F. Austin Walter from the director's role, and the Club's achievements in those twenty years speak to the value of such stability.[87] The enhanced reputation that the Club enjoyed under Gardner's leadership offered opportunities to further showcase the role of the arts at Rutgers, both within and outside of the university. One such moment occurred in the spring semester of 2014, when Rutgers would host the biennial seminar of the International Men's Choruses association (known since 2021 as IMC: The Tenor-Bass Choral Consortium) on the occasion of the one-hundredth anniversary of that group. One of the highlights of the seminar, which would take place on March 6–8, was the performance by the Glee Club, with the Rutgers Symphony Orchestra, of *Oedipus Rex*, an opera-oratorio scored for orchestra, speaker, soloists, and male chorus by Igor Stravinsky. Composed in 1927 in Stravinsky's neoclassical style, the work is based on a Sophoclean tragedy. The IMC performance on March 7 was repeated on March 9; both performances were given in the Nicholas Music Center.[88]

The Club embarked on another international tour in the early summer of 2015. This time, the Club would perform at venues in the United Kingdom and the Netherlands. The tour began on May 19, when the group departed from Newark Liberty Airport bound for London Heathrow Airport. On arrival, many of the

Club's members immediately availed themselves of the opportunity to partake in a walking tour of Windsor Castle. The following day, the group departed for Bath and then went on to Gloucester, where they gave a concert at Gloucester Cathedral. Subsequent performances were given in Bridgend, Wales (St. Mary's Catholic Church); Oxford (St. John the Evangelist Church); Henley-on-Thames (St. Mary's Church); Maastricht (St. John's Church); Nijmegen (St. Stephen's Church); and Utrecht (University Hall in the Academiegebouw). The final stop on the tour was Amsterdam, where the Club visited the Rijksmuseum and engaged in further tourist activities before returning to New Jersey on June 2.[89]

Director Gardner with graduate students Colin Britt (left) and John Wilson (right) in the chamber in Gloucestershire Cathedral in which Henry VIII received petitioners, 2015. Rutgers University Glee Club Archives.

The Glee Club at the *aula* (auditorium) at University Hall in Utrecht, 2015. Rutgers University Glee Club Archives.

The Glee Club performs at Gloucestershire Cathedral, 2015. Rutgers University Glee Club Archives.

The Glee Club in the town of Greenwich, county of London, 2015. Rutgers University Glee Club Archives.

A CD featuring performances from this tour—titled *Sudden Light*—was released in 2016, along with a DVD of the concert at Utrecht University. This latter effort—titled *The Rutgers University Glee Club at Utrecht University*—was recorded by a professional film crew. It offers the viewer a chance to experience some of the sights of this tour as well as the sounds.[90]

2016 marked the 250th anniversary of the establishment of Rutgers College. Not surprisingly, the focus of campus activities, as well as a variety of off-campus events, was squarely on this impressive milestone. The Glee Club was, of course, prominently featured in these celebratory expressions of university pride. The spring concert on April 23 of this year was once again open to alumni members. A series of joint rehearsals with the Club and the alumni were scheduled, as were catered luncheons and other activities, giving the current Club members a chance to imbibe in the relatively immediate history of the group through alumni interaction.[91]

Earlier that month, the Club had been featured at a legislative celebration in honor of the University's 250th anniversary at the Botanical Gardens in Washington, D.C. This invitation-only event, at which the Club performed the alma mater and other Rutgers songs, was attended by several members of the New Jersey Congressional Delegation, including Senator Robert Menendez and Representatives Frank Palone Jr., Scott Garrett, and Donald Norcross.[92]

The Club also had the honor of performing at the 250th commencement ceremony at Rutgers on May 15, 2016, at which President Barack Obama became the first sitting president of the United States to deliver the university's commencement address. At the event, the Club combined with members of the Kirkpatrick Choir, the University Choir, and the Voorhees Choir to create an ensemble of over 120 singers. Preparations for this performance were described as "intense and meticulous," and they were seemingly effective. Contemporary reports state that, at the conclusion of the combined group's performance of "The Star-Spangled Banner," President Obama was seen (and heard) saying "Wow" as he turned to university president Robert L. Barchi.[93]

The Club returned to the stage of the ACDA National Convention for the first time in seventeen years during the spring semester of 2017; that year's event was held in Minneapolis, Minnesota. The Club gave two performances—one at Orchestra Hall, home of the Minneapolis Symphony Orchestra, and one at the Central Lutheran Church in the downtown Minneapolis area—during the extended weekend of March 8–11. Included in the repertory for these performances were *Psaume 121* by the French composer and conductor Darius Milhaud and Franz Schubert's *Nachtgesang im Walde*.[94] The Schubert work was accompanied by a horn section consisting of members from the Minneapolis Symphony and the Minneapolis Orchestra.

Patrick Gardner and the Glee Club reenact the first intercollegiate football game in the United States (November 6, 1869) between Princeton and Rutgers as part of the annual spring concert on April 23, 2016. The concert was part of the university's 250th-anniversary celebration. ©Jody Somers, 2016.

Glee Club alumni join with the current Club members for the finale of the 250th-anniversary concert in the Nicholas Music Center on April 23, 2016. ©Jody Somers, 2016.

The Club's most recent European tour took place following the conclusion of school activities in the spring semester of 2018. As part of this excursion, the Club gave performances in Sweden, Finland, and Estonia. The first concert was on May 16 in Stockholm at Erik Erikson Hall, where the Club was hosted by a local choir, the Stockholms Studentsångare; a second performance was given in this city at the Sofia Church on May 18. Then it was on to Uppsala, where the Club performed at the Missionkyrkan (Mission Covenant Church) and received coaching from the renowned Swedish choral conductor Robert Sund. Crossing to Finland via ferry, the Club was hosted by the Academic Male Voice Choir of Helsinki for their performance at the St. Paulus Church.

2018 marked the one-hundredth anniversary of the establishment of the Estonian Provisional Government, which signaled the formation of the modern state of Estonia.[95] This occasion motivated the Glee Club to accelerate its traditional four-year cycle for European tours (2003, 2007, 2011, 2015) by moving this trip up one year. The Club further paid tribute to their Estonian hosts by including in their repertory several selections by the native composer Veljo Tormis. The Estonian

The Glee Club performs with a horn section featuring members of the Minneapolis Orchestra and the Minneapolis Symphony at the 2017 ACDA convention.

songs were presented by the Club at concerts in the cities of Tartu and Tallinn. As was customary on Club excursions, there was time for sightseeing; a tour of Tallinn's medieval Old Town was a favored activity.[96]

In the fall of 2019, the Club participated in a collaborative effort with the glee clubs of Yale University and Princeton University. Representing some of the oldest such organizations in the country, the three groups presented a concert on the Princeton campus on November 15. The oldest of the three clubs, that of Yale, was established in 1863, a mere nine years before that of Rutgers College, with the Princeton Club following not long after its New Jersey neighbor in 1874. The Rutgers group, however, is the only one of the three that is still constituted as an all-male ensemble; both the Yale and Princeton clubs transformed themselves into mixed ensembles in the 1970s. Collaborative efforts such as this represent a prominent thread running through the history of the Rutgers Glee Club. Throughout the Glee Club's annals, there are many references to such joint concerts, going back to the earliest days of the group. Joint concerts with glee clubs and choirs from Harvard, New York University, Cornell, Mount Holyoke, and a variety of other institutions have long been a part of the Rutgers Glee Club tradition. While invitations to participate in such collaborations had fallen off during the latter years of F. Austin Walter's directorship of the Club, Gardner's connections to the larger choral world led very quickly to the reestablishment of these projects shortly after his arrival. Mount Holyoke and Wellesley were particularly eager to schedule visits from the Club, and requests from Smith College were also received. Funding from the Richard Shindell Glee Club Concert Fund was helpful in underwriting the expenses for these concerts. And the Rutgers group planned to continue this tradition the following fall; a joint concert with the Wellesley College Choir, featuring a combined performance of the *Hymn of the Cherubim* by Pyotr Ilyich Tchaikovsky, was planned for April 4, 2020, at the Houghton Memorial Chapel at Wellesley College.[97]

2020: The Glee Club in the Era of COVID-19

Indeed, 2020 began with the Glee Club looking very much to the future. The group was again selected to perform at the ACDA Eastern Region Conference, which was scheduled to take place on March 7 in Rochester, New York. The joint concert mentioned above with the Wellesley Choir was also eagerly anticipated, as was the annual spring concert on April 25. But aside from the immediate concerns of preparing for these upcoming events, the Club was also beginning to discuss plans for the 2021–22 academic year, which would mark the 150th anniversary of the Club.

Having heard tales of the 125th-anniversary concert in Alice Tully Hall at Lincoln Center, the current iteration of the Club was determined to ensure that the 150th-anniversary celebrations would equal or surpass the events that marked the previous milestone.[98]

However, many of these plans would be canceled outright or, at the very least, put on hold as the COVID-19 pandemic began to take hold of the country. The ACDA Conference—which was held at the Hochstein Performance Hall in Rochester—was a highly successful event for the Club. Performing works by Christopher Marshall, Franz Schubert, Lewis Spratlan, and Nikolai Golovanov, the months of intensive rehearsal that the Club's members dedicated to this important appearance paid off; the group received a standing ovation and significant praise for their performance at this concert.

The Glee Club was, at this point, completely unaware that this would be the last time that the group would meet as such for over a year. Due to the increasing severity of the pandemic, however, this would be the final appearance in public for the group in 2020. Rutgers University—like many, if not most, such institutions in this country and abroad—switched to online instruction following the spring recess of March 2020. That status would remain in effect through the spring semester of 2021. Notwithstanding the preclusion of in-person performances that COVID protocols,

including this new online-instruction format, dictated, the Club carried on to the best of its ability, living up to the standard of previous generations of students who had endured far worse circumstances yet persevered. Inclusiveness and camaraderie are values that are held in high esteem by the Club, and methods by which the group might keep in contact and carry on with Club affairs were quickly adopted. Perhaps the most important step in this direction was the embracing of the video platform Zoom, which provided a virtual space for the discussion of Club business. This engagement with Zoom quickly led to the notion of a virtual choir, a concept that was embraced by all members. With Gardner coordinating these efforts, a video performance of the alma mater—edited by Club member and current president Ryan Leibowitz, '21—was released by the Club at approximately the same time of the academic year that the annual spring concert would have occurred, demonstrating the group's ongoing commitment to brotherhood and community.[99]

Having gained experience through this virtual performance, the Club decided to keep the tradition of the Christmas in Carol and Song concerts, an integral part of any normal Rutgers holiday season since its inception, alive through a similar virtual concert (see chap. 6 sidebar, "Christmas in Carol and Song: A Rutgers Tradition for over One Hundred Years"). This event—usually performed four times over two evenings at Kirkpatrick Chapel by the combined forces of the Glee Club and the Kirkpatrick Choir—was this year streamed on Saturday, December 12, on the Facebook pages of both participating organizations as well as that of the Mason Gross School of the Arts. "We didn't want to lose that tradition just because of Covid," Gardner stated. "We're better than that. So, we decided to get together and create something very, very special."[100] Many of the Christmas in Carol and Song traditions were maintained for this season, including the preconcert reception for the Colonel Henry Rutgers Society and the President's Council, which Gardner ran from home with his Christmas tree in the background. Officers from the Glee Club and the Kirkpatrick Choir joined him in greeting the major donors who attend this event each year. Over 3,000 people watched the premiere of the virtual performance on YouTube and Facebook; as of March 1, 2021, over 16,000 people had viewed the virtual concert.

Virtual events became the accepted standard for participation in performance situations as pandemic restrictions continued into 2021. Thus the Glee Club's presence at the 2021 National Conference of the American Choral Directors Association, originally scheduled to take place in Dallas, took the form of a video performance. To be invited to appear at a national ACDA convention, a group must submit three recordings for adjudication by a blind panel. It is not unusual for the association to receive seven hundred or eight hundred submissions for a national conference. That being the case, it is a rare occurrence for any group to be chosen to perform at the national level more than once. For Gardner and the Rutgers Glee Club, acceptance to the 2021 virtual conference, which took place between March 18 and March 20, 2021, marked their third such appearance, having been invited in 2001 and again in 2017.

The work performed at this event was "Wanting Memories" by the American singer, composer, and speech pathologist Ysaye Barnwell. The composer stated in an interview that the genesis of the piece can be traced to memories that were generated by the process of preparing for the sale of the house that she grew up in following the death of her parents. The work is, therefore, a tribute to those who came before us: our mothers, grandmothers, and all caretakers who have passed away, but whose memories evoke an unconscious wish or prayer for that which is gone yet remains within us.[101] As expressed in the lyrics, these are the things that "made us laugh, made us dance, made us sing," that made us into who we are. In this way, the work evokes a sense of becoming human through these caretakers.

The beautiful video was created by Rutgers graduate student Stephanie Tubiolo using video clips and photos of happy memories from current Glee Club singers. The resulting visual collage superimposed on

The Glee Club performs during the pandemic, 2021. Rutgers University Glee Club Archives.

Barnwell's music consists of video footage of the Club members as they perform the work interspersed with the photos and moving images of the students' families. Remarking on the impact of this performance at the ACDA conference, veteran choral director Jo-Michael Scheibe commented that "when I saw the images of children and their moms on the video and the connections that tied [all the elements of the video] together, I wept."[102]

Beyond to the 150th-Anniversary Celebration

With the future still not certain in terms of upcoming performance opportunities, the Rutgers Glee Club nonetheless finds itself at the time of this writing, on the brink of the 150th anniversary of its inception, in a position of strength, unity, and indeed, optimism concerning the next chapters in its storied existence.

CHRISTMAS IN CAROL AND SONG

A Rutgers Tradition for over One Hundred Years

One of the oldest and best-loved traditions of the Rutgers academic year is the annual Christmas in Carol and Song presentation during the month of December at Kirkpatrick Chapel. As has been the case for decades, the Rutgers University Glee Club and the Rutgers University Kirkpatrick Choir typically present four programs over two evenings on the final weekend of the semester. These concerts are quite distinct from the Glee Club's participation in the Christmas events of the Howard McKinney era, which are outlined below. Complete with student traditions ranging from decorating the chapel to the ringing of the Old Queens bell by the seniors after the performances, these concerts carry a weight of history all their own.

Notwithstanding, while the basic format for the present-day Christmas in Carol and Song performances—from the organ preludes to the thundering performance of the two combined choral groups in Arthur Honegger's stirring finale

Christmas in Carol and Song participants with Director Gardner, December 2019. Rutgers University Glee Club Archives.

to his 1921 oratorio *King David*—was the creation of David Drinkwater, these concerts do hold an elemental connection to the Christmas presentations that were so much a feature of the McKinney era. As can be seen in the Howard D. McKinney sidebar in chapter 5, McKinney was responsible for the development of virtually all musical activities at the college during this period. Among the innovations to the nascent music program that he instituted during the 1916 season, his initial year as a Rutgers employee, was the presentation of a Christmas service at Kirkpatrick Chapel featuring seasonal carols. An account in the *Targum* describes this event as follows:

> A service of Christmas music will be held in the [Kirkpatrick] chapel at four o'clock, on Sunday afternoon, December 17th. A number of carols, most of them having been written prior to the beginning of the nineteenth century, will be sung by a male chorus consisting mostly of undergraduates and a mixed choir composed of singers from the various choirs of the city churches. This is an innovation and gives an opportunity of hearing some of this music which has come down to us through the years, and which possesses a beauty so peculiar to itself.[103]

This particular modification to the Rutgers schedule, however, did not immediately establish itself as a perennial feature. The following Christmas season, no similar event was undertaken. In its place, McKinney presented an organ recital at 5:00 p.m. on December 23, 1917, the program of which included seasonal favorites such as selections from the oratorio *Messiah* by Handel.[104] No Christmas programs of any sort were offered in 1918 or 1919.[105] This is almost certainly due, at least in part, to the advent of America's participation in World War I and the resulting exigencies.

However, on December 18, 1920, the following notice appeared in a local newspaper:

> At Kirkpatrick Chapel on Sunday afternoon [December 19] at 4 o'clock . . . a service of Christmas Carols both ancient and modern will be given under the direction of Howard D. McKinney of Rutgers College . . .
>
> A choir composed of Rutgers College and the N. J. College for Women students will participate in the concert.[106]

The article goes on to list the proposed program, including Christmas favorites "A Joyous Christmas Song," "Adeste Fidelis," and "Holy Night," the last for solo voice and organ.

By 1924, this Christmas concert had been recognized as a much-anticipated annual event, which featured "the combined Choral Clubs of Rutgers University and the New Jersey College for Women." The combined group offered "traditional Christmas carols . . . presented by the seventy voices representing the two organizations." A program similar to the 1920 event was given on this occasion, with the addition of favorites such as "Bring a Torch, Jeannette, Isabella."[107]

By 1926, this event had become so popular that an additional concert was added. A special performance would be given at the regular morning chapel service time of 11:00 a.m. along with the now traditional 9:00 p.m. service. The combined group for this year was reported to number approximately ninety, with one-third of those from the Rutgers College contingent and the remainder from the women's college.[108]

In 1929, McKinney decided to change the format of the Christmas concerts at Kirkpatrick Chapel. On December 15 of that year, he presented an abridged version of an original composition of his own, titled "A Mystery for Christmas." This work was laid out as what McKinney described as a medieval miracle play involving several tableaux, complete with staging and lighting directions. Characters in the play include Mary, the archangel Gabriel, a variety of lesser angels, shepherds, and the Three Wise Men.[109] Throughout the 1930s, performances of McKinney's "Mystery" would alternate on a quasi-yearly basis with the more traditional performances of the combined choirs of Rutgers College and the New Jersey College for Women. In 1936, "Mystery" was presented; in 1937, the choir concert. Both versions of the Christmas presentation garnered enough interest that two performances were required to accommodate all patrons.[110]

As with many activities at Rutgers in the early 1940s, problems related to the onset of World War II caused a disruption in the presentation of these Christmas programs. The tradition was restored, however, in 1945, though not under the auspices of the Rutgers music faculty. Instead, this event was presented under the aegis of the Rutgers Protestant Fellowship.[111] This change in sponsorship notwithstanding, McKinney and the combined choirs remained the main components of the program.

In the 1950s, F. Austin Walter had taken over the duties of presenting the annual Christmas programs. Walter kept to the traditional arrangement instituted by McKinney; an alternation between the "Mystery" pageant and a more conventional service consisting of Christmas favorites. The latter was the format, for example, of the program Walter conducted at Kirkpatrick Chapel on December 17, 1950.[112] By the mid-1950s, however, Walter had decided on a hybrid arrangement. For the Kirkpatrick Christmas concerts given on December 16, 1956 (two, at 7:30 and 9:00 p.m.), the Glee Club, with Walter conducting, opened the performances with seasonal selections, including the Austrian carol "A Little Child is Born." This was followed by a rendition of McKinney's "Mystery," performed by members of the Rutgers Drama Club under McKinney's guidance.[113]

In 1957, David Drinkwater was hired by the university to fill the role of university organist. His duties included taking charge of the Kirkpatrick Choir. In this latter role, the presentation of the annual Kirkpatrick Christmas concerts became his responsibility. In 1958, Drinkwater designed the basic format for the program that is now known as Christmas in Carol and Song.

Drinkwater envisioned the format as a religious service interspersed with a number of carols and important choral works on Christmas themes. This configuration was adapted from one that was annually presented at the Union Theological Seminary in Manhattan,[114] which in turn was inspired by the service of the Nine Lessons and Carols, often associated with the university choral program at Kings College Chapel, Cambridge. The performances of the Nine Lessons at Kings College began in 1918, though they stemmed from a much older tradition. Their popularity quickly spread to the United States, where many universities embraced the format as a fitting Christmas offering, particularly the private colleges of the East Coast that still maintained chapel services. While Rutgers University became a public university via legislative acts in 1945 and 1956, chapel services under Drinkwater's direction were maintained until the beginning of the new millennium.

Among the differences between the traditional Kings College arrangement and that presented by Drinkwater at Rutgers were the use of a single reader (this role was originally filled by the Rutgers College chaplain), shorter readings, and more musical selections. In this format, the Glee Club and the Kirkpatrick Choir, now the two components of these performances, alternated vocal selections between readings.[115]

By the early 1960s, the designation "Christmas in Carol and Song" had been adopted for these annual concerts, as can be seen by the following announcement:

The combined Rutgers Glee Club and Kirkpatrick Chapel Choir will offer two performances of its traditional concert, "Christmas in Carol and Song," at 7 and 9 p.m. Sunday [December 13, 1964].[116]

But the appellation was also used during this period for holiday radio broadcasts featuring recorded performances by various groups affiliated with the university, as the following account demonstrates:

A program of "Christmas in Carol and Song," featuring three widely known Rutgers University singing groups, will be heard on some 30 radio stations, now [December 21, 1967] through Christmas Day.

The half-hour program . . . will feature the Kirkpatrick Chapel Choir directed by David A. Drinkwater, the Rutgers University Glee Club, conducted by F. Austin Walter, and the Douglass College Chapel Choir, directed by A. Kunrad Kvam . . .

Selections on the program are from the recent Christmas services held on the university campuses.[117]

These broadcasts were extremely popular, and indeed, there was by this time a long tradition of Rutgers choral groups presenting material from their Christmas concerts in the form of radio programs, dating back to at least the 1940s.[118] By the 1970s, these programs were being carried on nearly sixty radio stations throughout the state.[119] And by the late 1970s, on-campus demand for the Christmas in Carol and Song events had risen to the point that the combined groups had to begin offering four performances over the course of a weekend, usually two on Saturday and two on the following Sunday, both days at 7:00 and 9:00 p.m.[120]

The success of Drinkwater's basic format for the concert is apparent; the underlying design of the concert remained consistent throughout his tenure as director of these events and, indeed, has endured to the present day. Such a service would unfold as follows:

The published starting time of the concert is preceded by a set of organ voluntaries lasting approximately twenty minutes. When the organ preludes conclude, the members of the Kirkpatrick Choir emerge from the balcony of the chapel in near darkness and present the a cappella introit. This is followed by the processional hymn "O Come, O Come, Emmanuel," during which the audience rises and sings with the two choirs. During this selection, the Kirkpatrick Choir processes from the balcony to the altar, switching places in the hall with the Glee Club, each group singing while traversing the beautifully decorated chapel, candles in hand. After each group settles into their places, a reader presents the "Prophecy and Annunciation." For many years, the university chaplain filled the role of reader at these events; however, it has now become the custom for officiants from local churches to be invited to fill this role.

This is followed by three sets of pieces related to the narrative of the Christmas story. The first group of works concerns the annunciation itself. This is followed by a group of four or five pieces, alternating between the Kirkpatrick Choir and the Glee Club, that constitute the next section, the "Birth." The audience then rises to sing another carol, leading to the next segment of the story, the "Shepherds and Angels," and musical works pertaining thereto. Immediately following this last set, and serving as the "Expectation" in the narrative, comes the presentation of the final chorus from the Honegger oratorio *King David* mentioned previously. The resounding conclusion to that work, featuring the voices of the combined vocal ensembles, is one of the most powerful and memorable parts of the concert. A testament to that power came one year in the early 2000s when an alumnus proposed to his now wife while sitting in the audience during this portion of the service.

The singing of the traditional German carol "Silent Night" by the two vocal ensembles from across the chapel as the lights dim to almost nothing is followed by a reading. Following the "Benediction," the English carol "God Rest Ye Merry Gentlemen," the final selection on the program, is then sung by the Glee Club as the Kirkpatrick Choir processes with the organist and the reader to the back of the chapel.

The format that developed over the course of these Christmas presentations proved to be extremely popular and has remained in place to this day. For the first five years of his tenure at the helm of these concerts, Gardner conducted only the Glee Club while Drinkwater conducted the Kirkpatrick Choir, as was the case during F. Austin Walter's time as Glee Club director. However, during this period, interest in these concerts had ebbed somewhat. In the late 1990s, while many of the four concerts would typically sell out in any given year, some performances struggled to reach half capacity.

On David Drinkwater's retirement in 1998, the Rutgers Music Department, following up on plans designed by a faculty committee in the two years prior to Gardner's hiring, merged the Kirkpatrick Choir with the premiere mixed-voice ensemble of the Music Department, the Rutgers University Concert Choir. This latter ensemble had been formed one year prior to the start of Gardner's tenure, with then Glee Club director Bruce Kolb as its conductor. Singing at chapel services would no longer be a primary part of the new choir's function, and in fact, the interdenominational services held at Kirkpatrick Chapel ceased altogether two years after Drinkwater's retirement. While most vocal students, in performance as well as in music education programs, would now receive credit for their participation in the Kirkpatrick Choir, the ensemble still offered a place for the most advanced nonmusic majors to sing. Participation by members of the adult community at large, however, was no longer offered.

Thus, without the pressure of performing weekly Sunday services, the Kirkpatrick Choir could now focus on the performance of significant choral repertory of the sort in which Gardner specialized, including established choral masterworks as well as important works of the twentieth and twenty-first centuries. Engagement by the choir with this body of choral literature, particularly those works of a more modern disposition, allowed Gardner to take a contemporary approach to the programming of these Christmas concerts, an approach that was quickly embraced by the annual event's audiences. This new repertory included a broad range of selections from various cultures and societies across the globe, providing a cultural balance to the traditional European-themed holiday program, thus invigorating and energizing a cherished Rutgers institution. Adding another level of innovation, Gardner used these concerts as pedagogical vehicles, offering significant podium time to his graduate conducting students in the preparation and presentation of these holiday concerts.

A typical Christmas in Carol and Song program in the Gardner years—again following the design of a concert of lessons and carols—is exemplified by the performances given on December 9 (6:00 and 9:00 p.m.) and December 10 (5:00 and 7:30 p.m.) in 2006 at Kirkpatrick Chapel. The combined forces of the two choral groups involved—the Rutgers University Glee Club and the Kirkpatrick Choir—numbered 139 students, overwhelmingly undergraduates. The performance began with organ voluntaries, performed by the guest organist for this event, Justin Bischoff. Interspersed throughout the various sections of the performance—the "Introit," the "Processional Hymn," the "Prophecy and Annunciation," the "Birth," the "Shepherds and Angels," the "Expectation," the "Benediction"—were the mixture of traditional Western carols and selections by modern composers from a variety of cultures that Gardner had initiated. Thus the "Processional Hymn" offered the thirteenth-century plainsong "O Come, O Come, Emmanuel," as in Drinkwater's presentations. The section titled the "Birth," however, included the sixteenth-century English ballad "What Child Is This?" followed by a Nigerian/Yoruba carol, "Betelehemu," transmitted by Babatundi Olatunji and arranged by the twentieth-century African American gospel musician, educator, and minister Wendell P. Whalum, which featured traditional African body motions and hand clapping. Similarly, in the section titled the "Shepherds and Angels," "Los Reyes Magos" by the Argentine-born composer Ariel Ramírez (1949–2010) was followed later in this segment by the traditional "Joy to the World," often attributed to the German-born composer George Frideric Handel (1685–1759). Also included in this section was "Estampie Natalis" by the Czech American composer Václav Nelhýbel (1919–96), a choral work featuring accompaniment by a small instrumental ensemble consisting of solo piccolo, violin, and violoncello, with two percussionists.

Other concerts in the series would present variations of this basic format. For example, Gardner would often program South American works that featured accompaniment by guitars and percussion as well as other instrumentation, giving him a chance to utilize his skills on the guitar in concert. Several times he has programmed medieval Spanish processionals for the "Introit" and has further stretched the boundaries of repertory by including canonic twentieth-century compositions such as "Friede auf Erden" by the German composer Arnold Schoenberg (1874–1951). Gardner has also included works by twenty-first-century artists, including Jennifer Higdon (b. 1962) and other noted contemporary composers, and has presented works by Rutgers University faculty and student composers on the series as well.

It should be noted that the ambiance of these Christmas in Carol and Song performances is greatly aided by the physical surroundings of Kirkpatrick Chapel. The beauty of this performing space when decorated for these seasonal affairs is often commented upon. These decorations are initiated during the week prior to the performances by members of the Glee Club and the Kirkpatrick Choir, who gather to install candle holders, purchase garland and trees, and attach bright red bows to the chapel fixtures. The students are also on hand to set up the lighting equipment, chairs, and music stands for the concerts. Extra rehearsals are held, including dress rehearsals with the organist, and following the concert, the students remain in the hall to strike the decorations and store all the equipment.

In the 2010s, construction on the interior of the chapel led to the removal of the choir screen. This necessitated a rethinking of the design for the Christmas accoutrements. The current design for the decorations was produced by the Glee Club's performance manager Thomas Young, '17. Indeed, the removal of the choir screen had a major effect on many aspects of the series. The Kirkpatrick Choir is now visible to the audience during these performances, and while some sense of mystery has been lost, the ability for parents and audience members to see the choir seems to have been met with positive reactions.

Students gather before the concerts and between performances in the Old Queens building adjacent to the chapel. After the concert, students vacuum and clean the building. As soon as that task is accomplished, the seniors gather for a tradition that is enormously significant to both the Glee Club and the Kirkpatrick Choir—the ringing of the Old Queens bell. As students of Rutgers history know, the bell was donated to the school by Colonel Henry Rutgers in 1825. For over fifty years, graduating seniors of the two vocal ensembles have been allowed to ring the bell at this time.

One new tradition instituted during this period by Patrick Gardner and then head of the Rutgers University Foundation, James J. Dawson, was a donor event held each year in conjunction with the Christmas in Carol and Song performances. At both the Saturday and Sunday performances, major donors who are members of the Colonel Henry Rutgers Society and the President's Council gather for a meal prior to the concerts. It is not unusual to have over one hundred such donors

attending these events each night. At these gatherings, Gardner presents a short talk, thanking them for their support of the university and of the choral program. He then outlines the major activities of the immediate past and offers details on upcoming concerts and projects for the spring. Gardner also introduces the student officers and other Club leaders, who then assist in shepherding the audience into the chapel for the concert, just prior to the organ voluntaries.

An interesting aspect of these concerts is that the two ensembles keep the income from the sale of tickets. The singers themselves, as members of two of the most important student organizations at Rutgers, do all the work of decorating the chapel, interfacing with donors, and perhaps most importantly, advertising the concerts. Since these concerts predate the formation of the Mason Gross School of the Arts in 1976, the university directs the income from ticket sales to the two groups. This seems an equitable arrangement. Other ensembles at the Mason Gross School typically perform one concert at a time. To maintain this much-beloved project, which involves presenting four performances over a two-day period, in addition to the groups' regular series of events during the fall semester, involves an immense amount of work on the part of these students.

When the COVID-19 pandemic forced Rutgers University to resort to a curriculum of exclusively online learning in March of 2020, the initial response from many educators to this new mode of teaching was shock and confusion. However, most educators were highly motivated to preserve the essence of their disciplines and programs despite the new realities of the world. Teachers quickly adapted their materials and methods to the new educational environment and implemented innovative procedures, programs, and courses to ensure that the core elements of their disciplines were not lost.

By the winter of 2020, this new ethos of embracing the positive aspects of online education and performance was fully assimilated by the performing organizations under Patrick Gardner's direction. There is no better example of this than the continuation of the decades-old Christmas in Carol and Song tradition in December of 2020. Recognizing that this tradition was far too consequential to the morale of not only the students directly in his charge but the university community as a whole, Gardner set out to make the 2020 Christmas in Carol and Song performance a truly meaningful one.

"In this year when we've lost so much, not just traditions but daily connections—seeing our friends, being in our offices and classrooms, and greeting each other at everything from football games to choir practices—we wanted to find a way to give people some comfort," Gardner stated in an interview with a local online news outlet. Therefore, working closely with the students of the Rutgers choral ensembles, he brought in the noted young Italian projection designer and musician Camilla Tassi to produce an online concert experience that would transcend the by-now routine Zoom-squares performance model. Tassi was recommended to Gardner for

this project by one of his doctor of musical arts conducting students, Stephanie Tubiolo. With Tubiolo and Gardner making the primary design decisions, Tassi was able to blend ten individual concert videos not only showcasing the extraordinary capabilities of the Glee Club and Kirkpatrick Choir but also highlighting the striking American collegiate gothic architecture of Kirkpatrick Chapel that is so much a part of the Christmas in Carol and Song tradition. To be sure, the majority of the creative work on this project was done by Tubiolo. She produced seven of the ten videos, while the other three were put together by Tassi. While Tassi added a distinctive touch, the predominant creative force on the project was Tubiolo.

To achieve a novel effect, Tubiolo and Tassi collaborated to interweave their two distinct video styles into a finished product that showcases the talents of both women well. The video consists of a small coterie of Rutgers students/performers engaging in some of the traditional concert processions. This action takes place while the students decorate the chapel and is melded with visuals from ninety other members of the vocal ensembles, who each recorded themselves remotely while singing their parts to the works on the program.[121] The result is a magnificent fusion of the old and the new, the traditional and the modern, the pre- and existing-COVID-19 realities. It is a collaboration about which all involved can feel a sense of pride and accomplishment, and it represents a fitting continuation of a cherished Rutgers tradition.

STUDENT LEADERSHIP
A Glee Club Hallmark

Historical Outline

The Rutgers University Glee Club can rightly claim to be the oldest student-run organization on campus; it has maintained a fully functioning executive leadership board of some sort in place throughout its existence. From the Club's inception in 1872 to the present day, while specific organizational/supervisory titles may have been altered or modified, such changes have always been implemented as a reflection of the various needs and requirements of new and, often challenging, eras. Notwithstanding these alterations, the students have consistently maintained a significant role in the management and daily activities of the Glee Club.

To be sure, the original group that arose in 1872 was a completely student-run affair. Officers for this inaugural Club were taken directly from the ranks of the performing contingent; their complement included a president, a vice president, a secretary, a treasurer, and, considered as part of this governing group, a leader (or director). This configuration of officers continued during the tumultuous early years of the Club's existence, while it struggled to maintain its footing as a viable organization. And indeed, student participation from all Club members was necessary in these early days; an all-hands-on-deck ethos was required just to keep the enterprise afloat. It is telling, for example, that the first recorded performance outside the walls of Rutgers College took place in Flatbush in the borough of Queens, New York, in 1873 at the home of Mr. John Lefferts, father of one of the members of the '76 Glee Club. It would seem that all available resources, including family connections, were employed toward the goal of putting these early clubs on the path to a stable performance routine. (For details on the membership and configuration of these early groups, see chap. 1, "Birth of the Rutgers College Glee Club.")

The pursuit of greater institutional balance led in 1880 to the formation of a committee to review existing procedures of the Club and to implement improvements. Toward that purpose, the committee added a new position to the array of Glee Club officers—that of the business manager. The first gentleman to hold this post was George B. Fielder, '81, who was elected during the fall semester of 1880.[122] The role of the committee and that of the business manager would figure prominently in the subsequent configurations of the Club during the formative years of the 1880s. For it was at this time that the group had decided to abandon the idea of a student leader and opted instead to have the role of director/leader fall to a professional musician, the colorful and flamboyant Loren Bragdon (see chap. 1 sidebar, "Loren Bragdon [1856–1914]"). With Bragdon at the helm of the Club during this decade, impressive strides were made, both artistically and structurally. But aside from Bragdon's influence, much having to do with all aspects of the group's maturation could be attributed to student involvement and leadership through the student committee and the actualization of these ideas through the new position of (student) business manager.

The role of the business manager in the latter part of the nineteenth and early twentieth centuries was indeed substantial, as it continues to be in the Club's modern configuration. This officer was responsible for the arrangements for the tours—primarily to New York, New Jersey, and Pennsylvania locales, though that scope was occasionally widened—that the Club now undertook.[123] But the business manager also had the task of keeping the parade of engagements flowing for the group. The Glee Club was, above all, a self-supporting organization, and touring incurred expenses. Therefore, the business manager had to be sure that a certain profit margin was achieved. In the early twentieth century, a vigorous advertising campaign was implemented, with notices placed in local newspapers, including the *Targum*, and elsewhere proclaiming the Club's "high standards of excellence" and providing contact information for the business manager, with whom terms of employment could be discussed.

The arrival of Howard D. McKinney in 1916 as coach of the Glee Club was, in many ways, a reaction against the role of the professional leader that began with Loren Bragdon in 1881 and persisted until this time. Certain problems resulting from that structure had moved the Club in the direction of student leaders aided by professional coaches. This arrangement made good sense for a variety of reasons, not the least of which being that, by this time, the Glee Club had combined with the Rutgers College Mandolin Club. The complement of the combined groups in the 1916–17 season was fifty-eight members, clearly calling for various levels of leadership. Thus McKinney served as the overall mentor of the combined clubs and coached the Glee Club contingent, while the president of the combined groups for this season, William Phillips Thorp Jr., '17, coached and served as leader for the Mandolin Club segment of the combined unit.[124] Certainly, a large group such as this needed a good deal of management. To that end, the combined clubs now carried as officers a president, a vice president, a secretary, a manager, and two assistant managers—all taken from the clubs' ranks—to coordinate the groups' many engagements and activities. The manager, in addition to his duties arranging the logistics of tours and dealing with the vagaries of promoting the combined clubs, was also involved in selecting the members of the groups through the audition process, again emphasizing the importance of student involvement during this period.[125]

The idea of student leaders for the combined clubs took hold quickly during the ensuing years of McKinney's tenure. By the 1922–23 season, the combined clubs listed student leaders for both the Glee Club component (Dana B. Scudder,

'24) and the Mandolin Club contingent (Franklin J. Maryott, '25). McKinney is, of course, still listed as the director of the Rutgers College Glee and Mandolin Clubs.[126]

Clearly the most significant and impactful student leader to emerge from this system is F. Austin Walter. Walter joined the Club during the 1929–30 season as a sophomore, singing first tenor.[127] In his senior year (1931–32), Walter was named student director of the Glee Club component of the still-combined clubs. Following Walter's graduation, McKinney, having found Walter's contributions to the organization too important to do without, asked the erstwhile student leader to return to the Club as assistant director. To be sure, a student leader was still in place during the 1932–33 season, Ewald H. Bergmann, '33,[128] but Walter's role in the Glee Club would continue to expand. By 1933, the Mandolin/Instrumental Club component had been permanently severed from the Glee Club. This resulted in a change in the organizational structure of the now independent Glee Club; in the 1935 edition of *The Scarlet Letter*, the Glee Club page lists McKinney as director, with Walter claiming the title of assistant to the director. The student officers include only a president, Howard R. West, '35; a manager, William E. Sperling, '35; two assistant managers; and three "Sophomore Managers," all Glee Club members. While the role of leader may have been passed to the newly created position of assistant to the director, the emphasis of this robust forty-four-man independent group remained firmly focused on student engagement and responsibility.

Walter would take over in 1946 as the official director of the Glee Club following McKinney's appointment as the first director of the Rutgers Department of Music. Under Walter's control, the Club continued to expand following a period of decline during the war years. During the 1946–47 season, the group had fifty-two members; in the 1947–48 season, the number had increased to seventy-four men. Along with this growth in membership was a corresponding growth in the number of engagements in which they participated, again seemingly calling for a robust student corps of officers to administer the details of the various concerts. This became especially apparent in the 1950s as Walter's involvement with the University Choir increased. However, the ranks of the officers seem to have been pared down considerably during this period. The 1953 edition of *The Scarlet Letter* lists only Walter as director; Leroy Johnson, '53, as president; and William Snedeker, '53, as manager. Notwithstanding, the account of the Club's activities in the yearbook boasts that this, in terms of Club engagements, was "one of the most ambitious and varied seasons in the history of the group."[129]

This arrangement meant that, during Walter's time as director, the president and manager would have had a variety of duties assigned to them; this often included consulting with Director Walter concerning the musical aspects of the group. In any given year, the manager, in consultation with the president, would typically begin work during the summer preceding the academic year, during which he would execute all the business arrangements that needed to be made for the upcoming season. It was also during this time that preparations for the annual Club outing at Lake Minnewaska would be undertaken, which required much planning and, usually, a great deal of attention from the manager.[130]

In the 1970s and 1980s, international touring was one of the most prominent features of the Glee Club's schedule. The position of business manager had now merged with the new designation of tour manager. Together with the Club president, the tour manager would work with Director Walter on the logistical details involved with the proposed tour. Employing a similar model to that which was contemporarily in use at major universities throughout the country, Walter, as director, would set the itinerary for the excursion. This was often implemented with the cooperation of other institutions, such as the U.S. State Department or the Friendship Ambassadors Foundation, a nonprofit organization based in Manhattan that promotes cultural tourism. The director would also be responsible for the finalization of all concert arrangements. As is the case today, there was a significant amount of work on the ground executed by the members of the Glee Club Executive Council, including the collection of student payments, the setting of room assignments, checking students in and out of hotels, and arranging for social interaction with the various host choirs.

Soliciting funds from various academic offices and funding budgets was also part of the officers' duties during this time. The president of the Club had the responsibility of acting as liaison with university officials for the purpose of creating and assembling the yearly budget. This would require the president to solicit donations from the various university colleges and to represent the Club at budget meetings. On-campus fundraising events were also the purview of the president as well as the (tour/business) manager and other officers (the clubs in the late 1970s and early 1980s frequently added the post of executive secretary to the roster of officers).[131] One well-remembered event of this type was the annual Halloween concert presented by the Kirkpatrick Chapel Choir and its director David Drinkwater, in collaboration with members of the Glee Club. Launched in 1976, the Halloween events, which were sponsored by the Rutgers Music Department, involved the participation by and assistance of the Glee Club, the Queens Chorale, and the Kirkpatrick Chapel Choir. The basic format involved members of these organizations, in costume, attempting to frighten guests (hopefully also costumed) during a two-hour screening of the 1925 silent movie "The Phantom of the Opera" at Kirkpatrick Chapel. Organist Drinkwater would provide humorous improvisations as an accompaniment to the action on-screen, often succeeding in producing the desired laughter.[132] As a charitable endeavor, this event was successful for a number of years.

The tradition of strong and effective student leadership continued to be cultivated in the Glee Club configurations under Patrick Gardner following his arrival in 1993. Gardner was keen to reestablish the strong tradition of touring that had been all but abandoned following the departure of F. Austin Walter from the role of Club director. Gardner's years of experience in fundraising for tours for his previous ensembles bore fruit here. Thus, in preparation for Gardner's first European tour in 1996, the business manager of the Club, Scott J. Pashman, '97, and Director Gardner spent the season prior to this excursion organizing various fundraising events that would produce the estimated $120,000 needed to fund this tour.[133] One important new aspect to the fundraising efforts was the involvement of Robert Mortensen, '63, who continues to assist Gardner in these efforts to this day. Especially in the first decade and a half of the Gardner/Mortensen collaboration *re* fundraising, Mortensen's outreach to donors of substance was of prime importance for reaching the Club's fundraising goals.

While the number of officers on the Glee Club Executive Council changed very little from the 1970s to the present, the number of projects and the work needed to execute them

The Glee Club at Winants Hall, Queens Campus, Rutgers University. Rutgers University Glee Club Archives.

expanded exponentially during this period; the group began to receive more invitations to perform, and the complexity and significance of the events in which they participated grew. The list of senior officers for the 1993–94 season illustrates the scope of the officer ranks. Positions include a president (Daniel Alan Terner, '95), a vice president for special organizational affairs (Eric "Del" Chrol, '95), a vice president for alumni relations and development (Edward Potosnak III, '96), an executive secretary (Michael Singer, '97), and a business manager (Scott J. Pashman, '97). Further, a coterie of junior officers, whose specialized roles allowed for greater flexibility in the overall administration of the Club, included a financial coordinator (Mark Sharp, '97), a public relations coordinator (Jeffrey Shaman, '97), a performance coordinator for uniforms (Matthew Hooban, '98), a performance coordinator for music (Kevin Beach, '96), a tour manager (Nicholas Brown, '98), and a historian (Richard J. Fox, '97).

As we have seen, many of these offices had existed in previous iterations of the Club. Indeed, most were in existence and at least somewhat active on Gardner's arrival in 1993. Some offices, like that of historian, have been part of the Club on an intermittent basis for decades; the Glee Club roster first lists this post in *The Scarlet Letter* for the 1890–91 season, during the tenure of Loren Bragdon.[134]

The officers for the 2020–21 season perhaps deserve special praise for their efforts in maintaining and administering the various traditions and projects that continued throughout the COVID pandemic. The senior officers include president (Ryan Leibowitz, '21), vice president for alumni relations and development (Benjamin Kritz, '21), vice president for special organizational affairs (Matthew Lacognata, '21), business manager (Amartya Mani, '21), and treasurer (Aditya Nibhanupudi, '21).[135] Junior officers include executive secretary (Allen Li, '23), music manager (Kyle Cao, '23), performance manager (Gabriel Lukijaniuk, '22), uniform manager (Kolter Yagual-Rolston, '22), public relations manager (Ryan Acevedo, '22), technology coordinator (Seonuk Kim, '21), and historian (Caleb Schneider, '23).[136] Thanks to their efforts, the presence of the Glee Club as a representation of the best that Rutgers has to offer did not diminish during this dangerous and troubling time.

It should also be noted that from the middle of the twentieth century and continuing to this day, the members of the Rutgers University Glee Club—officers and rank-and-file performers alike—have greatly benefited from the assistance provided by various Rutgers faculty and staff members who have served as the Glee Club's advisor. Alumni of the 1960s, for example, may fondly recall Dean of Students Howard J. Crosby Jr., '41, and his supportive work with F. Austin Walter and the Club, as well as his presence on the international tours of that decade. Dr. Roger Locandro, a much-lauded and highly respected member of the Rutgers faculty followed Dean Crosby in that position; Locandro was in turn followed by Matthew J. Weismantel, '85. Weismantel, though not a Rutgers faculty member, was a full-time staff person at Rutgers, serving as senior director of the Campus Information Services during most of his time as Glee Club advisor. Rutgers University dean of students Dr. Marie Logue worked closely with Gardner in the period around the turn of the twenty-first century, providing particularly close contact to the upper administration of the university. Dean Logue also organized the first complementary friends and family tours associated with Club's concert excursions in Europe.

In 2002, the Glee Club was fortunate enough to obtain the services of Dr. Peter Gillett as the Club's faculty advisor. Dr. Gillett, who holds undergraduate and graduate degrees from Oxford University and a PhD from the University of Kansas, holds the rank of associate professor in the Rutgers University School of Business. Dr. Gillett immediately began working with the officers of the Club upon appointment, bringing his expertise in auditing practices to their efforts.[137] An accomplished vocalist who often performs with Gardner's Kirkpatrick Choir, Gillett was (and is) instrumental in providing a knowledgeable and sensitive link between the officers and members of the Club and the various administration officials and alumni that are so important to the financial and spiritual health of the organization. These capable and caring individuals are to be commended for their generosity in sharing their time and skills, all aimed at providing the best possible experience for the members of the Rutgers University Glee Club.

The Organizational Model of the Modern Glee Club

The Rutgers Glee Club as it is constituted today is a model of efficiency and organization. While the arrangement of the assorted student boards and leadership committees has changed from era to era, the discharging of the various duties necessary to the smooth running of the group has been largely consistent since the time of F. Austin Walter's leadership. There have been, as mentioned above, alterations to the process since the 1980s, particularly in the period between the departure of Walter and the arrival of Gardner (1983–93). However, Gardner's assumption of the directorship of the group at that time in many ways represented a continuation of the well-established organizational principles upon which the Club had relied for decades. The sheer number of events in which the modern Club engages, as well as the increased complexities of contemporary event organization, has grown exponentially over the past thirty years. As Gardner often remarks, "The Glee Club could not maintain the incredible roster of concerts and events without the terrific work of the student officers. We could easily present the norm for a collegiate choir, one or two concerts on campus, with the work of the music department staff. But to maintain our schedule of concerts, alumni events, performances at national conferences, and national and international tours, we depend on our student officers."[138]

In the modern era of the Glee Club, the professor in charge of the Club—who, whether employed as an adjunct faculty member or a tenure-track or tenured professor, serves as the director of the Club—has been largely responsible for the design of the season's musical and academic activities. The range of activities could encompass anything from a year of relative quiet—with the annual Christmas in Carol and Song concerts and the annual spring concert as the primary projects for the year—to a season in which numerous off-campus performances and overseas tours were planned. F. Austin Walter and Patrick Gardner both brought a large collection of contacts within the professional musical world to their positions. Walter's first international tours came about through his association with colleagues at Yale University, which in turn led to an invitation through the U.S. State Department in 1962 for a government-funded excursion to Europe. Further, Walter's contacts in the recording business led to the release of a long-playing recording of the music that was performed on this tour under the title *Yale Wind Symphony and Rutgers Male Chorus* on the RCA Victor Records label. Similarly, Gardner's contacts throughout the nation and especially his international contacts have led to numerous invitations for collegiate collaborations. Such opportunities include concerts at the University of Michigan, Cornell University, and Harvard University; multiple joint concerts with the glee clubs from Mount Holyoke College, Wellesley College, and Smith College have also been undertaken. Additionally, Gardner's connections have led to invitations to perform throughout Germany, the Netherlands, Sweden, and Estonia.

Current practice at many universities requires the staff work necessary for the realization of large-scale projects such as those described previously to be performed by employees of the respective music departments/schools/programs. However, at Rutgers, the tradition of the Glee Club has been for the student executive officers to do the lion's share of this work. The contracting of busses, the management of the flow of information, and the collection of required materials from the students (the documentation of passport information, checking the status of visas, the collecting of fees, and much more) are all routinely managed by the Glee Club business manager, with meaningful assistance from the junior officers. Scheduling of nonmusical events on campus, such as alumni gatherings, and the purchase of food for barbecues and student outings are further examples of the tasks that are managed by the student leadership.

This division of labor among the officers of the Club is well defined under the Club's constitution. The following is a summary of the respective duties of the officers of the Club:

The primary job of the president is to represent the Club in all official external affairs. If there is a need for a student representative of the Club to meet with the president of Rutgers University or with the Rutgers Office of the Chancellor or their respective staff members, it is the Glee Club president's job to do so. Such meetings, in fact, occur each year during the university commencement activities. The president also runs the weekly executive council meetings, organizes the election committee, and runs the Wednesday night postrehearsal business meetings. And of course, the president keeps in close contact with the membership to report on the esprit de corps of the group, informing the director and the Glee Club council when issues arise.

The business manager's job in the modern configuration of the Club no longer includes the day-to-day keeping of the checkbook and reporting on balances; these tasks are now performed by the treasurer. However, all contracts are created by the business manager; it is his job to make the arrangements for each event and then consult with the treasurer for the management of the necessary income and expenses. So typically, the business manager interfaces with the Office of Rutgers University Athletics when the Glee Club sings at the football games, with the bus companies when the contracting of such transportation is required, and with the pizza vendors for after-event snacks and performs a variety of other such duties. Further, the yearly retreat at the Engleside Inn in Beach Haven, New Jersey—the modern Glee Club's equivalent

of the bygone retreats at Lake Minnewaska—is contracted by the business manager, who arranges for the catering of meals, organizes the carpools, and checks the members into hotels for this event.

The business manager's job came to be viewed during the early part of Gardner's tenure as director as such a major undertaking that, as mentioned above, tasks involving the maintenance of Club accounts and invoicing, as well as other duties traditionally associated with the business manager, were transposed to a newly designed position, that of treasurer. By the year 2000, the treasurer was, in addition to other duties, placed in charge of keeping in touch with the Rutgers Division of Student Affairs and the Office of Student Involvement concerning the fiscal affairs of the Club.

While Gardner is well known for his ability to raise funds and for his oversight of the development process, the vice president for alumni relations (VIPAR) is heavily involved in maintaining the alumni contact lists, which are critical to the continuity of Club traditions. In recent years, the VIPAR has worked intensively with Gardner on the management of Rutgers Giving Day, an annual event dedicated to the raising of funds for students, schools, and programs. In its first year of eligibility for this prize, the Glee Club won the $10,000 first-place award in the competition for new donors. Many other alumni events are managed almost exclusively by the students, including the preparation of activities at the annual homecoming football games, arrangements concerning alumni concerts and the summer alumni gatherings, and a variety of other special projects. Another significant part of the portfolio of the VIPAR is the publication of each new issue of the Glee Club's newsletter, the *Glee Gab*. The VIPAR chooses the subjects for the articles, recruits and assigns authors, interfaces with the Club advisor and a professional designer on the layout of the document, and works with the business manager to contract with a printer and deal with the invoicing, delivery, and mailing.

The vice president of special organizational affairs (VIPSOA) has two major items on his plate each year. During the season, he is in charge of social events. For example, just as F. Austin Walter had a student managing the reservations and other arrangements for the Lake Minnewaska events, the business manager and the VIPSOA manage the details for the current rehearsal retreats, which are held at the Jersey Shore. These retreats at the Engleside Inn, as well as their precursors at Cape May locations and elsewhere, have created new memories for the "Gardner alumni." As with the student leaders and the Minnewaska events, the business manager and the VIPSOA currently make all the arrangements for the now traditional three-day weekend. Carpools are organized, meals are contracted through the hotel, and invoices are received and paid. This is all accomplished by the VIPSOA and the business manager.

The other significant assignment for the VIPSOA is the organization of recruitment efforts. Again, Gardner works with the staff of the Rutgers Office of Student Affairs and the university vice president's office to design the recruitment program, but the students attend the new student orientation sessions that occur during the summer preceding the season. The Club members also maintain an active level of communication with students who express an interest in auditioning for the Glee Club at these orientation sessions. Throughout the years, the VIPSOA has worked with the "el supremo"— a less formal position of student leadership within the Club—to design outside social events, from the gatherings at the well-known local eatery "Stuff Yer Face" to outside parties and interactions with other choirs.

In the late 1970s, Rutgers University entered an extended period of vigorous growth. During this period, administrative oversight of student-run groups such as the Glee Club was organized under the sponsorship of a variety of university divisions and offices dedicated to the necessities of student life.

From at least the 1980s onward, all student organizations were required to be registered with what is today called the Office of Student Involvement (OSI). Over five hundred such student clubs are registered with this office. Each organization is assigned an OSI advisor and furnished with certain mandatory requirements regarding the construction of their constitutions and the proper manner in which they may engage in their respective activities. One interesting aspect of the OSI model for these organizations is that for the most part, a club cannot simultaneously serve as an academic class. The choirs at Rutgers are exceptions to this standard; they constitute some of the very few academic for-credit courses that are also designated as student clubs. Since the Glee Club is the oldest continuously active student organization on campus, it made sense to grandfather it into the Office of Student Involvement structure. This seemed appropriate since the Club has functioned as both a class and a club since well before the establishment of the Office of Student Life and the current Club system. Indeed, this dual status for the Glee Club, as well as some other musical organizations at Rutgers, goes back to before the onset of World War II.[139]

This bifold status can create some complicated circumstances, especially concerning the administration of finances. Like the other campus groups, the Glee Club applies for and receives funding from student fees each semester. These funds are administered through the Rutgers University Student Association (RUSA), and the Office of Student Involvement maintains the Student Affairs Business Office (SABO) for the purpose of distributing those funds. The Glee Club works closely and carefully with RUSA and SABO to acquire and properly distribute this funding. However, the largest portion of the Glee Club's funding originates from donations and fees that flow through the business offices of the Mason Gross School of the Arts and its subordinate division, the Rutgers Music Department. This being the case, the Glee Club's executive committee does the vast majority of the day-to-day interfacing with RUSA and SABO, while Gardner manages approximately a dozen endowed funds that are administered through the Mason Gross Dean's Office and/or the Rutgers Music Department.

It would be conveying a false impression if this presentation were taken to imply that the officers and members of the Rutgers Glee Club go about their various duties, both musical and administrative, without recourse to endeavors of a more informal and relaxing nature. To conclude this section, therefore, a brief look at some of the more well-known student-led traditions engaged with by the current crop of Glee Club members is appended.

Casual Traditions

A history of the Rutgers University Glee Club would not be complete without noting the long tradition of gatherings on Wednesday evenings after Glee Club rehearsals. Like similar contemporaneous gatherings of students at the University of Michigan (who assemble at the Cottage Inn in downtown Ann Arbor), Harvard, and Cornell, the Rutgers Glee Club has long gathered on Wednesday nights to relax after their customary three-hour rehearsals. For many years, these after-rehearsal social hours took place at Patty's, a not-very-special restaurant and bar behind the College Avenue Gymnasium. Business meetings would often end with the admonishment "Go to Patty's!" For the past several decades, however, the gathering spot of preference has been the student hangout "Stuff Yer Face," which is located on Easton Avenue in New Brunswick, not far from McKinney Hall. Taking over the upstairs back room, and in some years the entire upstairs of the establishment, Club members typically sing through the complete repertory of Rutgers songs while awaiting pizza and drinks. Members from the other choirs and alumni often join in, with special alumni weeks specified in advance in recent years.

Indeed, a variety of events aimed at relaxation and diversion are traditionally a part of a Glee Club season. The beginning of each year, for example, is marked with an introductory pizza party for officers, new students, and a few current members at McKinney Hall. This is then followed up with a more comprehensive gathering at Gardner's house, and subsequently, a decidedly formal event called the Rookie Banquet, at which the new arrivals are welcomed. The gathering at Gardner's home continues a tradition that originated in introductory parties of this sort hosted by F. Austin Walter. The current iteration sees the Glee Club gathering in Gardner's backyard after the second Friday afternoon rehearsal of the year, with a Glee Club officer manning the grill, and a carefully organized meal set out by council members. Rookies gather in Gardner's music room to learn one of the Rutgers songs on their own. The returning members join in on a second verse, laughingly correcting wrong tempi and firing up the new class.

The Rookie Banquet is held in Winants Hall on the College Avenue Campus in New Brunswick. This event takes place in a luxuriously appointed room that is normally reserved for meetings of the university board of governors and board of trustees; the Glee Club is the only student group at Rutgers that is allowed to hold such an event in this room. Students dress in sport coats and ties, new members are introduced by the older members, and Rutgers songs are performed, all during a formal dinner. After the meal, the Club moves to the cannon on the lawn in front of the adjacent Old Queens Building—the oldest extant building on the Rutgers campus—and the el supremo leads the group in an informal songfest of all the Rutgers college songs in the group's repertory. The term *el supremo* refers to an unofficial officer in charge of

Glee Club members attend the Rookie Banquet. Rutgers University Glee Club Archives.

social events. Off-campus parties, announcements of musical events outside of the Glee Club activities, keeping track of birthdays, and all unofficial social duties are in the hands of the el supremo, an office that goes back at least to the late 1960s.

The end of the year finds the ensemble gathered for the bookend event to the Rookie Banquet, a concomitant affair appropriately designated as the Senior Banquet. The tradition of senior speeches has held true for decades and heartfelt memories are shared, awards are presented, and scholarships are announced, as is the appointment of the newest el supremo.

Informal traditions such as these serve to solidify the fraternal nature of the Glee Club and to provide a much-needed diversion from the serious business of the Club's various responsibilities. The value of these more casual customs and practices to the overall health of the organization should not be overlooked when considering the remarkable growth and development of the Rutgers University Glee Club as it celebrates its sesquicentennial.

ACKNOWLEDGMENTS

A book of this size and scope can only emerge as a coherent entity through the confluence of myriad influences and inspirations. Many individuals provided valuable information, insightful anecdotes, and tangible artifacts that contributed meaningfully to this undertaking. The following is a by-no-means-comprehensive list of those who contributed to the process of initiating and funding the venture; those who aided in the compilation of the material necessary for the historical and anecdotal background information; those who contributed to the publishing, editing, and distribution of the finished product; and finally, those who, in any way, supported the author by generously providing their experiences, attitudes, and general historical knowledge concerning the Rutgers University Glee Club.

In the first category, credit must be given to Patrick Gardner, current director of the Rutgers University Glee Club. This project was conceived by him and the initial steps toward implementing its realization were his. The contributions of Robert Mortensen, '63, who provided the funding for the majority of this enterprise, also deserve acknowledgment. Both men are—and indeed, have been for decades—dedicated to the advancement and development of all aspects of the Rutgers Glee Club, as can be seen in the narrative that the book advances.

The current officers and members of the Glee Club (academic year 2020–21) were extremely helpful in compiling and categorizing information for inclusion in this volume. Special thanks should be expressed to Caleb Schneider, '23, club historian, whose activities along these lines were especially noteworthy.

Many Glee Club alumni were extremely generous with their time in recounting their various experiences with the group. Several of these former members shared programs, photographs, and other Club memorabilia, of which as much as possible has been included in this book. I would like to especially thank Charles A. "Chip" Noon III, '67; Tom Struble, '81; and Matthew Cirri, '01, for their willingness to accommodate my requests for materials and information throughout the course of the project.

Many current and former members of the Rutgers faculty also contributed their recollections—and the historical context those remembrances provided—to the written record of Glee Club activities. These include the current chairman of the Rutgers Music Department, William Berz; retired university organist and director of the Kirkpatrick Chapel Choir, David Drinkwater; and former assistant director of the Rutgers Music Department and retired director of the Rutgers University Marching Band and RU Wind Ensemble, Scott Whitener. Thanks to these men for sharing their institutional memories, accumulated over their many years of dedicated service to Rutgers, concerning their interactions with the personalities and organizations mentioned in this text.

I would also like to thank Jo-Michael Scheibe, chairman of the Department of Choral and Sacred Music at the University of Southern California's Thornton School of Music and Frank Albinder, current conductor of the Washington Men's Chorale and the Virginia Glee Club for providing pertinent observations on the modern world of collegiate men's choruses. They offered informed and insightful context on the place in that world that the current iteration of the Rutgers University Glee Club occupies, as well as on the exemplary work of its current director, Patrick Gardner.

Thanks should also be given to Erika Gorder, interim university archivist, Special Collections and University Archives, Rutgers University Libraries for her help in obtaining archival material for this project and to Jonathan Sauceda, music and performing arts librarian at Rutgers, for facilitating communications with the Rutgers University Libraries system during the trying COVID-19 emergency.

The assistance provided by Peter Mickulas (executive editor for social sciences and history) and Micah Kleit (director) at Rutgers University Press in facilitating the publication of this book should also be mentioned here. Their experience and guidance in these matters greatly facilitated the procedures involved in the formatting and general design of the book. Working with them was a pleasant and fruitful experience.

These individuals, and many more not specifically cited here, provided much-needed support to a project that could easily have been derailed by the exigencies of the COVID-19 pandemic. I offer them my thanks and appreciation for their guidance and patience.

David F. Chapman
New Brunswick, New Jersey

NOTES

Introduction

1. William Henry Steele Demarest, *A History of Rutgers College, 1766–1924* (New Brunswick, N.J.: Rutgers College Press, 1924), 37.
2. Richard P. McCormick, *Rutgers: A Bicentennial History* (New Brunswick, N.J.: Rutgers University Press, 1966), 3–12.
3. McCormick, 40–41.
4. McCormick, 82.
5. McCormick, 92.
6. *The Scarlet Letter* (New Brunswick, N.J.: Rutgers University, 1972), 36–52; hereafter, *The Scarlet Letter* will be referred to as *TSL*. All editions of *The Scarlet Letter* can be found as physical copies in the division of Special Collections and University Archives of the Rutgers University Libraries. Additionally, many of these yearbooks, particularly for the years between 1871 and 1913, can be found digitally at https://collections.libraries.rutgers.edu/yearbooks.
7. McCormick, *Rutgers*, 65. McCormick gives the date of inception for the *Targum* as 1867.
8. Erika Gorder, "*Targum*," Rutgers University Libraries, accessed May 17, 2021, https://collections.libraries.rutgers.edu/targum.
9. Arnold Ray Thomas, "The Development of Male Glee Clubs in American Colleges and Universities" (PhD diss., Columbia University, 1962), 43. See also Jeremy D. Jones, "The Development of Collegiate Male Glee Clubs in America: An Historical Overview" (DMA diss., University of Cincinnati, 2010), 34.
10. "University Yearbooks," Rutgers University Libraries, accessed August 10, 2020, https://collections.libraries.rutgers.edu/yearbooks.
11. Rutgers Department of University Communications and Marketing, "Rutgers Editorial Style Guide," last modified July 2020, 6, https://communications.rutgers.edu/services-resources/editorial-style-guide.

Chapter 1: Early History

1. James G. Smith and Percy M. Young, "Chorus (i)," Grove Music Online, accessed January 5, 2021, https://www-oxfordmusiconline-com.proxy.libraries.rutgers.edu/grovemusic/view/10.1093/gmo/9781561592630.001.0001/omo-9781561592630-e-0000005684.
2. Smith and Young.
3. Smith and Young.
4. Smith and Young. Paul's instructions appear in Corinthians 14:34–35 (NIV): "Women should stay silent in the churches, for they are not permitted to speak, but are to submit themselves, as the law also says. If they want to learn something, let them ask their own husbands at home, since it is disgraceful for a woman to speak in the church." See

also Richard H. Trame, "The Male Chorus, Medium of Art and Entertainment: Its History and Literature," in *Choral Essays: A Tribute to Roger Wagner* (San Carlos, Calif.: Thomas House, 1993), 19–20.

5   Perry Jones, "The History of Women's Liberation in Choral Music," *Choral Journal* 16, no. 6 (February 1976): 12–14.

6   Indeed, the preface states, "In the expressing of these songs, either by voyces or Instruments, if ther happen to be any jarre or dissonance, blame not the printer, who (I doe assure thee) through his great pains and diligence doth here deliver to thee a perfect and true Coppie." William Byrd, *Psalmes, Sonets, and Songs of Sadnes and Pietie, made into Musicke of Five Parts* (London: Thomas East, 1588), preface.

7   "[Musicologists Joshua] Rifkin and [Andrew] Parrott . . . propose . . . that Bach's essential choir consisted of solo voices (with one singer on a part). These solo voices, known as the 'concertists,' were ordinarily made up of 4 male singers (SATB), but were sometimes expanded to from 5 to 8 singers." Roland Jackson, *Performance Practice: A Dictionary-Guide for Musicians* (New York: Routledge, 2005), 23.

8   Jones, "History of Women's Liberation," 12.

9   Jones, "Collegiate Male Glee Clubs," 14–15.

10 Horst Brunner, "Meistergesang," Grove Music Online, accessed January 5, 2021, https://www-oxfordmusiconline-com.proxy.libraries.rutgers.edu/grovemusic/view/10.1093/gmo/9781561592630.001.0001/omo-9781561592630-e-0000018291.

11 Mozart joined the Freemasons in 1784 and subsequently persuaded his father, Leopold, to do so. See H. C. Robbins Landon, *Mozart and Vienna* (New York: Schirmer, 1991), 192.

12 Trame's works for the Freemasons include the cantata *Laut verkünde unsre Freude*, K. 623, for tenor, male chorus, and orchestra. Trame, "Male Chorus," 20–21.

13 Jones, "Collegiate Male Glee Clubs," 14–21.

14 David Johnson, "Catch," Grove Music Online, accessed January 5, 2021, https://www

-oxfordmusiconline-com.proxy.libraries.rutgers.edu/grovemusic/view/10.1093/gmo/9781561592630.001.0001/omo-9781561592630-e-0000005164.

15 Michael Hurd, "Glees, Madrigals, and Partsongs," in *Athlone History of Music in Britain*, vol. 5, *The Romantic Age, 1800–1914*, ed. Nicholas Temperley (London: Athlone, 1981), 242–243.

16 Hurd, 242–243.

17 Johnson, "Catch."

18 Brian Robins, "The Catch Club in 18th-Century England," *Early Music* 28, no. 4 (November 2000): 527.

19 Paul Weaver, "Samuel Webbe (i)," Grove Music Online, accessed January 5, 2021, https://www-oxfordmusiconline-com.proxy.libraries.rutgers.edu/grovemusic/view/10.1093/gmo/9781561592630.001.0001/omo-9781561592630-e-0000044333.

20 Robins, "Catch Club," 523–524.

21 Weaver, "Samuel Webbe (i)."

22 Hurd, "Glees, Madrigals, and Partsongs," 245.

23 Robert D. Hume, "London (i), §V, 2," Grove Music Online, accessed January 5, 2021, https://www-oxfordmusiconline-com.proxy.libraries.rutgers.edu/grovemusic/view/10.1093/gmo/9781561592630.001.0001/omo-9781561592630-e-0000016904.

24 Robins, "Catch Club," 525.

25 Lawrence J. Fried, "Glee," Grove Music Online, January 31 2014, accessed June 6, 2020, https://www-oxfordmusiconline-com.proxy.libraries.rutgers.edu/grovemusic/view/10.1093/gmo/9781561592630.001.0001/omo-9781561592630-e-1002256658.

26 James H. Richardson, "The English Glee," *American Music Teacher* 21, no. 5 (April–May 1972): 45; see also 30.

27 Fried, "Glee."

28 Fried.

29 "History," Harvard Glee Club, accessed June 23, 2020, https://harvardgleeclub.org/about/history/.

30 William Alexander Barret, *English Glees and Part-Songs: An Inquiry into Their Development* (London: Longman, Green, 1886), 225–226.

31 Jones, "Collegiate Male Glee Clubs," 14.

32 Jones, 22–23.

33 Mabel Newcomer, *A Century of Higher Education for American Women* (New York: Harper, 1959), 46. Newcomer reports that in 1860, only 21 percent of college students in America were women.

34 Winstead sites musicologist H. Wiley Hitchcock, who expressed the dichotomy using the terms "cultivated" and "vernacular" traditions. James Lloyd Winstead, *When Colleges Sang: The Story of Singing in American College Life* (Tuscaloosa: University of Alabama Press, 2013), 51–53.

35 Winstead, *When Colleges Sang*, 81. *Songs of Yale* presented the texts of songs and associated tunes but did not print the music. See Winstead, 84.

36 Winstead, 84.

37 Winstead, 81.

38 Yale was not officially incorporated as a university until 1864; see *Encyclopedia Britannica*, s.v. "Yale University," accessed July 15, 2020, https://www.britannica.com/topic/Yale-University.

39 Jones, "Collegiate Male Glee Clubs," 34.

40 Jones, 34.

41 Jones, 34–35.

42 *TSL* (New Brunswick, N.J.: Times Steam Print, 1872), 46. John Oppie, '74, served as treasurer for the group and as organist; however, he did not participate in the vocal ensemble.

43 *TSL* (1872), 13.

44 *TSL* (1872), 42.

45 *TSL* (1872), 49.

46 *TSL* (New York: Griffith & Byrne, 1875), 34.

47 A calithump, or callithump, is a noisy, boisterous parade or mock serenade. See *GNU Collaborative International Dictionary of English*, s.v. "Calithump or Callithump," accessed December 23, 2021, https://gcide.gnu.org.ua/?q=callithump&define=Define&strategy=. The Rutgers chapter of the fraternity Alpha Sigma Chi instituted a troupe of "Thumpers" during the 1874–75 academic year. Their motto was "Go Calithump to-night." See *TSL* (1875), 69.

48 *TSL* (New York: Griffith & Byrne, 1874), 6–12.

49 *TSL* (1874), 8–9.

50 *TSL* (1874), 60.

51 *TSL* (1875), 63.

52 Fuller sang soprano for the group and served as an Instrumentalist (Flutist). See *TSL* (1872), 46.

53 Oliver Kip Westling, "On the Banks—1873," *Journal of the Rutgers University Libraries* 11, no. 1 (1947): 28–29.

54 H. R. Waite, ed., *Carmina Collegensia: A Complete Collection of the Songs of the American Colleges with Piano-Forte Accompaniment* (Boston: Oliver Ditson, 1868). Colleges represented in this volume include Harvard, Yale, Brown, Dartmouth, Williams, Bowdoin, Union, Hamilton, and many others.

55 Waite, preface to *Carmina Collegensia*.

56 *Targum*, November 1873, 6.

57 *Targum*, November 1873, 6.

58 *Targum*, November 1873, 6. This list is also cited in Westling, "On the Banks," 28.

59 Westling, "On the Banks," 28.

60 Westling, 29.

61 See, for example, Demarest: "A glee club was organized, not destined to have continuous life. . . . Edwin E. Colburn was the organizer of the club." Demarest, *History of Rutgers College*, 431. Also see Flora Boros et al., *On the Banks of the Raritan: Music at Rutgers and New Brunswick* (New Brunswick, N.J.: Rutgers University Libraries, 2014), 30, where Colburn is designated as the "founder" of the Glee Club.

62 Alexander Johnston's "Rutgers Foot-ball Song" appears in this volume; see Henry Randall Waite, ed., *Carmina Collegensia* (Boston: Oliver Ditson, 1876), 147. See also Oliver Kip Westling, "The Author of the First Rutgers Football Song," *Journal of the Rutgers University Libraries* 12, no. 2 (1949): 62–63.

63 William Clinton Armstrong, *Patriotic Poems of New Jersey* (Cranford, N.J.: New Jersey Society of the Sons of the American Revolution, 1906), 161. See also Demarest, *History of Rutgers College*, 431. This story is also presented in *Targum*, March 11, 1908, 428.

64 *Kings County Rural Gazette*, December 13, 1873, 4. This performance was part of a fundraising event for

the benefit of the Flatbush Mission School. Selections that evening included "Stars of the Summer Night," "As Fresh We Came to Rutgers," "The Bull Frog," and "Farewell. Good Night." The absent members were Isaac D. Vanderpoel and Le Roy Brumaghim (both of whom sang first tenor).

65 For details of this concert, see *Targum*, March 1874, 7.

66 *Targum*, April 1873, 8.

67 *TSL* (New Brunswick, N.J.: Times Steam Print, 1871), 28.

68 *TSL* (1874), 33.

69 *TSL* (1872), 39.

70 *TSL* (1872), 44.

71 *TSL* (1872), 46.

72 Demarest, *History of Rutgers College*, 430. Yale, Princeton, and Rutgers were represented, though Harvard and Columbia were invited to attend.

73 *TSL* (1874), 56. His position on the team was Fielder; see 57.

74 *TSL* (1874), 54.

75 *TSL* (1874), 2.

76 *TSL* (1874), 48. The Rutgers Philoclean Society, established in 1825, is one of the oldest collegiate societies of its kind in the United States. See "Philoclean Society (Rutgers University)," SNAC, accessed May 29, 2020, https://snaccooperative.org/view/75383486.

77 *TSL* (1874), 59.

78 *New York Times*, March 1, 1931, N7.

79 *Targum*, April 1873, 8.

80 *Targum*, February 1874, 9: "The Glee Club of '76 will make its *debut* at Newark shortly after the Sophomore Exhibition, and we earnestly hope it will be encouraging."

81 *TSL* (1874), 30.

82 *Targum*, March 1874, 6. "We have delayed this issue in order that we might give an account of the Concert, given by the Glee Club of '76, at the Academy, Metuchen, N.J. Home talent not only should be recognized, but also patronized." The article containing the specifics of the concert appears on page 7 and takes up nearly two columns.

83 *Targum*, June 1874, 6: "The Glee Club of '76 certainly deserves a place in the columns of the *Targum* by the excellent manner in which its members entertained their very select audience lately at Somerville." The article gives a detailed account of the event, encompassing nearly two columns.

84 *Targum*, January 1875, 9.

85 *TSL* (1875), 63.

86 *Targum*, January 1876, 9.

87 *Targum*, January 1876, 8.

88 *Targum*, May 1876, 7.

89 *Targum*, November 1876, 10: "We are delighted to hear that an effort is on foot to organize a Glee Club."

90 *TSL* (1875), 45.

91 *TSL* (1875), 34.

92 *TSL* (New York: Griffith & Byrne, 1877), 37.

93 *TSL* (1877), 2.

94 *Targum*, January 1877, 9.

95 *Targum*, February 1877, 10.

96 *Targum*, June 1877, 11.

97 *Targum*, December 1877, 6.

98 "The Freshmen Have a Glee Club," *Targum*, March 1878, 9.

99 *Targum*, December 1878, 7.

100 *Targum*, November 1879, 94.

101 *Targum*, December 1879, 105: "The Glee Club will sing in New York, on Wednesday, January 7th."

102 *Targum*, May 1880, 59.

103 *Targum*, May 1880, 58.

104 *Targum*, February 1, 1921, 4.

105 *TSL* (1885), 81.

106 *Targum*, October 15, 1880, 5.

107 *Targum*, December 17, 1880, 44.

108 *TSL* (New Brunswick, N.J.: J. Heidingsfeld, 1885), 81.

109 *TSL* (1885), 40.

110 *Targum*, January 7, 1881, 52.

111 This information is contained in a short essay titled "Sketch of Rutgers' Glee Club." It should be noted that, in this account of the history of the group, the visit from the Princeton Glee Club and the subsequent formation of the committee mentioned

above constitute "that time [from which] may be dated the beginning of the Rutgers College Glee Club." *TSL* (1885), 81.

112 *TSL* (1885), 81.

113 *Targum*, January 28, 1881, 66.

114 *Targum*, March 11, 1881, 93.

115 *Targum*, January 28, 1881, 62.

116 *TSL* (1885), 81.

117 *Targum*, March 11, 1881, 93. This article, titled "Success of the Glee Club," contains extracts from local press coverage of the concerts mentioned above. The reaction to the February 2 concert is excerpted from *New Brunswick Daily News Times* of February 3, 1881.

118 *Targum*, March 11, 1881, 93.

119 *Targum*, March 11, 1881, 93.

120 *Targum*, March 11, 1881, 93.

121 *Targum*, March 11, 1881, 98.

122 *Targum*, April 15, 1881, 101.

123 *Targum*, April 15, 1881, 101.

124 *Targum*, May 6, 1881, 119.

125 *TSL* (New York: Homer Lee Bank Note Company, 1882), 79.

126 *New York Times*, June 21, 1881, 5: "The commencement concert of the glee club was held in the Opera-house this evening [June 20] at 8 o'clock. The house was packed and many were turned away from the doors. The students were assisted by Mrs. Belle Cole."

127 *Targum*, February 16, 1883, 70. The Glee Club performed in Baltimore at the Academy of Music on February 6, 1883, for an estimated crowd of 2,500, with Mrs. Cole as guest soloist.

128 *Targum*, May 6, 1881, 121: "Musical Director, Mr. Bragdon, '76; President, Mr. Haring, '81; Vice President, Mr. Skinner, '83; Business Manager, Mr. Havens, '82; Secretary, Mr. Scudder, '82; Treasurer, Mr. Miller, '83."

129 *Targum*, May 6, 1881, 121.

130 *Central New Jersey Home News*, May 22, 1906, 1.

131 *Targum*, January 27, 1882, 59.

132 *Targum*, January 27, 1882, 58. The *Targum* states that this concert occurred on December 21, 1881.

However, the program for the event gives the date as December 19. Since the account in the *Targum* matches the selections of the program, including the appearance of Ms. Berger, it would appear that the *Targum* date is not correct and this concert did, indeed, take place on December 19.

133 Christine Ammer, *Unsung: A History of Women in American Music* (Westport, Conn.: Greenwood, 2001), 119–120.

134 *Targum*, January 27, 1882, 58.

135 *New Brunswick Daily News Times*, January 21, 1882, 3. The date of this concert is given in the *Times* as January 23, but in the *Targum* as January 21.

136 *Targum*, January 27, 1882, 59.

137 *Targum*, June 19, 1882, 143.

138 *TSL* (1882), 29. The two members listed on the Glee Club roster as P. G. (post-graduate) are James S. Wight and Bastian Smits; see *TSL* (1882), 78.

139 *Targum*, December 16, 1887, 46.

140 *New York Times*, June 19, 1888, 6. Howard MacSherry (1853–1930) was a prominent New Jersey lawyer and author who had strong ties to New Brunswick. See *Pittsburgh Press*, May 31, 1930.

141 *Targum*, May 1, 1889, 174–175.

142 *Targum*, June 15, 1890, 195.

143 *TSL* (New Brunswick, N.J.: J. Heidingsfeld, 1891), 109–113.

144 *TSL* (1891), 112–113.

145 *TSL* (1891), 113.

146 John Howard Raven, *Catalogue of the Officers and Alumni of Rutgers College (Originally Queen's College) in New Brunswick, N. J.: 1766–1909* (Trenton, N.J.: *Star Gazette*, 1909), 20–21.

147 *Targum*, February 1, 1891, 97.

148 *Targum*, February 1, 1891, 98.

149 *Targum*, February 1, 1891, 98.

150 *Targum*, February 14, 1891. See the detailed account of the inauguration of President Scott on 108–116.

151 *TSL* (1893), 94. A detailed account of this trip can be found in *Targum*, January 13, 1892, 81.

It should also be noted that between the years 1886 and 1931, *TSL* was put together and published by members of the junior class. Therefore, the 1893 edition features the senior class of 1892.

152 David O. Whitten, "The Depression of 1893," EH.net (Economic History Association), accessed June 20, 2020, https://eh.net/encyclopedia/the-depression-of-1893/.

153 *TSL* (New Brunswick, N.J.: J. Heidingsfeld, 1895), 123.

154 *TSL* (1895), 122.

155 *TSL* (1895), 121.

156 *Targum*, October 3, 1894, 24.

157 *Targum*, November 14, 1894, 104.

158 *Targum*, January 9, 1895, 163.

159 See, for example, Boros et al.: "The Glee Club's early directors included Loren Bragdon (1881–1896)." Boros et al., *On the Banks*, 32.

160 *Central New Jersey Home News*, October 27, 1929, 18; hereafter, *Central New Jersey Home News* will be referred to as *CNJHN*.

161 *CNJHN*, March 12, 1914, 1.

162 Raven, *Catalogue of the Officers*.

163 *New Brunswick Daily News Times*, March 9, 1894, 1.

164 See, for example, *Brooklyn Daily Eagle*, November 28, 1888, 3. Bragdon made an appearance on November 27, 1888, with the Amphion Musical Society, where he was a featured soloist. He also appeared in a minstrel show in the summer resort town of Asbury Park, New Jersey, on September 1, 1899. See *Baltimore Sun*, September 2, 1899, 7.

165 *New York Times*, December 1, 1892, 5.

166 *New Brunswick Daily News Times*, March 6, 1894.

167 *Buffalo Morning News*, October 27, 1889, 1.

168 *New Brunswick Daily News Times*, June 23, 1897, 1.

169 *CNJHN*, April 4, 1904, 1.

170 *CNJHN*, May 27, 1904, 1.

171 *CNJHN*, February 18, 1903, 1.

172 *Targum*, March 18, 1914, 498.

173 *CNJHN*, March 12, 1914, 1.

174 Waite, *Carmina Collegensia*. See the announcement of this edition in *Targum*, January 1876, 9.

175 See, for example, *Targum*, February 18, 1881, 74; and *Targum*, April 15, 1881, 108.

176 *TSL* (1882), 35–36.

177 *The American College Song Book: A Collection of the Songs of Fifty Representative Colleges* (Chicago: Orville Brewer, 1882), 3.

178 *American College Song Book*, 6.

179 *American College Song Book*, 148–151.

180 *CNJHN*, December 29, 1934, 1. Their father was the Reverend John Scudder, MD '57; see *Targum*, December 15, 1882, 47.

181 *TSL* (1882), 78.

182 See, for example, *Targum*, April 15, 1881, 108.

183 *Targum*, May 27, 1881, 126. Will S. Cranmer, '82, was also a member of the Glee Club (first bass) and an associate editor of the *Targum*. See *TSL* (1882), 78.

184 *Targum*, April 24, 1885, 104. The members of this committee, all involved with the Glee Club, were Alfred F. Skinner, '83; F. Parcell Hill, '83; J. Waterbury Scudder, '83; Henry Everton Cobb, '84; and Frank S. Scudder, '85.

185 *Targum*, December 14, 1883, 42.

186 *Targum*, December 12, 1884, 45. The other members of the committee were Edwin Knickerbocker Losee, '85, who participated in the Glee Club; W. Edwin Florance, '85, a member of the Philharmonic Club, of which Frank Scudder served as president in 1882–1883; and William Henry Barnes, '85, a colleague of Frank Scudder in several Rutgers organizations.

187 *Targum*, April 24, 1885, 97.

188 *Targum*, April 24, 1885, 104.

189 Dee Baily, "College Songs," Grove Music Online, October 4, 2012, accessed October 17, 2020, https://www-oxfordmusiconline-com.proxy.libraries.rutgers.edu/grovemusic/view/10.1093/gmo/9781561592630.001.0001/omo-9781561592630-e-1002228093.

190 Winstead, *When Colleges Sang*, 94.

191 *TSL* (1966), 41.

192 As cited in Daniel B. Comito, "'On the Banks of the Old Raritan': The History of the Rutgers University Alma Mater" (honors thesis, Rutgers University, 2011), 2–4.

193 David Parlett, *A Dictionary of Card Games* (Oxford: Oxford University Press, 1992), 104.

194 Comito, "On the Banks," 6.

195 Comito, 7.

196 Comito, 7.

197 Comito, 9.

198 Howard D. McKinney, ed., *Songs of Rutgers* (New Brunswick, N.J.: Rutgers Alumni Association, 1916). The letter appears in its entirety following the opening section titled "Especial Mention"; this part of the book is not paginated.

199 McKinney, n.p. The brief comments are titled "A Word from President Demarest" and appear on the seventh page of text in the volume.

200 See divergent accounts in *CNJHN*, October 28, 1922, 9; *CNJHN*, October 11, 1928, 4; *CNJHN*, April 10, 1930, 15; *CNJHN*, May 13, 1956, 10; and *CNJHN*, July 1, 1962, 12.

201 Comito, "On the Banks," 18. For the complete lyrics for the Camden and Newark revisions, see Comito, 21–22.

202 Patrick Gardner, personal communication with the author, March 16, 2021.

203 Gardner.

204 *CNJHN*, March 28, 2010, 1.

205 *New York Times*, September 21, 2013, https://www.nytimes.com/2013/09/25/nyregion/rutgers-updates-its-anthem-to-include-women.html.

206 *CNJHN*, September 24, 2013, A1.

207 *CNJHN*, September 27, 2013, A2.

208 *CNJHN*, September 27, 2013, A2.

209 *CNJHN*, September 24, 2013, A3.

210 *CNJHN*, September 24, 2013, A3.

Chapter 2: New Directions

1 *TSL* (1885), 80.

2 *TSL* (1895), 121.

3 *CNJHN*, December 3, 1933, 14.

4 Library of Congress Copyright Office, *Catalogue of Copyright Entries*, pt. 3, *Musical Compositions*, vol. 6, no. 1 (Washington, D.C.: Government Printing Office, January 1911), 3189 and 4277.

5 *Targum*, January 11, 1900, 212.

6 See, for example, Fred W. Wimberley, "The Private Music Teacher and the Public School Music Supervisor," *School Music Monthly*, 1906, 1. Wimberley quotes liberally from the views of Wilmot as expressed in the latter's paper, "School Music: Has It Made Music Readers?"

7 *Targum*, February 13, 1895, 249.

8 *Targum*, April 17, 1895, 370.

9 *Targum*, March 13, 1895, 316.

10 *Targum*, January 23, 1895, 200.

11 Paul E. Bierly, *The Incredible Band of John Philip Sousa* (Urbana: University of Illinois Press, 2006).

12 *TSL* (New Brunswick, N.J.: J. Heidingsfeld, 1897), 3.

13 *TSL* (1897), 78.

14 *Targum*, November 6, 1895, 91.

15 *Targum*, December 11, 1895, 167.

16 See the brief narrative in *TSL* (1897), 85.

17 *Targum*, June 16, 1896, 518.

18 *TSL* (1897), 80.

19 A detailed account of this trip can be found in *Targum*, January 12, 1898, 209–210, and continued in the January 19, 1898, edition of the *Targum*, 229–230, and the January 26, 1898, edition, 252–253.

20 *TSL* (New Brunswick, N.J.: J. Heidingsfeld, 1899), 105.

21 *TSL* (New Brunswick, N.J.: J. Heidingsfeld, 1900), 125.

22 *Targum*, May 12, 1897, 516. It should be noted that a separate quartet of this sort was an occasional component of the Club from its earliest incarnations; see *TSL* (1874), 60.

23 *TSL* (New Brunswick, N.J.: J. Heidingsfeld, 1901), 131.

24 *TSL* (New Brunswick, N.J.: J. Heidingsfeld, 1902), 43.

25 *TSL* (New Brunswick, N.J.: J. Heidingsfeld, 1903), 143.

26 *TSL* (New Brunswick, N.J.: Heidingsfeld Press, 1904), 153.

27 For example, the group had fourteen members in 1885 and thirteen in 1895 under Bragdon. See *TSL* (1885), 80; and *TSL* (New Brunswick, N.J.: J. Heidingsfeld, 1890), n.p.

28 *TSL* (New Brunswick, N.J.: Heidingsfeld Press, 1905), 152 and 157.

29 *Targum*, October 27, 1904, 70. This article also includes a detailed account of the New York trip.

30 *TSL* (New Brunswick, N.J.: Morrison & Blue, 1906), 126.

31 *Targum*, October 27, 1904, 70.

32 *TSL* (1906), 126–128.

33 *TSL* (1872), 46.

34 *TSL* (1874), 60.

35 *TSL* (1897), 8.

36 See *TSL* (1872), 46; *TSL* (1882), 78; *TSL* (1885), 80; *TSL* (New Brunswick, N.J.: Heidingsfeld Press, 1907), 124.

37 See, for example, *Targum*, October 6, 1904, 4.

38 See *TSL* (1905), 152.

39 See, for example, *Targum*, May 21, 1906, 473. In the description of a Club concert, Mr. (Frederick Adam) Kullmar, that year's reader, is listed as giving a recitation. In the "History" of the Club that appeared in the 1906 yearbook, he is described as "our noted elocutionist." See *TSL* (1907), 127.

40 *Targum*, May 21, 1906, 473.

41 *Targum*, May 21, 1906, 476.

42 *CNJHN*, May 22, 1906, 1.

43 *TSL* (1907), 136.

44 *TSL* (1907), 23.

45 *CNJHN*, May 24, 1906, 5.

46 *CNJHN*, May 29, 1906, 5.

47 *CNJHN*, May 29, 1906, 5.

48 *Targum*, June 6, 1906, 494.

49 *CNJHN*, June 13, 1906, 1.

50 *CNJHN*, June 14, 1906, 2.

51 *CNJHN*, May 22, 1906, 1.

52 *Targum*, June 1906, 527.

53 *CNJHN*, June 19, 1906, 5.

54 *CNJHN*, September 15, 1906, 1.

55 For more information on the group, see their website: http://www.mgcnyc.org/.

56 *CNJHN*, September 15, 1906, 1–2.

57 *CNJHN*, September 15, 1906, 2.

58 *CNJHN*, June 19, 1906, 1.

59 *CNJHN*, September 15, 1906, 1.

60 *CNJHN*, September 15, 1906, 2.

61 *TSL* (Asbury Park, N.J.: Pennypack, 1908), 121–122.

62 *TSL* (1908), 120.

63 *TSL* (1908), 124.

64 *TSL* (1908), 121.

65 *Targum*, June 5, 1907, 557.

66 *Targum*, June 20, 1907, 579.

67 *Targum*, June 20, 1907, 579.

68 *Targum*, June 20, 1907, 579.

69 *Targum*, June 20, 1907, 579.

70 *Targum*, October 2, 1907, 26.

71 *Targum*, October 30, 1907, 111.

72 *TSL* (New Brunswick, N.J.: Heidingsfeld Printer, 1909), 126. The Dutch expression "Een Dracht makt Macht" translates as "In unity there is strength." It is the national motto of Belgium and various other countries.

73 For details on this group, see the Cornell University Glee Club History website: https://www.gleeclub .com/history.

74 For details, see the Columbia University Glee Club History website: http://www.columbia.edu/cu/ glee/history.html.

75 See, for example, John Marks, "Banjos, Mandolins, and Glee," Historic Geneva, April 21, 2016, https:// genevahistoricalsociety.com/recreation/banjos -mandolins-and-glee/.

76 *Targum*, January 16, 1895, 179.

77 *TSL* (1890), n.p.

78 See *TSL* editions for the respective years.

79 There is no official listing in the yearbook for this group. However, in the "Personalia" provided in *TSL* for that year, the group is mentioned. The president was E. S. Conklin, '96. See *TSL* (1896), 188–192.

80 *TSL* (1897), 82.

81 *TSL* (1897), 35.

82 *Targum*, January 15, 1896, 210.

83 *Targum*, February 26, 1896, 275.

84 *Targum*, April 15, 1896, 344.

85 *Targum*, February 24, 1898, 337.

86 *Targum*, March 9, 1898, 374.
87 *TSL* (1899), 105.
88 *Targum*, June 22, 1898, 606.
89 *Targum*, February 9, 1898, 290.
90 *TSL* (1900), 125.
91 *TSL* (1900), 131.
92 *Targum*, May 2, 1901, 504.
93 *TSL* (1903), 153.
94 *TSL* (1903), 157.
95 *TSL* (1904), 143.
96 *TSL* (1904), 147.
97 *TSL* (1905), 162.
98 *TSL* (1906), 190.
99 *Targum*, October 30, 1905, 66.
100 *Targum*, November 20, 1905, 129.
101 *TSL* (1907), 132.
102 *TSL* (1907), 126.
103 *Targum*, June 20, 1906, 513.
104 *TSL* (1908), 120–122.
105 *CNJHN*, November 14, 1905, 5.
106 *TSL* (1908), 124.
107 The Harlingen concert is mentioned in a larger article on the Glee Club in *Targum*, January 16, 1907, 220–221; *TSL* (1908), 120. The Glee Club "History" is presented on 121–122; that of the Mandolin Club appears on 125.
108 *Targum*, February 27, 1907, 336.
109 *Targum*, May 29, 1907, 538.
110 *Targum*, October 2, 1907, 26.
111 *Targum*, October 30, 1907, 111.
112 *Targum*, October 30, 1907, 111. See also *TSL* (1909), 124–125.
113 *TSL* (1909), 126.
114 *TSL* (1909), 124–125.
115 *Targum*, November 6, 1907, 130.
116 *Targum*, December 11, 1907, 215.
117 *Targum*, December 18, 1907, 239.
118 *Targum*, March 4, 1908, 399.
119 *TSL* (1909), 125.
120 *Targum*, April 1, 1908, 494.
121 *Targum*, April 29, 1908, 543.
122 *Targum*, September 30, 1908, 11.

123 *Targum*, October 21, 1908, 83.
124 *Targum*, November 11, 1908, 153.
125 *Targum*, December 2, 1908, 198–199.
126 *Targum*, December 2, 1908, 208.
127 See *Targum*, December 16, 1908, 250–251; and *CNJHN*, December 14, 1908, 5.
128 *Targum*, March 3, 1909, 422–423.
129 *TSL* (New Brunswick, N.J.: Rutgers College, 1910), 110.
130 *Targum*, March 24, 1909, 492.
131 *Targum*, June 9, 1909, 693.
132 *Targum*, June 23, 1909, 720.
133 Library of Congress Copyright Office, *Catalogue of Copyright Entries*, pt. 3, *Musical Compositions*, vol. 6, no. 1 (Washington, D.C.: Government Printing Office, January 1911), 2567 and 2677.
134 *Targum*, October 20, 1909, 81.
135 *TSL* (New Brunswick, N.J.: Rutgers College, 1911), 120.
136 *Targum*, June 9, 1909, 693.
137 *Targum*, October 6, 1909, 37.
138 *Targum*, February 23, 1910, 395.
139 *Targum*, April 20, 1910, 640–641.
140 *Targum*, October 5, 1910, 30.
141 *Targum*, February 15, 1911, 345–346.
142 *Targum*, March 1, 1911, 420.
143 *Targum*, September 27, 1911, 9–10.
144 *CNJHN*, August 21, 1911, 5.
145 *CNJHN*, February 15, 1912, 2.
146 *TSL* (Plainfield, N.J.: Courier News Publishing, 1913), 174.
147 *Targum*, October 4, 1911, 31.
148 *TSL* (1913), 174.
149 *TSL* (1913), 175.
150 *Targum*, September 25, 1912, 5.
151 *Targum*, October 9, 1912, 57.
152 *Targum*, January 22, 1913, 333.
153 *TSL* (New Brunswick, N.J.: Rutgers College, 1914), 172. See also *CNJHN*, December 17, 1912, 1.
154 *CNJHN*, October 14, 1912, 2.
155 *TSL* (1914), 172.
156 *TSL* (1914), 173.

157 *CNJHN*, June 2, 1913, 5.
158 *CNJHN*, June 6, 1913, 5.
159 *CNJHN*, May 20, 1913, 5.
160 *Targum*, May 28, 1913, 669.
161 *Targum*, October 22, 1913, 112.
162 *Targum*, February 11, 1914, 378.
163 *Targum*, February 25, 1914, 420.
164 *Targum*, May 27, 1914, 666.
165 *Targum*, October 21, 1914, 110.
166 *TSL* (New Brunswick, N.J.: Rutgers College, 1916), 192.
167 *Targum*, January 20, 1915, 337.
168 *TSL* (1916), 193.
169 *CNJHN*, September 27, 1915, 2.
170 *TSL* (New Brunswick, N.J.: Rutgers College, 1917), 192–193.
171 *Targum*, February 23, 1916, 416.
172 *Targum*, February 2, 1916, 342.
173 *Targum*, March 22, 1916, 510.
174 *Targum*, March 29, 1916, 535.

Chapter 3: The Modern Era: Rutgers at 150

1 For more on this, see McCormick, *Rutgers*, 3–12.
2 *CNJHN*, October 14, 1916, 13.
3 *CNJHN*, October 14, 1916, 15. See also *Targum*, June 14, 1916, 717.
4 *CNJHN*, October 14, 1916, 6.
5 *CNJHN*, February 5, 1916, 3.
6 *Targum*, March 15, 1916, 491.
7 *CNJHN*, October 17, 1916, 7.
8 *TSL* (1914), 172.
9 See, for example, Boros et al., *On the Banks*, 30: "The Glee Club's early directors included Loren Bragdon (1881–1896) and Howard D. McKinney (1916–1946)."
10 *Targum*, October 13, 1916, 7.
11 Jones, "Collegiate Male Glee Clubs," 89–90.

12 *Targum*, December 20, 1916, 225.
13 *Targum*, January 24, 1917, 297.
14 See, for example, *CNJHN*, March 22, 1917, 9; and *CNJHN*, April 28, 1917, 7.
15 McCormick, *Rutgers*, 186.
16 *CNJHN*, February 17, 1917, 4. The complete program that Ganz presented on this occasion can be found in *Targum*, February 21, 1917, 369.
17 Jeremy Yudkin, "Chasin' the Truth: The Lost Historiography of American Vernacular Music," *American Music* 26, no. 3 (2008): 398–409.
18 *TSL* (East Orange, N.J.: Abbey Printshop, 1918), 208.
19 *TSL* (1918), 209.
20 *Targum*, December 20, 1916, 225.
21 *CNJHN*, November 27, 1916, 7.
22 *Targum*, March 28, 1917, 493.
23 *Targum*, March 28, 1917, 496.
24 *Targum*, April 18, 1917, 545.
25 *Targum*, May 16, 1917, 634.
26 Walter Karp, *The Politics of War: The Story of Two Wars Which Altered Forever the Political Life of the American Republic (1890–1920)* (New York: Franklin Square, 2003), 222–223.
27 *Targum*, May 16, 1917, 635.
28 *Targum*, October 3, 1917, 6.
29 *Targum*, December 12, 1917, 245.
30 *Targum*, January 24, 1918, 366.
31 *TSL* (East Orange, N.J.: Abbey Printshop, 1919), 208.
32 *Targum*, March 27, 1918, 586.
33 *CNJHN*, May 9, 1918, 5.
34 *Targum*, May 1, 1918, 727.
35 Lloyd. L. Brown, *The Young Paul Robeson: On My Journey Now* (Boulder, Colo.: Westview, 1979), 60.
36 Thomas J. Frusciano and Erika B. Gorder, *Rutgers through the Centuries: 250 Years of Treasures from the Archives* (New Brunswick, N.J.: Rutgers University Special Collections and University Archives Exhibition Catalog, 2015), 27.
37 Sheila Tully Boyle and Andrew Bunie, *Paul Robeson: The Years of Promise and Achievement* (Amherst: University of Massachusetts Press, 2001), 27.
38 Boyle and Bunie, 16.

39 Boyle and Bunie, 28–29.
40 Boyle and Bunie, 42.
41 Frusciano and Gorder, *Rutgers through the Centuries*, 27.
42 See, for example, detailed accounts of such occurrences in Brown, *Young Paul Robeson*, 60–62; and Boyle and Bunie, *Paul Robeson*, 49–51.
43 Boyle and Bunie, 53.
44 Alan H. Levy, *Tackling Jim Crow* (Jefferson, N.C.: McFarland, 2003), 15.
45 Boyle and Bunie, *Paul Robeson*, 54.
46 Paul Robeson Jr., *The Undiscovered Paul Robeson: An Artist's Journey, 1898–1939* (Hoboken, N.J.: Wiley & Sons, 2001), 28.
47 Martin Duberman, *Paul Robeson* (New York: New Press, 1995), 574.
48 Boyle and Bunie, *Paul Robeson*, 54.
49 *TSL* (1920), 44.
50 Boyle and Bunie, *Paul Robeson*, 54.
51 *New York Age*, June 7, 1919, 7.
52 *Washington Evening Star*, September 19, 1919, 32.
53 *CNJHN*, September 2, 1945, 8.
54 Boyle and Bunie, *Paul Robeson*, 258.
55 *CNJHN*, February 26, 1982, 22.
56 *CNJHN*, January 16, 1991, 11.
57 Duberman, *Paul Robeson*, 548.
58 *TSL* (1919), 209.
59 Brian Bond, *The Unquiet Western Front: Britain's Role in Literature and History* (Cambridge: Cambridge University Press, 2007), 22–23.
60 *Targum*, October 3, 1918, 6.
61 *TSL* (East Orange, N.J.: Abbey Printshop, 1920), 165.
62 *Targum*, November 13, 1918, 121.
63 *Targum*, December 18, 1918, 201.
64 *CNJHN*, December 13, 1918, 24.
65 *Targum*, December 18, 1918, 205.
66 *Targum*, January 8, 1919, 221.
67 *Targum*, January 15, 1919, 234.
68 *Targum*, January 15, 1919, 236.
69 *Targum*, March 19, 1919, 414.
70 *Targum*, April 2, 1919, 453; *Targum*, April 9, 1919, 475.
71 *CNJHN*, September 19, 1918, 1.
72 McCormick, *Rutgers*, 149.
73 Boros et al., *On the Banks*, 30.
74 *TSL* (1919), 211.
75 *CNJHN*, September 28, 1919, 12.
76 *TSL* (East Orange, N.J.: Abbey Printshop, 1921), 230.
77 James Tyler and Paul Sparks, "Mandolin," Grove Music Online, accessed January 8, 2021, https://www-oxfordmusiconline-com.proxy.libraries.rutgers.edu/grovemusic/view/10.1093/gmo/9781561592630.001.0001/omo-9781561592630-e-0000046239.
78 *TSL* (1921), 228–229.
79 *Targum*, January 13, 1920, 3.
80 *TSL* (New Brunswick, N.J.: Rutgers College, 1922), 239.
81 *TSL* (New Brunswick, N.J.: Rutgers College, 1923), 237.
82 *Targum*, February 1, 1921, 4.
83 *Targum*, February 1, 1921, 4.
84 *Targum*, February 8, 1921, 1.
85 *TSL* (1923), 237.
86 *Targum*, March 8, 1921, 1.
87 *TSL* (New Brunswick, N.J.: Rutgers College, 1924), 278–279.
88 *CNJHN*, December 11, 1922, 7.
89 *CNJHN*, February 10, 1923, 5.
90 *CNJHN*, February 23, 1923, 12.
91 *CNJHN*, May 12, 1923, 7.
92 *The Quair* (East Orange, N.J.: Abbey Printshop, 1923), 14. This is the yearbook for the New Jersey College for Women. Physical copies of these yearbooks, like all of *The Scarlet Letter* yearbooks, are held in the Special Collections of the Rutgers University Libraries. Most are available through RU Core, the online Rutgers database: https://collections.libraries.rutgers.edu/yearbooks.
93 *CNJHN*, February 29, 1924, 15.
94 *Quair* (1923), 91.
95 *Quair* (East Orange, N.J.: Abbey Printshop, 1925), 145.
96 *Quair* (1925), 34.
97 *CNJHN*, February 29, 1924, 15.
98 *CNJHN*, May 27, 1923, 10.

99   *TSL* (1923), 237.
100 *CNJHN*, May 27, 1923, 10.
101 *CNJHN*, May 27, 1923, 10.
102 *Scrappy Lambert*, Emanon Records (1978), LP liner notes. See https://www.discogs.com/release/8631975-Scrappy-Lambert-Scrappy-Lambert.
103 *CNJHN*, April 3, 1932, 15.
104 *Scrappy Lambert*, LP liner notes (1978).
105 *Scrappy Lambert*, LP liner notes (1978).
106 "Scrappy Lambert," Jazz Age, accessed August 4, 2020, http://www.jazzage1920s.com/scrappylambert/scrappylambert.php.
107 "Hawley Ades," Wayback Machine, accessed August 4, 2020, https://web.archive.org/web/20110715200018/http://www.rogerrossimusic.com/avemaria/arrangment.php.
108 *Camden Courier-Post*, October 25, 1984, 46.
109 *CNJHN*, December 23, 1940, 6.
110 *CNJHN*, January 31, 1936, 18.
111 McCormick, *Rutgers*, 186.
112 *TSL* (New Brunswick, N.J.: Rutgers University, 1925), 307.
113 *CNJHN*, December 13, 1923, 15.
114 *CNJHN*, February 22, 1924, 9.

Chapter 4: Change in Focus

1   *CNJHN*, April 22, 1925, 4.
2   *TSL* (1925), 306–307.
3   *CNJHN*, December 2, 1925, 3.
4   *TSL* (New Brunswick, N.J.: Rutgers University, 1928), 265–266.
5   *TSL* (1924), 279.
6   *TSL* (1925), 308.
7   *CNJHN*, February 28, 1927, 4.
8   *CNJHN*, February 28, 1927, 4.
9   *TSL* (1928), 31.
10 *TSL* (New Brunswick, N.J.: Rutgers University, 1929), 226.
11 *CNJHN*, May 25, 1928, 1.
12 Edith Potter Smith, "Cleveland Bohnet in Recital in Kankakee," *Music News* 11, no. 1 (1919): 11.
13 *CNJHN*, September 28, 1928, 23.
14 *New York Times*, March 13, 1961, 29.
15 *CNJHN*, September 8, 1928, 3.
16 *CNJHN*, November 12, 1928, 3.
17 *TSL* (New Brunswick, N.J.: Rutgers University, 1930), 335–336.
18 *CNJHN*, December 12, 1928, 7.
19 *TSL* (1930), 335.
20 *CNJHN*, January 19, 1929, 7.
21 *CNJHN*, December 12, 1928, 7.
22 *CNJHN*, October 18, 1929, 31.
23 *TSL* (New Brunswick, N.J.: Rutgers University, 1931), 299.
24 *CNJHN*, December 4, 1929, 3.
25 *CNJHN*, December 16, 1929, 9.
26 *CNJHN*, December 15, 1929, 5.
27 *CNJHN*, March 16, 1930, 9.
28 *CNJHN*, March 20, 1930, 2.
29 *TSL* (1931), 299.
30 *CNJHN*, April 10, 1930, 15.
31 *CNJHN*, March 19, 1930, 13.
32 *TSL* (1931), 299.
33 *CNJHN*, December 7, 1930, 25.
34 *CNJHN*, April 13, 1931, 7.
35 *CNJHN*, February 27, 1932, 17.
36 *CNJHN*, December 8, 1963, 8.
37 *CNJHN*, May 13, 1932, 23.
38 *CNJHN*, May 24, 1932, 1.
39 *CNJHN*, January 6, 1932, 9.
40 *CNJHN*, October 8, 1932, 10.
41 *CNJHN*, October 22, 1933, 5.
42 *CNJHN*, March 18, 1933, 7.
43 *CNJHN*, October 15, 1977, 51.
44 *CNJHN*, April 8, 1933, 7.
45 *TSL* (New Brunswick, N.J.: Rutgers University, 1934), 228.
46 *CNJHN*, February 1, 1934, 12.
47 *CNJHN*, January 12, 1935, 5.
48 *CNJHN*, December 20, 1935, 44.

49 *CNJHN*, May 6, 1935, 5.

50 *CNJHN*, December 21, 1935, 1.

51 *CNJHN*, January 31, 1936, 18.

52 *CNJHN*, April 24, 1992, 44.

53 *CNJHN*, February 22, 1948, 15.

54 *CNJHN*, December 4, 1936, 27.

55 *TSL* (New Brunswick, N.J.: Rutgers University, 1937), 244–245.

56 *TSL* (New Brunswick, N.J.: Scarlet Letter Council, 1940), n.p.

57 *CNJHN*, December 17, 1936, 1.

58 *TSL* (New Brunswick, N.J.: Rutgers University, 1939), 116.

59 *TSL* (1940), n.p.

60 *TSL* (New Brunswick, N.J.: Rutgers University, 1939), 115. See also *CNJHN*, March 21, 1939, 9.

61 *CNJHN*, March 12, 1940, 9.

62 *CNJHN*, January 3, 1940, 1.

63 *CNJHN*, February 10, 1929, 15.

64 *CNJHN*, January 8, 1940, 7.

65 *CNJHN*, January 9, 1940, 1.

66 *CNJHN*, November 27, 1937, 7.

67 McCormick, *Rutgers*, 225.

68 McCormick, 257.

69 *CNJHN*, October 10, 1940, 15.

70 Earl Robinson and Eric A. Gordon, *Ballad of an American: The Autobiography of Earl Robinson* (Lanham, Md.: Scarecrow, 1998).

71 Kevin Jack Hagopian, "'You Don't Know Who I Am!' Paul Robeson's *Ballad for Americans* and the Paradox of the Double V in the American Popular Front Culture," in *Paul Robeson: Essays on His Life and Legacy*, ed. Joseph Dorinson and William Pencak (Jefferson, N.C.: McFarland, 2002), 167–179.

72 *CNJHN*, September 20, 1940, 17.

73 *CNJHN*, March 30, 1941, 9.

74 *CNJHN*, September 7, 1941, 11.

75 *CNJHN*, September 11, 1941, 15.

76 *CNJHN*, December 8, 1941, 2.

77 *CNJHN*, December 11, 1941, 10.

78 Elizabeth W. Durham, "Soup," *Rutgers Alumni Magazine*, September/October 1983, 27–28.

79 *CNJHN*, February 6, 1942, 6.

80 *CNJHN*, February 6, 1942, 6.

81 Leonard Hansen, interview with G. Kurt Piehler and Stacey Morgan, Rutgers Oral History Archives, December 3, 1996, accessed August 8, 2020, https://oralhistory.rutgers.edu/interviewees/30-interview-html-text/542-hansen-leonard.

82 *CNJHN*, April 16, 1942, 20.

83 *CNJHN*, February 12, 1943, 6.

84 *CNJHN*, February 21, 1943, 3.

85 *CNJHN*, August 13, 1943, 10.

86 *CNJHN*, January 18, 1944, 7.

87 McCormick, *Rutgers*, 261.

88 *TSL* (New Brunswick, N.J.: Rutgers University, 1947), 60–61.

89 *CNJHN*, December 16, 1945, 13.

90 *TSL* (1947), 66.

91 *CNJHN*, May 12, 1946, 24.

92 *CNJHN*, April 13, 1947, 21.

93 *TSL* (1947), 208.

94 *CNJHN*, February 5, 1947, 13.

95 *TSL* (1947), 209.

96 *CNJHN*, September 2, 1945, 8.

97 *CNJHN*, December 7, 1947, 17.

98 *CNJHN*, February 22, 1948, 15.

99 *CNJHN*, March 16, 1948, 8.

100 *CNJHN*, December 7, 1949, 31.

101 "Glee Club," *TSL* (1940), n.p.

102 F. Austin Walter, "Memories on the Banks," *Glee Gab* (Fall 1983): 1.

103 *CNJHN*, September 20, 1940, 17.

104 *CNJHN*, September 11, 1941, 15.

105 Sam Levitt, "Lake Minnewaska Mountain Houses," About Town, 2009, http://abouttown.us/articles/lake-minnewaska-mountain-houses/.

106 Art Robb, "'Soup': F. Austin Walter," accessed June 23, 2020, http://www.art-robb.co.uk/soup.html.

107 Peter Jensen, "Minnewaska '69," *Glee Gab* (1969–1970): 6 and 10.

108 Bob Murphy, "Minnewaska . . . ," *Glee Gab* (April 1974): 4.

109 *CNJHN*, July 16, 1978, 75.
110 F. Austin Walter, "Memories," 1–2.
111 Ifeanyi Ezeanya and Edwin Trent, "Building Eternal Bonds, One Weekend at a Time," *Glee Gab* 34, no. 2 (Spring 2016): 5.

Chapter 5: Prestige and Travel

1 *CNJHN*, February 19, 1950, 9.
2 *CNJHN*, April 8, 1950, 1.
3 *CNJHN*, October 20, 1950, 19.
4 *CNJHN*, October 20, 1950, 19.
5 F. Austin Walter, "Memories," 1.
6 *CNJHN*, January 17, 1951, 21.
7 *CNJHN*, March 18, 1951, 14.
8 *CNJHN*, January 17, 1951, 17.
9 Nicolas Slonimsky, *The Concise Baker's Biographical Dictionary of Musicians* (New York: Schirmer, 1988), 724.
10 *CNJHN*, March 11, 1951, 20.
11 *CNJHN*, March 24, 1951, 1.
12 *CNJHN*, May 8, 1951, 14.
13 *CNJHN*, May 8, 1952, 22.
14 *CNJHN*, May 1, 1953, 14.
15 *CNJHN*, March 18, 1954, 14.
16 *CNJHN*, March 26, 1954, 15.
17 *TSL* (1955), 93.
18 *CNJHN*, January 15, 1956, 10.
19 *TSL* (1956), 181.
20 *CNJHN*, November 11, 1955, 24.
21 *CNJHN*, February 20, 1956, 11.
22 *CNJHN*, March 24, 1956, 1.
23 *CNJHN*, March 24, 1956, 1.
24 *CNJHN*, February 19, 1957, 10.
25 *CNJHN*, May 6, 1957, 10.
26 *CNJHN*, March 26, 1958, 28.
27 *CNJHN*, March 5, 1959, 2.
28 *CNJHN*, January 14, 1959, 29.
29 *CNJHN*, April 3, 1959, 26.
30 *CNJHN*, April 30, 1959, 34.
31 *CNJHN*, May 17, 1959, 5.
32 *CNJHN*, April 8, 1959, 18.
33 *CNJHN*, February 3, 1961, 9.
34 *CNJHN*, April 28, 1960, 33.
35 "The Julius Bloom Collection," Carnegie Hall Archives, accessed August 13, 2020, https://carnegiehall.github.io/archives-findingaids/namedcolls-fa/juliusBloom.html#ref646.
36 *CNJHN*, May 17, 1959, 5.
37 *Targum*, October 20, 1915, 80.
38 "Rutgers University Faculty Data File: Howard Decker McKinney," Alexander Library Special Collections, May 21, 1947.
39 *CNJHN*, September 28, 1919, 12.
40 *CNJHN*, September 28, 1980, D3.
41 *TSL* (New Brunswick, N.J.: Rutgers University, 1963), 17.
42 *CNJHN*, September 28, 1980, D3.
43 *CNJHN*, October 15, 1980, 41.
44 Paula Morgan, "Alfred Mann," Grove Music Online, accessed August 13, 2020, https://www-oxfordmusiconline-com.proxy.libraries.rutgers.edu/grovemusic/view/10.1093/gmo/9781561592630.001.0001/omo-9781561592630-e-0000017644.
45 *CNJHN*, November 19, 1959, 33.
46 Durham, "Soup," 20–21.
47 *South Florida Sun Sentinel*, December 24, 2020, accessed August 14, 2020, https://www.sun-sentinel.com/news/fl-xpm-2001-12-24-0112230419-story.html; *CNJHN*, March 22, 1960, 5.
48 *CNJHN*, May 3, 1960, 4. Details of the story of Nelson's rejection by the Glee Club are recounted in Ozzie Nelson, *Ozzie* (Englewood Cliffs, N.J.: Prentice Hall, 1973), 54–55.
49 *CNJHN*, May 3, 1961, 33.
50 *CNJHN*, January 25, 1961, 28.
51 *CNJHN*, May 3, 1961, 19.
52 *CNJHN*, February 21, 1962, 67.
53 *CNJHN*, February 27, 1962, 9.
54 *CNJHN*, July 1, 1962, 17.
55 *CNJHN*, October 7, 1962, 17.

56 *CNJHN*, November 10, 1963, 44.
57 *CNJHN*, November 21, 1963, 23.
58 *CNJHN*, December 8, 1963, 8.
59 *CNJHN*, November 26, 1963, 14.
60 *CNJHN*, February 23, 1964, 30.
61 *CNJHN*, November 14, 1965, 40.
62 *CNJHN*, November 14, 1965, 25.
63 *CNJHN*, February 23, 1964, 5.
64 *TSL* (1964), 213.
65 *CNJHN*, November 14, 1965, 40.
66 For more on tour preparations, see F. Austin Walter, "Touring," *Glee Gab* (April 1966): 1.
67 *CNJHN*, April 28, 1966, 47.
68 *CNJHN*, June 2, 1966, 19.
69 *CNJHN*, June 12, 1966, 15.
70 *CNJHN*, June 26, 1966, 13.
71 *CNJHN*, December 17, 1966, 10.
72 *CNJHN*, December 3, 1966, 2.
73 *CNJHN*, February 27, 1967, 9.
74 *CNJHN*, April 25, 1967, 6.
75 *CNJHN*, October 5, 1967, 36.
76 *CNJHN*, October 17, 1967, 1.
77 *CNJHN*, October 23, 1967, 13.
78 *CNJHN*, October 13, 1967, 15.
79 *CNJHN*, April 18, 1968, 37.
80 Keith Sattely, "A Concise History of Past Glee Club Tours," *Glee Gab* 5, no. 1 (Summer 1995): 8–9.
81 *CNJHN*, March 21, 1969, 10.
82 *CNJHN*, April 13, 1969, 12.
83 Yale, Princeton, and Rutgers were represented, though Harvard and Columbia were invited to attend. Demarest, *History of Rutgers College*, 430.
84 Boros et al., *On the Banks*, 31–32.
85 *Targum*, October 22, 1913, 106.
86 *Targum*, October 24, 1914, 104.
87 *CNJHN*, October 8, 1932, 10.
88 *Targum*, September 21, 1948, 1.
89 *Targum*, September 30, 1952, 1.
90 Steven M. Wolf, "From the Business Manager," *Glee Gab* (1969–1970): 2.
91 *CNJHN*, April 17, 1978, 18.
92 *CNJHN*, April 17, 1978, 18.
93 Tom Struble, personal communication with the author, May 28, 2021.
94 Vince Tirri, "On the Gridiron Now They Fight: Homecoming 2003, Glee Club Style," *Glee Gab* 21, no. 1 (Fall 2003): 2.
95 Scott Sincofe, "Taking on Yankee Stadium," *Glee Gab* 30, no. 2 (Spring 2012): 2.
96 John Padden, "Glee Club Readies Itself for Annual Soup Bowl," *Glee Gab* 20, no. 1 (Winter 2002): 2.
97 *CNJHN*, November 18, 2002, 1. See Max Ohring, "Glee Club Shuts Down the Band," *Glee Gab* 35, no. 1 (Fall 2016): 3, for the 1970 date.
98 ZuzuRU, "An Unsung Tradition Turns 50: The Tradition of a Football Game . . . between the Marching Band and Glee Club," SBNATION, November 17, 2017, https://www.offtackleempire .com/2017/11/17/16668266/an-unsung-rutgers -tradition-turns-50-soup-bowl-band-glee-club.
99 ZuzuRU.
100 Max Ohring, "Soup Bowl's Evolution," *Glee Gab* 35, no. 2 (Spring 2017): 6.
101 Peter Fabian, "Soup Bowl: Another Year, Another Victory," *Glee Gab* 27, no. 2 (Spring 2010): 1–2.
102 Ohring, "Soup Bowl's Evolution," 6.
103 *CNJHN*, February 23, 1969, 21.
104 "The First Game: November 6, 1869," Rutgers University Athletics, accessed August 19, 2020, https://scarletknights.com/sports/2017/6/11/ sports-m-footbl-archive-first-game-html.aspx.
105 *CNJHN*, February 26, 1970, 38.
106 "Rutgers Glee Club Discography," accessed August 19, 2020, http://www.art-robb.co.uk/soup.html.
107 *CNJHN*, September 15, 1969, 10.
108 *CNJHN*, October 28, 1970, 59.
109 *CNJHN*, February 22, 1971, 18.
110 Al Gilbert, "Europe, '70," *Glee Gab* (1969–1970): 1 and 4.
111 F. A. Walter, "Germination of an Idea for Friendship," *Glee Gab* (June 1971): 1–3.
112 Sattely, "Concise History," 8–9.
113 *CNJHN*, February 22, 1972, 10.
114 *CNJHN*, April 13, 1972, 43. This account lists the dog's name as "Tosca," but it would appear that Walter

always called his pet "Tosci." See F. Austin "Soup" Walter, "Tosci and Tanzi: 'Bow-Wow-Wow,'" *Rutgers Alumni Magazine*, September/October 1983, 21.

115 *CNJHN*, May 1, 1973, 14.
116 *CNJHN*, March 30, 1973, 22.
117 *CNJHN*, May 7, 1974, 10.
118 *CNJHN*, May 16, 1974, 45.
119 *CNJHN*, February 5, 1976, 14.
120 *CNJHN*, March 25, 1976, 19.
121 Richard Nemeth, "Americans in Paradise," *Glee Gab* (December 1976): 1 and 3.
122 *CNJHN*, April 30, 1976, 17.
123 *CNJHN*, October 16, 1977, 51.
124 *CNJHN*, October 23, 1977, 52.
125 *CNJHN*, November 4, 1977, 19.
126 *CNJHN*, February 19, 1978, 60.
127 Sattely, "Concise History," 8–9.
128 *CNJHN*, May 1, 1978, 16.
129 *CNJHN*, April 23, 1978, 33.
130 *CNJHN*, April 9, 1978, 14.
131 *CNJHN*, May 26, 1978, 11.
132 *CNJHN*, July 16, 1978, 35.
133 Durham, "Soup," 21.
134 *CNJHN*, November 30, 1978, 35.
135 *CNJHN*, December 7, 1978, 8; *CNJHN*, December 12, 1978, 8.
136 *CNJHN*, April 7, 1979, 29.
137 *CNJHN*, April 29, 1979, 47.
138 *CNJHN*, January 28, 1980, 13.
139 *CNJHN*, April 10, 1980, 38.
140 *CNJHN*, November 29, 1979, 23.
141 *CNJHN*, November 25, 1979, 54.
142 *CNJHN*, April 10, 1980, 38.
143 *CNJHN*, April 14, 1980, 7.
144 Ian Lowell Heller, "That Was the Tour That Was," *Glee Gab* (1980–1981): 1–2.
145 *CNJHN*, April 26, 1981, 64.
146 *CNJHN*, December 9, 1981, 34.
147 *CNJHN*, September 25, 1981, 19.
148 *CNJHN*, November 7, 1982, 66.
149 F. Austin Walter, "Tenth European Tour," *Glee Gab* (Fall 1982): 1.
150 *CNJHN*, April 23, 1983, 20.
151 *CNJHN*, April 21, 1983, 68.
152 *CNJHN*, April 5, 1984, 63.
153 *CNJHN*, May 7, 1985, 27.
154 Sattely, "Concise History," 8–9.
155 *CNJHN*, March 3, 1986, 12.
156 *CNJHN*, November 25, 1986, 37.
157 *CNJHN*, December 5, 1986, 79.
158 *CNJHN*, May 1, 1987, 66.
159 "Biography: Rob Kapilow," Colbert Artists Management, October 2021, accessed August 31, 2020, https://colbertartists.com/artists/rob-kapilow/.
160 *CNJHN*, December 19, 1987, 13.
161 *CNJHN*, December 11, 1987, 75.
162 *CNJHN*, February 19, 1988, 59.
163 *CNJHN*, April 24, 1988, 52.
164 "Biography: Rob Kapilow."
165 *CNJHN*, May 8, 1989, 11.
166 *CNJHN*, May 8, 1989, 11.
167 *CNJHN*, March 25, 1990, 25.
168 *CNJHN*, September 21, 1990, 50.
169 *CNJHN*, November 17, 1991, 29.
170 *CNJHN*, November 26, 1991, 1–2.
171 *CNJHN*, April 24, 1992, 44.
172 *TSL* (1898), 37.
173 *CNJHN*, December 8, 1963, 8.
174 *CNJHN*, October 23, 1977, 58.
175 *CNJHN*, October 23, 1977, 58.
176 *TSL* (1931), 299.
177 *CNJHN*, March 6, 1931, 19.
178 *CNJHN*, October 23, 1977, 52.
179 *CNJHN*, February 1, 1955, 11.
180 *CNJHN*, September 7, 1941, 11.
181 *CNJHN*, November 10, 1968, 5.
182 *Targum*, October 1, 1941, 1.
183 *CNJHN*, March 1, 1941, 9.
184 Durham, "Soup," 20–21.
185 *CNJHN*, October 20, 1950, 19.
186 *CNJHN*, December 17, 1936, 1.
187 *CNJHN*, December 8, 1963, 8.
188 *CNJHN*, September 20, 1940, 17.

189 Robb, "Soup."

190 *CNJHN*, October 23, 1977, 58.

191 Robb, "Soup."

192 *CNJHN*, November 10, 1968, 5.

193 Matthew Cirri, "The Passing of a Legend: F. Austin 'Soup' Walter, 1910–2000," *Glee Gab* 18, no. 1 (August 2000): 1.

194 Bill Rech, "Frederic Hugh Ford," *Glee Gab* (Fall 1983): 3.

Chapter 6: Into the New Millennium

1 Matthew J. Weismantel, *Rutgers University Glee Club History*, internal memorandum of the Rutgers University Glee Club, 1970s–1997 and 2019, accessed June 2020.

2 Richard J. Fox, "List of Officers, 1934–1995," *Glee Gab* 3, no. 2 (Spring 1994): 7.

3 Weismantel, *Rutgers University Glee Club*.

4 Weismantel.

5 Scott J. Pashman, "Why Tour Drive '96 Is a #1 Priority," *Glee Gab* 5, no. 1 (Summer 1995): 4.

6 Patrick Gardner, personal communication with the author, April 13, 2021.

7 *New York Times*, December 6, 2017, https://www.nytimes.com/2017/12/06/arts/music/best-classical.html.

8 Gardner, personal communication.

9 *New Yorker*, November 22, 1982, 181.

10 *Newsweek*, November 29, 1982.

11 Edith L. Bookstein, "Altman's 'Rake' a Staggering Success," *Ann Arbor News*, November 7, 1982.

12 University of Michigan Men's Glee Club, "U-M Men's Glee Club Sings National Anthem at World Series," ztrawhcs, streamed on July 29, 2008, YouTube video, 2:12, https://youtu.be/sQJR5C8ZOoQ.

13 Frank Albinder, personal communication with the author, March 23, 2021.

14 Jo-Michael Scheibe, personal communication with the author, March 23, 2021.

15 *New York Times*, August 29, 2000, E5.

16 *New York Times*, August 3, 2001, E4.

17 *Targum*, September 14, 1993, 1 and 5.

18 *CNJHN*, December 12, 1993, 70.

19 Patrick Gardner, personal communication with the author, March 23, 2021.

20 Patrick Gardner, personal communication with the author, February 19, 2021.

21 Christopher Treglio, "Celebrating 125 Years of Tradition," *Glee Gab* 3, no. 2 (Spring 1994): 4.

22 *CNJHN*, November 4, 1994, 67.

23 Treglio, "Celebrating 125 Years," 4.

24 Patrick Gardner, personal communication with the author, March 18, 2021.

25 Scott J. Pashman, "Eastern European Tour '96," *Glee Gab* 6, no. 1 (Spring 1996): 2.

26 Robert Mortensen, "Tour Committee Chairman Challenges Us," *Glee Gab* 5, no. 1 (Summer 1995): 1.

27 Pashman, "Eastern European Tour," 2 and 6.

28 Harry Allen IV, "Eastern European Tour '96," *Glee Gab* 11, no. 1 (Spring 1997): 2.

29 Patrick Gardner, *Let Thy Good Spirit* (New York: Ethereal Recordings, 1996), liner notes.

30 Keith Sattely, "Glee Club Prepares for 125th Anniversary," *Glee Gab* 6, no. 1 (Spring 1996): 1.

31 Weismantel, *Rutgers University Glee Club*.

32 John Mylecraine, "125th Anniversary a Rousing Success," *Glee Gab* 18, no. 3 (September 1997): 1.

33 *CNJHN*, October 14, 1998, 27.

34 "Past Concerts," Riverside Choral Society, accessed March 23, 2021, http://riversidechoral.org/past-concerts.

35 "Jane Shaulis," Metropolitan Opera Company, accessed December 31, 2021, https://www.metopera.org/discover/artists/mezzo-soprano/jane-shaulis/.

36 Shaun Baines, "Plans for European Tour Progress," *Glee Gab* 16, no. 3 (Fall 1998): 2.

37 Patrick Gardner, "Singing with Soup," *Glee Gab* (Summer 1999): 1.

38 "Glee Club Calendar," *Glee Gab* (Summer 1999): 3.

39 Cirri, "Passing of a Legend," 1.

40 Cirri, 1.

41 Larrej Drayton, "The Road to ACDA," *Glee Gab* 35, no. 2 (Spring 2017): 3.

42 "2000–2001 RUGC Update," *Glee Gab* 18, no. 1 (Summer 2000): 7.

43 *CNJHN*, April 13, 2001, 90.

44 *CNJHN*, April 15, 2001, 62.

45 *CNJHN*, April 20, 2001, 24.

46 Willa J. Conrad, "Rutgers Musicians Go Bigtime," *Newark Star-Ledger*, April 21, 2001, 27.

47 "Rutgers University Glee Club 2000–2001 Calendar," *Glee Gab* 18, no. 2 (November 2000): 7.

48 *CNJHN*, December 5, 2001, 50.

49 Masayuki Gibson, "Professor David Kimock Continues Excellence," *Glee Gab* 19, no. 2 (Spring 2002): 5.

50 Gibson, 1.

51 Christopher Nicosia, "Glee Club Performs Brahms *Nänie* with Women of Mount Holyoke," *Glee Gab* 19, no. 2 (Spring 2002): 3.

52 J. D. Shenton, "Glee Club Begins Work on European Tour Set for Summer 2002," *Glee Gab* 19, no. 2 (Spring 2002): 4.

53 Leslie Garisto Pfaff, "Patron Saint of the Arts," *Rutgers Magazine*, Winter 2014, https://ucmweb.rutgers.edu/magazine/1419archive/the-arts/patron-saint-of-the-arts.html.

54 Weismantel, *Rutgers University Glee Club*.

55 John Krasting, "Glee Club Proud to Welcome New Faculty Advisor," *Glee Gab* 20, no. 1 (Winter 2002): 1.

56 Peter Gillett, "Tour de Force," *Glee Gab* 21, no. 1 (Fall 2003): 1.

57 Patrick Gardner, personal communication with the author, March 31, 2021.

58 Gillett, "Tour de Force," 6.

59 Brendan Kelly, "Berlioz Is a Success," *Glee Gab* 22, no. 2 (Spring 2004): 2.

60 Chuck Delcamp, "A Busy Year Indeed!!!," *Glee Gab* 21, no. 1 (Fall 2003): 3.

61 Kelly, "Berlioz Is a Success," 2.

62 Patrick Gardner, personal communication with the author, March 31, 2021.

63 James O'Keefe, "Glee Club Impresses at IMC," *Glee Gab* 22, no. 2 (Spring 2004): 4.

64 Delcamp, "Busy Year," 3.

65 Matt Klimek, "Michigan Comes to Rutgers," *Glee Gab* 23, no. 1 (Summer 2005): 1.

66 Patrick Gardner, personal communication with the author, March 18, 2021.

67 Chris Dovas, "Glee Club Welcomes Back Dion Ritten," *Glee Gab* 23, no. 2 (Fall 2005): 1.

68 *CNJHN*, March 10, 2006, 15.

69 *New York Times*, September 29, 2006, E17.

70 *New York Times*, October 31, 2006, E5.

71 *Frankfurter Neue Presse*, June 6, 2006, 17–18.

72 Patrick Hosfield, "Green Room Dedication Event," *Glee Gab* 25, no. 2 (Spring 2008): 1, 5–6.

73 Hosfield, 1, 5–6.

74 Sean Plante, "Glee Club to Sing with *Cantabile Limburg*," *Glee Gab* 25, no. 2 (Spring 2008): 4, 6.

75 Mark DiGiovanni, "Glee Club Hosts *Cantabile Limburg* on the Banks," *Glee Gab* 26, no. 1 (Summer 2008): 3, 6–7.

76 Patrick Gardner, personal communication with the author, March 31, 2021.

77 Christopher Meiman, "An Exchange Weekend with Mount Holyoke," *Glee Gab* 26, no. 1 (Summer 2008): 6–8.

78 Jeff Smith, "Choral Extravaganza," *Glee Gab* 26, no. 3 (Spring 2009): 3.

79 *CNJHN*, March 27, 2009, 64.

80 *CNJHN*, April 27, 2009, 31.

81 Mark A. Boyle, "Glee Club Selected to Sing at ACDA," *Glee Gab* 27, no. 1 (Fall 2009): 1–2.

82 Patrick Gardner, "Alumni Concert: 'Soup' Walter Centenary," *Glee Gab* 28, no. 1 (Summer 2010): 1–2.

83 Brian Thomas, "Euro Trip," *Glee Gab* 28, no. 1 (Summer 2010): 1.

84 Daniel B. Comito, *Rutgers University Glee Club: Italian Tour* (New Brunswick, N.J.: Rutgers University Glee Club, 2011), 4.

85 Christopher Glass, "140 Years of Musical Excellence," *Glee Gab* 31, no. 1 (Summer 2012): 1–2.

86   Devin Flynn-Connolly, "Spratlan on Spratlan," *Glee Gab* 21, no. 1 (Summer 2012): 5.

87   Austin Tamutus, "Dr. Gardner Celebrates Two Decades," *Glee Gab* 32, no. 1 (Fall 2013): 1.

88   Austin Tamutus, "Club to Present *Oedipus Rex*," *Glee Gab* 32, no. 1 (Fall 2013): 6.

89   Edwin Trent, "Glee Club 2015 European Tour," *Glee Gab* 34, no. 1 (Fall 2015): 4–9.

90   Larry Fried, "Our Latest CD and DVD Have Arrived," *Glee Gab* 35, no. 1 (Fall 2016): 5.

91   Edwin Trent, "Celebrating an Amazing Birthday," *Glee Gab* 34, no. 2 (Spring 2016): 1.

92   Patrick B. Phillips, "RUGC Performs in Washington, D.C.," *Glee Gab* 35, no. 1 (Fall 2016): 6.

93   Axel A. Gonzales, "Singing for the President," *Glee Gab* 35, no. 1 (Fall 2016): 4–5.

94   Drayton, "Road to ACDA," 3.

95   Peter Calvert, *The Process of Political Succession* (New York: St. Martin's, 1987), 68.

96   Dan Robertson, "Tour Recap," *Glee Gab* 37, no. 1 (Fall 2018): 3–5.

97   Louis Lombardi, "Rutgers, Princeton, and Yale? Oh My!," *Glee Gab* 38, no. 1 (Fall 2019): 3.

98   Benjamin Kritz, "150 Reasons to Sing," *Glee Gab* 39, no. 1 (Fall 2020): 1.

99   Ryan Leibowitz, "The Virtual Choir," *Glee Gab* 39, no. 1 (Fall 2020): 7.

100   John Bathke, "Rutgers Holiday Concert to Be Performed Virtually This Weekend," News 12 New Jersey, December 11, 2020, https://newjersey.news12 .com/rutgers-holiday-concert-to-be-performed -virtually-this-weekend. See also Lisa Intrabartola, "Annual Rutgers Holiday Concert Reimagined in Pandemic," My Central Jersey, December 10, 2020, https://www.mycentraljersey.com/story/ entertainment/2020/12/10/rutgers-kirkpatrick-chapel -holiday-concert-reimagined-pandemic/3863852001/.

101   Ysaye Barnwell, "Composer's Notes," Ysaye Barnwell's personal website, accessed April 22, 2021, https://www.ymbarnwell.com/composers-notes-1.

102   Jo-Michael Scheibe, personal communication with the author, March 23, 2021.

103   *Targum*, December 20, 1916, 205.

104   *CNJHN*, December 22, 1917, 7.

105   *CNJHN*, December 20, 1919, 3.

106   *CNJHN*, December 18, 1920, 3.

107   *Targum*, December 9, 1924, 1.

108   *Targum*, December 11, 1926, 3.

109   *CNJHN*, December 15, 1929, 5.

110   *Targum*, December 13, 1937, 1.

111   *Targum*, December 12, 1945, 3.

112   *Targum*, December 15, 1950, 1.

113   *CNJHN*, December 9, 1956, 24.

114   David Drinkwater, personal communication with the author, March 14, 2021.

115   Drinkwater.

116   *CNJHN*, December 10, 1964, 24.

117   *CNJHN*, December 21, 1967, 29.

118   *CNJHN*, February 22, 1948, 215.

119   *CNJHN*, December 17, 1975, 56.

120   *CNJHN*, December 7, 1978, 8.

121   Intrabartola, "Annual Rutgers Holiday Concert."

122   *Targum*, December 17, 1880, 44.

123   *CNJHN*, May 22, 1906, 1.

124   *TSL* (1918), 208–209.

125   *CNJHN*, October 17, 1916, 7.

126   *TSL* (1924), 306–307.

127   *TSL* (1931), 299.

128   *CNJHN*, March 18, 1933, 7.

129   *TSL* (New Brunswick, N.J.: Rutgers University, 1953), 101.

130   Wolf, "From the Business Manager," 2–3.

131   Tom Struble, personal communication with the author, March 18, 2021.

132   *CNJHN*, November 1, 1979, 12.

133   Pashman, "Why Tour Drive '96," 4.

134   *TSL* (1892), 106.

135   *Glee Gab* 39, no. 1 (Fall 2020): 1.

136   *Glee Gab* 39, no. 1 (Fall 2020): 2.

137   Krasting, "Glee Club Proud," 1 and 5.

138   Patrick Gardner, personal communication with the author, May 22, 2021.

139   *Targum*, October 25, 1941, 1.

INDEX

Page numbers in *italics* refer to figures.

ABOUT THE AUTHOR

DAVID F. CHAPMAN received his PhD in historical musicology from Rutgers University, where he teaches courses in music history and literature, performance practice, and ethnomusicology. He is the author of the monograph *Bruckner and the Generalbass Tradition* and is currently preparing an edition of Anton Bruckner's *Nullte* symphony (WAB 100) for the New Bruckner Collected Works series. He has contributed articles and reviews to various scholarly journals, including *Eighteenth-Century Music*, *Ad Parnassum: A Journal of Eighteenth- and Nineteenth-Century Instrumental Music*, and the *Galpin Society Journal*.